JAMES G. ENDICOTT:
REBEL OUT OF CHINA

James G. Endicott: Rebel Out of China

STEPHEN ENDICOTT

UNIVERSITY OF TORONTO PRESS
Toronto Buffalo London

© University of Toronto Press 1980
Toronto Buffalo London
Printed in Canada
Reprinted 1980

ISBN 0-8020-2377-0 (cloth)
ISBN 0-8020-6409-4 (paper)

Canadian Cataloguing in Publication Data

Endicott, Stephen Lyon, 1928-
James G. Endicott

Includes index.

ISBN 0-8020-2377-0
ISBN 0-8020-6409-4 PBK.

1. Endicott, James G., 1898-
2. Missionaries – Canada – Biography.
3. Missionaries – China – Biography.   4. China – History – 1900-

BV3427.E52E52   266'.7   C80-094300-7

This book has been published with the assistance of the Canada Council and the
Ontario Arts Council under their block grant programmes

The woodcuts from the 1940s appearing on the part title pages are by the Szechuan
artist, Chang Yang-hsi

TO MARY AUSTIN

The sounding cataract
Haunted me like a passion ... I have felt
A presence that disturbs me with the joy
Of elevated thoughts; a sense sublime
Of something far more deeply interfused,
Whose dwelling is the light of setting suns,
And the round ocean and the living air,
And the blue sky, and in the mind of man:
A motion and a spirit, that impels
All thinking things, all objects of all thought,
And rolls through all things.

William Wordsworth, 'Tintern Abbey'

Contents

Foreword, by K.H. Ting ix
Preface xi

PART ONE
BEGINNINGS, 1898–1925
1 In the shadow of the white
  pagoda 7
2 The Methodist soldier 19
3 At university 33
4 Circuit-riding in Saskatchewan 43
5 Ideology and ordination 48
6 The gates of Eden 59

PART TWO
THE MISSIONARY YEARS,
1925–1944
7 Apprenticeship in Chungchow 75
8 China in ferment 86
9 The Wanhsien incident 92
10 Exodus to Shanghai 102
11 Preaching and teaching in
   Chungking 110
12 Furlough in Canada 124
13 Experiments in missionary
   work 134
14 Madame Chiang's New Life
   Movement 141
15 Furlough again 153

PART THREE
CHINA IN REVOLUTION,
1944–1947
16 Aboard the *S.S. Priam* 169
17 Save China by democracy 177
18 Secret agent 'Hialeah' 184
19 The mice of No 11 196
20 The battle of the embassy 208
21 Resignation 219
22 The *Shanghai Newsletter* 235
23 The 'Endicott controversy' 245

PART FOUR
THE PEACE MOVEMENT,
1948–1971
24 Founding the peace movement 261
25 War in Korea 278
26 Charges of germ warfare 289
27 The Stalin Peace Prize 303
28 Return to China 309
29 One divides into two 325
30 A time of decision 342

EPILOGUE
31 The happy warrior continues 359

Notes 367
Index 401

Foreword

More and more students of history are coming to see the inadequacy of viewing the modern Western missionary spirit simply as an isolated religious phenomenon representing the Christians' response to Christ's commission to his disciples. It was very much a manifestation, on the religious scene, of the broader socio-economic and politico-military movement looking beyond the limits of national boundaries. In spite of the good intentions motivating many individual missionaries, their whole upbringing and captivity to the prevailing understanding of the social and international situation within which the missionary enterprise operated made it very hard indeed for them to transcend their milieu.

Many missionaries are frustrated when they are confronted with the tremendous fact of human suffering. The social systems in countries to which they are sent are found to be producing poverty and misery and estranging and grinding men and women on a scale much too large for the few mission hospitals, orphanages, and vocational training centres to try to catch up. But they usually do not dare to think seriously in terms of some basic structural revolution.

Some missionaries, whose first concern is not so much the institutional church and its 'public relations' as the true welfare of the masses of the people, can achieve some sort of break-through as a result of their openness to progressive intellectuals and their ability to see signs of hope in the people's struggle for independence and liberation. They have not allowed themselves to be deterred by the fact that the struggle is under the leadership of persons who in large number profess an unbelief in God but have proceeded to make friends with them and to try to learn from them. They have found meaning for themselves in serving the people's cause.

Jim Endicott is a good representative of this breed. He has given Christianity an image which China in revolution can somehow begin to understand. Today, thirty years since liberation, there is in China a Christianity to which revolution is no longer such a stranger, and a revolution to which Christianity is not such a stranger either. Jim Endicott contributed much to the evolvement of both.

His indefatigable, interpretative work on behalf of China and of peace has generated international understanding and friendship in a remarkable way.

This biography is more than a significant monument in scientific historical research; because of his personality, it is a source of inspiration to those who hunger for a model of Christian engagement in the world.

Toronto, November 1979   K.H. Ting
Vice-president
Nanking University
People's Republic of China

Preface

Immediately after the Chinese revolutionary civil war of 1945–49, in which he had taken some part, my father began to write his life story, entitling it 'Roar of the Red Dragon.' It had exciting chapter headings such as 'Battle of the Embassy' and 'Maiden in Distress.' With less than twenty pages typed, however, he became involved in other battles in Canada and let his memoirs lapse in favour of what he considered to be more important tasks. Another attempt to tell his story was made by my mother, who took a more personal approach, calling her projected volume 'Life with Jim.' She knew all the highlights but left the work until it was too late and her health failed before she had progressed very far. Her writing and the materials she collected, now deposited in the Public Archives of Canada, provided none the less the voluminous sources upon which my own account of this remarkably vigorous, vexing yet lovable, inquisitive, controversial, non-conforming, uncovenanted, committed, and courageous man is largely based.

In recording what my father has said about people and social movements I have not forgotten that he had a flair for exaggeration at times. This flaw in an otherwise admirable character was a by-product of his intense emotional energy, his passion for social justice. It was sometimes seized upon by those who wished to distract attention from the burden of his message as a means of discrediting his influence; by and large they 'strained out a gnat and swallowed a camel' (Matthew 23:24).

Not a scientist or a professional writer, he was a preacher, a reformer/revolutionary, as well as an historian and presenter of information often omitted in the commercial press. He acted, not in the interests of a party or group in which he hoped to exert power, but in the interests of people whose sufferings were so vivid to him that he felt impelled to change the conditions that created them. He was concerned about truth also, as setting people free from the bondage of prejudice, the blindness of personal interests without concern for the broader welfare; but it is probably fair to say that only as the revelation of that truth would improve that welfare was he willing to give his life to it. Truth in itself may be a beautiful but barren possession.

The reader will find full references to sources at the back of the book. Apart from talking to my father and reading the private correspondence and family documents referred to above, the chief sources for this biography have been the transcripts of interviews conducted with him in 1966 by Marjorie McEnaney for the Canadian Broadcasting Corporation; the archives of the West China Mission of the United Church of Canada, located at Victoria University in Toronto; the files of the Historical Division of the Department of External Affairs in Ottawa; Federal Bureau of Investigation files held by the National Archives in Washington; newspapers, magazines, records of House of Commons debates, privately printed pamphlets; interviews with relatives, friends, and many associates in Austria, Canada, China, France, Germany, Great Britain, Hungary, Japan, Romania, and the United States. A request to visit the Soviet Union to conduct interviews was refused.

I am indebted to all those who contributed to the making of this book and acknowledge with special gratitude the criticisms and suggestions given by Kay Riddell, Shirley Endicott Small, Donald Willmott, Lena Endicott, and Richard Allen in the earlier stages, to Betsy Anderson and Nora McMurtry for help with research, to Marion Keresztesi for the index, and to Gerald Hallowell, my editor, for his skills, resourcefulness, and good humour in helping to prepare the final draft. I also thank the Killam Programme of the Canada Council for the Senior Research Fellowship that allowed me time free from teaching Chinese history and Third World politics to pursue this subject.

30 January 1980   Stephen L. Endicott
                                             Atkinson College
                                             York University

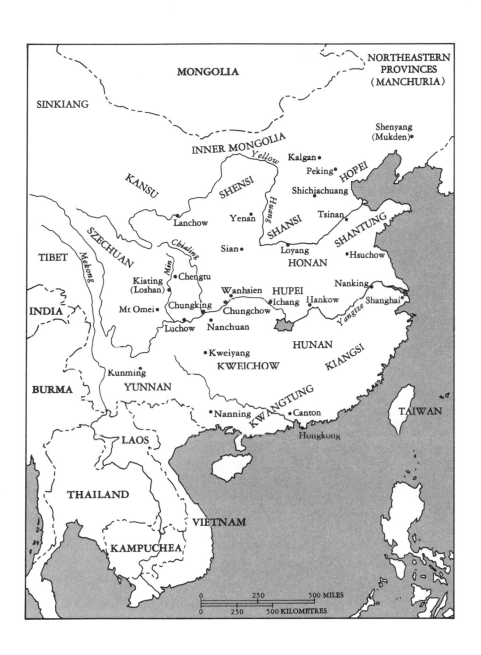

MONGOLIA

NORTHEASTERN
PROVINCES
(MANCHURIA)

SINKIANG

INNER MONGOLIA

Shenyang
(Mukden)•

KANSU

Yellow Kalgan•

Peking• HOPEI

SHENSI

Huang Shichiachuang

Lanchow

Yenan

SHANSI

Tsinan•

SHANTUNG

Chialing

Sian•

Loyang

•Hsuchow

TIBET

Min

Kiating
(Loshan) •Chengtu

HONAN

Mekong

SZECHUAN

Wanhsien HUPEI

Nanking•

INDIA

Mt Omei• Chungking•

•Ichang Hankow

Shanghai•

Chungchow

Yangtze

Luchow• Nanchuan

HUNAN

•Kweiyang

BURMA

Kunming•

KWEICHOW

KIANGSI

YUNNAN

KWANGTUNG

•Nanning

•Canton

TAIWAN

LAOS

Hongkong•

THAILAND

VIETNAM

KAMPUCHEA

| 0 | | 250 | | 500 MILES |
| 0 | 250 | | 500 KILOMETRES | |

PART ONE

BEGINNINGS
1898–1925

INTRODUCING
JAMES G. ENDICOTT:
VERY REVEREND JAMES
ENDICOTT BEFORE A CROWD
OF TEN THOUSAND AT
MAPLE LEAF GARDENS,
TORONTO, 11 MAY 1952

I do not find it any particular dishonor to be introducing my son. I suppose there is no one that ought to be made to do it more than I, for I had something to do with introducing him into the world. At any rate, I've known him a long time, and I've known him very intimately ...

But, first of all, I want to say this – that there are two things which stand out to everybody. One is that he was received and welcomed – an enthusiastic welcome – during the past few months, by the people of China of all classes – a welcome such as has never been granted before to any Canadian. And one would have thought, from a casual looking at the case, that Canadians would be rather glad of such a welcome for a member of the Canadian family, and an honorable member of society, an ex-soldier of His Majesty, a man who's given his life to good causes. One would have thought that we would all have rejoiced in this. But he comes back from that welcome in China to find himself Public Enemy Number One. Now I don't believe that that stigma comes from the heart of the Canadian people – not by any means ...

I doubt if any other man in the country could have had the type of welcome he got, in the quarters where he got it. He was able to preach in all the types of Christian churches there – and there *are* churches in China, you know, living, vital, working churches, yet. He was able to preach in them to packed congregations. He was introduced at meetings by the presidents of the greatest universities in China, and the students gave him tumultuous acclaim. He spoke to peasants; he spoke to learned groups. He did all that in China, and I say he comes back to be called Public Enemy Number One ...

You must remember this, that he was born in a foreign land, and in a city far from the coast, over 1,800 miles up in the interior of China, in a very ancient city. Now, we hadn't any cars in that city, nor radios, nor movie pictures. He missed the inspiration and the education – the sanctifying influence – of Hollywood. Yes, he missed all that ...

Now, what did he have, then – as a little lad born in a place like that? Well, he had his father and mother. And he had a thing that we used to talk about as Family Worship. Perhaps you have heard of it. It is a thing that used to take place. Now, that Family Worship business had something to do with making him what he has become. Anything about his development that isn't what it should be must be credited partly, or debited partly, to his father and to that Family Worship every morning – every morning – and to the Bible. He wouldn't have been Public Enemy Number One today if it hadn't been for those things ...

Now then, another thing about it was this: we didn't deal, in those Family Worship days, with a thousand and one things we might have dealt with, but we concentrated mainly on great personages in the Bible.

There was Moses, for example, and Elijah, and Amos, and Daniel. Now, you get a boy thinking that all over, and, presently, this is what you've got. You've got a young lad looking at these characters back there: *there* was Moses, *there* was Pharaoh, and the one was challenging the other. There was a situation of slavery and exploitation of the people, and there was this brave man who said: 'Let my people go!' Well, Jim had to take his choice; he either had to stand with Pharaoh or else with Moses. And he *plumped for Moses! ...*

And then we came to Daniel, you see, and he had to stand for Daniel. He took his time about it, and it became quite clear to him that Belshazar and Nebuchadnezzar and Darius and the rest of them were flimsy things compared with that man Daniel. Now, you know, we had a hymn about Daniel from our old Sunday School. We used to sing it sixty years ago in Canada. Do you know it? It wasn't high-class poetry but it had some sound substance in it. It went this way:

'Dare to be a Daniel;
   Dare to stand alone!
Dare to have a purpose true
   And dare to make it known!'

Now the difference between Jim and a thousand ministers today is this: they say, 'Dare to admire a Daniel!' but they seldom think of saying, 'Dare to be one.' And it makes a difference! ...

But most remarkable of all is this: Jim saw that if you're going to be effective you must be contemporaneous. If Jim had stood for talking about the old prophets and old martyrs and all the men who lived a long time ago, they'd never have made him Public Enemy Number One ... But the trouble is this, that he saw that every one of the prophets was contemporary. They spoke to contemporary men and contemporary situations. You see, it was a living Pharaoh and a living Moses that you see pictured in the Bible ...

So that here was where my son's troubles began. He said, 'If this was true in the days of Moses, it's true now. And it'll be just as true in China as it is anywhere else.' And so, five or six years ago, he was faced again with the necessity of choosing between two types of leadership. He astonished the people of Canada by declaring that the best man to lead China was a Communist by the name of Mao Tse-tung, and the worst man was Chiang Kai-shek.

Now that's the trouble. He should have kept away from contemporary things. But if you do, you are not quite so effective as we ought to be. He spoke out, and there wasn't a man from China in Canada that knew Chiang Kai-shek and his whole organization better than he did. He spoke to Chiang face to face about the situation in China at that time. He warned him that things were bad and must be changed. He warned our ambassador repeatedly and at length about what was going on. Yes, he played the game, all right. And then he announced, to my astonishment and to the astonishment of everybody, what the outcome of the civil war in China would be. Jim didn't wait until things had happened. He said then, in 1947, 'Although Chiang Kai-shek commands the finest army China ever had, the best equipped army – American equipped – and although he holds every important city in China but one, Chiang Kai-shek is doomed. He deserves to be kicked out and he will be kicked out.'

And all the leading papers in Canada, except two or three, denounced Jim for predicting Chiang's doom. You see, this attitude of the press today isn't a new thing. They've been after Jim for years, because he dared to see what was there to be seen and to tell what he had seen. And he has proven himself, up to date, a true prophet of how things would happen and what would turn out in China.

So that's my introduction to him. He hasn't failed us; he hasn't failed his father and mother. I still remember his mother when he came back from France after the first war ... she heard awful stories of what happened to the boys in Paris and elsewhere. And when he came home she took him aside ... [and] came back to me with these words, 'Daddy, he's all right. He's as good a boy as when he went out to France to fight.'

And that's my message to you tonight. He's as good a boy tonight, in spite of all the howlings of the lions. Most of them now have been manicured, as far as their claws go, and they occupy carpeted dens. But in spite of them all, I'm as proud of him as though they had sent out a ticker-tape welcome for him when he came back to Toronto.

CHAPTER ONE

In the shadow of the white pagoda

Less than a week after they first arrived in Kiating in 1895, having travelled down the Min River from Chengtu on a chartered junk, James and Sarah Endicott would be forced to flee.

A small city of fifty thousand in western China, Kiating was the hub of Loshan hsien (Happy Mountain County) in the prosperous and populous province of Szechuan, the region of four streams. Built upon a high ledge of rock, it was surrounded by an imposing wall of red sandstone, crenellated in medieval fashion.

The buildings of the magistrate's offices, on the high ground in the centre, blended with the graceful, curving, grey-tiled roofs of the residential and business quarters below. Crowded, noisy restaurants and inns, shops for making umbrellas and straw sandals and displaying copper and steel utensils, stores with quality silks or cotton fabrics from England, vendors selling incense and candles made from wax gathered off the 'insect trees,' all these and more lined the relatively wide and smoothly cobbled streets.

As the foreign travellers pushed through the crowded streets to the south-western part of the city, they looked across a vast expanse where the waters of three rivers, the Tatu, the Ya, and the Min, flowed together creating a large whirlpool. On the far shore, with the turbulent water swirling at its feet, sat a magnificent Buddha; sixty feet across the shoulders and 230 feet high, it had been cut into the cliff during the Tang dynasty and still gazed down on the city twelve centuries later. Off to the right, thirty miles distant but clearly visible, was Mount Omei, another giant symbol of idol worshipping: rising eleven thousand feet above sea-level, the mountain was a sacred place known throughout China for its Buddhist monasteries, 'thick as teeth on a comb,' dedicated to PuHsien, the Buddha of Universal Light. Priests and pilgrims, little old women with bound feet, groups of young people from distant villages, were to be seen passing through the city on their way to offer prayers on the Golden Summit. For all its beauty, Kiating was unmistakably the Buddhist stronghold of western China, a formidable challenge to any missionary who devoutly believed there was only one true God.

The journey that ended in Kiating had indeed been a long one. James Endicott, senior, had come originally from Devon in England, the fourth in a family of eleven children. His father, a farm worker, had moved about the valley of the Teign River, cutting hay and tending sheep for the gentry, unable to earn enough to provide the basic needs for his family. In 1882, at the age of seventeen, James left for Canada, having resolved not to spend the rest of his life 'tipping his hat to the squire' as his father had done. While working for his eldest brother as a house painter in Lucan, a village in southwestern Ontario, he was attracted to the Salvation Army and was soon singing in their street-corner rallies. One day his rich baritone voice caught the attention of a lively young Irish woman, who half-jokingly invited him to come to the Methodist church to sing in the choir; this chance encounter with Sarah Diamond determined his future career as well as his marital life.

Sometime after this meeting Endicott became a probationary minister and volunteered for missionary work in the Canadian northwest. The minister of the Methodist church in Lethbridge, the Rev. Charles MacKillop, was sufficiently impressed with the young man's gifts in the pulpit that he sponsored his application to Wesley College at the University of Manitoba. When Endicott graduated with the gold medal in philosophy in 1893, he was not tempted by the prospect of an academic career, for he had already been deeply moved by the experience of hearing the famous American evangelist, John R. Mott, speak at a student conference in Minneapolis. 'I have decided to offer myself to the church for foreign service,' he wrote in 1892, for 'there is awful significance in the figures presented concerning the great millions dying in darkness, and there seems to be great explicitness in the command, "Go ye into all the world." '[1] His classmates at Wesley College chose him as their representative to the newly opened Methodist mission field in Szechuan, and undertook to raise the funds necessary to keep him there until the end of the century. Upon graduation as an ordained minister, Endicott returned to Lucan and there, on the evening of the traditional 12th of July Orange parade, as Sarah had planned, they were married. Two weeks later the young couple were on their way to China.

The Endicotts were not the only challengers to the 'heathen' tradition in Kiating. A long-established French Jesuit mission stood outside the North Gate, and two Protestant groups, the British China Inland Mission and the American Baptists, were already located in the lower town. When their boat nudged into shore under the great banyan trees near the East Gate, the newcomers were greeted by Dr O.L. Kilborn of their own mission, who had preceded them and had acquired premises in the western residential section of the city.

They had, however, chosen a bad time to arrive. The ancient Chinese empire was on its last legs. The old empress dowager, Tzu Hsi, and the decadent Manchu Court she headed, had barely managed to crush the challenge of the Taiping Rebellion through pitiless repression, which had alienated the peasantry and caused disaffection among the educated élite. Now, with the nineteenth century drawing to a close, young scholars, Kang Yu-wei in the lead, were calling for the introduction of Western scientific knowledge and a host of reforms; Sun Yat-sen had issued the first of his revolutionary manifestos to revive China under a republican form of government; and Mao Tse-tung, Chu Teh, and Chou En-lai, who would organize the forces that eventually overthrew the feudal-landlord social system in 1949, had already been born.[2]

The breakdown of the Chinese empire is a story as complex as the decline of ancient Rome, and, as in the fall of Rome, it was the aggression of 'barbarians from without' that created the final, unprecedented crisis. The imperialist aggressors, 'sharpening their teeth and watering at the mouth,'[3] were spearheaded at first by Great Britain in the Opium Wars of the 1840s and 1850s and later by Japan at the time of the Sino-Japanese War of 1894–95. Thus new anti-foreign riots flared up in May 1895, shortly after James and Sarah Endicott and their baby daughter Mary reached Kiating. The troubles were largely instigated by influential Szechuanese who camouflaged their opposition to the Treaty of Shimonoseki, which had ended the war with Japan, by spreading rumours and stimulating the latent fears of the local Chinese about 'people of the ocean,' as foreigners were called. Behind a screen of superstition about foreigners, Chinese merchants and officials were protesting China's recent humiliation and the heavier taxes imposed to pay the war indemnities. The ways of Chinese politics were ever mysterious to the outsider: James Endicott and his colleagues were not aware of the plight of the Chinese merchants; nor, for that matter, did they bother much about the activities of foreign businessmen.[4] The missionaries had other enterprises in mind – preaching the Christian gospel, distributing tracts, healing the sick, and teaching the uneducated – preoccupations enough to occupy most of their waking hours.[5]

Within days of their arrival, then, the Endicotts were in for a rude shock, for angry crowds of demonstrators were pounding on the gates of their compound, throwing stones and refuse over the wall, and shouting: 'Knock down the foreign dog! Kill the big-nosed eaters of children, disturbers of the ancestors!' This terrifying behaviour was occurring as well at missionary compounds in Chengtu. The magistrate in Kiating sent a message to the mission that the foreigners had better go, for the people were upset and uncontrollable. The missionaries hurriedly consulted and decided to leave at dawn the next day. After a sleepless night, the Endicotts set out for the South Gate, taking only the clothes they had on; James carried the double-barrelled shotgun which he had brought from Manitoba for duck hunting. When they arrived at the banks of the river, a large jeering crowd stood between them and the junk, where the other foreigners were already on board. There was no choice but to run the gauntlet. Placing the cook, Lao Yang, in the lead, followed by Sarah and the baby, Endicott raised the gun and roared: 'Zhan Kai! Ngo Kai Qiang.' 'Stand aside! Or I fire!' 'The first one who touches them will be shot!' he added. The crowd parted and they passed through unmolested. As the junk turned its back on Kiating and set sail down the Min for Shanghai, a disheartening two thousand miles away, smoke and flames could already be seen rising in the air.

When the Canadian Methodists returned to Kiating in the spring of 1896, however, they held a trump card in their hands: an order from the Manchu provincial governor requiring the city to pay for the restoration of the buildings that had been wrecked in the riots the previous year. Bolstered with these Chinese funds, the missionaries embarked upon an ambitious programme, purchasing homes, renting a street chapel, building a church, dispensary, school, printing press, and a bookroom, and buying land for a hospital. Preaching, too, began in earnest.

For any foreign extrovert, and for James Endicott in particular, it was a simple matter to gather a crowd and to proclaim the Lord's name in Kiating. He was a strange-looking human, tall and energetic, with eyeglasses and, most curious to the onlookers, red whiskers. His appearance alone was sufficient to attract a score of people at the market or to the storefront street chapel at any time of the day. If, in addition, the missionary could recite the Lord's prayer loudly in Chinese and sing a hymn, he was guaranteed a mass rally of the curious, blocking all the traffic in the street. But it was not possible to win lasting converts without addressing the immediate needs of the people, and it was for this reason that the mission required schools and hospitals as well as chapels.

For the best part of a decade, except for furlough in Canada and absences to escape political disturbances, James and Sarah Endicott made their home in Kiating. Here, in the little Methodist mission compound at 212 White Pagoda Street, in an attractive, single-storey house built around a tree-shaded courtyard, their family continued to grow. In time, little Mary was joined by Enid, Jim, Norman, and Dorothy. James Gareth Endicott, third of the five children and the eldest son, was born on 24 December 1898. At the back of the house, in a cliff, there were caves, where the Endicott children would later play together by the hour. The local people called these caverns 'man tzu tung' (caves of the barbarians), but they were originally rock tombs for burial, dating back two thousand years to the Han dynasty. On the ridge above stood an ancient, nine-storied, white pagoda, which gave its name to the street below, Bei Ta Gai. According to legend, such was the malevolent influence of the pagoda that no son had ever been born under its shadow. It was a myth now shattered.

Jim Endicott's earliest years were spent in Kiating, but his most vivid childhood memories were of Chengtu, where the family moved after his father took charge of the Mission Press in 1904. The capital of Szechuan is a windy city in the middle of a flat plain, and for Jim one of the outstanding experiences of life there was the pleasure of flying kites. Some of them were shaped like dragons and as much as forty feet long. When flown high in the air, the strings on the kites hung down in great loops, which often came enticingly close to the walls of nearby compounds; the temptation to capture the kites of others, by tying a stone to the end of a string and tossing it over the loops, was irresistible. 'Father used to warn us that this was not an ethical practice; he certainly frowned upon it and I think he even forbade it. Nevertheless, we enjoyed it, and secure within our walled missionary compound, my brother and I, two little savages, enjoyed the exhilaration of predatory free enterprise.'[6]

In later life Jim recalled that his 'earliest memories of childhood life on the mission field are concerned almost entirely with the delights of doing those things which were forbidden.' The two small brothers used to sneak out onto the street to buy a particularly delicious brand of candy, although warned often that it 'would make you sick'; considering the complete lack of sanitation in China at the time, 'it is a wonder that we did not die of cholera, dysentery, or typhoid fever.' Another forbidden delight was to go over to the dining room of the apprentices who worked in the Mission Press and enjoy a good Chinese meal. 'We also used to sneak over to watch the presses which fascinated me. My old friend Pen Chi-ling would station one of the small printer's devils at the door to watch for my father's entrance. If he should come the boy would call out, "Red whiskers is coming!" and Mr. Pen dropped us out the side window so we would not be caught watching where we were not supposed to be. That was my first alliance with the proletariat.'[7]

Jim had pleasant memories of playing with Chinese children, mostly the offspring of the servants. This experience gave him an unusual ability to get along with people of different language and culture in later life. Contact with street children was not allowed for fear of catching smallpox or other diseases, but Jim was not aware of any racial differences.

I was only conscious of the fact that we were rather better off. The relations that we had with the servants were really feudal. They had the ideology of great loyalty to the master and they felt lucky to be hired by people who were reasonable and who helped their children to go to school, as we did. Our old cook, Lao Yang, was a man of considerable character who would not hesitate to discipline me. He would even slap me rather sharply occasionally and lecture me on proper behaviour. He was like an uncle and created the feeling in me of having a Chinese as one of the family. The result of this relationship was that I never had any racial prejudice. I had from my earliest childhood learned to regard people as people and that some were good and some were not so good. That had a great influence on my psychology later when I went back as a missionary. I had natural relations of trust and confidence with the Chinese in general. I was never afraid. There were times when we were perhaps threatened with riots but somehow I developed a feeling of friendliness.[8]

Among his memories of Chengtu were the Winter Fair with its colourful chrysanthemum show, soldiers going through the streets to pacify some rebellion in Tibet, and a public execution. Jim was not positive that he saw the actual decapitations, for when he was young, like Mark Twain, he often remembered everything whether it happened or not! Several officers had been caught being corrupt and were made scapegoats. Special tents were put up on the military parade ground which was next to the Mission Press compound and during three days there was music and dancing and good food for the victims. Although his father tried to discourage his interest in the affair, Jim climbed the fence to witness as much as possible; whatever he missed was vividly relayed to him by the Chinese children. At the end of the proceedings a section of the fence was torn down for the coffins to be taken out; it would have been a disgrace and bad luck to allow the beheaded ones to be carried out through the official gate.

The carefree innocence of childhood was interrupted at the age of seven when Jim, along with his older sisters and Leslie Kilborn, was taken three hundred miles downriver by his father to an English Quaker school in Chungking. The next two years at the Hill School were almost entirely unhappy. He was not good at mathematics and his writing was large and scrawly; he preferred to run around catching butterflies or to play tennis. His teachers came to the conclusion that Jim had limited mental capacity and wrote the Endicotts advising that he be apprenticed to some kind of manual work by the age of twelve.

School discipline was harsh and reflected the stiff moral standards of the day. Two incidents left a particularly deep impression on the boy. In the first, he had been juggling two stones when one of them suddenly disappeared and hit his sister Mary in the eye; she protested loudly but Jim insisted that he had not done anything wrong and refused to confess that he had thrown the stone. Miss Hunt called him a liar and caned him. Months later, one of the boys who had been walking behind Jim admitted that he had been twirling his tuque which had a tassel on it and the latter had deflected the stone against Mary's eye. The bitterness of this unjust accusation and punishment never left him.

The second incident reflected the school matron's zealous concern to uphold puritanical standards of sexual purity and modesty. In Jim's second year at the Hill School, James and Sarah were informed by Miss Hunt that their eight-year-old son and a friend had been 'severely punished' because they 'undid their pants and exposed themselves, threatening to relieve themselves on the wall.' 'Fortunately,' she added, 'only boys saw it ...'

To add to Jim's misery, in this authoritarian institution, a child's attempts at self assertion met with little sympathy. One of his most humiliating memories was of the Christmas concert when he had refused to have an adult counsellor and tried to do his own poem. After two lines he got stuck but would not get off the platform. He insisted he would stay there until he remembered it and was finally removed forcibly.

Jim's later hostility towards otherworldly theology may well have had its psychological roots in this two-year period of unhappiness at boarding school. Every night during the term the evangelistic Quakers had prayers and Bible readings and Miss Jones led the singing of the *Glory Song* – the epitome of the theological stance Jim would later call 'reactionary':

When all my trials and labours are o'er
And I am safe on that beautiful shore
Just to be near the dear Lord I adore
Will through the ages be glory for me.
Oh that will be
Glory for me, glory for me ...
When by His grace I shall look on His face
That will be glory, be glory for me.

Had the negative experience at the Hill School been allowed to continue, it might have nipped a theological career in the bud. Forever after Jim associated the *Glory Song* with those years of rigid discipline and negative evaluation. However, after two terms of evident misery on their son's part, his parents decided to keep him at home the following year. He was taught by his mother until Miss Leah Ker was sent out from Canada in 1909 to found the Canadian School in Chengtu, which Jim attended as a day pupil. Schooling at home allowed a wider perspective of Christian theology than that contained in the *Glory Song*.[9]

The Endicott household was a stimulating environment in which to grow up: old-fashioned in its severity but supported by the warmth of love, high in expectations but tolerant of diversity, tense during transient outbursts of temper but united around evolving family traditions. There was a social distance between parents and children typical of that day; for many years meals were eaten separately. But the parents were keen to encourage any enthusiasm the children showed and gave strong support whether to flying kites, collecting butterflies, playing tennis, learning music, or reading. As the family grew older, the emphasis was placed upon intellectual matters and music; dancing and cards were not allowed, and theatre was frowned on except for Shakespeare. Birthday anniversaries and Christmas celebrations, however, were always exciting occasions. Sarah, an outstanding cook, decorated the Christmas table with pressed maple leaves brought out from Canada, and James would read aloud *How John Norton the Trapper Kept His Christmas*, by W.H.H. Murray, an affecting story about a poor woman who was brought aid and comfort.

The marriage of James and Sarah was typical of the patriarchal relationships so prevalent and acceptable in their time: where the father was stern and a disciplinarian, the mother was soft and reassuring. But in moments of desperation mothers too invoked the threat of patriarchal authority to restore order: 'I'll hand you over to your father!' was frequently heard by Sarah's offspring. Once when James was absent and she was reduced to tears by the children, Sarah frightened them badly by threatening to run away.

Family finances – always a problem for missionary families coping both with large families and with the ubiquitous Chinese corruption or 'squeeze' – were a source of friction. As Jim's brother, Norman, later recalled: 'Father was punctual and accurate and kept accounts; he taught himself double entry bookkeeping for the Mission Press and applied it to house affairs. Mother had an allowance but wouldn't keep within it and never quite knew where the money went. Father would yell and intimidate her. There was enough bullying to make us resentful of Father but we did wish Mother was more logical.'[10] Jim also disliked the bully in his father, but such patterns are hard to break: his own children would have similar memories of him scolding their mother and of her tears that followed in consequence.

It was his father's roles as religious teacher and story-teller that had the greatest impact on Jim's adult life. James Endicott believed strongly in the Methodist doctrine of justification by faith. He avoided the narrow fundamentalism of literal acceptance of the Bible as well as what he conceived to be the futile superficiality of the humanist versions of the 'social gospel.' Although he supported the medical and educational work of the Christian missions, the central purpose of the church in his view was to preach the gospel in order to convince people that salvation depended upon repentance and regeneration through acceptance of God as revealed in Jesus Christ, that future punishment or reward depended on keeping the Sabbath holy, and that the virtues of devotion to duty and self-improvement should be cultivated. In addition to his commitment to evangelism, Endicott also had a lively interest in the broad sweep of history beginning with the prophets of the Old Testament down to the lives of men like John Bunyan, Garibaldi, and Abraham Lincoln. From the example of such people he set high standards for the measurement of human achievement and he imparted to his children a sense that true greatness was related to sympathy for the poor and the oppressed.

In the daily family worship sessions after breakfast, James Endicott exposed his family to both of these themes – personal evangelism and the Judaeo-Christian prophetic tradition. From Jim's recollection of these sessions, it was clear that the latter theme made the greatest impression upon him: 'I found it a little hard on the knees when his prayers got a bit long, but the parts that I remember are of his marvellous voice and his ability to read the Bible and make it live; his reading of the Book of Job I can still recall, and he taught me, anyway, to admire the great heroes of the Old Testament, Moses as against Pharaoh, Daniel as against Nebuchadnezzar. I have the impression that he made them much more realistic to us than he was able to do with the New Testament and the more theological aspects of St. Paul.'[11]

Like all British missionaries of the day, James Endicott was an ardent supporter of Queen Victoria and her empire. During the Boer War, for example, he had startled an American colleague by shouting excitedly: 'Take off your hat! Mafeking has been relieved! Mafeking is free!' In 1901, a year after 231 missionaries had been killed during the Boxer Uprisings of North China, he participated in British 'gunboat diplomacy' by securing a pilot for a Royal Navy boat and then accompanying a military mission to rescue Roman Catholic Christians allegedly in danger upriver in Penshanhsien.[12]

Later, Endicott became aware of the unscrupulous dealings of some missionaries and regretted his gunboat venture. The Roman Catholic bishops and priests, in particular, had assumed the status and prerogatives of officials of the Chinese empire, setting up their own courts, securing the best land, and offering powerful assistance to their Chinese converts in case of lawsuits.[13]

He came to believe that the way to make Christianity, at least the Protestant version, succeed in China was not through the use of foreign temporal power.

In 1906, when his son Jim was aged seven and old enough to remember the incident, Endicott helped to undermine plans to establish a British consulate illegally in Chengtu; a missionary was to purchase a piece of land ostensibly for a school but really for a consular building. What incensed Endicott and some of his colleagues was not the basic principle of imperialism inherent in the plan but rather the deviousness of the scheme which would be a 'standing disgrace to our country' as well as 'embarrass missionary operations.'[14] The basic admiration for the empire remained, however, and reinforced the messages Jim was receiving from Miss Ker at school. In later years Jim remembered that the British empire seemed to be something very special:

We sang 'God of our fathers, known of old, Lord of our far flung battle-line ...' as if the Empire were guided by God. We were taught that it carried a white man's burden – we had gone out to the corners of the world with the best of goodwill to help the natives who were backward and ignorant and stupid. Livingstone was a great example of our noble nature, not emphasizing that Liverpool was built up on the slave trade but selecting a few prominent people like Wilberforce who did something to stop slavery which proved how good we were. I remember with what great pride I managed to get a Union Jack up on the mast of our junk as we floated down the Yangtze River into the Port of Ichang where we were going to board a steamer for Shanghai on our way home to Canada in 1910. I was proudly displaying my flag when I noticed a small boat putting off from the British gunboat which was anchored there and an officer came over and very discreetly informed us that the king had died, would we please fly the Union Jack at half mast. I was greatly impressed with this attention.[15]

When James and Sarah Endicott brought their family back to Canada on their second furlough in 1910, the delicate health of their youngest daughter, Dorothy, made it seem unlikely that they would ever return to China as a family. Then, when the church decided that James should become general secretary of the Board of Foreign Missions, a post that he held until the end of his working life, the move to Toronto became permanent. In the early years they lived at 715 Shaw Street in a working class district, but after James' promotion, when the family income improved, they moved up to the more fashionable Walmsley Boulevard. At Dewson Street public school, where he was first enrolled at age eleven, Jim felt nervous about the strange routines and doubtful about his ability to keep up with the class. Fortunately, an early geography lesson was on Asia; when the class started talking about the Yangtze River he mentioned that he had been there recently. The teacher,

Miss Cheer, persuaded him to talk about it, and under her personal interest, which he would never forget, he overcame the negativeness that had been instilled in him as a result of the earlier, unhappy experiences of school.

From that time on he did fairly well in his studies. Records from Brown School and Oakwood Collegiate show that he lacked the patience of a scholar, but his sense of curiosity and quick intelligence, combined with an extraordinary memory, made him above average scholastically. Oakwood Collegiate was new and the classes were small. 'We had a good personal relationship with the teachers,' Jim recalled. 'Miss Evelyn MacDonald was very influential in encouraging me to read widely.' On the urging of his teachers and with the permission of his parents Jim was jumped from the second form to the fourth, skipping third, with the idea that he would put in two years in the fifth form and try for a scholarship. At the age of fifteen he won a gold medal in public speaking on 'The Glories of the British Navy.'[16]

James Endicott was ambitious for his children and scornful if they did not always stand first. Jim adopted the same stance and was jealous of those who stood ahead of him. His egocentricity developed in him a habit of criticizing and even ridiculing those who could do things better than himself. This attitude persisted into adult life even though by that time he was consciously trying to eradicate it. 'To be able sincerely to enjoy the achievements of others is part of the joy of life,' he would tell his children, 'and if one can't then one needs overhauling in the mind and heart.'[17]

At the age of thirteen Jim came to the realization that he wanted to follow in his father's footsteps and preach the gospel as a foreign missionary in China. This idea came to him during a missionary rally at the old Elm Street Methodist Church in Toronto, a few months after the abdication of the Manchu dynasty in China in 1912. Many Canadians were curious to know more about the dramatic turn of events in China, and Jim's father, who had taken the boy along with him to the overflow meeting, used the occasion to speak on the opportunities for Christianity provided by the current anarchy in China. Beginning in biblical times with the text, 'In the year that King Uzziah died I saw also the Lord' (Isaiah 6:1), moving down through history – the collapse of the Roman empire and the triumphant rise of Christianity above its political ruins to conquer the conquerors under Augustine's missionary work – Endicott predicted that once more Christianity faced a challenge to help restore unity and peace to the millions who were suffering from destruction and despair resulting from the removal of China's leaders. The historical analogies were compelling and young Jim made an inward decision to accept the challenge. When he shared this ambition with his parents, they gave it their blessing in both spoken and unspoken ways. There was thus no adolescent rebellion against parental values; nor did Jim's childhood hero-worshipping of his father turn into its opposite, as is frequently the case. Instead he became a lad with a sense of vision and purpose who frequently turned to his father and his mother for advice and friendship.[18]

In spite of James Endicott's promotion, the family was not well off financially and the children were encouraged to find part-time or summer jobs to help out. Two experiences made a deep and lasting impression on Jim's youthful mind. In the summer of 1914, before the Great War broke out, he was seeking a job at Eaton's, a large department store in Toronto. He went down one morning and lined up at a window. There were about fifty people in the line, waiting for ten jobs. Suddenly a man came to the window and shouted: 'You must go to the office in the next building.' Everyone started to run, regardless of who was first in the line. As Jim was running quickly he passed a rather old, lame man who could not travel fast. Something in his heart gave a tug as he passed him, but he kept on running and got near the head of the line. When he told his father how he felt, Endicott explained that in trying to get himself a job Jim was not harming anyone else. But this explanation left Jim troubled; such ethics implied the 'survival of the fittest,' which might be a law of nature, but was it ethical?[19]

The other experience occurred in the summer of 1916 while Jim was working in a munitions factory. Unaware he was even in a lion's den, Jim had his first experience of daring to be a Daniel:

I remember that the pay for those times was very good, although we worked very hard, twelve hours. I was running a six-way lathe making nose caps for shells. The most vivid memory I have was the awful feeling of how terrible factory life would be if anything should happen to my father and I would have to go to work in the factory. You just were so tired when you came home that you had no energy or interest for anything else. You would really become a cog in a machine and the idea horrified me. One night in a lunch hour we started some discussions. I had no knowledge of the trade unions or of any kind of struggle, but it came to me that men should organize together and maybe even bargain collectively. There was rather a silence and some sharp looks from the foreman. When I came out from work a day or two later through a narrow alley, a big 'plug-ugly' stepped out from somewhere and said, 'You're the so and so that is talking trade unions are you,' and he hit me a terrific wallop on the mouth, knocked me semi-conscious for a while. The result was I lost a tooth. The dentist tooth that I have in the front came as a result of that blow.[20]

He lost a tooth but came away from this encounter with greater moral sympathy for the underdog in society.

CHAPTER TWO

The Methodist soldier

Tall, spare, weighing barely 130 pounds, Jim Endicott hurried down to the old Toronto armouries a few days after his eighteenth birthday in December 1916. Flanked by posters declaring 'Your King and Country Need You, Now!' he volunteered for active service in the army, and as he posed for photographs in his new uniform it was clear that he was well pleased with his decision.

Endicott joined the army believing it was a chance for service and adventure in a righteous cause guided by the hand of God. Everything in his environment – school, church, family, and the Toronto *Globe* – contributed to the felling that it was his personal duty to take up arms against Kaiserism, the popular name for German imperialism. W.B. Creighton, a close family friend and editor of the Methodist *Christian Guardian*, wrote that this was 'God's battle,' and making one's contribution to help win the war was 'a supreme manifestation of faith, a supreme act of decision and of sacrifice for Christ.'[1] Ministers became army chaplains and the churches took an active hand in recruiting, collecting victory bonds, and providing recreation for soldiers stationed away from home. Several conferences of the Methodist Church reported that within their bounds there was not an available minister's son of military age who was not in khaki. With few exceptions, such as J.S. Woodsworth and William Ivens who were pacifists, or social reformers like Nellie McClung, Salem Bland, and William Irvine, everyone supported the war effort in its early years.

Within the family circle, the view of his father, rich in historical perspective, had a powerful influence on Endicott's mind and shaped his feelings about the war. He was particularly impressed by the arguments his father used at a conference in the United States in 1916 to convince his neutral American brethren of the reasonableness of the stand taken by Canadian Methodism on the war. 'We have viewed with scorn all jingoistic flag waving,' James Endicott began, 'and we were in deep sympathy with Lloyd George when he maintained that when the flag waved over a slum it was as deeply disgraced as when it dropped over a battlefield on which the nation had met defeat. Such a people before the war we were, and such a people, essentially, we remain.' Yet, when war had actually been declared, Canadians responded with amazing unanimity of conviction and were continuing with steadily deepening purpose: larger military forces had crossed the Atlantic Ocean from Canada than had crossed altogether since the days of Columbus. The subject was too tragic for empty rhetoric, but, judged by every test, the citizen soldiers of Canada had fought a good fight. He went on to describe the inner spirit that moved them in their valorous deeds and unmeasured sacrifices, and concluded that, in spite of their military efforts, Canadians were still great lovers of peace:

the heroes of St. Julien and of subsequent battles were fundamentally one with the heroes of Marston Moor and of Valley Forge and it would not be a desecration of the immortal words of Lincoln were we to stand where our brave lads lie buried in France and say as he said on the stricken field of Gettysburg over your slain heroes, that they died in order that 'government of the people, by the people and for the people shall not perish from the earth.' And because such things are of priceless value, we have paid a great price and we shall continue to pay, however great the price may be ... We sing no songs of hate, nor do we propose to teach our children to sing them. We are fighting as free men for freedom and for freedom to be shared by all the world, and we do not intend in the process to become the slaves of hatred ... From out this weltering chaos of bloodshed we hope to see emerge a new world order, the coming of 'a new heaven and a new earth wherein dwelleth righteousness.' May the Lord hasten the good day ...[2]

If the premise was granted – that the leaders of the British empire deserved trust – and if opposition to the war by French Canadians was overlooked, then the logic was powerful, the words eloquent and deeply soul-stirring.

As might be predicted, army life at Lansdowne Park in Ottawa, where Jim Endicott arrived for basic training on 30 January 1917, did not measure up to the rhetoric of his father and was a profound shock to the idealistic 'son of the manse.' To him the men seemed crude and coarse, utterly lacking in what he had been taught were the necessary qualities for a good life. The Protestant churches had been successful in introducing the prohibition of alcoholic beverages in Ontario,[3] but Endicott wrote home that he was surrounded by men 'who made frequent trips to Hull, etc.' in Quebec. It depressed him greatly to have to rub up against and listen to men whose chief interest seemed to be in finding a bar and chasing whores.

Endicott had been assigned to the Signal Training Depot, Canadian Engineers, where he became sapper No 507564. He was under the impression that the engineers were the élite corps of the Canadian army. But as he scrubbed the barracks floor, peeled potatoes in the officers' mess, did guard duty, hospital duty, and marched around the parade ground at 6:15 a.m., he joked that he was 'nothing but a blooming fatigue specialist.' His basic training also included such matters as lectures on signals, musketry, route marches through downtown Ottawa in full battle dress, and practice in riding horseback. One day he made the mistake of volunteering to go on stables for a boy who was sick. It was his first ride. He got along all right with the trotting and cantering, but then the two- and three-foot hurdles were brought out. His horse was balky and did not go over evenly, 'but kind of "bucked" over and lit stock-still on the other side.' Endicott shot over its neck and landed on the seat of his trousers ten feet away. He avoided injury, but from then on did not think he would care for stables, for 'there is too much everlasting grooming and smell.'

As Endicott watched one overseas draft after another leave Lansdowne Park he became restless. There was no fulfilment for his ambitions in the mindless fatigues of an Ottawa barrackroom. Like many, he was convinced that the war would be over by summer or fall, and he wanted to get to England at least and better still to France. Then one day towards the end of March 1917 he was given only a few hours notice to take the place of a soldier who had broken his leg. The march through the streets of Ottawa to the waiting train was a memorable event. The new members of the Canadian Corps, a force already famous for battle honours in France, received a roaring send-off. Led by a pipe and drum band, half the depot went ahead with rifles as an honour guard, half came behind with flags, and the overseas draft marched in the centre – 120 men easily distinguished by their rolled overcoats, mess tins, haversacks, and water bottles. In spite of showers, the streets were packed with people who cheered and clapped; cut flowers, candy, and cigarettes rained down from the windows on the upper floors. Endicott had never heard a Canadian crowd cheer its troops; for the moment he felt like a hero. His memory flashed back to the time he had first arrived in Canada, how he had thought what a wonderful place it must be. 'No one could ever have dreamt that in a few years I would be splashing through the streets of its capital in the uniform of a soldier.'

His diary reveals his further excitement about discovering the eastern part of Canada; his early views on Quebec are those that might be expected from a teenager who had reached the fifth form in the orange-tinted Ontario school system.

March 27, Near St. Charles, PQ The track runs near the river for some miles before you come to Point Lévis and the opposite bank of the St. Lawrence and the hills before Quebec are very pretty … When I got the first glimpse of the Plains of Abraham I thought various things. I have always wanted to see them since Mother gave me *With Wolfe in Canada* when I was ten. I never dreamt that when I should see them it would be from a troop train on my way to England. I liked the look of Quebec, especially the citadel. The Montmorency Falls are frozen over but we could see them quite distinctly across the river which I guess is about two miles wide. We stayed in Point Levis about ten minutes … got a good view of a small part of the great river … saw the famous bridge with the middle span missing. Quebec, especially around Quebec City, seems too fine to be owned by these — Frenchmen. I can't stand them. They are most queer. Their farms are about one hundred yards wide and very long and you see farm houses all in a row …

His opinion of French Canadians, already low because of their failure to implement prohibition, was not improved by a hail of stones that hit the troop train near Point Lévis from sources unseen. He had no understanding of the French-Canadian reluctance to fight for an empire whose supporters refused them equality inside their own country.

April 8, Elmsdale, Nova Scotia (near Halifax) Easter Sunday, spent on a side track. When I woke up in the morning there was a white-throated thrush sitting on a tree about thirty feet away singing like everything. Travelled through Moncton, Amherst, Truro, one of the prettiest little cities I have seen in all Canada … there were all kinds of girls wanting to shake hands, some chaperoned, some not, and we had a great deal of fun. There was more yelling, more hooting, more promiscuous handshaking …

On the voyage from Halifax to Liverpool Endicott was too seasick to notice much; as a friend said: 'the first day you are afraid you are going to die and the second day you are afraid you are not going to die.' But when settled at Crowborough Camp in Sussex he felt once more 'like a young Sampson ready to face the rigours of training camp for another eight months.' Army life in England still held out the same alluring attractions in the way of 5:30 a.m. reveilles, mess duties, and Officer Commanding inspections. Now and then something turned up to break the stillness, a visit from royalty or a threatened air raid – 'one as bad as the other' – or a long route march on Saturdays when it invariably rained.

Through all the physical toughening of training camp, Endicott was determined, if possible, to maintain the habits and manners of his Christian upbringing. 'Do not forget,' he wrote to reassure his mother, 'that I am just that much of a Christian that I am not ashamed to kneel and ask God for guidance and pray for those at home.' He disapproved of the massed church parades which the military brass hats favoured: too often the preacher could not be heard, and when the troops had to stand from 7:30 a.m. to 11:00 a.m. some inevitably fainted. There was little religion, too, in the comments that floated through the air on such occasions. He preferred the Bible study classes which a fellow engineer, Rev. Bill Howey of Owen Sound, organized at the 'Y' on Sundays, or the efforts of the chaplain to create a group consciousness among some of the Christian boys in order to prevent them from becoming discouraged and losing ground as individuals 'because they thought they were the only ones in the whole outfit trying to fight clean.' As Rev. Endicott's son, Jim was asked to speak at one of the meetings held out in the woods. Choosing as his text 'Grant unto thy servants, that with all boldness they may speak thy word' (Acts 4:29), he talked for fifteen minutes not so much on 'to speak' as 'to act' the word. At the age of eighteen it was necessarily a patched up job, but he felt that the other boys appreciated it.

To escape the coarseness and monotony of army life, Endicott visited several aunts on his father's side who lived in London or went down to the coast to see the holiday crowds and to walk by the seaside hotels. A Canadian serviceman with a bandolier was a target for smiles all along the promenade, especially from the young women. On trips to Brighton and Worthing with Bill Howey, however, the two soldier-Methodists found it difficult to strike up acquaintances. The strange cockney accents were unnerving. And, deep within, Endicott was frozen for fear of getting involved in some way that his church and his parents, especially his mother, might disapprove. Several lines of poetry stuck in his mind:

Somewhere a woman watches thrilled with pride ...
Oh! keep for her dear sake, a stainless name,
Bring back to her a manhood free from shame.

A year after he had enlisted in Toronto and a few days after he became eligible at nineteen, Endicott was called for active service in France, where he was assigned to the 2nd Brigade, Canadian Field Artillery, attached to the

First Division of the Canadian army. With economy of words his diary entries record the events that shaped his existence and the general current of his mind.

1 January 1918 It is not the circumstances of life that count but how you take them; and God never closes one door but he opens two.

13 January 1918 This is my first Sunday on active service and it does not in the least feel like Sunday. They carry on as usual ... Had a bath at the Corps bath house today. Was lucky enough to get issued with a complete new outfit. Tea with Capt. Otter. Read some R.L. Stevenson. I like him because he makes me laugh at myself. Service at 'Y' in Villiers aux Bois.

24 January 1918 Warned for the 1st Div. and sent up by truck. Started right in on the horse lines. They are altogether too regimental here and I do not wonder at the length of the war. Had a fine discussion with Ellis last night on 'Ethics and the War.' I think the time has come for Britain to offer an armistice.

8 February 1918 Stables and dump cart. Went down to the 13th Batt. Concert party and it was pretty fair ... Heard the following discussion today. They had been talking filth, telling stories, etc., and I went out for a bit and they did not give me time to get away till they let out:

  1st Voice: (Laughing) 'I guess we've shocked his modesty.'

  2nd Voice: 'Well he's a damn nice fellow anyway.'

  3rd Voice: 'Yes, he's a hell of a good sort and it's a case of do as I do with him and he never tries to tell you what you should do.'

  Then I got out of range.

3 March 1918 Sunday. Church parade and beaucoup shining. The speaker both morning and evening was very short and not very good but he had some good ideas. It does not do to be too critical. In contrast to last week, this week I have been pretty cheerful and every day I feel more and more the power of the Personality of Christ in the development of true life. I would be hooted at as an idiot were I to express it aloud but day by day I feel more and more the magnitude of the cause in which we are partaking; the mighty appeal there is in this struggle of freedom against military oppression and the unique experiences one is privileged to undergo. It is a continual source of wonder to me what will come of it all. How will all these men and their habits of life fit back into the clean manhood of Canada. What great movements will be started and must not the trend of life for the ultimate realization of a notion of social rightness and reformed living be directed by the teachings, the Ruling Spirit of the

Jesus of History? I am at times inclined to be almost cynical at the petty righteousness and narrow-minded religion and dogma of church people but it is my Christian home and parents, my Christian friends and the strange appeal the gospel has to me now, since last January, the strange confidence within me at times, which makes me feel superior, even to death itself which roots my faith in the 'Man of Galilee.'

8 March 1918 Out on the forward lines all morning and cleaned up a bit in afternoon. Read Omar Khayyam and Fitzgerald's essay and I am beginning to appreciate it in the right way but it made me angry at first. The pretense that sensual pleasure is the serious pursuit of Life does not go well with me. Viz:

Yesterday *this* day's madness did prepare;
Tomorrow's Silence Triumph or Despair.
Drink! for you know not whence you came nor why,
Drink! for you know not why you go nor where.

That does not go well up here in a dugout where Fritz makes merry.

5 April 1918 In Arras today and Fritz was shelling the R[oyal] E[ngineers'] Dump. Most of the boys were drunk tonight and some were sick. I sleep with one.

9 April 1918 Vimy Ridge. Worked on lines all day. Fritz shelled and I was afraid. Beaucoup drunkenness tonight.

On 21 March 1918 the German high command launched its last major offensive of the war in an effort to separate the British armies from the French and to capture the Channel Ports. The British Fifth Army cracked as 106 German divisions moved forward on a fifty-mile front immediately to the south of the sector held by the Canadian Corps. As the Canadian artillery was called into supporting action for the hard pressed Fifth Army, Endicott found himself alternately on picket duty with a rifle or thirty feet down in a damp dugout, wearing a tin hat and a gasperator around his neck, operating a signal box to direct the gunfire. Rumours were flying, about the old battlefields of the Somme being piled once more with enemy corpses, but when Endicott overheard from the signal box Field Marshal Haig's order of the day on 11 April, he knew the situation was serious: 'Every position must be held to the last man. There must be no retirement. With backs to the wall and believing in the justice of our cause each one of us must fight to the end.' Wet and cold, and after two days and a night without sleep, Endicott accepted a ration of rum.

The German offensive ground to a halt in May and the tension began to subside. There followed a three-month respite during which the Allied armies reorganized and prepared for the final hundred-day offensive which was to end the war on 11 November 1918. Jim had more time to read and to reflect upon the core of his beliefs.

5 May 1918 Sunday. No church parade on account of rain. The men were expressing themselves in most degraded language of the padre, the church and in fact anything good. Read 'Closed Doors' by Begbie last night and it is very real. He also rubbed me about Christianity. For a long while now I have been waiting for some definite settlement in my own mind of the mysteries of my religion. I cannot see why there should be the Virgin Birth, or the miracles of the bodily resurrection etc. What most men need to get instilled into them is a standard of sexual morality, a respect for all women and a little true religion which is to do justice, love mercy and walk humbly with God. I wish I could get somewhere in a quiet comfortable place and be alone for a while. I laughed for a few minutes at a joke tonight:

Tommy: 'Ow far is it to camp?

Native: About five miles as the crow flies.

Tommy: Well, 'ow far is it if the blooming crow has to walk and carry a rifle and kit bag?

9 May 1918 Yank threw me today. It took all my nerve to walk back and ride him again. They expect some fighting here shortly.

10 May 1918 Rode Yank successfully and played football. I am in poor physical condition these days ... I am in strange circumstances and one of the greatest joys of life is to write a cheerful letter home or to sit and recall the past. The old innocent days in China, the Christian strength and beauty of my home, and my happy helpful school days. How strangely those contrast with the present! How shall I learn to love them, these fellow men of mine, with their scorn of goodness, their vile attitude towards women and the sacred things of life and their ultimate selfishness. I thank heaven I am honest and strong enough to take an infinite pride in my Christianity.

11 May 1918 Carried on with the usual routine. Went picking mushrooms tonight and gathered a hat full. And they say there is a war on! Here I am having fried mushrooms to the extent of a pound or so and in London 1 lb. would fetch $1.00.

11 June 1918 I was worried today somehow, caused no doubt by the discussion I had with Watson about the church. I came across an article in the 'Canadian Magazine' about the Church. It is evident that the Church as an institution must wake up. Also the C. of E. is dead in England and the R.C. is a relic of medieval superstition. The Church must drop its dogma, its deeper philosophy which goes over the heads of the members and its worship of respectability. True religion and undefiled is that ye visit the sick and widows and keep yourself unspotted from the world and thou shalt love thy neighbour as thyself. I believe with R.L.S[tevenson] that Christ came 'not to give views but a view,' not to give a 'code of rules but a ruling spirit.' To instill in man a love for the beautiful in all things, reverence for God and for manhood and womanhood, to teach men to be honest, truthful, and unselfish, surely this does not require the deep-dyed dogmatists and foolish arguers. I enjoyed Beauchamp on 'Prayer' and Pope on the secret of happiness from his 'Essay on Man' ...

5 July 1918 Practised baseball twice today and read. Had another discussion with McCandlass on Literature, Poetry and finally from Porphia's Lover into the disillusions of life. He claims that the cynics knock the bottom out of all our beliefs and that we cannot stand on anything. I argued that when the cynics were through it was then the man of real stuff set a firm chin and started out with strong Faith to make the best of life and if he be a lover of Nature and Humanity and be accustomed to intellectual honesty he can laugh the cynics to scorn. Mac. proved his worth though, when he spoke his appreciation of a brave little woman here who is bringing up a fine little family. Her husband is a prisoner ...

About this time an unusual and intriguing request came to Endicott: the British War Office asked that he be transferred to serve as an officer with the Chinese Labour Corps. An unprecedented number of Chinese workers and student-workers, about 150,000, had come to France under temporary contract to help with the war effort. Some of the Chinese worked in French factories, mines, and workshops, but the majority were attached to the British army where they were assigned to the heavy work connected with road repairs, ammunition dumps, construction of barracks, exhuming and re-burying the war dead. Because of the nature of this work and the social environment where race-conscious British officers tried to impose strict discipline, the national and class consciousness of the Chinese workers developed rapidly and led to the growth of militant protective organizations, such as the Chinese Labourers' Society, the Labour Union, and other semi-political or Marxist groups.[4] In order to cope with the disaffected Chinese workers, the War Office was recruiting British China missionaries as officers for the Chinese Labour Corps. Captain Bert Brace of the Canadian Methodist mission in Szechuan had discovered that Endicott was in France and put in a request for his transfer. In response to a message to report to divisional headquarters, Endicott cleaned the dirt of the trenches from his boots and rode Yank back to report for an interview.

The first officer to question him wanted to know if he could speak any

Chinese. 'Well,' he replied, 'I can speak a little,' although he actually only remembered some nursery rhymes and a few individual words. The immediate task for the Chinese was to paint some rectangular boards as markers for the First Division, so the officer wanted to know if Jim could tell the men to paint the boards red. 'Oh yes,' was the response, 'I certainly could.' It was a strange coincidence, but the only sentence that Endicott could say in Chinese at that time was 'You must paint it red.' The reason for this piece of knowledge lay in an incident that occurred while his father was supervising the building of their house in Chengtu in 1906. An old Chinese painter became very enthusiastic about a cellar way and didn't notice that there were no steps as yet. He walked into the doorway and as he was saying 'Yao shua hong di, yao shua hong di!' 'We'll paint it red!' he stepped off into the void, fell, and knocked himself unconscious on the cement floor below. The cement was still wet, and all the time the Endicotts were in Chengtu the mark of the painter's head was still there. The old man recovered and Jim never forgot how to say 'Yao shua hong di.' The unsuspecting officer, noting that the Chinese workers did as Endicott had instructed, approved his linguistic abilities and passed him on to the colonel. Here he was not so fortunate. Eyeing Endicott's underfed horse and trench-scuffed boots, the colonel asked: 'Soldier, what makes you think you'd make an officer?' Endicott protested that he was not applying for anything, only willing to be of service if required. The interview was terminated abruptly. Later his brigade captain showed him the terse report that said: 'No. 507564 marginal material; unsuited to be an officer.' It was a judgement with which Endicott was inclined to agree, and he was content to remain a sapper for the last months of the war.

The final assault of the war began on the morning of 8 August near Amiens. To surprise the enemy, the fifty thousand shock troops of the Canadian Corps, proud of their reputation for 'frontier ingenuity,' had rapidly moved forty miles south and assembled under cover of darkness and careful camouflage in the broad valley of the Luce River.[5] Four days later, not having washed or shaved since the attack began and with his unit having such trouble keeping up with the retreating Germans that they carried no blankets or coats and nothing except rations in their haversacks, Endicott sat down and wrote an account of the events, which his father sent on to the *Christian Guardian*:

I will never forget the morning of the 8th. As soon as the guns opened up four of us started out to lay a line from our advanced headquarters to Fritz' support lines. The mist was very heavy in the Valley where Fritz was and it lent excitement to the whole affair. The great tanks came creeping up and the reserve artillery came galloping across the fields of wheat.

Before long our wounded began to come back. We stopped and dressed three men who will get away to Blighty I hope but the fourth lad died while he was being fixed up. After that there was a bit of dirty work in the shape of a small barrage. We got through. There was only one shell which landed near enough to cover us with dirt. By this time there were endless lines of cavalry coming through the mist formed up in squadrons. Before it was over it was all the artillery could do to follow up our own infantry, let alone bombard the retiring Hun.

The second day the fight was stiffer and the German machine guns showed great pluck in holding a wooded valley. The infantry failed to take it and also the cavalry but by this time the heavy tanks were up and soon Fritz was in full retreat ... There is still a lot of hard going and there will be much dirt flying but still we are here for that and at any rate I'll bet we'll put a bee in old Ludendorff's bonnet.

August 8th was indeed, in Ludendorff's words, 'the black day of the German Army.'[6] But Endicott had also had some bad moments. By mid-morning, as he walked to the crest of a hill unreeling wire behind a tank, he suddenly took fright at the sight of a German sniper with his gun pointed straight at him. Gripped by fear and nausea, he fell to the ground. When nothing happened, he looked up cautiously and saw the sniper in the same position. He found that the German had been shot through the heart but his head remained propped up by his rifle. As Jim walked on that morning the sight of hundreds of dead and wounded men had its affect. Ignoring orders, as German shells began landing nearby, he and a comrade took shelter for half an hour while the rest of the attack moved forward. Later, having advanced almost five miles and run out of cable, he grew weary and lay down to sleep in a shell crater. When he awoke it was daybreak the next morning and his unit had moved on, shifting south by a mile; he was in unspeakable panic for some hours trying to rejoin it.

With the demolition of the supposedly impregnable Hindenburg fortifications in October, German morale collapsed and most of the fighting of the war was over. As the First Division joined the pursuit across Belgium, villagers assembled at the churches to ring bells and to cheer 'les braves Canadiens.' At one place where Endicott stayed the woman brought out a bottle of the very finest aged wine, which she said she had been carrying around in her forced exile in Germany for the purpose of drinking to the health of Belgium's liberators and to the day when freedom triumphed. There was a time when he would have walked out rather than take a mouthful of wine. But here, amongst these cultured and generous people, he felt that the hard and narrow ideas of prohibition were irrelevant. He drank the toast.

It was not the first break in his strict Methodist moral discipline. His family had been warned in letters home that things would not be all plain sailing when he got back. 'A man cannot be out here for so long,' he wrote, 'without getting his ideas changed. I used to consider smoking wrong. Now I consider it an undesirable habit but not to be looked down on in one's friends. I have smoked a bit out here.' It was not as easy to dismiss feelings of guilt related to his sexual urges. After flirting with a girl named Maria at Roudorf, near Cologne, in Germany, he felt ashamed:

My code of morals has been so hard and stiff that when I did made a small slip [he had kissed her goodbye at her request] it assumed large proportions. It makes one savage to think that after sailing straight and true for the war I should make a slip at the end. I have no one to blame but myself and I am lucky that I left when I did. It is not the thought of what I did that hurt, for I did nothing, but the thought of what I might not have had the strength to resist, which makes me repentant and very, very thoughtful. These, in the eyes of the world, small sins will please God be healed twice as strongly and perhaps the character formed under these knocks will be more worthy and twice as strong. Too much saintliness would perhaps make us too overbearing but such temptations are to be strongly overcome.

As the victorious troops marched across Germany, Endicott recorded some of his reflections on the people he had been taught to view as the enemy: 'I am afraid I was not cut out to be a conqueror, and am inclined to sympathize with these folks very much. They have sung their hymns of hate; they were told it was the correct thing; and like many others they were not accustomed to reasoning for themselves so they cheered for victories and prayed for the defeat of their enemies. The world will be long in forgiving their selfishness and crimes but these people here never heard of "world power." They were surrounded by enemies on all sides and were told to defend their "Vaterland." Of course, they may have been extra willing to be duped but they are going to suffer some real hardships now to pay for it.'

When Endicott had to go on 4 a.m. bridge duty in Bonn he was billetted in a home where two sons, also tall and fair, had been killed in the war. 'You can't lie very cold and distant,' he reflected, 'when some jolly old frau about five feet high and six feet broad, insists on going through your kit to see if your socks etc., need mending and wants to know if you get lots to eat and that if you don't you must eat with her. A man would need a heart of adamant to be high and mighty after that.' Earlier, during the battle for Amiens, Endicott had stumbled across the body of a young German soldier whose appearance was not unlike his own, whose face he liked, and he felt he could have made a friend had they met in peace. Eventually he mailed to the German mother the picture and other keepsakes he had taken off the dead enemy. The grateful mother wrote back to him and in later years he sent her parcels from Canada.

The contrast between Endicott's expectations of what the war might accomplish and the harsh realities of the blood-soaked struggle in Europe was extreme. The horrors of war and the coarseness of the barracks destroyed any illusions he had had about military service; he had seen men degraded and brutalized and his sensitive personality had revolted. At the same time, his inherited ethical norms, especially the prudish moral codes of Methodism, had been shaken, giving way to the uncertain searchings of a young man for some philosophy of life to give meaning to his changing mental and spiritual universe. Although he still believed in the church, he wrote his father to say that he was 'not anywhere near deciding on studying for the ministry' because he was not sure he had the necessary personality to make good as a preacher. Nevertheless, the bravery, the sacrifices, and the comradeship that he had also seen in the war gave him hope and kept alive his dream of going back to China as a missionary in order to demonstrate international brotherhood as God's plan for the human race.

On political matters, his naïve belief in England and in the goodness and justice of the British empire was undermined by various observations, not least by the prominence given to the frivolous activities of the aristocracy in the British newspapers: he had complained that 'they fill up pages and pages with fool pictures of the duchess pouring tea or some such national crisis'; once he had stumbled across a fox hunt in Sussex at a time, he knew, the working poor of London were forced to queue up for bones to make soup.

As for his thoughts on the war itself, he was most impressed by the dramatic, yet questioning, lines from 'The Hosts,' written in 1915 by Alan Seeger, a young American poet who by now had had 'a rendezvous with death, at midnight in some flaming town.' He memorized some lines and after the war copied them onto the cover of his photograph album:

There was a stately drama writ,
By the hand that peopled the earth and air,
And set the stars in the infinite,
And made night gorgeous and morning fair,
And all that had sense to reason knew
That the bloody drama must be gone through.
Some sat and watched how the action veered,
Waited, profited, trembled, cheered.

> We saw not clearly nor understood,
> But yielding ourselves to the Master Hand,
> Each in his part as best he could,
> We played it through as the author planned.

Apart from an instinctive, almost inarticulate, resentment that he felt about those who waited and profited, these lines expressed an idealism and fatalism about war which Endicott shared at this stage of his life: fatalism because, if God arranged history, then the war must be part of the arrangement; idealism because it is assumed that there is a righteous purpose, even if its design cannot be seen clearly. By the end of this grim conflict, when he marched into Germany as one of the survivors and conquerors, Endicott had not shifted to a pacifist position as some had done, nor had he begun to question what lay behind the slaughter or ponder the deeper causes of war. But through his contact with ordinary German people he at least understood better than before the potential universality of human brotherhood. He saw that this potential could only be realized by dedication and prolonged effort, and this conclusion strengthened his resolve to become a missionary as a means to support such a goal.

CHAPTER THREE

At
university

After the Great War ended in November 1918, Jim Endicott spent six months at Khaki College in Yorkshire, a school, set up by the army for men who agreed to defer their repatriation for a few months, intended to qualify young soldiers for entrance to university in Canada. Amongst other things, Endicott studied history, under Professor George Wrong of the University of Toronto, and Latin and Greek. But it was not easy, after the horrors and stimulation of wartime, to settle into the routine of academic study. As he headed out to Scarborough with a class picnic to celebrate the end of lectures in June 1919, he was certain he would fail the approaching examinations. When the picnickers returned, however, they found the parade ground laid out with steel helmets and trenching tools. 'Has the war started again?' someone asked. Ordered at once to line up, his class was then marched down to the train to be taken to Epsom in Surrey, south of London. There had been a riot among the disgruntled Canadian troops waiting in their dreary camps on the Downs to return to Canada; the university boys, considered reliable, were instructed to quell the disturbance. Fortunately, by the time they arrived at Epsom order had been restored, though they were kept on stand-by for several weeks. By this time Endicott was praising the Almighty for his great good fortune, for Khaki College had decided to grant the men their examinations without having written them. As a result, when the young soldier returned to Toronto in the summer of 1919 he was able to enter his chosen honours course without having finished the fifth year in high school.

The Canada that Endicott returned to, in which he would spend the next six years as a student, was entering an unusual period of social and intellectual ferment.[1] The boom years of the early twentieth century, which had seen unprecedented feverish railway building and massive immigration to populate the Canadian West, and had culminated in the expansion and industrialization that had taken place during the war, were over. Beginning with the general strike in Winnipeg in 1919, the country was embroiled for several years in a wave of strikes and labour agitation, as Canadian workers, whose union membership had doubled during the war but plummeted thereafter, struggled to resist employer wage-cutting and union-breaking. Meeting in a barn near Guelph, scattered factions of militant socialists joined together to form the Workers' party, a precursor of the Communist party, with the avowed revolutionary aim of overthrowing the capitalist system.[2] Even more success-fully, the farmers too strengthened their organizations; and, on the basis of reform platforms calling for reduced tariffs and freight rates, graduated taxes on private and corporate incomes, votes for women, and the public ownership of utilities and the processing of natural resources, they elected a government in Ontario in 1919, became a force to be dealt with in other provinces, and in 1921 formed the government in Alberta.

At the federal level, too, there was political instability, and Prime Minister Arthur Meighen's policy of favouring the vested interests combined with his repressive measures against labour only served to increase social unrest. Popular discontent and disillusionment thus led to the defeat of the lingering wartime unionist government in December 1921; the new Liberal administra-tion of W.L. Mackenzie King faced in the House of Commons not only the decimated Conservatives but also the representatives of two new parties: the sixty-five member, farm-based, National Progressive party, now the official opposition, and the Independent Labour party consisting of two socialist members, J.S. Woodsworth and William Irvine, both of whom were clergy-men turned politicians.[3]

Confronted by the industrial conflict and rural discontent apparent at the end of the war, the Canadian churches, especially the Methodist Church, began to criticize strongly the existing social system. The long-standing emphasis on evangelism and the saving of individual souls was increasingly challenged by a radical social gospel that argued that the capitalist system itself should be changed; it was not enough to seek personal salvation in the hereafter, the Kingdom of God must be built here and now on earth. Accord-ing to a resolution adopted by the Methodist General Conference in 1918, the war had made clearly manifest the 'moral perils inherent in the system of production for profits'; the undying ethics of Jesus demanded 'nothing less than a transference of the whole economic life from a basis of competition and profits to one of co-operation and service.'[4] In the teeth of opposition from businessmen and fundamentalist, conservative clergy, few practical means were suggested for bringing about this revolutionary change; nevertheless, the conference action was another sign of the social turbulence and intellectual agitation that were occurring across the land as Jim Endicott began his university training.

Victoria College in 1919 was a small, intimate community;[5] its ivy-covered, redstone Victorian architecture, creaky hardwood floors, spacious halls, and wide, friendly staircases, whose steps were already wearing thin at the edges from the endless tramp of book-laden students, made it a comfortable place to be. It was not difficult to forget the world beyond. Endicott enrolled in a triple honours course known as English, History, and Philosophy, and participated enthusiastically in the extra-curricular programme of tennis, teas, and debates. He was especially fascinated by the works of Shakespeare and Wordsworth, and by the study of the French and American revolutions. Although he did well in logic and philosophy generally, he felt there was too much idle, unscientific speculation. In his second year he enrolled in a three-year course as a probationer for the ministry in the Methodist Church, a programme including such topics as Old and New Testament history and literature, systematic theology, John Wesley's sermons, church history, comparative religion, Greek – altogether twenty-four courses. Even with seven courses off for military service, it was a heavy load.

Endicott's classmates considered him to be a happy, buoyant personality, generous and open-hearted, a 'clear thinker, keen critic, [with] high executive ability,' whose assets included 'a magnetic smile and capacity to make friends.'[6] He was recognized as an able debater and was chosen along with Clarence Halliday to represent Toronto against Queen's University on the eve of the federal election in 1921. The Toronto team lost a dramatic contest about tariffs, but afterwards there was a surprise: O.D. Skelton, a Queen's professor closely connected with the Liberal party, contacted Endicott saying he had never heard an undergraduate who had such a good platform presence, ability to think on his feet, and forceful speaking manner; he urged him to consider a career in external affairs.[7] In his final undergraduate year in 1923, Endicott won the Moss Scholarship signifying the university's best all-round man of the final year; during the same year his younger brother, Norman, who had been too young to be in the war, was awarded the Rhodes Scholarship for Ontario. Later, while doing an MA thesis on the poet William Wordsworth, Endicott was elected to an uneventful year as president of the Student's Administrative Council of the University of Toronto. Perhaps the most encouraging assessment came after he graduated, when Salem Bland, the veteran Methodist preacher, described him as 'brilliant, popular, a born leader, especially in the Student Christian Movement, following from boyhood the highest things, [who] bids fair to shatter the rule that distinguished fathers do not have distinguished sons.'[8]

Endicott did not have such high estimations of himself, because the war had left him with inner doubts, a kind of shell-shock. Sometimes he fell into moods of black depression. Merely to survive each day at college he found that he needed two or three more hours of sleep than his younger brother, with whom he shared the attic room in their parents' house. He felt an intellectual fuzziness. Although he had aligned himself definitely with the modernist school of religion which accepted the findings of evolution, as opposed to the fundamentalists with their literal interpretations of the Bible, that was not enough; he wanted to discover in Christianity a faith without *any* dogmatism, a faith that could accept the methodology of science and still retain an openness, a sense of wonder, about the unsolved mysteries of the universe.

While overseas he had been captivated by a book written by the British theologian, T.R. Glover, called *The Jesus of History*, which had brought Christ out of the clouds into the realm of ordinary living so that a young person could better understand the meaning of Jesus' actual life and teachings. Endicott was so fascinated that he had read on by candlelight in the barracks after 'lights out' and was given a day in the lock-up as a result, where, to his satisfaction, he finished the book. He was now able to continue this kind of open, critical study in the basement of Victoria College, where the popular Bible study groups of Dr H.B. Sharman met. Dr Sharman was a chemistry professor who had turned his scientific training to the subject of the records of the life of Jesus; he established a method of study which scores of students declared was the most stimulating experience of their university life. By comparing the gospels to ascertain how and why they were written, the confusion caused by their various versions was clarified. The result was a simplified but more profound picture of the life and teachings of Jesus than could be obtained in any other way. Sharman's text, *Studies in Jesus as Teacher*,[9] was a dragon of a book, full of penetrating and difficult questions about the records of the synoptic gospels of Matthew, Mark, and Luke.

While Dr Sharman was a kindly and mild-mannered man, he conducted an exacting study: if the group member had not prepared the questions he dared not show up; but, if his attendance was slack without good reason, he would be asked to leave the group. Dr Sharman insisted on pressing for all the evidence and on inculcating a respect and practice of the principles of democratic discussion, although the groups did not run on consensus. He was against any formulas, any concept that the religion of Jesus could be reduced to a set code or standard. Through non-directive leadership his goal was to help seekers discover for themselves 'who is this man, what is he saying?' Group members discovered that Jesus took a path in opposition to the traditions and great institutions of his day and that the central guide of his life's activity was the fulfilment of the paradox: 'Whosoever shall seek to gain his life shall lose it; but whosoever shall lose his life shall preserve it' (Luke 17:33). The conclusion to be drawn about such a life of service was that a follower of Jesus must commit himself to do the 'right' no matter what the cost. There were guides and suggestions in the teachings of Jesus, but each person would have to find the 'right' for himself with the realization that it might, would likely, change in new circumstances.

Although Sharman was 'non-directive' and tried to avoid giving any opinion, Endicott realized that one of his purposes was to show that Jesus rejected the idea that he was the Messiah of the Jewish tradition; as well he wished to show that the 'miracles' might have scientific rather than miraculous explanations. Sharman was opposed to working out any application from the study. 'If we cannot rest confident in the belief that when Jesus is adequately known the implications of his thought will be obvious, not only so but likewise compelling,' he said, 'then we would regard ourselves as engaged in a hopeless task.'[10] This restriction upon the study groups bothered many students, including Endicott, but they mainly respected Dr Sharman's wishes. Once Sharman was asked by his students to give a lecture on his idea of God: it became known as 'the black sermon'; after an hour of circumlocutions everyone was more perplexed than ever, not knowing if they had heard something profound or simply confusions. Another Victoria professor, Samuel H. Hooke, once wrote a satirical verse on Sharman's effort by depicting a discussion of theologians trying to decide how to press the crease in the trousers of aboriginal man; while they were engrossed in their disputations the poor man died of the cold. This was a biting comment, but not entirely undeserved.[11]

Hooke himself was a storm centre at Victoria College in those days. A scholarly, poetical professor of Old Testament history,[12] he had more students who loved him and hung on his words than any other professor in the university. People who preferred the conventional ways and thoughts finally drove him out of Victoria; but before that happened he had startled many generations of students into thinking, and he made the life of Jesus a challenge to stir their souls. The year that Endicott was chairman of the committee preparing the annual revue, known as 'The Bob,' Hooke stole the show by doing an impersonation of himself as 'A Personal Devil': in one scene he imitated Chancellor R.P. Bowles by walking in saying 'Consider the lilies of the field, they smoke not, neither do they swear' because Hooke had been criticized for doing both.

Although Hooke led Bible study groups using the Sharman method, his effect was entirely different. Hooke was both more practical and more mystical. His advice to students was to get involved 'up to the neck.' A person should be prepared to sacrifice for what he believed in; Christian knowledge of God would be disclosed in the doing, for the Word was a creative event rather than a concept. Hooke thus favoured applications of study, and since he was profoundly critical of the acquisitiveness of capitalist society he made wide use of the brilliant studies on the subject by the socialist professor, R.H. Tawney of London. It was at this time that Tawney gave his famous lectures on 'Religion and the Rise of Capitalism' in which he demonstrated how the commercial class of the seventeenth century perverted Protestant ethics, isolating the realm of economic interest and thus condoning the sharp antithesis between personal morality and the practices that became permissible in business; the capitalist system departed most sharply from the teachings ascribed to 'the Founder of the Christian Faith' because of its assumption that 'the attainment of material riches is the supreme object of human endeavour and the final criterion of human success.' Tawney suggested that compromise was impossible between the Church of Christ and the idolatry of wealth that was the practical religion of capitalist societies. He further predicted that industry would be paralyzed by recurrent revolts on the part of outraged human nature because it neglected the truism that 'since even quite common men have souls, no increase in material wealth will compensate them for arrangements which insult their self-respect and impair their freedom.'[13] This strongly argued case was bewildering and difficult for the study group members at Victoria. The students of that day had little inclination to practise Tawney's conclusion and become socialists or join a labour party. But neither could they feel happy any longer with the other option, which was to support the YMCAs and service clubs in order to ameliorate, during an evening hour or two, the damage which the business corporation did to workers during an eight- or nine-hour day. Hooke prudently avoided suggesting specific courses of action to his students, although Endicott heard vague reports about the existence of a Diggers Club, named after the most egalitarian group in the Puritan revolution. Twenty-five years later, after returning from the China mission field, he was surprised to learn that the Diggers, who were associated with the founding of the *Canadian Forum*, a radical, anti-establishment magazine, included Hooke, Huntley Gordon, Margaret Fairley, Gilbert Jackson, and Harold Manning, and that some of them had been considerably interested in Marxism.[14]

S.H. Hooke's socialism did not deter him from believing that if a person worked, heart and soul, without self-seeking, to further God's design for the establishment of His Kingdom of righteousness and peace on earth, then God would respond. This was the mystical side of his thought. God was at the pinnacle of a pyramid, and the course of evolution, of which Darwin had discovered only the beginning, was straining upward towards deity. Hooke's favourite passage to describe this creative continuum was from Revelations 21:2 and 4: 'And I John saw the holy city, new Jerusalem, coming down from God out of heaven, prepared as a bride adorned for her husband ... And God shall wipe away all tears from [men's] eyes; and there shall be no more death, neither sorrow, nor crying, neither shall there be any more pain: for the former things are passed away.' Endicott realized that for Hooke, the messianic socialist, there was a politics of God, which revealed itself in the Exodus: Israel was aware not only of having liberated itself from the oppressive power of Egypt's ruling class but of having been liberated. The Christian hope was an invitation to continue such responsive action between God and man.

Hooke found the same spirit in the romantic poets. With Shelley he would 'hope till Hope creates from its own wreck the thing it contemplates.'[15] And in unforgettable, measured tones, strangely tuned by a cleft palate, he would recite Wordsworth's poem in praise of an imprisoned revolutionary to illustrate his view about the nature of immortality:

Toussaint ...
Live, and take comfort. Thou hast left behind
Powers that will work for thee; air, earth, and skies;
There's not a breathing of the common wind
That will forget thee; thou has great allies;
Thy friends are exultations, agonies,
And love, and man's unconquerable mind.[16]

Out of a fierce loyalty to his own background, perhaps, Endicott argued at times against Hooke's criticisms of the church. But in the lecture hall, study groups, and informal gatherings of the poetry circle in private living rooms, Hooke could see the leaven at work in the young man's mind. One day as Endicott hurried into class a few minutes late, Hooke paused and was heard to say: 'Here comes James the Old Pretender.' The class was mildly amused, but for Endicott it was a premonition of hard times ahead. In the back of his mind he knew that at the end of four years he must appear before the Toronto Conference to be questioned by the 'orthodox' on his doctrinal beliefs. Only after this test could the laying on of hands, which signified acceptance into the ministry of the church, take place.

Endicott already had reservations about several articles of church doctrine.

The articles on the nature of sin suggested that sin was rooted in man's constitution from the beginning because our first parents, being tempted, chose evil and so fell away from God and came under the power of sin. As a result of his encounters with Sharman and Hooke, the legend of Adam's fall and original sin no longer had any literal meaning for him; moreover, that legend cast too pessimistic a shadow on human nature. He continued to believe that all people sin and fall short of the glory of God and that all people have need of repentance and forgiveness; but, in his new view, sin was a wrong choice, a mistake, an error made consciously, a deliberate act which something within one warns is not the best way to act. To sin was to act contrary to the dictates of conscience, it was to lack self-control, but it was not a yoke that one carried from the day of birth. As to salvation from sin, Jesus' story of the return of the prodigal son (Luke 15:11–32) seemed to show how a person could be saved from sin without the dogma of the church about the Cross. According to this reading of Jesus, forgiveness could be achieved by repentance for wrongdoing, preparedness to live differently (in this case as a hired man), and by seeking the forgiveness of those who had been wronged – a willingness to live a changed life. In so far as people's sufferings were their own fault, they were the consequences of sin, not God's punishment for wrongdoing.

Similarly, S.H. Hooke's notions about prayer called accepted beliefs into question. Hooke explained prayer in two ways. Early religions attempted to control the unknown forces of nature by prayer: gods could be bound by spells or appeased by sacrifice and in this way the cosmic forces were favourably influenced on behalf of the individual. It was in this same self-centred manner that the articles of doctrine of the Methodist and later the United Church described the role of prayer: a confession of sins and 'seeking of Him every gift needful for this life and for our everlasting salvation'; in response, God will 'grant us every blessing.' By contrast, Hooke presented prayer as an attitude of surrender to the facts of the universe, an attitude of patient and humble observation of the actual workings of the universe and of learning 'how to cooperate intelligently with the cosmic forces to whatever end they may be moving.' Such an attitude involved an acknowledgement of limitations in place of much that formerly seemed divine certainty, but in the end it might prove to be the true way of life, 'the real surrender to the "will of God."' Seen in this fashion, divine salvation became, for Endicott, not so much an individualistic hope for an immortal, celestial life as it was a belief that God required everyone 'to do justly, to love mercy and to walk humbly with God' in order that the 'brotherhood of man wherein the Kingdom of God is to be made manifest' could be fulfilled.[17]

The third, and perhaps most decisive, influence on Endicott as an under-graduate was the work of Albert Schweitzer, musical genius and missionary, whose position was somewhere between that of Sharman and Hooke. Where-as Sharman rejected the idea of Jesus as a supernatural Messiah and Hooke counted upon it, Schweitzer said that it did not matter. Schweitzer's book, *The Quest of the Historical Jesus*,[18] shocked people by the thesis that the historical Jesus had to be accepted as capable of error because 'the supernatu-ral Kingdom of God, the manifestation of which He announced as imminent,' did not appear. But Jesus did not think dogmatically. Nowhere, according to Schweitzer, did Jesus demand of his hearers that they sacrifice thinking to believing; on the contrary, he bid them meditate upon religion. Schweitzer concluded that 'they serve Christianity better by the strength of their devo-tion to Jesus' religion of love than by acquiescence in all the articles of belief.' Schweitzer's research showed that Jesus as a concrete, historical personality 'remains a stranger to our time, but his spirit, which lies hidden in his words, is known in simplicity and its influence is direct.' In a tribute to Schweitzer when he died in 1965, Endicott wrote that the last paragraph in *The Quest of the Historical Jesus* had been for all his life the best explanation of what being a Christian means: 'He comes to us as One unknown, without a name, as of old, by the lakeside, He came to those men who knew Him not. He speaks to us the same word: "Follow thou me!" and sets us to the tasks which He has to fulfill for our time. He commands. And to those who obey Him, whether they be wise or simple, He will reveal Himself in the toils, the conflicts, the sufferings, which they shall pass through in His fellowship, and as an ineffable mystery, they shall learn from their own experience Who He is.'

Schweitzer's viewpoint was at once historical, ethical, practical, and mys-tical. He became one of Endicott's heroes because he gave a lifetime of service in obedience to what he believed were the basic teachings of Jesus and at the same time exercised his individual right of historical research and personal moral and intellectual judgement; he heard the words of Jesus and he did them.

The impact of Sharman, Hooke, and Schweitzer on Endicott's thinking was profound and lasting, especially in grasping the need to avoid the kind of faith that depends upon no change. As far as one's personal life was concerned, if some idea, some teaching, or some philosophical analysis made an appeal or stirred a response in the heart, the mind, or the conscience, then he was convinced that one must respond to it, test it in practice, and try to find out if it proved to be justified. He reflected that it was a common psychological experience that at certain times in a person's life a new understanding results from some flash of insight. Such experiences came in different ways to

different people. Wordsworth as a young poet had found that in a feeling for nature, observing and reflecting on the 'sounding cataract' or the 'violet by a mossy stone, half hidden from the eye,' he received what he described as 'authentic tidings of invisible things.' To the scientist the new truth might suddenly leap to mind as the result of many years of painstaking research and analysis. At this early stage of his life, Endicott's most exciting discovery was the sense that it was a fundamental fact of the universe that there is a force in human life and in evolution which pushes forward towards the new, towards the solution of contradictions in the direction of making life better; by seeking to align oneself with this creative direction one could find a sure basis of optimism and could build a life of inner integrity.[19] Throughout his life this sense was his moral compass.

CHAPTER FOUR

Circuit-riding in Saskatchewan

In 1921 Endicott became a probationer for the Methodist ministry and consequently spent the next two summers circuit-riding in Saskatchewan. During the first summer he was based in a hamlet called Gledhow, south of Saskatoon, where he stayed in the home of a farmer by the name of William Gleave. Each Saturday he rode a horse twelve miles to Rabbit Foot Lake, a glorified alkali slough, staying overnight at the farm of the Kerrs, a congenial middle-aged couple who had moved up from the United States. John Kerr was a socialist and had half a trunk full of pamphlets; but he kept to himself because, he said, all the farmers had become hostile. Something about Endicott appealed to him. 'If I had a preacher like you,' he told him, 'I'd go every Sunday.' The church service took place in the schoolhouse, and sometimes during that first summer the congregation consisted of no more than three or four people. Refusing to be down-hearted in the face of the obvious, Endicott chuckled one day as he said to his flock: 'I'll put my hat on the front seat; it'll make it appear as if there are more people here.'

The competition was stiff. The Pentecostals organized an assembly at Rabbit Foot Lake and brought up a silver-tongued American orator, whose peroration ended with a promise that 'We will be changed in the twinkling of an eye; we will be caught up in Heaven and we'll go so fast that you won't know we're gone until you see our clothes falling.' A humorous old farmer then turned and remarked to Endicott: 'You know, I've no doubt God loves the Pentecostals, but I don't think he admires them.'

Following the morning service, Endicott rode a few miles over to O'Malley for an afternoon meeting in a private house. He often had a lively time afterwards at lunch with another branch of the Gleave family, which later produced a Co-operative Commonwealth Federation member of Parliament. To complete the day he returned to Gledhow, about five miles distant, for an evening service in a little church that stood as a forlorn outpost on the bald prairie. Monday through Thursday he visited schoolhouses in the area, and with the permission of the teachers, who were usually younger women from the East, he conducted Bible classes. Shying away from evangelistic soul-saving he would teach from biblical history, concentrating on the stories of the prophets – Moses versus Pharaoh, Daniel versus Nebuchednezzar – and explaining how valuable it was to have a general knowledge of the Bible because of its effect on literature.

In making his rounds he rode about fifteen hundred miles each summer, not always without incident. When cars came near, his spirited little mare often reared. 'Sometimes,' he wrote in a letter home, 'she jazzes on all fours ... Today she happened to waltz over the edge and did a most fascinating glide and roll into the water. Little Jimmy slid back over her tail in time to avoid a bath. I always did dislike the water.'

At first, Endicott did not know how to develop a sermon and his early ones lasted barely three or four minutes. He would have two or three main ideas, usually related to some local or world event of the previous week, say them, and then it was over. A farmer named Norris, who was held in awe locally because he was the nephew of the great Harry McGee, the general manager of the T. Eaton Company, complained to him: 'When I come such a long way I expect to hear more, a longer sermon.' This Sunday it had been a seven-minute effort. Influenced by the fact that the uncle was a tough-minded tycoon who had once told a board meeting at Timothy Eaton Memorial Church that he wouldn't give a dollar to Ernest Thomas and his Department of Evangelism and Social Service, Endicott reacted subjectively to Norris and decided to put him on the defensive. 'Well, you were here last Sunday. Do you remember what I preached about?' He didn't. 'That was only a five minute sermon and you didn't remember it,' Endicott said with a grin, 'so if you come again next Sunday I'll try a four minute one and see if you can remember it.'

Next year the Home Missions Board moved him closer to North Battleford to cover the little communities at Meota, Prince, and Scentgrass, and he tried to associate himself more closely with local activities. 'I am having a great time with the "dancing crowd,"' he wrote his mother, 'only the trouble is that about fifty percent of the young men do not like to see me there "sticking my nose into what is not my business." You see I go to their shine if they come to my service. Part of the trouble at the dances here is that the north of Saskatchewan is out of control of the police and "home brew" is rather easy to get and some of the young sh'entlemen turn up a little worse for moonshine.'

But even more bothersome than dancing and intemperance was the aggressive propaganda about the second coming of Christ, which seemed to be as pervasive as the dust storms that whipped across the prairie that summer. The fundamentalists had canvassed the whole district selling books at four to seven dollars apiece. Even the Anglican priest at Meota, Endicott complained, was 'narrow, literal and "Second Coming." '

Ultimately, Endicott decided to go on the warpath on the subject of the millennium. People were heart-broken because of the drought. Farmers who had wheat up eight or ten inches saw it become so dry that the little hard grains of sand lifted by the wind cut the crop to pieces. Preaching about the second coming in a static, three-storey universe composed of heaven, earth, and hell was as senseless as praying about the weather. Surely a more helpful understanding, Endicott thought, was that man was engaged in a struggle against natural forces in which irrigation, crop insurance, an adequate price for wheat, and the social cohesion necessary to achieve these objectives should be the prime focus of the farmers and their spiritual advisers. He commenced his campaign by preaching on 'The Christian and His Bible,' trying to present a more living and readable view of the Bible. On that background he began using a parcel of 'second coming' criticism sent out from headquarters by T. Albert Moore, general secretary of the Board of Evangelism and Social Service. Endicott tried to show that if we know the principles on which Jesus based his life, why he prayed, what he taught, we should realize that the 'second coming' doctrine is a practical denial of all that; it is a pessimistic, escapist doctrine which denies the Christian hope about life on earth, that men 'might have life and have it to the full.' Endicott became so enthusiastic about his subject that he found he could preach a respectably long sermon without notes of any kind. As he emphasized the prophets' demand for social justice and hit out at the wickedness of the war system which allowed private profiteering in armaments, his congregations started to increase. Meota went up from 20 to 35, Scentgrass to 25, and Prince stayed at 40. The financial prospect also became more promising: 'My collections for the last four Sundays have gone $8, $9.50, $10 and $13 ... More than that, I am enjoying the work.'

One Sunday evening in August 1922, as Endicott was sitting in the little farmhouse of Austin Mair at Scentgrass, having a quiet cup of tea, his host suddenly said: 'You know, Jim, you always seem to be hammering at something. How would you like to give us a hand in organizing the Wheat Pool?'

Endicott looked at him questioningly: 'What do you mean?'

Mair explained that he was one of a group trying to get farmers to sign a contract to sell their crops through a proposed farmers' co-operative wheat pool.[1] 'This is the only way we can protect ourselves from the power of the Eastern grain monopolies. This is the only way we can get a fair price for our labour. Our union has to sign up 51 per cent of the acreage in order to get it through. In the last couple of weeks we've discovered that the Royal Bank has sent a carload of hostile printed material, and paid agents are canvassing farmers saying, "If you sign this Wheat Pool contract they'll have a mortgage on your farms. You might lose your land through foreclosures." This is a lie. But we're afraid that if you don't help us, we may not succeed.'

As he listened to the farmer telling stories of bitter hardship and observed his weather-beaten face and calloused hands, he thought for a moment of Professor Hooke expounding the implications of Jesus' remark: 'by their fruits ye shall know them. Not every one that saith unto me, Lord, Lord, shall enter into the kingdom of heaven; but he that doeth the will of my Father ...' (Matthew 7:20-1). When Mair fell silent he responded doubtfully: 'But what could I do?'

Mair brightened: 'A lot of the foreign born farmers, the late arrivals, are falling for the propaganda. Because of language problems we can scarcely talk to them. We propose that you go around with us in our car and because you have been teaching the children of these people in Sunday School, and because they have respect for the preacher, the children will interpret for us.'

It was settled, and in characteristic fashion Endicott soon warmed to the task. He used the story of Moses and said that the Pharaohs were to be found down in Winnipeg on the Grain Exchange; he explained the benefits of co-operation and mutual self-help which would protect the farmers from exploitation. As the signed contracts began to pile up the pool organizers marvelled at his powers of advocacy. They even worried that he was being too overpowering. Aaron Sapiro, one of the team, found an opportunity to tell a story about not trying to be too comprehensive in dealing with machinery. 'There's a simple rule,' he said. 'Put oil on where the squeaks are.' Endicott tried to take the hint.

Victory for the pool brought inevitable reaction and Endicott received his first letter of reprimand from church headquarters. Had the Pharaohs in Winnipeg complained? Perhaps. Or perhaps the complaint arose from a chance visit by his Uncle Charles, then Superintendent of Home Missions in Saskatoon, who came to take part in a concert to raise some money for mission work. One parishioner made a fatal remark. 'I'd like to tell you, Dr. Endicott,' she said, 'your nephew is such an interesting preacher. He talks about so many things besides religion.' Uncle Charles may have made further enquiries. In any event, Endicott received a letter from Lloyd Smith at the church head office criticizing activities other than what were considered strictly religious. He wasn't sent out to help farmers to organize a wheat pool; he should confine himself to activities suitable for a preacher. Endicott felt hurt and made no reply, but he did a lot of thinking.

This was the first of many censures by church authorities. Later on in his career, similar conflicts would be interpreted by some of his colleagues as stemming from his egocentric personality. According to this argument, if he were more sensitive in interpersonal relations he would not make so many enemies. His student ministry experience suggests, however, that it was his understanding of the responsibility of a Christian preacher to give leadership on public issues that got him into trouble. It was basically what he did, not the way he did it, that annoyed his critics.

CHAPTER FIVE

Ideology and ordination

When Endicott returned to Victoria College in the fall of 1922 for his final undergraduate year, his resolve to be a missionary in China grew in spite of strong criticism's of foreign missions put forward by people whose opinions he otherwise respected. Two groups were competing for his loyalty at this time: the Student Volunteer Movement for Foreign Missions and the newly formed Student Christian Movement. Had he been completely won over by the SCM leadership, his missionary years in China would never have taken place.

The Student Volunteer Movement, which was an expression of the more conservative wing of North American Protestantism, had been founded some thirty-five years earlier by a group of American clergymen, of whom John R. Mott was the most dynamic spokesman. Mott, backed by a laymen's movement that included some of the most prominent businessmen of the United States and Canada, organized giant quadrennial rallies around the call for 'the evangelization of the world in this generation.' The emotional atmosphere of the rallies, which included appeals from converts in foreign lands to 'come over and help us,' had helped to persuade over eight thousand American and Canadian university graduates to live in Asia and Africa, and half as many again had signed up as volunteers should there be a call for them to serve.[1] Endicott was one of those who had volunteered.

At the same time he was attracted to the Student Christian Movement which began after the Great War. Although founded upon Christian beliefs and concern, it was to be an open movement, including the questioner and the doubter; through study, prayer, and practice it aimed to unite all who were willing to test the truth of the conviction 'that in Jesus Christ are found the supreme revelation of God and the means to the full realization of life.'[2] Even though Endicott was active in the group at Victoria College, was leader of the

Toronto SCM delegation at the first national Canadian student conference in 1922, and was part of the SCM national council in his senior year, the ideological direction of the movement came from people like S.H. Hooke and Davidson Ketchum, a young, erudite, and witty graduate student in psychology who had spent four years in a German prisoner of war camp.

The *esprit de corps* of the SCM, its willingness to needle the establishments of church and state, was displayed in the satirical song, *Poisoning the Student Mind*, which Ketchum wrote in response to an attack on the SCM by a conservative, fundamentalist paper. The song expressed the divine discontent and irreverence that has marked most of the subsequent history of the SCM, and, for the rest of his life, Endicott remembered the words to all its seven verses, and could sing them with relish:

> The SCM has found its true vocation
>   In poisoning the student mind;
> Its leaders by astute manipulation
>   Are poisoning the student mind.
> The pious souls are sure that we will go
>   To toast our toes at furnaces below
> If we give heed to leaders who they know
>   Are poisoning the student mind ...
>
> Now old Prof. Hooke may seem a harmless critter
>   But he's poisoning the student mind;
> Within that pipe he brews a potion bitter
>   Just for poisoning the student mind.
> With views extreme his victims he'll beguile
>   And tell them with a supercilious smile
> That Noah marched his stock in single file –
>   Ah, yes he's poisoning the student mind ...
>
> CHORUS:
> They're poisoning the student mind.
> They're poisoning the student mind,
> Bad men, bold men, villains double-dyed,
> 'Neath their smiling countenances hide
> Spiritual arsenic, moral cyanide,
> For poisoning the student, poisoning the student,
>   poisoning the student mind.

Although Endicott admired Ketchum's talented leadership in many ways, he did not accept the latter's scornful attitude to foreign missions. Ketchum, while admitting that the ideal of missions was good, maintained that the system was lacking in results; he spoke of the uselessness of trying to turn heathen countries into likenesses of the nominally Christian, Western countries with their middle class culture. The 'heathen,' and especially the 'inquisitive and searching mind of China,' was asking questions: why does Christianity preach resignation to fate and teach superstitions, such as the virgin birth, miracles, the resurrection, and so retard the development of science? Capitalism was seeking to exploit China and Christianity was its vanguard and lure; when the gospel of love and the practice of imperialism came from the same people, how could such people be regarded as sincere and consistent? In case anyone should miss the point, Ketchum said that these criticisms, set forth in the *Canadian Student*, the SCM's magazine, and elsewhere, were specifically meant to benefit those who might at some later time be themselves called upon to answer such questions in China. The SCM held that if Canada was to continue sending missionaries, they 'should be picked people [who] go as comrades, willing to work with or be subordinate to the native Christian leaders.'[3]

Although these arguments spoke to many of the issues that were to cause Endicott great concern in later years, the would-be missionary remained steadfast to his long-held choice for a career. Had he engaged in some genuinely independent soul-searching at this time about his motivations for becoming a foreign missionary, he might have been spared years of inner turmoil. Instead he chose to retain a middle position between the ideas represented by Ketchum and those of Mott, a stance that became evident in the role he played in the conflicts between the two ideological camps.

During 1922 and 1923 the Canadian SVM leaders wanted to merge with the SCM in order to implement a policy of placing less emphasis on evangelism as the main purpose of foreign missions. John Mott, however, rejected merger with the SCM and refused to hear of any broadening of the content of the Declaration Card: a change in 'evangelization of the world' would mean 'dropping the keystone out of the arch' and would 'neutralize the influence of the entire movement.' The ageing American chairman was adamant. The Canadian student leaders then proposed an independent Canadian SVM which would co-operate with the New York headquarters but would be free from American control. The leaders in the United States insisted, however, that their general secretary must be recognized as 'the ultimate authority.'[4]

For the moment the student leaders did not challenge American domination any further, but senior Canadian church leaders were nervous. Dr Jesse

Arnup, assistant secretary of the Board of Foreign Missions, called Endicott into his office for a chat. Dr Arnup was concerned that the SCM was becoming political and would move to the left. He did not want that to happen. He was afraid that would weaken the missionary effort. 'Will you become chairman of the Canadian Student Volunteer Committee,' he asked, 'and try to bring the aims of the two organizations into harmony?'[5] Dr Arnup stressed that the year ahead was crucial because a large Canadian delegation would have to be sent to the quadrennial SVM rally to be held in December 1923 at Indianapolis.

Endicott felt unhappy and awkward about Dr Arnup's request. Because of his father's influence, he had great respect for John Mott, Sherwood Eddy, and the other American leaders, and he himself was aiming to become a missionary; but he also felt strong sympathy for the Canadian concerns and social gospel politics of the SCM. He tried to excuse himself by pleading the need to concentrate on his studies. Eventually, under Dr Arnup's heavy pressure and promise that he would be constantly available to help, Endicott agreed. He was appointed one of the SCM representatives on the SVM, and at the end of January 1923 he was elected chairman of the Canadian committee of the SVM.

During the following year, leading up to the Indianapolis convention, Endicott and Hugh MacMillan, the full-time secretary of the SVM, conducted a running battle with the prevailing SCM position. Dr Arnup, in the meanwhile, had succumbed to sleeping sickness and was out of action for the whole year. The first test came when Helen R. Nichol, one of the other SCM representatives on the SVM committee, resigned because she was 'not wholeheartedly in sympathy with the purpose of the SVM of Canada as it is at present constituted'; the SCM general committee followed up by deciding that 'it would be neither wise nor possible' for Canada to be as well represented at Indianapolis as it had been at Des Moines in 1919. In the end, however, Endicott led a fairly respectable delegation of 150 Canadians to Indianapolis, including Ernest Clarke, Norman A. MacKenzie, Helen Nichol, and Gertrude Rutherford of the SCM general committee. He appeared as one of the featured speakers on the programme, along with Walter H. Judd, a medical student from Nebraska who was his counterpart as chairman of the Student Volunteer Council in the United States. But when the conference, which attracted 6800 delegates, was over, the SCM continued its sniping, commenting that 'the convention in the end was much greater than the programme'; there had been 'sufficient careful planning and safeguarding to kill any spontaneity ... it was on the whole a very average group.'[6]

Although Endicott was more positive in his appraisals of Indianapolis, he was also restrained in his enthusiasm. While the students at the convention showed considerable willingness to ask 'What can I do?' they did not give evidence that they held any common basis for action or belief in the practicability of the Kingdom of God. 'If they do,' he reported in the University of Toronto *Varsity*, 'they hide their light under a vacant look.'[7] Much evidence had been provided, he admitted, to justify the suspicion that the present generation of students did not regard the challenge of foreign missions as of paramount importance in the Christian programme. While not wishing to detract in the least from the importance of the problems of peace or war, a Christian social order, and the eradication of racial prejudice, which had been called the 'unoccupied mission fields at home,' Endicott continued to argue that the missionary enterprise, linked as it was with all these questions, was still the most important concern of every Christian. How could Canadian students forget the testimony and appeal which came from the native Christians of India, Japan, and China? He also suggested taking a lesson from history to notice that whenever Christianity had grappled most thoroughly with social conditions, as, for instance, during the Wesleyan Movement, at the same time there was a new emphasis on the need for missions. Whenever Christians had felt that Christ and Christianity were real and true they 'have known they had a world programme on their hands.' He did not want to imply that he considered it to be more Christian or adventurous or the least bit more religious to be a missionary than to be a businessman or a plumber; there were some fields of industry where it was far more difficult to live and act as a Christian than it was to go to a far-off country as a missionary. Anyone who was working for the Kingdom to come on earth shared a common fellowship 'where there is neither first nor last.' And with that appeal for support to missions, Endicott ended his term of office as a student volunteer.

The General Board of the Methodist Church appreciated his efforts and appointed him as a missionary to West China 'without a single vote of opposition' – a unanimity which was sufficiently unusual to warrant notice by the Toronto *Globe*.[8] His appointment would take effect, the Chinese revolution permitting, after his ordination in June 1925.

Ordination was one of the major moral crises in Jim Endicott's life. Like many young, idealistic probationers for the ministry, he wanted to remain honest and true to himself and to his own feelings and at the same time he felt hypocritical in accepting some of the classical creeds of the Christian church. In the end, it was necessary to put his doubts to the back of his mind and to accept the teachings of his church with something considerably less than enthusiasm, but the apparent dishonesty of the compromise troubled his conscience for many years to come.

Endicott's moral conflict over ordination coincided with the last stages of the controversial campaign for church union, in which the Presbyterians, Methodists, and Congregationalists ultimately agreed to come together to form the United Church of Canada. His father played an important role in the public controversy, as well as helping to resolve his son's inner ordeal. When large sections of the Presbyterian Church tried to prevent union, arguing that they could not compromise on the statement of ancient creeds, the Rev. James Endicott made an inspired address before the parliamentary committee considering the issue, which made banner headlines in the *Toronto Star* on 9 May 1924: 'Creeds are milestones in religious life. Our opponents would have them millstones to hang about our necks.'

As the day of his ordination approached, young Endicott brooded unhappily about the 'millstones' of Methodism, for many of the creeds were being carried forward virtually unamended into the Twenty Articles of Faith of the new church. Of the germinal events requiring Christian acceptance – God's dealings with Israel through the voices of the Old Testament prophets, the birth, life, death, and resurrection of Jesus, and the hope of the Kingdom of God – only four were central to his belief; the virgin birth and bodily resurrection of Jesus were practically irrelevant. How would he respond to questions on a creed requiring such affirmations when he came before the Toronto Conference to be examined on his 'life, doctrine, learning and gifts' as required by the ordinances of the church?

The issue troubled him greatly and the more he studied the New Testament, the more troubled he became. As he read the Acts of the Apostles verse by verse he was appalled at the beliefs, which he considered to be mere superstitions of the early Christian church, that still survived as the touchstone of people's ideas. Christianity, he reflected, was a diamond buried at the bottom of a slag heap. The slag heap would have to be removed, he felt, before there would be any effective and intelligent understanding of the way of Jesus.

As for the ordination examination, there were three possible choices: to state frankly those things he could not accept; to attempt to endow the ancient sacraments and symbols with new meaning; to answer the questions of the committee evasively, giving the truth but not the whole truth. His heart led him to the first position, which was also the one most likely to put his chosen career in jeopardy. He would like to have said that he was entering the church because he believed it did the most in the world for decency and kindness and peace; that he had been led to that feeling largely by the influence of his father; and that as for all the creeds and notions which generally prevailed he believed it would be better if they were all pitched out in favour of some new ones. Instead of trying so desperately to preserve the old values, why not gather up the new ones that science and enlightenment in general had been spreading around so lavishly? He even toyed with the idea of coming out and stating the sad intellectual discredit into which religion in general had fallen; this would precipitate a church trial, where he would at least be given a chance to state carefully his case for the harmony of truth between Christianity and science.

Reluctantly, he abandoned this position because he felt it would very likely lead to his dismissal as some kind of humanist, and therefore probably rule out the possibility of fulfilling his boyhood dream. It remained as an unfinished agenda in his mind, however, and three years later he was still so haunted by not having taken the stance he truly believed in that he wrote out what he would have said at a church trial had one occurred. He would begin, he wrote,[9] by asserting that the pre-scientific beliefs of the Christian religion were the real framework of most of the closed minds that occupied the pews. 'It isn't dishonesty that I don't preach what I think ... If I preach what I think people will only succeed in getting an idea that I think exactly what I don't think. He that hath ears to hear let him hear, but he must first have heard of Galileo and Darwin and Historical research. And be willing to receive what seems reasonable.'

At his make-believe trial he answered many questions.

'Do you believe in God the Father Almighty, maker of Heaven and earth?'

'No. I believe in Life as I see it and trust to the good purposes that are evident in it. I want humbly to commit my life to those good purposes. I believe that we can get into communion with Life so that there comes a sense of personality ... Yes, call it God, but not the God who answers by fire or fishes and stops the sun in order to boost the peacock pride of an inordinately conceited little tribe in Asia Minor.'

'Do you believe in the divinity of Jesus?'

'No. Because that word implies a scheme of thought in which the fall of Adam, the Virgin Birth, the special incarnation ... are bound up as if they were certainties. I pledge my life to the "beauty and honesty and simplicity of Jesus." I am willing to try his way of life always endeavouring to conform to the right as I know it and keeping my mind open to the discovery of more right as I study Him.'

'Do you believe in the Bible as the Word of God?'

'No. I believe it is an ordinary history, full of mistakes but extraordinarily well written and of immense value to all men as a source book for study. True religion and sound learning are in no way completely dependent on it. The records of the life of Jesus are invaluable, the world's most precious document.'

The second choice, to which he did not give much serious consideration, was at the opposite extreme: it was to endow the ancient sacraments and symbols with a new and more contemporary meaning. This stand was suggested by the lectures of Professor Hooke, and by the books of Walter Rauschenbusch[10] and other liberals and modernists of the time. It would be taken much further by the intrinsically political theology of liberation which developed in Latin America fifty years later; through an imaginative reading of the Resurrection these theologians fused all the contexts in which this belief was presented in the New Testament – 'all will rise,' 'Christ is risen for our justification,' 'we have risen with him,' 'powers and dominations have been defeated' – to confirm the triumph of God's love and solidarity with man against the powers of oppression and evil. Such an eschatological faith, which embraced the concepts of heaven, hell, and the seat of judgement, it was claimed, kindles the imagination about a vision of the future and makes it possible for a human being to invest his life in the building of a new order with the certainty that even if it is temporary or imperfect neither he nor his effort is meaningless or lost.[11]

Endicott could have accepted the conclusions of this theology, but not the involved process: to employ the myths of the ancient Jews and credulities of the early Christians as a framework for believing required an immense investment of intellectual and emotional energy. Such theological proposals had their place in a college classroom, but in preaching they might simply contribute to the slag heap, obscuring the promise of the Kingdom illuminated by the simple life and profound teachings of Jesus.

Endicott confided his spiritual trials to his father and it seems likely that the latter's advice helped him to resolve the issue. 'There lives more faith in honest doubt, believe me, than in half the creeds,' he quoted from Tennyson,[12] and he assured his son that 'in the end every person makes up his own theology.' And so it was the third choice, the safe but obvious middle ground of restating and preserving the old acceptable values, that Endicott adopted as he, I.G. Perkins, Jack Kell, and several others – the last class to be ordained in the Methodist Church of Canada – prepared to face their examiners on the first weekend of June 1925.

'Do you think, in your heart, that you are truly called, according to the will of our Lord Jesus Christ, to the office of a minister?' was the first question.

'I think so.'

'Could you explain when or how you received that call?'

'It was not one event. It was a series of insights beginning with my childhood in China and sensing the suffering of the people; an occasion in the army when I was awakened after midnight and called to kneel in prayer at the foot of my bunk; an inspiration received at a missionary rally and during family Bible study led by my father; a conviction formed during a visit to a farm family while circuit riding on the prairie. As nearly as I can recall it was these and similar events which gradually formed my decision to commit my life to the way of Jesus and, should you see fit, to offer my service to the Church.'

'Do you believe in the Virgin Birth, the deity of Jesus?'

'I affirm my belief in the scriptures of the Old and New Testaments as the primary source and ultimate standard of Christian faith and life.' He chose his words carefully. 'I acknowledge the teaching and creeds of the ancient Church, of which the Virgin Birth is one aspect.'

The terminology was evasive. Isaac Bowles and one or two other fundamentalists on the committee pressed on relentlessly. 'Do you believe in the physical resurrection of the Lord?' 'Do you believe that the Bible is the Word of God?' Had the grilling continued he would not have been successful. But after a few minutes Salem Bland stood up and said: 'Brethren, this young man is being subjected to an intensive questioning of the kind that none of us now would care to undertake to go through ...'

A silence fell, and then the chairman said: 'I think perhaps we've had enough.' When the vote was taken the men who had been pressing him on the narrow, literal interpretations did not vote against him, but abstained, thus giving him the necessary majority. [13]

The next day, 7 June 1925, at a special service in Toronto attended by S.D. Chown, the general superintendent of the Methodist Church, the ministers present laid their hands upon the head of each of the young men, charged them to be faithful dispensers of the Word of God, and gave them each a Bible. Endicott was now ordained to the Universal Church of God to minister the Word and Sacraments and to exercise pastoral oversight. Ordination was an emotional occasion, but not one he would look back upon with any feelings of joy. His real sense of exultation and the return of his confidence came later in the week at the Mutual Street Sports Arena in Toronto during a speech by his father at the founding conference of the United Church of Canada.

The older man was perplexed and a little angered by the narrow spirit at work in some corners of the church, especially as exemplified at his son's ordination examination. Although he was a conservative on social questions, he made up his mind to make his speech to the founding conference of the new church into an appeal for more liberal horizons.

His turn to speak to the conference came at the end of a long programme; the first moderator, a Presbyterian, had already been elected and most of the business was completed. With his opening story James Endicott brought a hot, jaded audience back to life and held them spellbound, as he always did, through his entire address. He was a master orator, speaking in a direct, conversational manner without purple patches, without reference to notes (because he was short-sighted), who won his listeners by a powerful appeal to the emotions backed by a rational approach to his subject. According to the transcript of proceedings, he began humorously by referring to the two previous addresses: one was theological and the other geological; he supposed there was nothing left for him but to be religious (laughter). But there were difficulties about that. The great preacher, Collier of Manchester, went to visit a sick parishioner on one occasion and was met by the wife of the sick man, who said to him: 'Mr. Collier, I am very glad to see you, but you won't talk to my husband about religion, will you? He is miserable enough as it is' (laughter).

With five thousand eyes now riveted upon him, Endicott declared that he had been asking himself about the future of this United Church, which had been launched in such an imposing and glorious fashion. 'Now that we have launched it, what shall we do with it?' He suggested that there could not possibly be anything better than to follow the great principles which had brought the movement about. The first great principle was that of unity.

Let us hold by unity ... because by means of this principle we have today transcended sectarianism (applause), a very ugly thing, a distressing thing that blocks the highway for the march of the hosts of God today. That does not mean that we are here blaming our fathers, much less apologizing for them. We have no word of complaint, because even in the first days Peter and Paul found it hard sometimes to agree and Peter said he found some things in Paul's Epistles which were rather difficult for him; and I may say that the successors of Peter to this day have the same difficulties ... we have no word against Luther, no complaint about Calvin. We would never dream of apologizing for John Bunyan, or Oliver Cromwell or John Milton, or Robinson, or John Wesley, or the Pilgrim Fathers. That is all clear. We owe more than we can ever repay to men like these. But nonetheless we have lived long enough to know that there are tremendous difficulties in respect of denominationalism. A thing which may have been good at the start may become evil. Is it not said in one of the lines of our own poet, – 'Lest one good custom should corrupt the world' [Tennyson].[14]

Jim stole a look at Isaac Bowles, and noticed he wore a frown.

I am glad too we have a unity that transcends creeds. I have no objection to creeds provided other people want them (applause). But I tell you this, that very often the longer the creed the shorter the faith, and as far as the world is concerned 'these little systems have their day and cease to be.' A thing which might have made a great appeal five centuries ago somehow loses its power to reach us in this day. Even the manna could not be kept over one day or it stank, and sometimes credal statements have the habit of doing the same thing (laughter). I am not saying that we do not want creeds. I am not saying that we do not want faith, but I am saying that the world today has enough of creeds for the people who must have them, already drawn out ... We have not taken out a single thing that ought to be in, and we have done a great service in cutting things out that ought never to have been in (applause) ... let no one charge us with disloyalty to Christ in doing that. It is in the name of Christ and because of His Spirit that we have done it.

By now Bowles and his friends were sitting on their hands. Endicott enumerated some other principles more briefly.

If we must choose between the past and the future, we will always choose the future (applause). It is not that we reject the past, we have grown out of it. We are debtors forever to it. Yes, but if ever we are to choose between yesterday and tomorrow, we ought to choose tomorrow. Our fathers are not one whit more sacred than our children, and our children's children, and if we are tied down because of the past we can never serve the future ... In this union, we have manifested the true principle that if we are to choose between the weak and the strong we will take the side of the weak (applause) ... in the days to come ... it will mean that if in any crisis in our history we have to choose between Toronto ... or any other great city and the Peace River country we will choose the Peace River country. That is a sound principle. That is Christianity, and that we must never forget ... The Church does not exist for itself but for the welfare of the world and that is why it is here (applause).[15]

The speech left a deep impression on his son: it not only temporarily calmed his inner turmoil, churned up by the ordination ordeal, but remained a long-lasting source of inspiration when other Isaac Bowles would confront him in the future and censure his style of ministry.

The North Gate, Chengtu, from the outside (United Church Archives)

Canadian Methodist Mission compound
on White Pagoda Street, Kiating (Loshan),
Szechuan province, where Jim Endicott
was born in 1898; the mission chapel is on
the right (United Church Archives)

The great Tang dynasty Buddha at
Kiating

Missionary James Endicott, Sr, his wife Sarah, and family, Chengtu, China, 1906; the
children, from the left, are Mary, Dorothy, Jim, Norman, and Enid

Children of Lao Yang, the Endicotts'
cook, 1901

Examination halls, Nanking, in use until the system of imperial examinations was
abolished in 1905 (United Church Archives)

Mary Austin and her friend Lester B. Pearson, c. 1917, Chatham

Endicott at nineteen, about to embark for France

Mary Austin, graduation from the University of Toronto, 1918

Jim and Norman Endicott at Muskoka, 1921

Mary with her father, Charles Austin,
1921

Professor S.H. Hooke, Victoria College,
1924

Professor H.B. Sharman, Victoria College,
c. 1923

Jim Endicott and Mary Austin at the time of their marriage, 1925

Jim and Mary Endicott aboard the *Empress of Australia*, Vancouver, 1925

CHAPTER SIX

The gates
of Eden

In the midst of the crisis surrounding his ordination, Jim Endicott met and fell in love with a slim, fair-haired young woman who made him feel that he had stumbled on a mount of transfiguration.

Mary Elsie Austin was a strongly committed, sensitive, but unorthodox Methodist from Chatham, whose family was typical of a social class that had long been prominent in the Methodist Church in Ontario. Her father, Charles Austin, was a hard-working and financially successful entrepreneur; born in the Ottawa Valley, he had begun his career as a clerk in a hardware store in Eganville, later moving from one enterprise to another in various parts of Ontario until he settled in Chatham, where he married Minnie Chapman, the daughter of the Methodist preacher. The Charles Austin Company dry goods shop soon became the largest department store in Kent County – a development Austin attributed to honest dealings, hard work, and God's timely interventions on his behalf.

In contrast to Jim, the son of missionaries, Mary grew up in relatively affluent surroundings, living in a large turreted house built to her father's specifications on the banks of the Thames River. The Austins were the first family in town to own an automobile. In 1910 Charles Austin was elected mayor of Chatham; he continued to prosper, especially through the war years, and in the late 1920s, planning to live on his invested wealth, he sold his business to the highest bidder.

Mary had been quick in school and was ready to enter Victoria College in Toronto at the age of sixteen. She had been overly sensitive as a child, and suffered from a certain amount of emotional insecurity. Perhaps in response to some shock, which her parents thought might have been a teacher threatening the class with the strap, at the age of seven she developed a stutter; try as she would to overcome it, this speech impediment stayed with her for the rest of her life. In matters of daily prayer and regular church attendance, Mary obediently accepted the strict religious practices of her family, but under the influence of Professors Sharman and Hooke at Victoria College, which she attended during the war, her ideas began to mature; she gave up the idea of God as an imaginary general manager in favour of seeing Him as a life-giving power waiting to be understood by science and available for the benefit of mankind.

As Mary grew up the Austin home was a centre of sociability and warm hospitality, especially for church people. With her slim attractiveness and strong-featured face, Mary had many admirers, including Lester Pearson, a future prime minister, whose father was for a time pastor at Park Street Church. At the age of sixteen she and her cousin, Allan Austin, of Renfrew, fell in love, but they kept it a secret for fear of parental disapproval. This relationship continued for seven years. However, one day Allan came to Chatham to announce that he was going to marry an Englishwoman he had met while serving overseas during the war. Mary was crushed. Only after two years did she begin again to find her bearings by engaging in a relentless programme of religious activities: she joined the executive committee of the Chatham Literary Guild, worked on the editorial board of the SCM's *Canadian Student,* formed a Canadian Girls in Training group at Park Street Church, participated in the Girls Work Board of the church in Toronto, attended the Bon Echo Bible study camp of Dr Sharman, and was on staff at the Camp Bruce leadership training course of the Young Women's Christian Association. During this period she made a striking impression on those with whom she came into contact; once, after being a house guest of the Austins over a Sunday while preaching for missions, James Endicott reported to his son: 'Jim, I met just the girl for you on this trip.'

In 1924, Mary, now in her twenty-eighth year, decided that the age of romance had passed her by; she would walk the whirlwind alone. Encouraged by her parents' long-standing interest in foreign missions, and wanting to broaden her vision for a career in youth work, she decided to seek an appointment with the Board of Foreign Missions of the Methodist Church to spend a year in China, followed by a year in Japan and India. It was this decision which took her to the North American Foreign Missionary Conference in Washington, DC, on the last weekend of January 1925, where she and Jim Endicott became mutually spellbound.

Mary had first seen the dynamic young divinity student two years earlier at the first national student conference in Canada, held over the Christmas holidays in 1922 at the University of Toronto. Late in life she remembered the occasion: 'I can see him yet, tall and slim, rising to a point of order every now and again. I sat on the other side of Convocation Hall but I could see his smile from there. He didn't make long speeches but they were very much to the point, and the students responded to his lead.'[1]

The meeting in Washington altered the course of both their lives; a common search for a rational, and at the same time practical, religion laid the foundation for the mushroom growth of their friendship. 'As we met at meal-times and walked the beautiful avenue between the Capitol and the Lincoln Memorial, exploring each other's ideas and experience as only newly-found friends can do,' Mary later recalled, 'a miracle was taking place in our hearts and minds. We each felt the inner excitement of the discovery of mutual interests but were unaware that our faces shone and that one old friend among the delegates was so struck by this radiance that she went home and reported to relatives of mine that we were engaged!' Thus, while Dr Arnup was fruitlessly searching the convention halls to ask him to speak to the final session on 'Why We Go,' Jim was walking along Pennsylvania Avenue with Mary, totally absorbed in his new-found romance.

Mary's effect on Jim was overpowering; in addition to the turmoil over his religious doubts he now faced emotional upheaval of a different kind. Four years earlier, during his first year at Victoria College, he had become friends with Nina Yeomans; as their friendship deepened they had made plans to be married, Nina breaking off another engagement to become his fiancée. The relationship had been strong and steady, even after Nina had dropped out of college following the death of her father and returned home to Belleville to help support the family. But now everything was changed. Would marriage based on friendship instead of romantic love, Jim wondered, be sufficiently satisfying to him? He knew how much the break would hurt Nina, and he knew as well of the criticism that was sure to come from family and friends.

When Mary came to Toronto in the third week of February to attend a meeting of the National Girls Work Board, she met Jim to go over the details of her proposal for work in China and to seek his help in presenting it to the Board of Foreign Missions. On the first day Jim arranged an invitation for them to have dinner at the home of their mutually favourite professor, S.H. Hooke, and his wife. On the way they dropped in to meet Jim's mother. The next day he wrote Mary a note: 'I walked home in the fascinating night light a little thrilled at the mystery of life and praying that love and faith do triumph in this sorry scheme of things. I did so want to return your kiss as you stood at the door looking so bewitching in your wistfulness.' Two nights later, on 19 February, the whirlwind romance reached its climax: after only seven meetings, Jim asked Mary if she would go to China and spend the rest of her life there with him. It was a double-barrelled proposition, suggesting that he was more committed to China than to anything else. But Mary's whole being leapt to accept it. For once in her life she did not hesitate to ponder pros and cons; she knew that something wonderful had happened to her.

The next day, a dismal, rainy, winter's afternoon, Jim went to Belleville to ask Nina for his release. When the moment came to part, after several years of happiness, it was not easy: two distracted hearts attempted to understand life and the ways of the human spirit, but they soon arrived at a mutual decision to separate and to accept their friendship as something belonging to the past.

Mary returned to Chatham to break the news to her parents, who were stunned by the suddenness of her decision and saddened too by the prospect of future parting. But they were understanding beyond her expectations; her father hoped some way would open up for Jim to wait another year before going to China and offered to pay for a year of study at Union Theological Seminary in New York.

Back in Toronto, Jim moved more cautiously. Keeping his proposal to marry a secret, he first talked over with his father his worry that he could not explain to Nina why things had gone so far and why prayer and questioning had not made any difference; his father would not allow the validity of any supposition that prayer can curb or change the natural, fundamental reactions of personalities: 'It is not intended for that,' he said, and ended up with a twinkle in his eye about the likelihood of Jim praying that he would get Mary Austin to love him. Jim remained silent, feeling it was too soon to let his family know of his new engagement. He reasoned that they would be much more satisfied and would accept Mary more readily if they felt that she was simply an indirect cause of his break-up with Nina; that was the fundamental truth of things anyway, he rationalized.

However, it was not possible to stall too long because of his plans to sail for China in the summer. Two weeks later he went to break the news to his father with an empty feeling in the pit of his stomach. Down in Chatham he had found acceptance and peace, but in Toronto, his father, who had waited ten years between the time of his engagement and marriage, was appalled at Jim's rashness: 'You're an expert at getting yourself into scrapes and consulting the family about getting out,' he roared, 'and then not consulting them about getting in again. How long will it be till you break this one? You can only do that sort of thing about six times before someone puts a bullet into you ...' After letting his son stew in his misery for a day, the older man regained his composure. Although he was opposed to Jim getting engaged so soon after his break with Nina, he was quite positive that, if Mary and her family were agreed, no change should be made in Jim's plans to go to China; they should go ahead and marry in time for a summer departure to the Orient.

The censure of Jim's friends and associates was even sharper and more prolonged. Marion Hilliard, an old friend, was particularly offended by what she considered to be his disloyalty and infidelity to Nina and accused him of having 'no sense of honour.' Furthermore, she continued, in a confrontation during a walk in Queen's Park, Mary Austin lacked the stable qualities necessary to be a missionary's wife. In response to her criticisms, Jim retorted that Marion was 'trying to dissect love with a surgeon's meat axe.'

Meanwhile a rumour circulated that one of the church brethren was going to raise the question of Jim's moral fitness to be accepted into the ministry at the Toronto District examination of candidates; he was relieved, however, to have Dr Arnup's reassurance and Dr W.B. Creighton's friendly comment that he had found the right girl. Even then it was difficult to concentrate on preparing his weekly preaching engagements, much less study for the ten final examinations in theology that loomed on the horizon.

Then one day Nina acted to disarm the critics. She came to visit Jim and said she proposed to see or to write Mary and tell of her acceptance of the changed situation. As Mary read Nina's letter she was amazed at her wonderful spirit and strength. To think she could have come to this point in six weeks! Mary had a horrible feeling that it would be she and not Nina who might break down. Such firmness, such calmness, such daintiness as her handwriting showed. 'She is the chastened daughter of adversity,' Mary thought, 'but it has given her the very things I need so much.'

Once again Endicott walked through Queen's Park with Marion Hilliard. This time she was gay and breezy and wished to send her love to Mary Austin. She told him she had recovered her trust in him and hoped they would be happy. Twenty years later she would deliver their first grandchild and in the 1950s she joined the Endicotts in the struggle to stay the hands of those who threatened nuclear war to solve East-West conflicts.

Jim felt comforted. The breath of spring in his veins refused any more regrets; he was bubbling over with a sense of freedom, with a glad confidence that without any restraint or fear he could let the returning new life of nature draw out all the love and joy and strength there was in him to give to Mary. To express his sentiment he gave her an unusual ring, set with a blue lapis lazuli into which the outline of the Capitol dome had been carved, his interpretation of Mary's preference for a ring with personal significance for both of them: blue and gold were the colours Mary wore that winter and the stone itself came from China; the carving was a symbol of that weekend in beautiful, snow-mantled Washington when their love sprouted and bloomed during long walks overshadowed by the great dome.

With Jim's personal moral crisis resolved, wedding plans could be made;

they were to be married in June, just ten days after his ordination examination. The intervening months were frantic: in addition to his anxiety about his impending ordination, the weekly preaching assignments, and ten theology examinations in May, his courtship of Mary churned up a variety of deep and intense feelings.

For ten weeks they exchanged almost daily letters and Jim took the train trip from Toronto to Chatham for weekend visits whenever he was not preaching. Amidst endless discussion of their future in China, what it would be like and what they should take with them, meetings with friends and relatives, some of whom looked askance at their brief engagement and the uncertainties of their life together in China, there were tense moments of mutual criticism, revelations, openness. 'I love you more after every letter you write,' Mary once responded. 'One day you carry me away on a magic carpet to the land of Lutany, the tract of Elenore, where the atmosphere is so rare with ecstasy that breathing almost ceases to be necessary; the next day you let me live with you in the ordinary round, the ups and downs of exams, the mean things and the nice things that people say to you. Your wooing may be swift and sudden, O Terrible James, but it is sweet and it fills me with wonder.'

Thus, their courtship took place after the decision to marry had been made and was a portent of their future life together. Living with Mary would be no humdrum, domestic existence for she was a complicated being, by temperament a person who found it difficult to repress spontaneous desires to share experience. In contrast to Jim's preoccupation with the external world, Mary was fascinated by the subjective, inner side of life. She wanted him to share her enthusiasm for introspection, an objective she never attained, but not for want of trying.

When they first met, Mary was particularly interested in the insights offered by the new discipline of psychoanalysis, which stressed the impact of repressed sexuality on one's personality, and was herself undergoing therapy for her long-time stutter; as well, she was fusing this experience with her religious convictions, thus forming an unconventional brand of theology. Jim, she felt, should know about her personal emotional problems as well as her theological ideas, self-revelations that left him both disturbed and pleased. At one point he became quite upset by the discovery of a side of her he had not known about, her desperate sense of inadequacy and inferiority, which undermined her health and expressed itself in her inability to cure her stammer; she believed she had some kind of witches' cauldron bottled up in her subconscious, the cause of serious shortcomings that might undermine her ability to cope with the strenuous life that lay ahead. At her request, he talked to her therapist, Dr Margaret Strong, but he could not make out what it was all about: if it was so serious perhaps they should postpone going to China in order to have a trained practitioner handle the case, rather than a blundering lover. Having given her assurance that revealing intimacies of her own life would not make her afraid of the loss of his love, Mary explained in detail what she felt she had learned from Dr Strong, that her stuttering was the result of strong parental disapproval of normal childhood sexuality. While the therapy was unsuccessful in eliminating her stutter or feelings of inadequacy, it did enable her to discuss sexual matters very frankly; Jim appears to have been pleased by this frankness and responded freely. For their day, their communication on sexuality was remarkably open and free.

Above all, Jim was interested in the place of psychoanalysis in Mary's theology, in her conviction that

in the last analysis one *is* an individual, who must live and die alone – with God. Perhaps if I ever truly find Him I shall be satisfied. Secretly, I wonder if anyone finds anything but the great longing for God, which rises to the point of being sure He is there – but just beyond the veil. Psychoanalysis is trying to analyse one's desires and fears, to know oneself and so to attain self-mastery and to discover the real faith by which one lives. God is beauty, goodness and truth, and to me, science is the handmaid of truth ever finding new means of revelation. Since our minds are so closely inter-woven with flesh and so deeply concerned with the outcome of spirit, the science of the knowledge of the mind and its workings is, to me, supreme among all the sciences.

It was a mystical perception of life, which led to a sense of personal fulfilment and social usefulness. Although Jim could not accept all of these ideas, Mary's personal creed would certainly be no barrier to come between them. He agreed with her hope that in the end one is an individual and would always be so; he could not enthuse about a God of 'absorption of all spirits,' such as the Buddhists proposed, because for him so much of the meaning of the universe was explained by the production of free, intelligent spirits. If God was 'just a dull level sea of spirit' wherein everyone sinks back like the rivers do into the ocean, then 'He must be awfully lonely.'

This shared unorthodoxy would be a great source of comfort to Jim in later years, even if Mary could not entirely understand his continuing obsessions with the problem of outdated creeds. Mary, of course, was not an ordained minister, with all the obligations that implied, but truly a free agent, theologi-cally speaking, a difference in position that limited in some ways the mutual understanding and support that would be possible in their future relationship.

In the spring of 1925, however, their concept of life together was expressed in highly romantic and idealistic terms. For Mary romantic love meant that Jim's dominant personality would compensate for her neurotic tendencies; she, in turn, would make being his wife and helpmate her vocation: 'You are strong enough and experienced enough to go with me through any garden of pain ... together we shall not be crushed ... somehow in a way I cannot know, now, through you I shall find the Loving Purpose behind and in all life.'

Nevertheless, there were certain limits to the amount of mutuality that was possible in a marriage, she thought: 'In spite of the closest union possible between two souls, we are individuals, with an inheritance and a life-history that have made us what we are. I do not know yet, how completely these twain can become flesh, one mind, one soul.' Jim replied that togetherness did not mean that the marks of individuality are blurred but rather are sharpened, and yet there is a realm created where 'I am you and you are me' and there is neither loneliness nor fear but mystic communion. 'It is out of this communion,' he wrote to her, 'that the strength for life comes.'

Mary was not altogether content to let matters rest on this abstract plane. She was determined to discuss aspects of Jim's behaviour that bothered her: his delight in shocking others by telling risqué jokes or jesting about religion and the general intolerance of etiquette when they were with other people. She found these actions offensive, considered them to be impolite and insensitive to the feelings of others, and let him know how hurt she felt. His confidence about his ability to make her happy was again shaken, and after some tearful sessions he promised to be more humble and thoughtful. But the criticism stung none the less: 'You and I cannot be a mutual improvement society,' he asserted. 'We must live and love and be free.' Mary disagreed: 'We can't help but be a mutual improvement society, dearest, but we can have a lot of fun being it, and mostly we won't know when it's having sessions.'

The major themes of their future life together had all surfaced in this intense ten-week period. Jim would endeavour, albeit with little success, to help Mary overcome her irrational fears and feelings of inadequacy, while valuing her creative intellect and emotional warmth. For her part, Mary would let him have the public limelight, be supportive of his unconventional theological and political ideas, but insist on convening sessions of the 'mutual improvement society.' Forty-two years, four children, one revolution, and two careers later, the relationship forged in the spring of 1925 had weathered the storm and remained intact, but it was hardly the conventional union of two conventional people.

On the eve of their wedding, which took place at sunset on 19 June 1925 in an outdoor setting on the bank of the winding Thames River behind the Austin home, Jim wrote a letter which expressed the meaning of Mary Austin and the promise of their courtship as prologue to their life together: 'You are more than a symbol of life, you are a challenging spirit – God's way of stabbing my spirit broad awake – and my life rises to meet that challenge and the joy of battle is in my eye. So while you may have lost faith in my maturity and judgement – and my manners – I care not just so long as you do not lose faith in what is now a reality, that my love for you and the meaning of yours to me is a real challenge to growth. Besides that it is the sweetest and most delightful thing in the world and I wish you were here in my arms at this moment. The overwhelming thought has just struck me that this is the last letter I shall write you before we are given the freedom of love and the social cherubim lift the flaming swords that guard the gates of Eden.'

These lines were written from the northern woods of Muskoka, where Jim had gone to prepare a lakeside cottage for their honeymoon. There they began their life together. When they returned to Toronto early in July, expecting to leave immediately for the Orient, they discovered that all new missionary postings had been delayed because of the rising tide of resentment against foreigners that had broken out in China. It was not until the end of October that the Endicotts were able to board the *Empress of Australia* at Vancouver, bound for Kobe and Shanghai.

PART TWO

THE
MISSIONARY
YEARS
1925–1944

We landed in Shanghai on the 17th [November 1925] as the Empress of Australia was one day late because of the rough weather earlier. If the Japanese streets had seemed crowded and chaotic, the Chinese were infinitely more so, in spite of the beautiful and imposing foreign buildings in the financial centre on the Bund. Such endless mobs of unkempt, bare-footed ricsha coolies in ragged, faded blue tunics ... oh, the dirt and the struggle for a livelihood, the competition for every little way of earning a bit! ... The kicking of ricsha coolies by some half-baked youths from abroad creates an impression which it is difficult to cope with ...

We stayed at the Missionary Home, which exists for the benefit of transients of every faith and creed ... All the 'guests' were expected to assemble morning and evening for prayers, which included a twenty minute homily from one of the elderly defenders of the faith. The morning that we went we got a strong sermon on the sins of the eye and the foot (the cinema and dancing) and the hottest warning about hell fire that I have ever heard ... We have learned since that the fundamentalist atmosphere which one encounters as an introduction to China is a standing joke ... and that the back stairs leading from the dining room is known as 'the prayer escape.' (If any one is inclined to read from our letters to any church societies, as they threatened to do before we came, they must use their own judgment in censoring the material.) ...

One of the most interesting things about the missionary's position is the attitude of the British press in China to the missionary. One may suppose that the missionary may quite legitimately and honourably try to influence his home government in the readjustment in China, according to his opinion of what would be most just and right for those concerned. But the press gets almost hysterical in its demands that the missionary 'should stick to his own business, if he has any business' ... To quote an editorial: 'They tabulate a line of conduct with regard to the treatment of the Chinese which is far beyond the ability of the ordinary mortal to make good but which looks nice and exceedingly pious in print.' And so it goes –

'The good are unkind to the clever
and the clever are rude to the good.'

But it may even be that the way of good will, if it prevail, be the best for the trade also ...

We were supposed to rise before dawn so as to be down at the river, in case the boat got in on time but none of us wakened until the rickety carriage with its scraggly horse was at the door. However, as we had to wait two hours for the boat after we did get there, we are thinking of adopting as our family motto:

'Let us with a gladsome mind
Always be an hour behind.'

... The four days from Ichang to Chungking were the most exciting of any on account of the gorges, the rapidity of the rapids and the tales of recent military and robber activities ...

The Yangtze River is so much narrower in spots than one could guess from the pictures – the cliffs come very close until from the side of the deck they seem to fill the sky. The formation of the rock and the caves therein and the tier upon tier of mountain peaks fading into a ghostly distance were sources of never-ending delight. An occasional group of trackers pull a junk as they walk along the narrow path often cut out of the sheer cliff, but the steamers have driven most junks off the river. Most thrilling is the Wind Box Gorge, even as Jim remembered it as a boy in houseboat days. As the steamer rounded the curve into the Wind-Box the siren gave a long blast of warning which started six different waves of echo. That shrill whistle is one of the weirdest sounds – like the shriek of a lost soul, with the volume of a dragon's roar.

The steamers on the river have their own troubles ... The channels of the mighty torrent are always changing and the water levels vary considerably from day to day. We saw two steamers perched high and dry on the rocky banks and heard detailed accounts from the captain of steamers that had gone to the bottom within the last two years ... The Yeh Tan rapids, situated below the twenty-five mile stretch of the Witches' Mountain Gorge, seemed to be in an angry mood; the large whirlpool near the left bank looked very fierce with the centre about four feet lower than the edges. The spray from the force of the current hitting our boat as it entered the rapid near the right bank at full speed blew up over the bows. In spite of all the power we could muster, the effect of our full speed against the current was to ferry the ship straight across the river onto the edge of the whirlpool where it seemed as if we would surely be thrown up on the bank. We hung on the edge of the whirlpool for some minutes and then tried to cross the rapid at an angle, only to land back where we started on the right bank. Once more we butted up into the current only to be driven toward the whirlpool again. By this time the funnel was getting very hot. While the ship hung on the edge of the whirlpool once more the crew threw a steel cable to the trackers on shore. As two hundred men pulled it up and fastened it to a high pile of rock the ship stood still on all the power it could summon, with two fire hoses playing on the smoke stack. The water ran down it in boiling streams. The vessel swayed back and forth on the edge of the raging, swirling water until the cable was fastened and the anchor engine heaved on it and pulled the boat through. The captain said we used three or four tons of coal in that half hour …

'Foreign devils!' is one of the first phrases we learned to recognize on the streets of Chungking. The little urchins call it out saucily as they throw gravel or spit as we go by …

If any of you lack the inspiration for a creepy nightmare I wish you could go through the streets of Chungking, particularly carried in a sedan chair at night. It is like going through a labyrinth of winding tunnels lined with caves on either side, weirdly lighted with torchlights or oil lamps except in a few sections where there are electric lights. Until about ten o'clock the labyrinth is crowded with unfamiliar forms and faces jostling each other and all talking at once. The caves are the little shops and eating places with food of all sorts exposed. Later boards are put up for the night and one catches glimpses of piles of bedding being made up for the night. Chungking is built on hills and one has to go up long flights of stone steps to go almost anywhere … Every few minutes the chairmen stop and change shoulders with varying ease and awkwardness. The streets, including the steps, are so narrow that two chairs can barely pass and even one chair in a crowded street creates a disturbance; people get poked with the poles in spite of the shouting of the carriers … once a woman nursing a baby as she went along, and I kept wondering if they are feeling resentment for their discomfort and how much resentment is directed towards the person riding in state, how much towards the carriers who stop for nobody except a group of soldiers drawn up before a shop to arrest someone.

It is like going from purgatory into heaven to pass through gates into the quiet and cleanliness and comparative spaciousness of a foreign house in its high-walled compound.

CHAPTER SEVEN

Apprentice-ship in Chungchow

Encircled by blue, misty hills, and washed by two rivers that meet, swirl over reefs, and then race eastwards fifteen hundred miles to the sea, Chungking is the commercial centre of Szechuan province and gateway to all West China. Built upon a rocky peninsula, this ancient city had an estimated population of 700,000 in the 1920s. Since it was an open port, the commercial houses and steamships of most of the great trading nations of the world were well represented, as were their consuls and gunboats. The missionaries, too, had made Chungking a central mission station: Christian churches, hospitals, schools, a business agency, and Bible societies were run by half a dozen different denominations. The tallest landmark in the city, rising above the great wall, was a church spire built on the model of Toronto's city hall tower with funds supplied by Canadian Methodists. The Endicotts, who arrived in December 1925, would spend most of their years in China in this vicinity.

Normally young missionaries were expected to proceed onward to Chengtu for twelve months of language study at the West China Union University, followed by a posting to one of the numerous outstations of the mission. Through unforeseen circumstances, the Endicotts never reached the language school in Chengtu. One reason was that Mary was already six months pregnant by the time they reached Chungking and the further ten-day trip over the bumpy road to Chengtu by rickshaw and sedan chair looked uninviting and might be hazardous to her health. There was also the incredible size of their baggage shipment: thirty-nine wooden packing cases of various shapes and sizes contained such items as a Gurney coal and wood stove, furniture for three bedrooms, a dining room set, and a Heintzman piano! Through misplaced parental affection, Charles Austin had outdone himself in providing the furnishings from his store. At the time when plans for these gifts were being hatched Endicott had protested, preferring to buy simple furniture

in China and proposing they content themselves with taking out their carefully selected library of three hundred books and some gramophone records
as well as the bare necessities. But Mary, who expected to be living in
Szechuan for the rest of her life, saw no compelling reason to leave 'the
fleshpots of Egypt' behind; surprisingly, she found support from her father-
in-law. As this huge cargo was trans-shipped laboriously from one boat to
another on its way up the various stages of the Yangtze, the leader of the
party, Dr J.E. Thompson, a dentist returning from furlough, became exasperated and suggested that Chungking was quite far enough. Endicott
readily agreed; already almost half a year's salary advance had been spent on
the freight charges.[1]

In these circumstances the new arrivals were glad to accept the invitation of
college friends from Toronto, Harold and Donalda Swann, to share their
house for the winter months. They lived at Duckling Pond, a small hamlet
across the Yangtze River, outside the city proper, where Harold Swann was
teaching in one of the mission's middle schools; Endicott would teach there a
decade later. While the Endicotts awaited the birth of their first son, Norman,
they found congenial company as well as all the comforts of an established
home, with servants to do the cooking and other chores. The large, grey,
brick house, surrounded by a compound wall, had fireplaces in every room;
on three sides of the building verandahs on two levels were invaluable in the
summer heat and useful for drying clothes in wet weather. Mary, especially,
doubted if they would ever live in more beautiful surroundings in China than
here in the countryside, with the great city spread out across the river and hills
on all sides broken into endless patterns by curving rice fields, dotted with
innumerable graves more or less elaborately marked by stone enclosures, the
occasional gnarled old tree, and squat, mud farmhouses. Along the narrow
footpaths a few ponies could be seen and occasionally a string of small
pack-mules, but mostly men were the only beasts of burden: groups of
coolies, stripped to the waist, came along at a trot carrying everything
imaginable, water, coal, building materials, food, fertilizer, in baskets or
loads hung on the ends of a pole balanced across their shoulders.

The main occupation of all new missionaries during their first two years in
China was language study and the Endicotts began their programme of
independent study at Duckling Pond. With the advantage of early, dimly
remembered, childhood knowledge, now fifteen years in the past, Endicott
was determined to become a Chinese-language specialist. The mission had
specialists for eyes, teeth, soil chemistry, why not a language specialist?
Particularly, he thought, since in the near future a missionary would need the
ability to confer and discuss matters in a free and easy way with members of

the growing Chinese church. He hired a Chinese tutor who spoke no English and worked diligently in his study from nine to twelve and two to four, six days a week, to gain this 'gift of tongues.' R.O. Jolliffe, who was in charge of the language programme, inspired him with the idea of a complete mastery of this difficult language, and urged the reading of the colloquial stories of Chinese history that every schoolboy knew, but no teacher of Chinese would recommend because they were not written in the high classical style. Endicott's efforts were remarkably successful, so much so that Kuo Mo-jo, president of the Chinese Academy of Sciences, told him in the 1950s that he was one of the few foreigners whose Chinese was so good it was indistinguishable from that of a native speaker.[2]

Although immersed in his studies, Endicott tried at the same time to become aware of conditions in the country and of the mood of the people around him. His chief impression was that there were so many disturbing circumstances that it would be difficult to do any missionary work at all. Warning his sponsors, the Timothy Eaton Memorial Sunday School in Toronto, that his were the observations of a missionary only two months in the field and should be judged accordingly, he nevertheless wrote out his impressions in considerable detail.

The most obvious difficulty was militarism. Various generals were struggling for power and for the right to collect taxes. The previous week, when he had gone into the city to visit a dentist, Endicott had been held up for an hour at the city gate by the arrival of a warlord with his army from up-country, who was demanding a million dollars before he would leave; there was fighting in the city and the larger shops had put up shutters for the day. Recently, too, another warlord had forcibly billeted his soldiers in the school in one of the mission stations. 'How would you try to get them out?' Endicott wondered. 'What is the Christian way?' Such militarists, he thought, would be a continual barrier to the formation of a stable, national government, and until the country was rid of them there would be little hope for progress: travel and shipment of goods would continue to be difficult because of robbers and bandit gangs; local famines caused by military operations would increase; and the opium trade would continue to grow at an alarming pace.

Another obstacle to missionary work, Endicott observed, was the current social unrest illustrated by student activities. Many schools had to close temporarily because the students refused to have discipline of any kind. 'When you see a statement that the old system of family government in China is giving way before democratic ideas,' he wrote, 'it seems easy to understand.' However, it was not so easy to live and work where this change was taking place, especially when democracy was interpreted by students as 'the right to frame their own curriculum, to sack their teachers if they do not please them, to refuse examinations and then to demand their diplomas at the end of the term.' He believed that many of the students were childish and ignorant, more or less unbalanced by their new taste for freedom, and that they were usually the tools of student union organizers from Shanghai who were trying to break up the school system.

Another challenge the missionary faced was the strong anti-foreign feeling that surrounded him. Some anti-Christians had come and spat on the church door at Christmas. To appreciate fully the anti-foreign feeling, however, Endicott thought it should be seen in the light of the rising spirit of nationalism; he sensed that a certain amount of the hostility was justified. An industrial revolution was underway in the country and conditions in factories, many of them foreign-owned, were primitive and cruel; on the river the foreign steamers had thrown thousands of men out of their accustomed jobs, for one steamer could do the work of a hundred Chinese junks because of its size and speed. Also, the fact that many of the foreigners despised the Chinese added to the resentment. Finally, an increasing number of Chinese were beginning to realize that the position of the foreigners in China was guaranteed by unequal treaties and extraterritoriality imposed on the country by the Western powers through armed force.

For the benefit of anyone who did not understand the words 'unequal treaties,' 'extraterritorial rights,' and 'toleration clauses,' Endicott offered a brief explanation: 'These *treaties* are agreements which were signed as far back as 1842 and 1860 ... They grant the foreigners certain rights of trade, residential areas in certain cities where they are in complete control and may, as in Shanghai, prohibit the Chinese from entering the public parks which the foreign residents build. *Extraterritoriality* means chiefly that the foreigners do not come under Chinese Law but are given their own courts. *Toleration clauses* refer only to missionaries and grant them rights of travel, acquiring property for religious purposes and free the Chinese Christians from government persecution.'[3] Some of these treaty privileges, he felt, especially those relating to missionaries, would probably be granted by a modern government, but the people of China desired a revison of the treaties so that they could give what they wished of their own free will and not under the compulsion of foreign armies and navies. There was a great foundation of good in the rise of Chinese nationalism, he was convinced, for it would make the Chinese more impatient with evils in their own country, and would draw them together as a nation, thus making possible a system of organized education and a strong government. To illustrate his point, he drew parallels with the nationalism of Elizabethan England.

Not all the obstacles to missionary work, as he saw them, were political or social. There were such things as 'the loneliness of the human heart for a touch of home, the longing for old friends, the constant guarding against disease and the difficulty of getting used to a new climate.' But these were more personal problems, some of which could be experienced in other ways whether one stayed at home or went abroad.

In spite of the myriad uncertainties of China, Endicott did not admit to discouragement, and he was heartened by the vitality and courage of many Chinese converts in the midst of the storms of anti-foreign and anti-Christian feeling. He found joy also in being able to put his own ideas and convictions to the test. 'We have been charmed all our lives,' he wrote, 'by the beauty of Paul's description of the love which never faileth, which is never resentful, which is always eager to believe the best. We have been ... urged that, "if we live by the Spirit, by the Spirit let us also walk." Well, there is a new thrill to that doctrine when you have to try it out in the face of real opposition. I [have] walked down the streets and been called "foreign dog" every few hundred yards. Little ragamuffins come up and tell us that we are all soon to be killed, and occasionally after dusk they throw mud.'

Endicott's views about working with the Chinese were shared by many missionaries, especially the younger ones, but his outspokenness caused lasting resentment among some of the senior members of the mission. At the annual meeting of the mission council, held in Chungking from 6 to 15 February 1926 to coincide with the Chinese New Year holidays, the Endicotts were given observer status and invited to attend as part of their orientation experiences. Much of the discussion centred around what to do about the rising Chinese nationalism with its attendant anti-foreign feelings and attacks on Chinese Christians as 'running dogs' serving privileged foreign overlords. The missionaries were gently pressured by their Chinese colleagues to give up the special status provided by the unequal treaties as a gesture to show that they separated themselves from the bullying tactics of the Western military and trading interests. But most missionaries in the field, fearful of the intense patriotic outbursts of radical students, rejected any move to give up their special privileges or gunboat protection until their safety could be guaranteed by a stable Chinese government.[4]

Unable to contain himself, Endicott made a short speech urging accommodation with the demands of Chinese national sentiment, ending provocatively with the cutting statement: 'I never read anything in the Bible which says "Go ye unto the world and shoot the Gospel into every creature."'

In the stunned silence that followed his remark, Dr C.B. Kelly rose and, speaking slowly, said: 'I'm prepared to leave it to the idealists like young

Endicott to try to work with the Chinese on a new basis. I'll be interested to see what happens. But for myself, I'm not prepared to work here without some protection for my wife and children. When the gunboats go, I go.' Kelly spoke for the majority.[5]

Challenging opportunities to try to work out new ways of relating to the Chinese were not lacking, especially in the streets. Even as Endicott and Harold Swann walked away from the meeting, on their way to catch the ferry to the south bank, they came upon some students who were reading aloud from tracts they were distributing on the street:

Great Chinese Student Body, do not go to foreign schools. Foreigners have complete control. Chinese books are not seriously taught. They put all your time on the Bible. These dog-teachers teach history only to the Ming dynasty because recent history they are afraid to teach. You give your money and are cheated of full teaching.

In their churches they have girl members on the reception committees [that is, to attract men] ... Fatty [nickname of a woman missionary] is especially successful at this, surpassing the best at the South Water Gate [professional prostitute area] ...

The two men happened to appear as they were reading the words 'these three dog-things,' referring to Christian schools, hospitals, and churches. Endicott and Swann took advantage of the situation to pause before the orators, bow and grin, in response to which the crowd roared and laughed. A little further on a group of students who were trying to address the bystanders surrounded them and shouted the usual anti-foreign epithets; one threw an over-ripe orange at Endicott, who ducked, the orange landing squarely in the face of one of their own number, whereupon everyone joined in general laughter. The students were surprised and impressed to hear Endicott speak a few sentences in Chinese, explaining that he understood about the principle of nationalism, for the foreign countries had it too. 'Some of its points are good, some bad. At present my Chinese is insufficient,' he said with a chuckle, 'but someday I would like to discuss it with you. See you again.'[6] It seemed to be better to try to respond with goodwill rather than to lose one's temper, and one's dignity, over a little rudeness.

By action of council the Endicotts were posted to Chungchow, a sleepy town of about ten thousand, some 125 miles down the Yangtze River from Chungking. There they could continue their language study as well as provide company for the Pincocks and the Morgans, the two remaining missionary families in the station.

Thus on 4 May 1926, after less than five months in China, the Endicotts were on the move once again. Jim was advised to take their freight down to

Chungchow on a junk, since by treaty foreign steamers were not allowed to unload cargo at any port in West China except Chungking, and then to return to accompany Mary and the six-week-old baby by steamer. All the belongings from Canada, except the piano, were therefore duly loaded at the East Water Gate under the watchful eye of two Chinese soldiers, whom the British consul insisted should be taken as an escort, and under the constant inspection of Endicott himself, to make sure that the boat captain did not try to run opium or war contraband under the protection of the foreigner.

As the junk moved out into the current in the late afternoon, the captain made his bow to the big Buddha just below Chungking and requested the dragon of the Yangtze to be kind to him; a chicken was killed and the feathers, dipped in the blood, stuck to the prow of the forty-foot craft. Before dropping anchor for the night they passed the Wild Mule Rapids, which were not dangerous at that particular height of water.[7]

Later, Endicott described to his wife some of his impressions of the three-day trip:

From the low deck of a junk a few feet above the swift water the height of the mountains on either side is seen in truer perspective [than from a steamer] and you have plenty of time to feast the eyes on the colours of the steep hills or the intensely cultivated slopes, ever green with the rich shades of the fluffy, graceful bamboo. If you pass a high rocky corner your pilot can probably tell of the days not long ago when it was a bandit stronghold and how he was robbed of a cargo there, until you can almost imagine you can see the fierce and dirty rascals with their black headbands and red sashes coming down the bank to stop your boat and discover that a kind providence had delivered Miss Austin's wedding presents into their hands. We were called in several times to be inspected by the military but had no trouble at all. I argued with them that I was a noble fellow doing religious work and should not have to pay the likin [transit tax]. They knew of course that foreigners were not supposed to pay and that if they insisted they might have a visit from the British gunboat on guard at Chungking.

Chungchow proved to be a typical little riverside city, perched high on a hillside, with crooked, steep streets. When all the goods had been safely unloaded and carried on the backs of men and women up some two thousand steps to the mission compound, Endicott hailed a steamer back to Chungking, returning a few days later with Mary and the infant.

When the Endicotts arrived at Chungchow they went immediately to a bungalow a few miles above the city, in the Muli mountains, where the foreign families usually spent several months each summer in order to escape the torrid heat of the Yangtze Valley. Nevertheless, the most exciting thing at the moment was the little house in Chungchow that was to be their first real home together. Mary's heart sank when she first saw it, for it was not like the other foreign houses with their grey bricks and large verandahs. It was a made-over Chinese house built of mud and white-washed, with the woodwork in brown, and a curving roof sadly in need of repair; down in its hollow it looked like a hopeless, helpless heap, with several other equally sad-looking buildings around it that turned out to be the servants' quarters, storeroom, and cow stable. The roof was the saving grace for Mary: 'I hoped I would live under a roof like that when I came to China,' she wrote, 'and few of the foreign built houses have them.' The more often she went, the more possibilities she saw in the house, and as Jim unpacked the furniture, fixing the damaged items – a leg off here, a back off there – and christened the building with Chinese characters meaning Luxuriant-Growth-of-Happiness House, she became impatient for the autumn when they could finally settle in. Endicott chose the name of a legendary character meaning Moon's Glory for Mary and, when added to the surname in reverse order according to the Chinese style, her name was Wen Yueh-hua. Jim's own Chinese name was Wen Yiu-chang, which meant 'Young Chapter of Literature'; 'Wen,' meaning literature, had been chosen in the first place for Jim's father because of the similarity of the sound to the first syllable in Endicott.

As spring ripened into summer, Jim became more and more interested in the work that Dr Alex Pincock was doing. He went with him on several emergency cases outside the hospital, which gave him some insight into Chinese family life. In one instance Pincock was called to see a woman who had eaten opium in a fit of anger towards her husband who had taken unto himself a new, young wife. Although this was a custom long accepted in China, individual women often resented it bitterly. The patient's home was dark and dingy, even though they were a family of considerable means. Pincock remarked that there was seldom a window in the bedroom and he usually found a score of relatives crowded around the patient. Twelve women were living in this house, the wives and daughters of one old man. Pincock said it was not uncommon for a member of such a household to attempt suicide by taking opium in the knowledge that she could be rescued by the foreign doctor and his stomach pump.

Then there were the tragedies of the very poor. One day when the Endicotts and Pincocks were out for a walk they came upon a little woman sitting on the street in her rags trying to sell two benches, probably the last of her household necessities. By the drawn, thin faces they could tell that she and her two children were near starvation. Her husband and two other children had died of fever two days earlier. The neighbours from the street all gathered around, fat, well-fed people, but none of them gave her a bowl of rice in her extremity. Pincock explained that if anyone offered assistance they would be held responsible for whatever happened to her, another old Chinese custom. He took the older boy up to the hospital, gave him enough food for several days, and looked after the family for some time.

Apart from such individual neighbourhood experiences, there were frequent encounters with homeless, starving beggars, some of whom ended up lying dead on the street until someone put them in the plain, wooden coffins provided by some charitable society.

'It makes you feel ill,' Mary wrote home, 'to see how some people suffer and others live in ease. The worst of it is that some of the Chinese themselves wax rich over famines, for instance, by hoarding their rice crop until the price is exorbitant. Relief doled out to the victims can never really cure the evil. One longs to be able to find the root of the terrible economic distress in this country. As one of our colleagues said, "If only the conscience of the better class can be roused." '

While Jim was able to take a more detached, philosophical view of their new experiences, Mary often felt confused and anxious. She realized that she had no experience with 'the masses' of her own race and kept trying to imagine that there must be many 'just as dirty, just as ignorant and just as greedy and untrustworthy' as the people with whom she was coming into contact. Unlike Jim, she had not been born in China, and did not have a keen ear for picking up new languages; she was impatient with having to ask constantly, 'What is he saying?' or else trying to be indifferent like a deaf person. On their first Sunday in Chungchow, she could not understand a word of the service, but she softly sang the English words to familiar hymn tunes. Afterwards all the church members gathered around to welcome the newcomers with beaming smiles and much bowing, clasping their own hands, which was their style of handshake. Some of the older women, told that she had given birth to a son, were intrigued by the fact that Mary nursed the baby herself, and thus felt her breasts to see if she had enough milk for the baby as part of their congratulations; she would have been even more startled had Ida Pincock not already told her that Chinese women of means used a wet nurse for their babies.

Sometimes feeling caged or imprisoned in the early days in China, Mary had a great longing to run along a lakeshore or dash about in a car as at home. Jim urged patience but she was often homesick; never having had a profession, friendships and her family formed an unusually large place in her life. It was a naïve, schoolgirlish confession, she admitted, but she felt more unsophisticated than ever: 'If you want to read a proper account of the glory of being a missionary's wife,' she wrote her friends, 'you must go to more saintly or more official sources.' In spite of her tribulations, however, Mary continued to be interested in the purpose of their coming to China and she believed in Jim's ability to fulfil that purpose.

One of the most important events that deepened the Endicotts' understanding of the Christian community during their early weeks in Chungchow was the funeral of the oldest and wealthiest member of the church. On the day Lee Yeh-yeh died, Dr Pincock was there as he had been twice a day for two weeks. The old man was seventy-six and very confident in his Christian faith; he reminded Endicott of a remark in John Wesley's *Journal* to the effect that 'our people die well.' The doctor had hardly announced that the old man was dying, however, when his wife, daughters, and relatives grabbed him, put him on the table in the guest room, and hastened to put on his new garments, which had been got ready in case he should die. The idea behind this old custom had something to do with the ancestral spirits and the possibility that his spirit would be cold if the new clothes were not put on before he died.

The funeral lasted several days and on the last morning the whole family knelt down at the front of the coffin while the old man's history was read out. At appropriate pauses, the mourners gave loud wails. When this was over the Christian pastor took charge of conducting the service, with several church members giving testimony to the worth of Mr Lee. Then the procession wound through the streets of the city and out to the Christian burial ground. First came about a hundred poor folk paid to carry the gift scrolls and banners on which eulogies were written. About every ten yards or so in the procession there was a long pole with a string of firecrackers that were set off at inspired intervals. The boys of the Christian school were there all dressed in white with borrowed band instruments from the government middle school. The son-in-law, a general, walked at the head of the procession, followed by the Endicotts, Pincocks, and Morgans with their heads bound round with white cotton; behind them came the coffin borne by four paid carriers. By the graveside all the noise, the beating of drums, the explosion of firecrackers, the wailing, ceased. The chairman of the church district read the Christian burial service and led in the singing of a hymn. It was a strange and impressive sight to see the little group of Christians surrounded by a great crowd of curious spectators and to hear suddenly after the noise and the blare the clear tones of the Chinese pastor reading: 'I am the Resurrection and the Life, saith the Lord.'

On the way home Endicott thought of the strangeness of most of the proceedings from a Western point of view and wondered what sort of customs the Chinese church would eventually make for itself. He asked one of the Christian teachers in the school if he wanted a noisy funeral like that and the latter replied enthusiastically in the affirmative. He also asked the pastor, who said only: 'Our Christian customs are not established yet.' Endicott was glad he had joined in with the native customs in spite of his Christian beliefs; to fail to do so would make people think the foreigners really did not care. An attempt by the missionaries to insist the Christian service should be practised exactly as in the West, omitting the colourful old traditions of China, would seem just as strange to them as if a Chinese turned up at a Christian funeral in Canada with a drum and a string of firecrackers.

CHAPTER EIGHT

China
in ferment

Throughout Jim Endicott's first term in China, from 1925 to 1933, his conscience wrestled with the tension between his increasing sympathy for Chinese nationalism and his own vocation. He had come out of the First World War with some strong doubts about the workings of the British empire and now he could not escape the uncomfortable fact that fulfilling his life's ambition as a missionary in China required the protection of British military might. This tension, as well as a private uneasiness about the outdated liturgical creeds he was expected to repeat each Sunday in the pulpit, provided the main thrust in the development of his political, social, and theological ideas throughout these early years.

The upsurge of Chinese nationalism was first led by Dr Sun Yat-sen, who is still revered in China as 'the father of the Republic.' Following the abdication of the Manchu emperor in 1912, Sun and his friends had organized the Kuomintang or Nationalist party in an effort to unify the country under a republican form of constitution.[1] The attempt failed, however, and China entered a dark age of political disunity, social disruption, and civil war as various factions gathered their military forces in an attempt to rally the country under their own banner. The leaders of these factions became known as warlords, men who exercised control over a fairly well defined geographical area by means of military organizations that obeyed no higher authority than themselves.[2] Within the shifting alliances of half a dozen major warlords who controlled the wealthier provinces, each avowing that their objective was to unite the country, hundreds of smaller warlords established their little kingdoms, ravaging the land through their struggles for survival.

From Canton, in 1921, where he had made a temporary alliance with a local warlord, Sun Yat-sen made yet another proclamation of a national government to end the chaos. The government was to be based on his famous three principles of Nationalism, Democracy, and People's Livelihood, doctrines that would become as well known to every Chinese as the Declaration of Independence is to every American. Briefly stated, nationalism for Sun meant the liberation of China from foreign control; democracy consisted of a period of political tutelage during which enlightened leaders would guide the people to self-government; people's livelihood was a form of socialism, vaguely defined, which would bring 'restriction of capital' and 'equalization of rights in the land.'

Sun Yat-sen's initial attempts to establish Canton as the centre for a national government met with failure and his appeals for support from Western countries fell on deaf ears. So it was that, when the Soviet Union offered to ship arms and ammunition to aid Sun's movement, the resulting negotiations led to an uneasy alliance between his party, the Kuomintang, and the Chinese Communist party, which had been formed at Shanghai in 1921.

Backed by material support from the Soviet Union, Sun was able to re-establish himself in Canton late in 1923. With the help of Michael Borodin, a remarkable adviser from the Soviet Communist party, the Kuomintang was reorganized and a military academy for training officers was established at Whampoa, near Canton. Sun's young disciple, Chiang Kai-shek, was placed in charge of the Whampoa Academy and was sent to Moscow for several months' advanced training. Since the Chinese Communist party had accepted the policy of working as a 'bloc within' the larger group, the first congress of the newly organized Kuomintang took place on 1 January 1924, adopting a programme and giving formal recognition to the united front; to cement the alliance, Sun announced that 'essentially, there is no difference between the Principle of People's Livelihood and Communism.'[3] Within the loosely knit coalition, the Kuomintang controlled the government and the army, while the Communists concentrated the efforts of their small, but talented, membership on military training, propaganda, and mass organization. It was their success in helping to build revolutionary mass organizations among the basic social classes of China, the peasantry, the industrial workers, the modern intelligentsia, and, to some extent, among the native capitalists, which gave the Communists a relatively influential position within the Kuomintang. All members of the alliance accepted Sun Yat-sen's 'Three Principles of the People'; based on this text, the Kuomintang was now committed to mobilize the Chinese people for a nationalist and social revolution. Although Sun himself died in March 1925, the victories and defeats, coalitions and divisions, of members of this new movement would dominate the politics of China for the next twenty-five years.

The first major impact of Chinese politics on Endicott's plans had occurred even before he left Canada. He and Mary had been forced to postpone their sailing date to China because on the afternoon of 30 May 1925, three weeks before their wedding, riots had erupted in Shanghai; the demonstrations that followed were the beginnings of a revolutionary upsurge in China that lasted almost three years.

The famous May 30th incident was triggered by the British chief of police in the 'International Settlement' of Shanghai, who is reported to have said: 'Give them a bit of lead; that's what they understand.' Militant students and workers had been demonstrating to protest the murder of a striking Chinese textile worker by a foreign factory guard and the subsequent arrest of sympathetic university students. When the parade, ten thousand strong, reached Louza Police Station on Nanking Road, the British authorities, acting on the orders of their chief who had been reached by telephone out at the golf course, opened fire on the unarmed demonstrators, killing twelve students, and arrested over fifty.

Shanghai was thrown into turmoil. Meetings and demonstrations took place in all quarters, leading to a general strike of over 200,000 workers in the foreign-owned enterprises. Fifty thousand students quit classes, servants left foreign homes, and many merchants closed their shops. Among the seventeen anti-imperialist demands adopted by the mass meetings were: withdrawal of all foreign land and naval forces from China; abrogation of consular jurisdiction; freedom of speech and assembly for the Chinese residents in, and Chinese representation on the municipal council of, the 'Settlement.'[4] Strikes and demonstrations spread over the land to Peking, Tientsin, Wuhan, Canton, and other places where there were foreign concessions. Never had there been anything quite like this since the great powers forced their way into China eight decades earlier. Westerners became panic-stricken.

More was to follow. On 23 June a demonstration of 100,000 Chinese was held in Canton in support of the anti-imperialist May 30th Movement; as the parade passed the foreign concession at Shameen, British and French machine-gunners fired across the creek, killing fifty-two students and workers and wounding over one hundred. A Western journalist living in China at the time described the result: 'A boycott of British goods and a general strike were immediately declared. Hongkong, fortress of Britain in China, was totally immobilized. Not a wheel turned. Not a bale of cargo moved. Not a ship left anchorage. More than 100,000 Hongkong workers took the unprecedented action of evacuating the city. They moved en masse to Canton. The strike halted all foreign commercial and industrial activity. It drew 250,000 workers out of all principal trades and industries in Hongkong and Shameen. In Canton workers cleaned out gambling and opium dens and converted them into strikers' dormitories and kitchens.'[5]

The strike and boycott enabled the Kuomintang to consolidate its power in the southern province of Kwangtung, and on 1 July 1925 a new national government of China was once more proclaimed in Canton. Following two years of tumultuous revolutionary civil war, the new movement established its capital on the Yangtze River, first at Wuhan and then in Nanking; in 1928 it was formally recognized by most foreign countries as the government of China.

For Endicott, then, the immediate effect of the May 30th Movement had been to put all his plans in jeopardy. Mission administrators in Toronto were alarmed by the reverberations of the coastal disturbances in Szechuan province. In Chungking, where British marines landed with fixed bayonets and wounded a number of Chinese who were demonstrating at a foreign firm, servants had gone out on strike and pickets were posted to prevent food reaching the foreigners. The British consul ordered British women and children to board a British steamer, which immediately departed downriver for Ichang. The local warlords seemed unable or unwilling to control the anti-Christian propaganda and the anti-foreign actions of the unionized workers and radical students.[6] The time did not seem right for sending out new missionaries.

Even before the Shanghai events, George E. Hartwell, secretary of the West China Mission Council in Chengtu, had written home to report that 'the air is electric with all kinds of ill-reports of the foreigners these days.' The age when the missionary had opportunities to reach the masses, 'who flocked around him wherever he took a stand,' he thought, were perhaps past, and more reliance would have to be placed upon Chinese leadership.[7]

Fortunately for young Endicott's plans, such suggestions for a reassessment of the missionary's role in China were received coolly in Toronto. Hartwell was assured that 'this burst of anti-foreign feeling will blow over.'[8] James Endicott, Sr, general secretary of the Board of Overseas Mission, was a man whose belief in the foreign missionary endeavour was unshakeable. He himself had encountered anti-foreign riots a few days after reaching Kiating in 1895, but had gone on to witness a great upsurge in Christian activity. Following the short-lived, anti-foreign, Boxer rebellion and the subsequent occupation of Peking by eight foreign armies in 1900, the missionary movement had gained further momentum. It had been pushed to even higher levels after the overthrow of the Manchu dynasty in 1912. In 1913 the veteran missionary, O.L. Kilborn, had written that 'foreign ideas ... are held in such regard, even by the highest in the land [that] the advice to study the Bible, even to have it put upon their course of study for schools, does not sound so strange in our ears or theirs. The exhortation to follow Jesus Christ falls with a force upon our hearers not possible formerly.'[9]

Subsequent events, however, demonstrated the naïvety of this assessment. Whether the West China missionaries and their colleagues in Toronto recognized it or not, another development, known as the May 4th Movement, had become a watershed in Chinese history. Taking its name from the day on which widespread demonstrations occurred in 1919 to protest the decision of the Versailles peace conference to transfer Germany's possessions in Shantung province to the Japanese, the May 4th Movement was much more than a momentary outburst of Chinese nationalistic pride. It was a 'new culture movement' in which the vernacular language, accessible to ordinary people, replaced the old Confucian classical forms as the medium of literature and education. It was a 'new thought tide' bringing the ideas of progressivism, liberalism, and Marxism to China. Science and democracy, catchwords in the West, became the standards by which all things, old and new, Chinese and foreign, were tested and measured.[10] Increasingly conscious of their country's national humiliation at the hands of foreign powers, Chinese students searched for useful knowledge and methods to strengthen China.

In this search, Christianity, at least the way it was being presented in China, was tested by many young Chinese and found wanting. Christian preaching about miracles and literal acceptance of ancient myths did not meet the tests of the scientific method; China, they felt, already had too much superstition. Christians, with all their separate denominations, were also vulnerable to the charge of being divisive elements, a hindrance to national unity. Western Christian schools intruded upon China's sovereignty with a denationalizing effect. What other nation would allow aliens to have such strong control over the educational system? And now, at Versailles, the Christian liberal West was siding with China's enemies to rob her of her territory!

By 1922 the impact of the May 4th Movement was already being felt by the West China Mission. D.S. Kern, educational secretary in Chengtu, wrote to James Endicott informing him about the changed circumstances. A leading student at the Christian university, who had been asked to explain the recently observed anti-foreign, anti-Christian feelings on the campus, was reported by Kern as follows: 'At the time of the Revolution when the Manchu Dynasty was overthrown the rulers and the people were afraid of the Foreign Powers, remembering what they had to pay after the Boxer trouble but now they have lost that fear, and so the anti-foreign feeling which has existed all the time has come to the surface. Since they no longer fear the Foreign Powers, they no longer hide their real feelings. Consequently many who were Church members have left the Church while others fear or have no wish to join.'

The missionaries also came in for criticism and were charged with oppressing the people. Chinese critics pointed out that the majority of Chinese preachers and teachers working for the mission were paid only $10 to $15 a month in 1922 while the missionary engaged in the same work was receiving eight to ten times that amount. This was a form of oppression. For servants the disparity was even more glaring; they received only $3.50 or $4 per month when it cost about $2.50 for their food. It didn't matter that many of their compatriots were even less well off. Kern agreed: 'Since the Missionary lives in comfort and plenty [hence] the talk about the Missionary oppressing the Chinese. I fear,' he said, 'it is the same old story of Labor and Capital.'[11]

By 1925, when the anti-imperialist united front of the Kuomintang and Communist parties, centring around Sun Yat-sen's Three Principles, had been active for a year, Chinese students at Christian schools and universities responded to the rising tide of nationalism by launching a 'Restore Educational Rights' movement.[12] Hartwell wrote to Endicott, Sr, on this awkward development. Foreign administrators, he said, were being accused of dictatorial and paternalistic behaviour, of having no respect for the Chinese students and the Chinese nation. A common taunt hurled at Chinese preachers and teachers was 'Wang Guo Nu!' – slaves who have forgotten their country. Students obstructed the operations of foreign schools, especially at examination time, hoping to provoke government intervention. They demanded that religious education be separated from the rest of the curriculum and that it be voluntary. They proposed that all education should be supervised by the government and that foreign schools must register and be regulated by provincial departments of education.

These were the factual developments that had led the West China Mission into its mood of questioning. In spite of the difficulties, James Endicott, Sr, chose to ignore any uncertainties with the confident optimism that was characteristic of most Methodist preachers of his day. Endicott's lack of doubt was matched only by his great success, along with Jesse Arnup, in finding money to finance the missionary endeavour: during the previous five years the Methodist Church in Canada, under their leadership, had been raising approximately $300,000 annually for the West China Mission – more than three times the amount the church spent on immigrants and native peoples.[13] This combination of ideological and financial vested interests would brook no opposition. The threat to the younger Endicott's future career turned out to be only a five-month delay in travelling plans. What his father had refused to acknowledge in Toronto, however, Jim would have to confront in person very soon after his arrival in China.

CHAPTER NINE

The Wanhsien incident

On Monday, 7 June 1926, at high noon, Mrs W.E. Sibley, who had been a Canadian missionary in West China since 1907, was attacked and killed as she walked along a crowded street in Chengtu. A lone swordsman came up from behind, cut off her head with a single blow, and threw it into a latrine as he made his escape.

This shocking occurrence was the first of a series of events beginning in the summer of 1926 which created mounting uneasiness and tension among the missionaries in West China. An inquest into the Sibley tragedy determined that the murderer was a member of the Red Lantern Society, a traditional anti-foreign secret society similar to the Boxers, rather than a part of the new nationalist agitation. Swift action by district authorities to check the growth of a violent anti-foreign outbreak, by rounding up members of the society and by announcing the execution of two leaders, temporarily reassured the foreigners. But within a few weeks there were new shock waves in the form of reports about the sweeping successes of the revolutionary army of the Kuomintang–Communist party united front as it left its base in South China on a northern expedition. The feelings of insecurity increased early in September when the southern forces, with their Bolshevik advisers from Soviet Russia, entered Wuhan on the Yangtze; concurrently, the British navy shelled the city of Wanhsien in eastern Szechuan in the course of a minor incident involving British shipping on the Great River.[1]

Missionaries were thus forced to rethink the purpose for which they had come to live in China, to consider whether the value of their contribution was worth the risk involved, to face more clearly the conflicting demands of living in a new, nationalist China at the same time as they felt the constraints of citizenship in the British empire with its pressing business and military interests.

Shielded from the immediate impact of events by the remoteness of Chung-chow, Jim Endicott took the attitude that 'so far, nothing has happened,' and went on about his work. For ten hours a day, that summer, he studied Chinese characters, and spent his free time climbing the hills chasing butterflies, moths, and dragonflies, demonstrating once again an awareness that 'the earth and common face of nature spoke to him rememberable things' (Wordsworth), a characteristic which throughout his life allowed him to keep a sense of proportion and an inner serenity amidst turmoil and trauma. He saw three specimens of the real leaf butterfly, which he had dreamed of seeing again since boyhood days, and he caught one. There were thousands of dragonflies around the rice fields and from five staple colours – red, green and black striped, blue, yellow, and copper – a great variety of mixtures arose. He caught and carefully noted forty-two dragonflies with distinctly different markings. When Cornell University happened to hear about his dragonflies they were fascinated; ultimately he discovered a new variety, which was christened 'gomphus endicotti' in a study published by that university.

The recent events in Chengtu had made the mission executive feel that it was now more dangerous to be a missionary, but Endicott got much inspiration from noticing that according to the dictates of nature those who achieve beauty and freedom and show signs of spontaneous joy are those who live in the sunlight and are not safe. It seemed to him that those who live sheltered, unadventurous, selfish lives, like worms, flukes, and other parasites, were dull, ugly, without inspiration of any kind. While missionary life with its dangers could bring rewards, as nature rewarded the adventurous insects, it did not necessarily do so. Some missionaries impressed him as being theoretically inspired by the life of the spirit but practically harassed and worried and cramped by the dangers of one kind or another. With the Chinese as touchy as they were now, it was easy to mistake or misname cowardice for meekness; Christian graces were not very inspiring unless they were superimposed on some solid pagan virtues such as courage and endurance.

In response to worried relatives in Canada, who wanted to know if the Endicotts felt they had 'special protection' of any kind, Jim reflected upon one of his favourite texts: 'For God hath not given us the spirit of fear; but of power, and of love, and of a sound mind' (II Timothy 1:7). He wrote of his attitude to danger, which was both appealing and naïve in its simplicity. As far as human beings harming one another, he believed that the Spirit of Love created by its power a condition of goodwill which would gradually rule out hatred and harm. Because a person was doing what he believed to be the Will of God, there was no guarantee whatever that he would not die of plague, be shipwrecked, or perish by any other cause. The facts did not bear out such belief. Job had wrestled with the problem of 'righteous' suffering and had been unable to arrive at any 'special protection' faith. The only way was to continue seeking knowledge, mastery of disease and accident, and then go on happily not worrying about possibilities. It was perhaps intended by the Creator of it that life should be a risky and adventurous thing. There were those who thought they 'must be forever worrying about living a long time and they fuss and worry and get their lives cramped and fearful and are a burden to themselves and everyone else.'[2]

Such thinking led to the conclusion, for both Endicotts, that, once they were assigned to some responsibility, to go the way of Jesus implied that they must stay at their post, unless otherwise advised by their Chinese colleagues; only by sharing the dangers of the Chinese Christians and giving them encouragement could a strong church be established.

It was the bombardment of Wanhsien, by British gunboats on 5 September 1926, that rapidly increased tensions and led to a new round of arguments as to whether the British missionaries should stay or leave Szechuan. The British navy wanted to clear the way for the possibility of more forceful action, and therefore wished, at a minimum, to have the women and children evacuated; the missionaries, on the other hand, were aware that if they appeared to panic their work and reputations among the Chinese would be ruined.[3]

The Wanhsien incident arose out of a dispute between British shipping companies and General Yang Sen, the warlord in that city. The latter, claiming that one or two of his junks containing soldiers and silver had been sunk by the wash of a speeding steamer, the *Wanliu*, seized two steamers with their officers and demanded reparations. When negotiations failed, the British authorites in Hankow sent a camouflaged merchant vessel with orders to secure the release of the six officers by negotiation or by force. Before the *Jia Ho* had arrived, the gunboats *H.M.S. Cockchafer* and *H.M.S. Widgeon* were already on the scene. When the *Jia Ho* put her bridge alongside one of the captured ships, her three officers walked off unharmed. After that no one was quite sure what happened, and, since all the responsible British naval officers were killed, no investigation was possible. Apparently when the commander of the expedition saw how easily the three imprisoned officers walked off, he decided on the spur of the moment to board and seize the ship. There seemed to be no Chinese troops ready for action. But there were troops hidden in the cabins and when the boarding party struck they opened fire. Meanwhile, the *Cockchafer* with a six-inch gun and the *Widgeon* with a three-inch gun bombarded the city, starting a number of fires; a large number of Chinese troops along the shore were killed by the use of machine-guns. While a foreign observer estimated that three thousand civilians and troops had been killed before darkness fell and the gunboats departed for Ichang, the British press in Shanghai made a great occasion of this incident with an editorial appearing under the heading, 'Wanhsien Epic,' describing the fight of the 200 against 20,000; it was felt that 'foreign prestige' had been maintained and the Chinese taught a lesson and 'put in their place.'[4]

During the Wanhsien incident the Endicotts were still up at the summer bungalow in the Chungchow hills, about sixty miles from the scene of the fighting. At midnight on 8 September 1926, Alex Pincock came over to awaken them, saying he had received word of the bombardment by wire from the British chamber of commerce in Chungking and it was feared that there would be popular demonstrations against all British citizens. Accordingly, the Chungchow missionaries were advised to get down to the city and be prepared to be picked up by steamer as soon as possible. The American consul, acting for the British consul who had gone to the scene of the fighting, had ordered the American vessel *Chi Ping* to stop at Chungchow to get them, but since they had not been at the shore it had gone on. The two families decided to move back to the city without delay.

This was Endicott's first real lesson in the relation of the missionary movement to the gunboat policy of the Western traders. Whether he liked it or not, just by reason of citizenship he was involved by such happenings as the bombardment of Wanhsien. He brooded on these things all the way down from the hills, his adrenalin flowing freely as he imagined being welcomed by an angry mob. Nobody bothered them, however, and, perhaps to clarify his ideas, he began to write letters home. To his father, who was now moderator of the United Church of Canada, he wrote:

There are some unpleasant things about our position. We are more apt to die for being British than we are for being Christian and nobody in his right senses would want to do that here in the Yangtze Valley. I would not mind 'dying for the flag' if the flag stood for what governments teach school boys that it stands for. But out here you are next thing to a traitor if you act on the principle that the flag stands for justice and freedom and the strong helping the weak. You lower the 'prestige' of the foreigners. Some day when the Chinese write the last chapter of the Washington Conference [of 1922, promising the end of extraterritoriality] they will announce that,

'Earth is sick,
And Heaven is weary, of the hollow words
Which States and Kingdoms utter when they talk
Of truth and justice [Wordsworth].

...and they will chase out the foreigners and probably massacre the wrong people, the missionaries instead of the editors who will give as their interpretation of history that the trouble was that 'foreign prestige' was not maintained.

The common argument that was given to those who were beginning to think as Endicott did was to say they were 'too pro-Chinese.' He answered this argument in the same letter about Wanhsien:

I am not particularly pro-Chinese. I think the Chinese are no better than they ought to be, in fact, I think they are worse than they ought to be or I would not be here. I am a meddler in people's morals. But politically it is easy to be sympathetic when you see with your own eyes the Westerners getting control of the industries of the country under the protection of armed force and the plea that they are more 'enterprising.' The Chinese could do just as well if China were given what every other country has the right to do, the power to limit foreign competition within her own borders until her own industries get established. France, Belgium and Italy have not paid any debts for years but we do not go and seize their customs. Nor did we insist on sending in troops to establish a cotton trade because there was civil war in the United States. Why then should we take advantage of China's civil wars to get our foot in first ... my head is more or less teeming with ideas of Chinese politics because there is grave fear that her foreign relations are bringing the missionary up against a blank wall.[5]

To the University of Toronto Historical Club, of which he was a graduate member, he philosophized in a letter of 24 October:

At the present time I am chiefly impressed with these two or three facts. The attitude of the foreigners, merchants, as also many missionaries, towards the Chinese is such as to preclude any friendly settlement until such time as China is able to talk from behind ten million troops ... any Chinese reading the English papers of China, and there are thousands now who do, could not help but feel that our attitude to them is that of conquerors, a relic of the frame of mind that foreigners had twenty-five years ago.
The foreigners are due to be hated in this country because they have precipitated an industrial revolution ... The steamers coming up the Gorges have thrown thousands of Chinese junkmen out of work ... there is animosity which comes as the result of economic disturbance ... while the Chinese merchant is hampered by the military and political situation and subject to all kinds of taxation, the foreign merchant under the protection of his gunboat is able to trade with freedom from interference and without taxation.

Endicott learned later that the freedom from taxation enjoyed by foreign business interests was constantly being infringed by local warlords who needed funds. General Yang Sen had forced all steamers to pay some taxes, and the captain of the *Wanliu*, the steamer that precipitated the Wanhsien incident, told Endicott that the shipping people had been hoping for something to happen so that the gunboat could 'take a crack at Yang Sen.'[6]

While Chungchow remained calm in the aftermath of the shelling of Wanhsien, the situation was different in central and western parts of Szechuan. In Chengtu sympathizers of the Kuomintang organized demonstrations in which thousands of soldiers, civilians, and students took part. No violence occurred during these demonstrations but the Union University Students' Association proposed a 'Declaration on the Wanhsien Tragedy,' which led to the closing down of the university for a few days. The English 'are always fierce and naturally cruel,' the declaration began. With the 'mien of the lion' they deceive the weak and small of the world with the strength of their ships and the prowess of their guns. These 'perverse barbarians' have recently drowned 'two boat loads of soldiers without the slightest attempt to indemnify'; the bombardment of Wanhsien is in violation of national rights and a 'direct contravention of the laws of rectitude among men.' In stirring tones, the students declared that fellow countrymen were being pushed 'into the slavery of dogs and horses and into an environment of bitter distraction.' They demanded the severance of all economic relations with Britain, an indemnity for the loss of life and property in Wanhsien, and the withdrawal of British rights of navigation in the interior.[7] When all servants and workmen in Chengtu withdrew their services and a food boycott of British families was put into effect, the situation began to appear desperate for the foreigners. Before long, however, when a representative of General Teng Hsi-hou, the local warlord, 'whispered' to Joseph Beech, president of the university, that the soldiers would soon be encouraging the students to return to classes, the foreigners knew that they were not in any danger.[8]

The position at Chungking was more alarming. Events moved so rapidly that the British chamber of commerce, which took charge in the absence of the British consul, recommended that all British subjects seek safety on ships in the river or on shore nearby. A giant demonstration was planned by Chinese groups for Saturday, 18 September, and before daylight that morning the Committee of Safety of the British chamber of commerce, which was waiting to the last moment hoping for a whispered message from the military, panicked and advised all British women and children and a number of the men to leave for safety downriver. The first boat left at dawn.[9]

The Chinese authorities prevented violence in the city of Chungking but the bungalows on the hills of the south bank, all unoccupied, were looted irrespective of nationality and most of the bungalows of Britishers were destroyed.

One or two families quietly but firmly defied the evacuation order, including Harold and Lal Swann with their two children. They elected to ride out the storm with their Chinese Christian brethren in much the same spirit as the Endicotts had decided they would try to act. On the Saturday of the great demonstration in Chungking, Harold Swann sat on the front steps of his house with the big gate open so that all passing might look in and see that things inside were normal. In reply to a long letter from Endicott, Swann gave his views of the present flare-up:

Lal and I ... both feel that work here, even though not in the most flourishing condition should have the first consideration and that our plans should keep that always central ... From what I saw last summer [after the May 30th incident] to stay on and suffer with the people links us to them more closely ... We stay because we represent Brotherhood as opposed to Force as the hope of the New World ... Sometime sooner or later we have to step out from the protection of the consular powers. I see no more opportune time than now ... if with retreating trade and naval interests we beat a hasty retreat we will be forever identified with them.

You remember the feeling one had the night before a scrap, Jim. Well last night I had it only infinitely worse. The kiddies never seemed more dear to me, oh they are sweet. We surely owe them safety. But to come to facts. About one o'clock a message came from the Chamber of Commerce saying that the body had met and decided we should move the women and children. We decided painfully, I don't need to go into all the reasoning, for I know you two will understand, that we could not get out with the first shot or rather before it. We know that no one else here approves of our action. We may move later as opportunity offers. Now we stay put. The Chinese teachers agree with our stand. The next four days will see us past the worst gusts and then it will be a long slow pull back to normal again.

A week later, after the clouds of wild rumour had drifted away and a quieter atmosphere had returned, the Swanns took great satisfaction in telling the Endicotts some of the amusing stories about the evacuation. Their favourite dealt with the panic of the British businessmen on that Saturday when they decided to evacuate completely: 'they were up in that Club area – Roll call – Nicholson missing – Search. Finally in desperation they decide to go and let Nick die at the hands of the noisy mob. But just at the gate they were met by messengers from Commander Tsao of the Militia who assured them that in spite of the noise there was no danger at all – And old Nick was discovered dead drunk right down on the boat on which they were to make the "run for freedom." Should be headed "British Businessmen in Dire Danger Saved by 'Black and White.' " "[10]

Needless to say the Endicotts heartily approved of the Swanns' stand, even while Jim conceded that 'some nerves will give out'; in the army the shell-shocked soldier was held in as much honour by his comrades as the wounded, and so it should be among the missionaries. Endicott had no criticism for those whose nerves had failed, for some of them had had loaded revolvers held to their heads and bayonets stuck before their throats in the last year or two. But there were others who were scared whose defence mechanisms made them either try to stampede everyone else or say anyone was a fool to stay. The murder of Mrs Sibley brought out that tendency. 'These people have every right to retire if they wish,' Endicott argued, 'but they have not the right to make everyone else do so ... Their criticism of some of us who are not so sure that the time has come to leave for a while is of such a nature that I am inclined to suspect that they are really afraid that we are right.'[11]

Although Endicott was anxious to take a firm and principled stand, he too was uneasy about the possibilities that lay ahead. It looked to him as if Britain intended to launch armed intervention. Had Yang Sen not turned over the two steamers by the end of September, Endicott learned that the British were preparing six gunboats, four of them carrying six-inch naval guns, to blow Wanhsien off the map.[12] If this was an indication of future policy, the Chinese would either make a stand and fight or be quelled by fear and retire with hate in their hearts to take it out on isolated people or in places like Szechuan that were difficult of access to foreign navies. In either case, missionary work would be more dangerous and perhaps impossible for a time. In view of the need to work out contingency plans, he and Alex Pincock decided to make the long journey up to Kiating to attend the annual mission council meeting, taking their families as far as Chungking.

The trip to western Szechuan, which began by passenger junk early in the new year, ended abruptly at Chungking. The joyful reunion with the Swanns was interrupted by a message from the British consul inviting all the British missionaries to attend a meeting: he reported that the British concessions in Hankow and Kiukiang on the lower Yangtze had been overrun by mobs directed by the Kuomintang nationalist forces, that the consulate at Chengtu was being closed, and that all British subjects in the nine consular districts west of Nanking were being evacuated. American citizens were also leaving the interior of China. 'I plead with you,' he said, 'to take the next boat; it will be leaving at noon tomorrow.'[13]

The heated discussion that followed focused less on the broader realities of political change than on balancing the probabilities as to hostile action on the part of the local Chinese, but it also had much to do with the ethical demands based on the possibility of martyrdom. As the consul listened to the talk of some of the more stubborn missionaries he grew exasperated. He was aware that at that moment troop ships were rushing 25,000 British and American marines and Japanese soldiers to Shanghai. 'If you knew what I know,' he said, 'you would not hesitate.' When asked what it was that he knew, he assured them it was a secret. He even suggested that if they disobeyed a government request they might in future be refused passports. 'Does the British Government have the right to deport us if we refuse?' someone asked. The consul declined to commit himself on this issue.[14]

In the end it was decided that everyone should obey the evacuation order. There remained behind in Chengtu only five male members of the mission, led by Walter Small and Frank Dickinson, who refused to accept the decision; thereafter they were called the 'gold star missionaries.' Oddly enough, these men were not among those most noted for standing in judgement on the imperialist aggression of their own country or for a sympathetic attitude to Chinese nationalism. They simply wanted to preserve the work and property of the mission by retaining a presence and by relying, as in the past, on the support of the local warlords to avert any real danger. General Liu Wen-hui had assured one of them that 'it is my personal duty to render assistance and give every possible protection to all foreigners no matter what circumstances may arise.' In spite of an unsigned telegram asking 'What in hell is delaying you five men?' they stayed on.[15]

By the middle of January 1927 the West China group, including the Endicotts, were part of the exodus of seven thousand missionaries fleeing the interior of China. The majority of them continued on to their homelands, and many, including the Swanns and Pincocks, never returned to China. The heyday of the missionary movement in China was over, leaving only a lengthy Indian summer of frustration.

The reaction of the missionary body to the Wanhsien incident made a deep adverse impression on Endicott, an impression that often came back to his mind in the struggles twenty years later when China, torn by civil war, was once more the object of gunboat diplomacy. Of the approximately two hundred British missionaries in West China, 'all but a half dozen' defended the British action in 1926. Their defence varied from outright endorsation and expression of satisfaction that the 'Chinese had been taught a lesson' to qualified support of the kind that said the action was 'regrettable but necessary.' The American missionaries as a whole had deplored the action and a large group of them issued a statement not only condemning the bombardment but suggesting that America was different. However, Endicott knew that American gunboats had also been involved indirectly in the Wanhsien affair by helping to escort the British ships through the hostile lines of the southern armies on the way down to Ichang and Hankow.[16] He began to suspect that as the Christian church was then constituted, financed, and educated, the missionary movement it sponsored would be such as would always endorse the national interests of its own country. He had obeyed, reluctantly, the order to evacuate to the coast, but for the time being he thought it worthwhile to stay in China and somehow 'try to give the idea that the missionary movement is altogether apart from any government action.'[17]

CHAPTER TEN

Exodus
to Shanghai

On the long voyage down the Yangtze as a refugee, a trip that was a repetition of that taken by his parents thirty-two years earlier, Endicott harboured strangely mixed emotions and contradictory ideas. At first he brooded un-happily over the thought that he was running away from his job; the consul had caught him away from home and he had found it hard to do anything but go with the others. But his conscience felt better when, below Wanhsien, the ship was attacked several times by soldiers and unemployed native boatmen turned 'bandits.' While passing through one gorge, in dangerous water, those firing were not more than fifty yards away, and the rifles had a most un-pleasant crack. Fortunately an upstream boat had given warning so that the passengers were upon the bridge behind the armour plates; nevertheless, one bullet entered the Endicotts' cabin and drilled a hole in the baby's diaper pail. At another point when firing began without warning one of the missionaries was caught in the bathtub.[1] In the face of such obvious dangers, escorting his family to safety seemed to be more clearly the right thing to do.

By mid-January 1927 the Endicotts had set up housekeeping in a flat in the French Concession in Shanghai. Here they lived as refugees for more than a year, continuing their language study and waiting for a return to peace in West China.

Within a few weeks they participated in the 'Exodus Council' of the West China Mission, and, as well, witnessed one of the critical, tragic climaxes of the Chinese revolution. The latter, however, made little impact on Endicott's thinking. Apart from the horror of the things he saw, he made no effort to analyse the class struggles that occurred in Shanghai during the spring of 1927. 'I was taught history and philosophy at the University of Toronto by Oxford-trained dons in such a way,' he later recalled with chagrin, 'that although I studied the French Revolution rather intensely, when I saw a revolution happening under my very nose in China, I was unable to comprehend it, unable to know why it was happening or to have a proper historical estimate of its significance.' China's internal revolutionary struggle, as distinct from her struggle for independence as a nation, appeared to him at this stage as the work of 'a mob of laborers and ne'er-do-wells,' the pawns of a 'red element' and 'Russian influence.'[2]

The atmosphere in Shanghai during these days was decidedly hard on the nerves of the missionaries. Quite apart from its notoriety for having the 'longest bar in the world,' for its opium dens, gambling casinos, race courses, brothels, and for the close liaison between gangsters and politicians, the city of 3.5 million was overcrowded by people from upcountry who had fled from places occupied or about to be overrun by the advancing Nationalist armies. The International Settlement, with 28,000 foreigners and 1.1 million Chinese, was largely British-controlled, and was run by a municipal council elected on a narrowly restricted franchise of about ten per cent of the foreign population, a fact that made it a highly vulnerable target for Chinese nationalism and what was called 'Bolshevist propaganda.'[3] As the city awaited the arrival of the Nationalist army, military sentries, barbed wire, and sandbags were everywhere. Especially unnerving were the daily occurring strikes, which turned greater Shanghai into a cauldron of social discontent. A large part of the work force was on a starvation basis because of low wages and the high cost of living. In the previous year alone, 200,000 workers had been involved in 169 strikes over the effects of high prices and inflation, the exploitation of child labour, and the brutal treatment of workers by foremen.[4]

When the news reached Shanghai on 19 February 1927 that the Nationalist army led by Chiang Kai-shek was south of the city, the General Labour Union, which had been organized a few years earlier by the fledgling Communist party of China, called a general strike to celebrate the victory and to weaken the position of the independent warlords who ruled Shanghai. The strike lasted only five days because, for reasons known only to insiders at the time, Chiang's forces halted in their tracks well short of the city.[5] Taking advantage of this lull, the warlord gendarmerie immediately set about beheading labour leaders in the streets. Endicott's new language teacher, a Szechuanese with leftist leanings, wanted him to see the worst for himself and took him out beyond the concession limits to the Lunghua pagoda. There, as Endicott watched, several men with arms bound behind their backs were forced to kneel and then had their heads chopped off.[6] Similar gruesome scenes of the reign of terror were described by the correspondent of the *New York Herald Tribune*, on 22 February, as the heads of victims who had been denied any semblance of a trial were placed on platters or poles and carried through the streets.

Although Endicott was shocked by these acts of violence and savage behaviour, there was fear of worse to come, which he blocked out of his mind, when the division of the Nationalist forces into right and left wings became manifest. The latter development was signalled by J.B. Powell, the outspoken, independent-minded, American editor of the *China Weekly Review*, who declared bluntly on 12 March 1927 that 'the struggle between liberty and property is on.' General Chiang Kai-shek, said Powell, was being supported more and more by the propertied interests, while the radicals or Communists derived their main support from the labour unions and students. The social revolution of peasants and workers had begun to pinch the pocket-books of the landlords, merchants, and bankers who wanted 'to call a halt now.' 'Foreigners,' Powell added, 'prefer the Right or Conservative wing of the party, chiefly due to the fact that when it comes to compromise or peaceful negotiation, they, the foreigners, usually come out on top.'

The chief obstacle in the path of Chiang Kai-shek and his friends was the militant labour movement in Shanghai. The British business community in the city had learned as early as December 1926 that Chiang's policy was 'not an out and out "red" one' and that once the Kuomintang had consolidated its position along the Yangtze he would be prepared 'to check the extremists.' In order to encourage this tendency they had joined with Chinese banking groups to raise $30 million in Shanghai currency, and pledged it to Chiang on the understanding that a proposed new government at Nanking, replacing the Kuomintang-Communist united front regime in Wuhan, would be anti-Communist.[7]

While these secret negotiations were in progress, the British government adopted a well-publicized dual diplomacy, announcing a willingness to modify its traditional attitude of rigid insistence on the strict letter of treaty rights and affirming the need to abandon foreign tutelage and to go as far as possible towards meeting the legitimate aspirations of the Chinese nation.[8] This policy was calculated to disarm the radical critics of imperialism. At the same time, the threatening presence of British troops at Shanghai and Hongkong, not to mention one-third of the British navy, was aimed at producing a stabilizing effect,[9] enabling the conservative elements in Chinese politics to regain their feet. On 20 March 1927, as the Nationalist forces once more approached the city, the unsuspecting General Labour Union called another general strike to welcome Chiang's army. This time the strike, which soon involved 800,000 people, turned into an armed insurrection and by 21 March, before the army entered the city, the workers had seized control of the police stations and had raised the new flag over all government buildings outside the foreign concessions. Within hours the Endicotts were amazed to see the Nationalist flag 'flying all over the place,' hanging from shop and apartment windows; they hoped that it was 'the symbol of better days for China.'[10]

Chiang Kai-shek lost no time in laying plans to break the power of the Shanghai trade unions. An incident in Nanking, where several foreigners lost their lives and which led to the shelling of the city by British and American warships, was conveniently blamed on the Communists and was seized upon by Chiang to develop anti-Communist opinion. 'One of the good results of the Nanking tragedy,' Endicott observed, reflecting the general attitude of the missionaries, would be 'the upsetting of the Red applecart and letting the more moderate elements of the Kuomintang have control.'[11] With the help of Du Yu-sheng, leader of the Shanghai underworld, who later regretted that he did not 'kill all the Communists,'[12] Chiang Kai-shek planned a strategy to disarm several thousand pro-Communist trade union pickets and to sabotage the formation of a new people's municipal government. The dramatic events that flowed from this plan became widely known in the West through *La condition humaine* (1933), the famous existentialist novel by André Malraux. At a pre-arranged signal, members of Shanghai's underworld gangs, wearing white armbands with the Chinese character *kung* (labour) to camouflage their mission, rushed out of the foreign concessions into the Chinese city, before dawn on 12 April 1927, and began attacking the headquarters of working class organizations. By mid-morning, with the help of selected army units, hundreds of trade unionists had been shot and thousands were missing, including Wang Shu-hua, chairman of the General Labour Union. Among the few leaders who succeeded in escaping the sudden reign of terror was Chou En-lai, whom Endicott would come to know well and view in different terms two decades later.

Chiang Kai-shek's 12 April coup, backed by the conservative faction of the Kuomintang, the Shanghai capitalists, the military men, and the foreign interests, dealt a stunning blow to the revolutionary forces. The counter-revolutionary momentum gathered strength in other centres as well. Before long the Wuhan government fell to pieces and Borodin was forced to return to the Soviet Union. In Szechuan, where the West China Mission was most concerned, 25,000 people had gathered at the Da Chang Ba (rifle range) in Chungking to protest the shelling of Nanking by foreign gunboats. At the height of the rally, plainclothes policemen, who had been sent by the military governor to mingle with the crowd, drew revolvers, shot the speakers, and caused a stampede that led to the deaths of 256 people. This disaster was blamed upon the Communists; their most prominent leader, a newspaper editor, was arrested and executed the following day after being accused of conspiring to kill the remaining foreigners and of planning to destroy the Christian buildings.

The local Christians were convinced the Chungking incident was a direct answer to their fervent prayers; church members referred to it as the 'Chungking passover' and called the killing of the Communists a 'necessary sacrifice' to get rid of the 'sinister element within the Nationalist ranks.' Violence against the Communists was justified on the grounds that the Communists used violence in their anti-Christian, anti-foreign campaigns. 'Are not Communist methods and aims comparatively well-known in the Western world as well as in the East?' wrote a Canadian missionary on furlough in 1927. 'Is not the example of Russia still fresh in the memory of all?' The answer to these rhetorical questions was self-evident. Communism had become the clear enemy in China. From now on the aim of Christianity, in the political realm, would be to unite with the 'sane' variety of the Nationalists to defeat the Communists.[13] It was a point of view with which Endicott, at this stage of his development, was in full agreement.

The remaining challenge of working out an accommodation with the conservative wing of Chinese nationalism, although not as difficult as navigating the shoals of social revolution, was, nevertheless, a major undertaking for the West China Mission Council. It required a revolution in thinking. The missionary of the future could no longer be a promoter and administrator but must be an interpreter and friend. This required a decision and a willingness to seek the devolution of power from the missionaries' hands into those of the local Chinese church. The aim of devolution was not new. The purpose of the missionary society in Canada had always been 'the creation of a self-governing, self-propagating, self-supporting Christian church in each Mission Field.'[14] But now there was an urgency where delay might prove fatal.

Endicott was a full-fledged, though junior, member of the West China Mission Council when it opened its thirty-first annual meeting in Shanghai on 19 March 1927. His father, as moderator of the United Church of Canada, led a small delegation from Canada to attend this important session. James Endicott, partly as the result of letters from his son pressing the case for Chinese self-determination, pushed hard on the question of devolution. If missionaries kept asserting the principle of devolution but did not agree in detail, he warned, the principle would soon be meaningless. 'In our church,' he pointed out, 'we claim the right to govern ourselves and determine all that affects the life of the church. We will not be dictated to by anyone outside. Has the church in China any less privileges than the church in any other land? If we have a real church in West China, then treat it as a real church.'[15] Nobody could make him believe that China had rejected Jesus or had rejected the missionaries because they were too much like Jesus. Life was difficult, he said, 'not because you are too much like Jesus, but too much like John Bull.'[16]

Some of the leading Chinese converts also came to attend the 'Exodus Council.' They did not want to eliminate the missionary, they said, but, as presently organized, the missionaries were the victims of denominationalism, of the fundamentalist-modernist controversies, and a conservative outlook often aligned them with reactionary tendencies in China. The Chinese Christians wanted the sole authority in China to be the Chinese church, to deal directly with the mission boards at home without the missionary acting as middleman. The Chinese church would then ask only for the number and kind of missionary that it wanted and grants from abroad would be made without any strings attached. The missionary would become the servant of the church in his adopted country, with his station, salary, and furloughs controlled in China. These proposals, had they been adopted, would have eased one of the most serious obstacles in the way of truly fraternal relations between missionary and convert – that of the missionary being an employer of Chinese Christian labour.

One of the more outspoken converts to address the council was Dr Cheng Ching-yi, secretary of the National Christian Council of China. He reminded his listeners that in the first place Christianity had come to China following upon the heels of military conquest, with the result that a good many people felt Christianity was in some ways the political tool of foreign countries, a suspicion that was 'not altogether unfounded.' He proposed a new emphasis in Christian work to clear the Christian movement from the protection of foreign countries. China desired a church in keeping with her own history and culture, her national psychology and national aspirations.

Another speaker pointed out that the Chinese Christians had not felt free to alter the old customs the missionaries had introduced 'of a fixed hour of worship, the singing of western tunes, the standings and sittings and kneelings in unison, as if under a drill-master, the listening to long prayers and longer sermons, and the sudden evacuation of the house of worship at a given signal, as if it were a prison from which it were a joy to be free for another seven days.' The time had come for experiments in finding fresh ways of worshipping God according to Chinese ideas of spontaneity and prayerfulness.

Treading onto even more controversial ground, Cheng Ching-yi, and other well-known Chinese converts such as Shen Ti-lan, stressed that in their opinion the church in China could not and should not avoid political matters. To be a follower of Jesus did not merely mean to build up one's own character and long for the life hereafter; the principles of Jesus were made to penetrate all phases of human life, whether personal, family, social, national, or international. In so far as the church was more or less 'standing aloof from the great surging tides of human need in China,' it was 'becoming a luxury rather than a necessity in China's national life.'[17]

Endicott responded to the Chinese appeal with enthusiasm. 'Personally I am prepared to accept the advice of the National Christian Council and become a full member of the Chinese Conference and take my orders from them,' he wrote Dr Arnup, adding that this would be much easier for the younger men like himself who had not taught the Chinese members or been their masters.[18]

The mission council, however, was more reticent. While officially expressing warm approval of the Chinese desire for spiritual autonomy and ecclesiastical freedom, many missionaries felt privately that much of what was being said by the Chinese Christians was 'entirely unreasonable ... a desire to save China and the Chinese Church from an imaginary foreign exploitation.'[19] The missionary majority therefore, while changing some committee structures to allow more Chinese participation, rejected the cardinal suggestion that the mission council should be abolished; at the same time, they affirmed an intention to effect a transfer of authority to the Chinese Conference at some future date.[20] It was the old cry of St Augustine, 'Lord save me, but not now.'

During the remaining two decades of missionary activity in China, the Chinese converts never did succeed in becoming 'self-governing, self-propagating, and self-supporting.' Such an outcome was not surprising since the familiar patterns in all relationships of dependency and domination were being played out between the missionary colonizers and the converts. By insisting upon their basic structures the colonizers frustrated attempts to achieve genuine independence; and by accepting the colonizer's gifts for development within their structures, the colonized were doomed to perpetuate their own dependence. This was especially true in the case of the Christian movement in China because, as the missionaries realized too late, in the revolutionary currents of the 1920s the church lost the cream of a whole generation, the brightest and most active young people,[21] who might have helped bring needed changes in church policy had they not come to the conclusion that the church, by its attitudes, was irrelevant to China's needs.

All this did not become apparent until much later, and Endicott had a sufficient measure of missionary optimism not to allow pessimism to cloud his horizons. Someday soon, he believed, there would be a real job for people like himself, who found it possible to be truly sympathetic to Chinese national aspirations and who had sufficient fluency in the language to share in their councils as an equal. Also it had been a great inspiration to see his father in action again. He treasured his father's expressed faith in him and he never forgot the sight of the older man waving his hat on the Dollar Steamship wharf at the end of his visit, calling out 'China Forever!' Endicott was more determined than ever to wait out events in Shanghai. This prospect was made easier when in the summer of 1927 Mary's parents, Charles and Minnie Austin, came to Japan and invited the Endicotts over to spend a month's holiday with them.

By the end of 1927, after a year of the exodus, the British consuls began to grant permission for single missionaries or married men without their families to return to the interior. For the Endicotts this posed a difficult decision, but they both agreed that, for the sake of the foundation Jim would get for all his future work, he ought to get back to Szechuan, even if it meant separation for a time. Accordingly, after their second son, Stephen, was born in January 1928, Mary returned to Canada with the children for eight months while Jim proceeded to Chungking.

CHAPTER ELEVEN

Preaching and teaching in Chungking

Upon arrival at Chungking in February 1928, Endicott received invitations to preach, to teach Sunday School, and to lead Bible classes in the middle school and at the YMCA. Barely six weeks later he was struck down with typhus fever, a dreaded disease that was usually fatal; of the three other people in the mission who had contracted typhus, two were in the little foreign cemetery above Chungking and the third had completely lost his memory. Mary was not informed of his illness until after the first three weeks when Dr Retta Kilborn, who had given him steadfast care, became convinced that he was going to survive.

During the long weeks of recovery, Endicott learned by heart the score of *The Gondoliers* and several other Gilbert and Sullivan operettas, and played recordings of Beethoven, Schubert, Brahms, and Chopin, finding their music had a beneficial effect on his spirits. He also used the time to study the works of Walt Whitman, whose appeal, he felt, was 'an unshakeable belief in goodwill and human friendliness and understanding, a religious conviction, amounting almost to mysticism, as to the immense possibilities of the new American experiment in Democracy, a huge admiration for human achievements in the way of machinery, roads and all the great pulse of commerce.' These were some of the ingredients of success the young missionary thought were badly needed in China, and he incorporated these ideas into his preaching.

His health restored, Endicott began spending much of his time itinerating in the rural district east of Chungking, down as far as Lanchuan (South River). For up to a month at a time, with his cook and a man to carry his bedding and pamphlets, sometimes accompanied by a fellow missionary in education work or by a Chinese probationer, he would make his way through the fertile valleys, visiting the schools and the local preachers, talking to anyone who would listen. Mostly he found this work depressing as he did not feel that he was able to influence the inert rural masses through the native workers and equipment available. However, a close acquaintance with the rhythm of life in the vast countryside and with the living conditions of the majority of the people began. In the process he developed considerable ability and tact, with his now fluent Chinese language, in winning the attention of a crowd or in handling a potentially difficult confrontation.

About to land after crossing the Yangtze one day, he was met by some shouting students who tried to prevent his boat from coming in. They took some sticks of firewood from a passing carrier and started shouting anti-foreign slogans to attract a crowd. From something in their manner Endicott decided that they were simply trying to be smart, so he said nothing, but took the first opportunity to jump onto an adjacent boat, thereby getting on shore. Once there, he felt that the crowd of coolies who had gathered to watch were rather friendly and so he said in the best colloquial he could muster: 'Have they gone bugs?' There was a roar of laughter and one of the coolies called out to the students: 'He wants to know if you have gone bugs.' Then Endicott rattled off a couplet from the Three Character Classic, 'Yang bu giao, fu dsi go,' which meant 'To feed a child without also educating it is a fault in the father.' That greatly amused the crowd, which applauded enthusiastically. One of the chair carriers thereupon said: 'Teacher, you speak such good Chinese! I will carry you up to the gate for half price.' Endicott thanked him without accepting his offer, gave him some money to have a drink of tea, and everyone parted well pleased with himself.

In trying to teach religion on these trips Endicott avoided the older method of salvation by information ('Believe in the Lord Christ and be saved') in favour of informal preaching in a way that was real to him. Once when he was crossing the river he saw the ceremony of 'bringing in the spring,' a relic of primitive magic similar to the Greek rites described in *The Golden Bough* by James Frazer. Noticing Endicott's scepticism, the boatmen asked: 'Why don't you believe in the ceremony?'

Endicott replied that he believed there was one true God and that one's beliefs about life and one's conduct ought to be in conformity to that belief. 'Therefore we should get rid of all superstitions,' he said. 'There are no devils to be feared. The lightning does not single out an unfilial son, nor will the reading of the Buddhist scriptures by a priest on the fifth of the fifth month keep away all fevers. You had better be inoculated. Instead of our trying to influence nature by magic rites we should search and investigate and struggle to find out how God works.'

The men, who had allowed the boat to drift along, were fascinated by Endicott's knowledge of Chinese folk religions and customs and wanted to know more about his God. 'Is it not a superstition also?' they asked.

'No,' he replied without hesitation, 'because we conform our actions to such truth as we find in nature, truth which can be tested out. As for man,' he continued, 'we should believe, because there is evidence that makes it reasonable so to believe, that man has developed in order to fulfil some purpose of God. As far as we can see now, Love should be the law of life at the human level and we should try to live a life in accordance with this principle.'

'And how do we find this life of Love?' asked the sceptical, weather-beaten sons of the Yangtze as they puffed lazily on their pipes.

'By studying the life of Jesus,' was Endicott's confident answer.

The good-natured curiosity of the people was endless on such informal occasions. If Endicott could succeed in getting people sufficiently interested in coming to study the life of Jesus, he felt he had achieved his purpose. After that 'the wind bloweth where it listeth [and] so is every one that is born of the Spirit' (John 3:8).

As these experiences show, the people were friendly wherever he went. Endicott found, however, that the previous few years had left local church members deeply discouraged and loath to attract any attention to themselves. At some places along the Yangtze, student agitators had caused the church to disband and he found several of the pastors in the district discouraged and ready to quit. Church members rarely came to church anymore, although they still welcomed a visiting missionary to their homes.

Reasons for the decline of rural Christianity were as easy to find as the solutions were difficult. Endicott sensed that the Chinese Christians felt that the missionaries ran away from their jobs in the face of adversity and that 'we have lost in their eyes the right to consider ourselves the moral or spiritual prop that we are supposed to be under the new conditions.' The anti-imperialist and anti-Christian literature which students had flooded into the area in the 1925–27 period had also worked to isolate the Chinese Christians. Their confidence was shaken by the criticism of the Bible as being unscientific. The preachers felt they had been hoaxed by missionary evangelists and led from one set of superstitions to another. One young convert said to Endicott: 'Why do you foreigners put such emphasis on the virgin birth? We Chinese claim to have thirteen authenticated cases of that in our history.' Socially the converts were bewildered and had taken to running kindergartens and schools in their churches as the only kind of work they could do to gain support from the people.[1]

Even more important, perhaps, was the failure of rural evangelism to address itself to relieving the burdens of the poor, whose numbers and hardships were increasing rapidly in the changing rural society of Szechuan. The province, divided into several garrison areas each controlled by a major warlord, had spawned a composite landlord class of military men and new urban bureaucrats who supplanted the old landlord élite and used their monopoly of power and government authority to gain control of large estates. More and more of the small, free-holding peasants were forced into tenancy. By 1933 three out of every five rural households were tenants, the highest percentage of any province in the whole of China. The armed landlords used their power ruthlessly, collecting as much as six years' land tax per annum and obliging peasant households to give up between one-half and three-quarters of the value of their annual output. This created a desperate situation for millions of people. A favourite method by which the heaviest tax burdens were shifted to those least able to pay was to falsify or destroy the local land registries; by 1937 over half the land in Szechuan was unregistered and its owners were able to escape provincial taxation while still collecting from the tenants.[2]

There was no doubt that the Canadian missionaries were well aware of the acute social struggle that was taking place in rural Szechuan – a fact of more than passing interest in view of the critical role played by the peasantry in the revolution of 1949 which led to the expulsion of the missionaries by 1952. The subject of rural conditions and rural evangelism began to receive more attention than any other subject at mission council and conference meetings in the 1930s. Missionaries were urged to 'think as deeply as we can into the whole question and reach unshakeable conclusions as to what our problem really is, and to what our strategy, therefore, should be.'[3] 'The selfishness and greed of the militarists is appalling,' wrote the Rev. Gerald Bell, secretary of the West China Mission, adding that the militarists occupied 'a somewhat similar position to certain capitalists in Western countries.' Another missionary, Howard J. Veals, in commenting upon the distress of the 'farming class of China,' had a clear analysis of the roots of the problem:

Very few of the farmers of China own their land. They are practically all tenant farmers and they usually have to pay about fifty per cent of their intake over to the owner of the land. Life is bound to be hard under such conditions. There is no more industrious class on earth than the Chinese farmers. They may be seen in their fields from dawn till dusk, rain or shine, every day of the year and as far as their knowledge goes they farm well. But they have no one to help them with seed selection or kindred problems and... they are in the power of the landlord and the money-lender. Many have to borrow to buy fertilizer or some other necessity with their share of the crop as guarantee... conditions here are much harder than at home.[4]

In spite of these accurate insights, the rural service work of the missionaries remained at a superficial level and never made vital contact with the forces in Chinese society that were moving to challenge and then overthrow landlord oppression. At that time neither Endicott nor his fellow missionaries were emotionally or intellectually prepared to challenge the existing structures of power that rested upon the landlord class. The agricultural project of the mission that received the most publicity and was considered to be a feather in the cap of the missionaries involved cattle improvement and acclimated fruit trees; the practical result, however, was to strengthen mission ties with the landlord élite, which alone had the necessary capital to invest in orchards and dairy herds.

Endicott had his own experience of failure with the problem of agrarian reform. While travelling through the town of Windy Gate one day with Yang Tsao-ran, a local preacher, he learned about the difficulties of the peasants in trying to borrow enough money to get seed and fertilizer, how they paid enormous rates of interest to the landlords and therefore got very little benefit from their crop. 'If I had five hundred u.s. dollars,' Yang declared, 'I could start a revolving fund which could eradicate poverty in my county among the lowest peasants.'

Remembering his own effort as a student minister in helping to organize the co-operative wheat pool on the Canadian prairies, Endicott asked the mission to allocate five hundred dollars which had been sent from Canada for famine relief.

The mission agreed to the request with the result that Endicott and his friend were able to start a non-profit revolving loan fund. The co-operative experiment ran for a year and seemed to be working well until Yang died of typhoid fever. Before long the local landlords infiltrated one or two of their agents into the co-operative for the purpose of creating quarrels and thus breaking it up; one of them, who had some education, contrived to get himself elected treasurer and disappeared with most of the funds. The Windy Gate experiment showed, therefore, that the provision of credit for improved seed selection, for better methods of cultivation, pest control, and the promotion of health and literacy, if administered for and by the peasantry, had revolutionary implications in a landlord-dominated society and could only succeed if the power of the landlords was curtailed or broken.[5] Alas for a gospel based upon the first sermon of Jesus (Luke 4:15–20), whereby the poor heard him gladly because he preached deliverance to the oppressed; the mission itself depended upon the goodwill of the warlords for its continued operation.

Following the sudden death of three more of the leading Chinese Christians in Chungking, from typhoid or cholera, including Wang Lieh-guang, pastor of the self-supporting downtown church at Little Cross Roads, the local Chinese church board invited Endicott, a foreigner, to take the position. A tribute to the way he had won the confidence and goodwill of the Chinese, this appointment was nevertheless a post that would soon try his mettle. In the first place it created personal difficulties, because after Mary had returned from Canada in the fall of 1928 the Endicotts had taken up residence at Whang Gin Miao, on the south bank of the Yangtze, on the grounds that the air there would be healthier for the children. Owing to the hours involved in crossing the river, especially at high water, the new assignment meant staying over in the city four nights a week. More important, Endicott was worried because of the reputation Little Cross Roads Church had as a hot-bed of conflicting personalities and factions, with tension between missionaries and converts never far below the surface; he had no enthusiasm for entering into the quarrels among the elders.

In spite of these drawbacks Endicott accepted the challenge, determined to use the pulpit to try to find a suitable answer to the question asked so often by many church members and young people: 'Now that we have become Christians what do we do?'[6]

As the following incident makes clear, Endicott felt that a man without liberal views could not get two steps with Chinese youth. Towards the end of term a group of about fifteen boys from a government middle school came and asked him the following questions: 'We know that your purpose in coming to China is to teach Christianity. What is your objective in teaching Christianity? Is it to persuade us to believe a certain set of doctrines so that we can get to Heaven when we die? Or is it to persuade us to be more humanitarian? The first we have investigated and don't believe and China has just as good humanitarian teaching as the West.'

'My objective is primarily to get men to study the life and teaching of Jesus,' Endicott replied. 'If you divorce the teachings of Jesus from his life it is quite true that many of his sayings can be paralleled in the sayings of the sages of China. But the sayings of Jesus cannot be understood and appreciated properly, nor can they stir the heart and the imagination, unless they are studied carefully as they were given during the course of his life. Therefore, if you want to know why I am in China you must study the life of Jesus, because Christianity cannot be explained as a set of beliefs nor defined as a few fundamental principles; it is a way of living which is derived from the supreme Religious Life in history.'

The boys agreed to come and start a study group on the life of Jesus. Endicott recorded an example of the kind of discussion that took place in the group:

We had been discussing the criticisms of Jesus by the Pharisees for his association with sinners, his healing on the Sabbath and his working on the Sabbath, what was it about their system of religion which made Jesus refuse to observe it and drew down these criticisms.

The group decided that the Pharisees had taken an original good principle and

speculated on it and made so many small rules about it that they burdened life with
rules instead of giving life freedom to work out the principle.

Then someone asked if this was not what the Chinese had done with the principle of
Filial Piety. The basis of Chinese moral and social teaching is 'thou shalt honour thy
father and thy mother.' But onto this originally good idea they had added literally
thousands of rules and regulations, going down into the smallest relations of life until
the observance of them had become a burden and killed all initiative and adventure. A
church member whose father died caused a great scandal by coming to church on the
third day when traditions said that he must not appear outside for seven days. Don't
you think that this was an excellent illustration of what the Pharisees were like in their
religion?

An astonished church elder summed up after the class saying 'Here we have been
condemning the Pharisees all these years and then we find out that we are like them!'[7]

From that experience Endicott believed that non-Christian Chinese students could be brought to see what the freedom and spontaneity of Jesus
might mean in one's personal life, and if they could see this it would do much
towards changing the old Confucian tradition of China which lay like a wet
blanket on the efforts at reform. He also believed that any attempt to impose
theological straight-jackets, or to insist, in traditional fashion, that Christianity could never have got its start without the miracles attributed to Christ,
would have no appeal or relevance to the youth of China.

Many of the older missionaries did not agree. Angered by Endicott's liberal
theology, one of the senior missionaries, Dr W.J. Sheridan, wrote to the
moderator saying: 'Jesus Christ is being betrayed in the pulpit of our church
every Sunday.'[8] The bitter and outspoken opposition to the method and
content of his evangelistic work by a fairly large circle of missionaries dampened Endicott's spirits, sometimes almost to the point of despair. But it was
his involvement in a lawsuit over a serious financial entanglement in which the
Chinese elders had placed the church that led to lingering unpleasantness.
Rumours about his supposed financial schemes and inability to get along with
the Chinese grew to such proportions that they reached the ears of the
superintendent of Timothy Eaton Memorial Sunday School in Toronto, who
demanded an official explanation. Endicott repressed his anger, replying
simply that the difficulties had been caused largely by a gift that turned out to
be a serious liability and a church treasurer who turned out to be dishonest.
'Neither of these factors are so Oriental or psychological,' he added, 'that
they are unheard of, even in the mother church.' That ended the discussion.[9]

In spite of his clear conscience, however, the fact remained that Endicott's
usefulness as pastor at Little Cross Roads was finished and he resigned from

the position after less than two years of service. Although this dénouement was a blow to his morale at the time, it had unexpected benefits. The ending of his full-time pastoral work allowed the emotional strain of presenting the creeds to recede into the inner recesses of his mind; as an occasional preacher or guest speaker he could be a true believer without hypocrisy.

Moreover, the temporary work to which the mission now assigned him, filling the gap for a colleague on leave who taught English as a second language, provided an opportunity to pioneer new methods – a role that suited Endicott's personality admirably. After this accidental beginning, a programme for reform in English teaching became the chief preoccupation of his remaining years in China and was the channel through which he became increasingly involved in Chinese political life.

The 'Direct Method' English course, of which he became a fiery apostle after a visit to its inventor, Harold E. Palmer, and the Institute for Research in English Teaching in Tokyo in the summer of 1927, was based upon the theory that a second language should be learned by speech first, giving students an opportunity to hear, observe, and imitate the same way as a small child learns a language. The further object of the method was to teach students to read rapidly and to compose accurately without the medium of translating mentally into their own language. Together with Mary, Endicott prepared simplified English versions of such exciting books as *Swiss Family Robinson*, *Lorna Doone*, and *Moby Dick* as practice readers to enable the pupils to 'learn to read by reading.'

Anyone who showed a glimmer of interest in the method would be held, if not by Endicott's glittering eye at least by his fluent tongue and smiling enthusiasm, while he expounded his theories, illustrating them by the latest charts and teaching devices. Mary used to smile when an unwary guest in their home would ask a polite question about his new work as she knew what he was in for. Nearly always the guest caught some of his enthusiasm and went away armed with complimentary copies of his texts, vowing to spread the word far and wide and determined to try out the method in his own classroom. After much agitation by Endicott, and many interviews, General Liu Hsiang, the warlord of Chungking, agreed to have the direct method texts sponsored and published by the English Department of Chungking University; in addition, Endicott was appointed as lecturer in English language and literature to demonstrate the method.

In gaining acceptance of the direct method, Endicott had to defend it against another method known as 'Basic English,' which had powerful academic and commercial backing in Britain and the United States and whose sponsors were attempting to make inroads in China by claiming to have perfected linguistic magic, a 'pocket edition' of the English language within the scope of 850 words. From his experience Endicott was convinced that English, although it could be simplified, was far too idiomatic to fit into such a narrow framework; attempts to make one word substitute for several meant doubling up, unnatural phrases, and confusion.

Any Chinese beginner who fell for the Basic advertising, 'that by learning 850 words, five simple rules and one gramophone record, he can acquire English,' soon found, according to Endicott, that he had been hoaxed. He liked to choose amusing examples to illustrate his contentions. The student, he said,

will find plenty of 'weasel' words in Basic. 'He let off a gun' is the Basic way of saying 'he shot a gun.' But, 'The judge let off the prisoner' doesn't mean 'He shot the prisoner.' 'Let off' is counted as *one word* in Basic ... The unsuspecting and trusting Basic student is going to be taught to make an ass of himself or herself without knowing it ... It is so easy to sell five simple rules! But what about the fifty times they don't apply? 'Ess' is a feminine ending, e.g. Prince – Princess. Having learned that, the student has to learn more if he is going to write; he has to learn when it cannot be used ... A Chinese student who had learned the rule, but not the exceptions, once wrote asking for financial help: 'In my family there are three adults and five adulteresses, and I am responsible for them all.'[10]

As the author of about fifteen texts and teachers' manuals published by the Chung Hwa Book Company in Shanghai, the fame of Wen Yiu-chang (Endicott's Chinese name) spread to various centres across China. For a brief instant after the Second World War Endicott was a millionaire, when Chung Hwa sent him an accumulated royalty cheque for $54,074,100; unfortunately, the dollar signs were Chinese, and with inflation raging in China the cheque was worth only $54 in United States funds.

With Michael West, whom he met while on furlough in Toronto, Endicott also later wrote a best seller entitled *The New Method English Dictionary*, published by Longman, Green and Company in 1935. This dictionary, which was written especially for foreign students of English, was an answer to Basic, and within a definitely limited vocabulary of 1490 words it succeeded in defining 24,000 words and expressions. The dictionary filled a need of which progressive language teachers had long been acutely conscious and one reviewer correctly predicted that it might well go through edition after edition with scarcely any change in the list of defining words, 'so well had that piece of work been done.'[11] It continued to be widely used in Africa, Asia, and Quebec, and by 1976 it had gone through forty printings totalling over four million copies.

Teaching English brought many pleasant by-products. Endicott became acquainted with educationalists and also met many Chinese officials with whom he had an opportunity to discuss not only English but also the objectives of the Christian movement in China. One of the most interesting of his Chinese friends was Ho Beh-hen, an official of the Navigation Bureau, a Buddhist, who believed that the essential points of Buddhism could be transmitted into social service for the community in co-operation with practical innovations borrowed from Christianity. Through Mr Ho and his friends, Endicott received invitations to speak to groups outside the church: 'The Christian Ideal of Marriage' at a non-Christian wedding; 'My Experiences in the European War,' 'Christianity and Science,' to the Knowledge Seekers' Club; 'Sex Education,' 'The Necessity for Birth Control in China,' at the YMCA; 'A Foreigner's Idea of the Three Principles,' to the 21st Army of the Kuomintang; 'Democratically-minded Officials: The Basis for a Democracy,' to the Association of Ba Hsien (County) Officials, with about five hundred attending. His fluency in Chinese and his forceful way of dealing with his themes, whether serious or humorous, made a strong impression on his hearers; they often crowded around him afterwards to say that they had never heard a foreigner speak Chinese so well.[12]

Perhaps the most stimulating and disturbing piece of work that fell to Endicott's lot near the end of his first term as a missionary was the teaching of English to Communists in the Court of Meditation, as the local prison was called. In his report to the Mission Board for 1932 Endicott wrote: 'In this prison there are about one hundred and thirty men of all walks of life, university teachers, middle school students, Chinese men of literature and common coolies. These men have all been under sentence of death and as I stand before them and discuss the life of Jesus, I am often overwhelmed with the sickening feeling that the Christian Church as it exists on the average has very little to offer to a keen young spirit that has tasted of death for a Cause.'

Firmly convinced that the Jesus of history had much to offer, Endicott nevertheless found himself up against stiff competition from the Buddhists. The latter were advising the prisoners to repent of living dangerously and to withdraw from the world to build up their inner life by religious meditation; they seemed to be winning as far as numbers went, but Endicott said he was more concerned to reach those who were still unconquered and to turn them into Christian channels of service.

The Communists were lonely, highly intelligent, and appreciative of the time and energy Endicott gave to them four afternoons a week. As the Christmas season drew near the prisoners prepared a concert for the missionary children. Inside the grey walls of the building they constructed a small stage festooned with numerous streamers of coloured paper and signs in

English saying 'Merry Christmas' and 'Welcome'; some of the Communists had obviously been students in missionary schools. After musical contributions by both the missionaries and the prisoners, and appropriate speeches, a spokesman for the prisoners announced they had prepared a symbolic skit in mime, 'The Good Shepherd,' which they wished to put on for the children. The skit, dramatizing the triumph of good over evil after necessary struggle, made a deep impression on the foreign guests.

Afterwards, a group photograph, the inevitable accompaniment of every Chinese festivity, and a basketball game in which the prisoners triumphed over the missionary men, concluded the festivities.

As the Endicotts were on their way out the gate, their six-year-old son, Norman, whispered: 'Aren't the prisoners coming out too?'

'No,' was the reply. His eyes grew wide with wonder and he began to ask questions about Communists and about what they were trying to do in China. The question came up again at dinnertime and showed he had been doing some thinking on his own. 'Do Communists try to help the poor people?' he asked.

'Yes,' answered his parents.

'Well, isn't that what Christians try to do?'

'Yes, certainly,' was the reply.

'Then why are the Communists in jail and you aren't?'

It was not an easy question to answer. The standard reply about the Communists believing in violence sounded hollow, especially in the Chinese setting. 'Out of the mouths of babes and sucklings hast thou ordained strength,' the Psalmist once suggested. 'Wise men are sometimes foolish,' Jim reflected to Mary afterwards. 'Is this a case where the young and innocent know better?'[13]

In spite of the frustrations, disappointment, and doubts arising from his early experiences, Endicott continued to have a strong sense of the worth of foreign missions. In response to the scepticism of university friends about his choice of vocation, he occasionally wrote letters to Canada expressing this sense. What the mission could do, he emphasized, was largely a matter of what a certain individual could do with a certain group of individuals to bring about a way of life that would make things infinitely better in China. He knew of farmhouse after farmhouse near Duckling Pond where the people lived in superstition and fear of all kinds of evil spirits. 'They put up their fierce-looking pictures of gods to drive away the demons who haunt their lives,' he wrote. 'They continue to bind the little girls' feet for fear of displeasing ancestral spirits who would bring curses on them if they broke from ancient custom.' There was no sanitation, people squatted their children on the streets spreading dysentery and cholera and then sacrificed to the gods to bring cures. When it came to such practical things as breaking the ground for the freedom of women, giving them the right of education and some rights of individual choice in marriage, all the old religions of China combined to oppose these changes. A few years ago, he commented, when a student in Chungking undertook to propose to a girl of his own choice, instead of his parents' choice, the Confucianists denounced such filial impiety by throwing him in jail and demanding his execution. 'The Kingdom of God,' he concluded, 'is really and truly like treasure which a man found, and went and shared it with his friends.'[14]

By the end of their first term in China the Endicotts' social life was a far cry from what it had been eight years earlier in the quiet backwater of Chungchow. Although Mary, especially, was still often lonely, in spite of a second visit by her parents in 1929 when they stayed in Chungking for several months, the Endicotts met many interesting people, both foreign and Chinese, whom they invited to their home. There were bridge parties, literary evenings, and play readings in which everyone took part in some way or other. On Saturday nights they frequently had open house for those who wished to listen to their new records.

When Mary was in Canada in 1928 she discovered a former professor who had taught himself to play the violin by following a book of instructions. Inspired by his example she had taken a violin back to her husband, to his great surprise and joy. Jim was one of those boys who refused to practise the piano in his youth and later greatly regretted his loss. He did fairly well in mastering the technique of the violin but it was rather discouraging. Then one day he heard that the captain of one of the Yangtze River steamers played the violin and was supposed to be self-taught. He headed for the ship the next time it was in port and brought home in triumph Captain Donald Brotchie, a genial Englishman whose love of music had led him to buy a violin of very fine quality and to teach himself with the help of a book, plus a few lessons from a Russian in Shanghai. He was not typical of the river captains and probably was considered rather strange by most of them, to Brotchie's own amusement. At night he used to take his violin up on the dimly lit top deck out of earshot of the crew and passengers and practise the lessons he had painstakingly memorized in his cabin on muted strings. Wherever he found a kindred spirit in port there would be evenings of music, on whatever instruments were available, in the range of semi-classical pieces and old favourite songs. From that time until nearly the end of their stay in China, Captain Brotchie's arrival in port, always announced by three toots on the ship's horn, was anticipated as a highlight in the Endicotts' lives, not only because of the music but also because of the friendship that grew up between them, the exchange of similar views of life, and the good humour that coloured his thinking and came to them as a fresh breeze from the sea. The zenith of their musical efforts was the mastery of Henry Purcell's *Golden Sonata*, with Brotchie taking the first violin, Jim the second, and Mary as accompanist on the piano.

Some of the Endicotts' happiest hours of relaxation were spent around the fireside or at the dinner table with the younger missionaries. Quite naturally they discussed the current questions to do with their religious ideas, the problems of the individual, the liberation of personality. They also often talked of the Great War, in which all the men in their circle had taken part, and of the disillusionment that followed the war.

Since these young missionaries were beginning to raise families of their own, a new book, *The Revolt of Modern Youth* (New York 1925), by Judge Benjamin B. Lindsey of the Denver Juvenile Court, was the basis of many discussions. Lindsey had observed that sexual delinquents matured physically too early and had not the soundness of judgement to deal with experiences as they came to them. He said that a large percentage of them were young people of marked ability and good background, and in some cases the cause of their troubles could be traced to the well-meant training wherein they were encouraged, if not urged, to develop too quickly mentally. Lindsey also identified other causes of delinquency, such as the enormous stimulus for early maturity afforded by the automobile, the telephone, and a thousand other conveniences of living, that did so much to engage the faculties, to arouse the mind, and particularly to arouse the desires. The Endicotts resolved to be guided by these warnings in raising their own children – of whom by 1932 there were two more, Shirley Jane and Philip Michael – a task made easier by the absence of modern gadgetry in far western China.

The new spirit of freedom for the individual, which was the subject of Bertrand Russell's *Marriage and Morals* (1929), was a stimulus to the thinking of the Endicotts' circle of friends. The most controversial element of Russell's book was the theory that marriage partners could have friendships among the opposite sex without disturbing the foundations of marriage; the difficulty was how to draw a line around sexual freedom. Was there not a danger of the separation of sex from affection and an increase in frustration, tension, and jealousy? Much of this discussion was purely academic, but there were episodes.

Whatever the effect of the unconventional aspects of some of their thinking and their social relationships, the marriage relationship of the Endicotts grew progressively happier during these years. Now in their mid-thirties, Mary and Jim found it hard to believe that many people at the same stage could get as much sheer enjoyment out of each other's society, whether alone or with other people, as they found together.[15]

As they boarded the *S.S. Kingwo* with their family at Chungking to begin the journey home for their first furlough in April 1933, they felt they had achieved some reasonable successes in their work and were looking forward to a time of renewal and relaxation. Their high spirits, as well as their baggage, were dampened only temporarily when the little British steamship struck a rock in the dreaded Kong-ling rapids of the Yangtze gorges, at a place where eight steamers had gone to the bottom in twenty-three fathoms of water. With the bow visibly sinking and the passengers scrambling for the upper deck, the captain managed by good fortune to turn the crippled vessel upstream; engines racing, smoke pouring from the stack, he brought it to rest at a dangerous angle on a sandy beach. The balance of the journey, first by Chinese junk, then on a relief steamer, and finally aboard the *Empress of Asia* Vancouver-bound from Shanghai, was by comparison uneventful.

CHAPTER TWELVE

Furlough in Canada

When the Endicotts and their four children arrived in Toronto on furlough in the summer of 1933, the country was in the grip of the Great Depression that enveloped all the countries of the Western world. Although their salary was cut in half, they did not feel the full economic impact of the crisis because, in common with most middle class urban families, they at least had a steady income, and in their case it included free accommodation for a year at the missionary apartments of the United Church. Nevertheless the depression, beginning in 1929 after the bottom fell out of the New York stock market, had led to a quarter of the Canadian labour force being forced onto bread-lines,[1] and deeply affected the thinking of the returned missionaries.

The striking paradox of the 'hungry thirties' was the existence of plenty amidst abject poverty. Coming from China where there was widespread famine, Endicott, as a member of an international famine relief commission, had seen that man's greatest struggle was against shortages and natural disasters. In China the problem was so immense there seemed to be no possible solution; but as he travelled across Canada he found that there was actually an abundance of food in the country. In some areas drought and grasshopper plagues had ruined the crops, but considering the country as a whole Endicott observed that 'we were having a depression because we had too much.' Professors and right-wing politicians 'were telling us that we raise a huge mountainous pile of wheat and because we can't sell a very big pile abroad we can't even afford to eat the small pile which was left here in Canada.'[2] This seemed like idiocy, and he asked himself how such logic could exist short of insanity.

From this time on, since to him the capitalist system seemed to be creating needless human suffering, Endicott became seriously interested in the social-ist ideas of planning, public ownership of the means of production, and production for human need instead of for private profit. The fact that his jolt towards the left came in Canada and not in China, where conditions were a hundred times worse, suggests that in order to become radicalized politically people must first become convinced, either by intuition or from experience, that a workable, alternative way of organizing human society is within the realm of possibility.

The Endicotts' political awakening, as well as that of some other missionary families such as the Jolliffes, was stimulated by the new forms of political and religious protest that were springing up in Canada at the time. The most significant new political movement was the Co-operative Commonwealth Federation, which was founded in Regina in 1933 by farm, labour, and intellectual groups and led by J.S. Woodsworth. The 'Regina Manifesto' of the CCF declared its aim to replace the capitalist system, 'with its inherent injustice and inhumanity,' by a new social order 'from which the domination and exploitation of one class by another will be eliminated, in which economic planning will supersede unregulated private enterprise and competition, and in which genuine democratic self-government, based upon economic equality will be possible.' The glaring inequalities of wealth and opportunity in the existing order, with its instability and waste, it was argued, condemned the majority of people to a life of poverty and insecurity in an age of plenty. A small and predatory group of financiers and industrialists had concentrated power more and more into the hands of an irresponsible minority to whose interest the majority was constantly sacrificed. 'When private profit is the main stimulus to economic effort,' the manifesto continued, 'our society oscillates beween periods of feverish prosperity in which the main benefits go to speculators and profiteers, and of catastrophic depression, in which the common man's normal state of insecurity and hardship is accentuated.' In a ringing finale, which in later years the CCF tried to forget, the manifesto declared that no CCF government would rest content until it had 'eradicated capitalism and put into operation the full programme of socialized planning.'[3]

Paralleling the political protest movement was a brief outburst of radical Christianity. This development was given direction to a large extent by the American theologian Reinhold Niebuhr, whose writings Endicott read with keen interest. Western society, according to Niebuhr in *Moral Man and Immoral Society* (1932), was in the process of disintegration, as illustrated by such things as the powerlessness of disarmament conferences to stop activity that would inevitably produce war and by the unwillingness of the rich to allow a more equal distribution of wealth, with the inevitable outcome of bitter class struggle. The fatal characteristic of modern Western life was that it provided for the private ownership of the productive processes upon which the health of the whole civilization depended. Unfortunately, much of the force of spiritual life represented by religion, Niebuhr argued, was wasted in covering the arbitrary and transient forms of life such as capitalist forms of ownership with an aura of the absolute. Religion as it was practised thus frequently became a dangerous source of moral confusion in the larger social relations. Nations and classes, cultures and civilizations, were often able to use religion, not to reveal the imperfection and partiality of their life and values, but to give the prestige of the absolute to what was relative and tentative.

In Canada, radical Christianity found expression not in the Student Christian Movement, which the Endicotts found had veered to the right and was more concerned with theological explanations for metaphysical questions, but through the new Fellowship for a Christian Social Order. Professors R.B.Y. Scott and Gregory Vlastos, who were prominent spokesmen of the FCSO, acknowledged that religion, as the Marxists claimed, had 'often functioned as an opiate,' but they affirmed the belief that Christianity was an historic faith which had revolutionary resources for the crisis of the Western world. Within Christianity they saw 'the same dialectic of reaction and revolution' that marked other phases of the social process; the faith of the prophets and of Jesus was really 'a disturbing, renovating force.' The persuasive message of the FCSO was that the true path for religion was to search for a socialist commonwealth.[4]

The result was that many FCSO members also found themselves active in the CCF and some supported the communist party. These forces of protest, reform, and potential revolution gathered such momentum that eventually the Conservative government of Prime Minister R.B. Bennett was induced to reverse its original position of non-intervention in the depressed economy and to offer a 'New Deal' for Canadians providing for unemployment and social insurance, minimum wages, and farm credits. But that was still a few years ahead.

After spending the summer holidays with the Austin and Endicott grandparents at their respective cottages on Erie Beach and Lake Muskoka, the Endicotts returned to Toronto, hired a maid, and proceeded to enrol all members of the family in schools. Mary pursued studies in early childhood education at the University of Toronto. Endicott himself enrolled in the Ontario College of Education, thinking that it would be useful to his work in China. He found the course irksome and the other students seemed immature; the prevailing methods of teaching appeared obsolete, especially in modern languages in which he had experience in China. The climax came when he was doing his criticism of a French class under one of the ablest teachers in the city.

In his written assignment he compared the methods used, in which less than eight per cent of the time was given to hearing and speaking, with the direct method he had used with marked success in China. The professor of French was furious and Endicott was asked to come to the office of the dean where he was told in no uncertain terms that he must change his ways; he was reminded that he had come to the institution to learn, not to teach. He shook off the dust of the College of Education after about six weeks, but before leaving he met Michael West, who was doing research work on language teaching, with whom he struck up a partnership to produce the *New Method English Dictionary*.[5]

Endicott managed to find some time for his hobby of playing the violin. The Mission Board had the custom of arranging for missionaries on furlough to take music lessons from the best teachers without having to pay tuition; in this way Endicott studied under Alexander Chuhaldin for twelve weeks. At first they both enjoyed this experience greatly. Chuhaldin was impressed by how much Endicott had learned on his own and had hopes of making a concert artist out of him. This was far from Endicott's mind; he merely wanted to play for his own pleasure and on the odd occasion for his friends. He had little time for practice and, worse still, he developed arthritis in one shoulder at Christmas time. He and the teacher agreed that it was no use taking their valuable time to go further. When Endicott expressed his appreciation for what he had learned, the teacher asked him to play one last time; at the conclusion of this effort Chuhaldin threw up his hands and cried: 'My God, don't tell anyone you studied with me!'[6]

Endicott's main concern that year was to accept the invitations to speak as arranged by the church headquarters in response to requests from various parts of the country. The Missionary and Maintenance Fund was in dire need of support since it could not meet its quotas in the face of rising doubt and criticism both within and outside church circles. Prominent Canadian newspapers were saying that it was absurd to talk of sending missionaries to the countries of the Far East, especially when university departments in Canada were being closed up for want of money. 'The Far East has been over missionary-ized,' declared the *Vancouver Sun*, adding that much missionary work in Asia was wastefully duplicating 'the civilizing work' that was now done by commerce, radio, and newsreels.[7]

Even more serious was the criticism of missions by the Laymen's Foreign Missions Inquiry of 1930–32, sponsored by the Protestant churches of the United States, which inevitably spilled over into Canada. The laymen's report, *Re-Thinking Missions* (New York 1932), criticized the missionaries for arrogance of spirit and for teaching a narrow, superstitious form of religion which any intelligent recipient would be reluctant to see fastened upon his or her people. This kind of missionary was making the lives of wretched people even more sad and hungry-hearted. The emphasis upon mechanical results such as the number of converts and the financial success of local projects, as often demanded by the home churches, was creating the wrong kind of atmosphere. The laymen's commission called for a new type of missionary, more tolerant, more scientifically minded, and less denominational, someone who could inspire by example of work rather than by endless preaching. The primary purpose of foreign missions should no longer be looked upon as saving souls from eternal punishment but rather to help people, through Christian revelation, to discover God as the supreme good; the foreign mission, at its best, 'should aim to develop individuals who – physically and mentally as well as spiritually – are fit to be accepted as citizens in a social order founded upon the ideas that Jesus preached.'[8]

The laymen had given full support to the Jerusalem meeting of the International Missionary Council in 1928, which had adopted as its motto: 'We believe in a Christlike world. We know of nothing better; we can be content with nothing less.'[9] Needless to say, Endicott was more than happy to go out speaking for United Church of Canada missions in the light of this perspective.

As Endicott's reputation as an inspiring speaker spread, tours were arranged from coast to coast. Mary went with him whenever he was driving in Ontario and never tired of watching the response of a congregation to his dynamic way of presenting the life of the Chinese people and what the mission was doing and hoped to do. This enthusiasm was not shared equally by all members of the family. On the Sunday when Endicott was to preach at Park Street United, her home church in Chatham, Mary took the two eldest boys with them. As time wore on the five-year-old began to fidget. Mary whispered to him: 'Daddy's talking about Chungking! Listen!' The small, bleary-eyed worshipper looked up and said loudly: 'Is he talking English or Chinese?'[10]

After Endicott had made his way through Ontario and across Manitoba and Saskatchewan, warm letters of appreciation for his masterly 'putting of the case' began to arrive. On the back of one of them he wrote: 'I shall line my rear pocket with these when I get kicked in the pants at Chungking.'[11]

In addition to preaching on Sundays, he spoke at many week-night meetings – Rotary and other service clubs, women's auxiliaries, and young people's societies. During the first months of furlough he spoke about China, Japan, and the League of Nations, dwelling on the weak-kneed action of the league in allowing Japanese militarism to run rampant in Manchuria since 1931.

While careful to point out that the Japanese were simply following the example of Western countries in expanding their empire by force, the burden of his plea was for intelligent sympathy for the Chinese, especially the students who were trying to bring new life to the warlord-ridden country.[12]

The most controversial speech of this period was made in a return visit to the Chatham Rotary Club in August 1934, a few days before he and his family were to depart for China. He explained that his thinking on the question of empire had gone through three stages: first there had been the stage of romantic illusion, then the stage of realism and disenchantment, and now that of hopeful waiting for its defeat. The stage of romantic illusion had begun in his high school days when he had orated to fellow students, confining himself 'largely to the mixture of piety and paganism which was dished out by Mr. Rudyard Kipling and which was fed to us in school in the name of patriotism and good citizenship.' In his enthusiasm he had learned yards and yards of

> God of our fathers, known of old ... .
> Beneath whose awful hand we hold
> Dominion over palm and pine ...

and, like Mr Kipling, he too had praised God in his prayers 'that He had seen fit in His infinite and inscrutable wisdom, to give one quarter of the earth's surface to us British to boss.' This phase of illusion had stayed with him during the Great War, 'even when I was risking my neck for a dollar ten a day,' and it had lingered on 'in the days when as undergraduates we flocked to hear the Hon. Newton Rowell deliver his lectures on "The British Empire and World Peace"'; he and his classmates had believed that the League of Nations was to be the new Magna Carta of international life and of the labouring classes. When he had gone to China to work for the Kingdom of God, the period of realism and disenchantment had begun, especially after he learned the story of what happened to China from the time the foreign powers had forced their way in until the Japanese seized Manchuria. He suggested to his listeners that an empire, 'whether it be political or economic, whether it be an accomplished fact like the British, a dream of desire like those of Hitler and Mussolini or in the process of making like the Japanese, may be defined as: a group of predatory interests which seek to expand and enrich themselves by the conquest and exploitation of other countries so that the common people are separated from their natural resources and robbed of their economic security.'

The dreams of empire, Endicott continued, were now being played out in two zones in the world where the predatory interests were laying the foundations for war. One zone was composed of the new countries of Yugoslavia, Czechoslovakia, and their neighbours, and the other was northeastern Asia. The spectacle of Europe revealed that throughout the new countries, in the factories, mines, and mills controlled largely by British, French, Italian, and Belgian capital, the worst horrors of the industrial revolution were being re-enacted; women worked in some extreme cases eighty hours a week for twenty-six cents a week; even in the depression years dividends as high as 300 per cent had been paid. Thus instead of the solemn covenant of the League of Nations being a new Magna Carta of political and economic life, the world was now witnessing an angry gang of European Al Capones, King Alexander of Yugoslavia, Mussolini, and Hitler, trying to hold together the crumbling, acquisitive, and exploiting civilization of Europe with gangster methods of government. To this bad-tempered crew there now came the startling announcement of Stanley Baldwin, leader of the British Conservative party, that 'the frontier of Great Britain lies on the Rhine.' 'That remark,' Endicott predicted, 'is a tacit declaration of the next war.' At the other side of the world, in the second zone, the Japanese imperialists were 'drunk with the sight of power' and the seizure of China was a natural step in their dream of empire. Long before these dreams were fulfilled, however, he predicted that some upheaval would occur. Thus had ended his period of disenchantment.

Anyone who offered a solution, Endicott admitted, was like the school board that resolved to build a new school, resolved to use the bricks of the old school to build the new one, and further resolved to use the old school while the new school was being built. But he was not without hope. In contrast to the difficulties of capitalism, Endicott declared that he felt a new sense of respect for the socialist road of the Soviet Union, a confidence he had gained from hearing the reports of J.S. Woodsworth and others who had been there, and from the writing of the Yugoslav author, Louis Adamic.

Russia stands between these two zones of conflict. I see her with the new state which her idealists are creating as a great giant, reaching out her right hand to the exploited Balkans and her left hand to the disinherited masses of China and lifting them up to an intelligently planned and controlled civilization. In all that area, from the Balkans across to China, Russia is the only state which is firmly linked to the future: a stronghold of the new social and economic morality which is based on the principle of production to meet the needs and for the benefit of the producing masses and not for the profit of a few rugged individualists. I consider that Russia, by making justice and equality practical politics, and by teaching the youth a new morality in regard to man's acquisitive instincts, has made the most important contribution to the progress of the world since Lincoln freed the slaves.

So I shall go back to China and say to the youth of the country, 'Behold yourselves surrounded by Empire builders who would oppress and exploit you. Go left, young man, go left. Look to Russia. And if you are a Christian you can learn from Russia that "The earth is the Lord's and the fullness thereof" and the natural wealth of it should be administered intelligently for the benefit of all His children. This cannot be done by the principles of empire building.'[13]

The local newspaper gave full and accurate coverage to the speech of the son-in-law of the influential Austins, while commenting that Endicott's address was 'as startling as it was cynical upon modern economic conditions.' Most of the audience was stunned into silence. Hostile reactions were typified by that of Endicott's mother-in-law, of whom he was very fond, who deposited the newspaper clippings of the speech in the garbage. Some thirty years later a businessman came up to Endicott and said, rather gloomily, that he remembered the speech and unfortunately what had been prophesied had come to be true.

The Chatham Rotary Club speech reveals that Endicott's views about the source of new wars within the capitalist system, his positive re-evaluation of the role of the Soviet Union in world affairs, and his sense that China would be one of the storm centres in the coming world upheavals, contained a prophetic element. His notions about socialism, on the other hand, obtained from casual reading or conversation, without any practical experience in the socialist movement, were less clear and rested mainly on the idea of speeding up the pace of social reform rather than in any inherent ideology of social revolution. His was a type of Christian socialism. Even so, if he had not been returned to China for missionary work, there seems little doubt but that he would soon have found himself with J.S. Woodsworth and the other ministers who were no longer able to work for the Kingdom of God as they understood it within the framework of the church.

As the time drew near to leave Canada, family problems and his growing political awareness made him uncertain as to whether or not he should return to China. Mary worried that there were no local school or playmates for the children in Chungking, and few if any congenial friends there owing to shifts in personnel; at times she was overwhelmed with tears by the thought that China was no fit place to bring up her children. Jim was confident that the personal problems could be worked out, but within himself the old feeling of futility had grown stronger concerning the mission's emphasis on trying to save the Chinese people individually by theological means. His reflections about Canadian experience during the depression led him to think that if China's problems were to be solved it would have to be through the energies of the Chinese people themselves, acting mainly at the level of political change.

Apart from these rather general thoughts, there were some specific inducements to stay in Canada. On one of his speaking tours, chance brought him to the seat next to J.S. Woodsworth on the train. Woodsworth had talked about his own experiences which finally led him to leave the ministry of the church to find a more practical way of building the Kingdom of God; he felt Endicott would also be more useful in the same search by throwing in his lot with the CCF, where he assured him there would be a place for him.[14] Endicott had also enjoyed the work with Michael West on the dictionary and had applied for a Carnegie fellowship for research and publication of methods of teaching English to foreigners; both men felt this work could do a great deal to aid relations between Eastern and Western countries and would justify Endicott staying in Canada. In addition, several churches had offered him their pulpit.

The main argument in favour of returning to China was that Endicott felt a loyalty to the church, which had invested so much in his training, and that it would be wrong to leave just when he was able to make his best contribution. Also, if the fellowship did not come through, China would be a better place to continue working on his own direct method readers. There were also the unspoken wishes of his father who would have been sorely disappointed if he did not continue the work in China. And so the decision to return to China was made, although the subject kept coming up for discussion with Mary until the boat sailed.

The most unsettling matter, however, was a long letter of complaint about Endicott from Gerald S. Bell, secretary of the West China Mission, to James Endicott, Sr, in the latter's official capacity as general secretary of the Board of Foreign Missions. Jim received a copy of the letter only the day before he left Toronto for China.[15] Bell spoke of problems connected with Endicott's stationing, of confusion for the mission arising from his turning away from pastoral to educational work, of criticism for his lack of tact and good judgement both in his personal relations with fellow missionaries and Chinese converts and in some of his public utterances at mission council and while on furlough as reported in the Toronto *Globe*. Endicott was held responsible for the 'present state of gravity' in the Chungking church. After going into many details, Bell tried to end on a conciliatory note, but he reiterated with considerable emphasis that Endicott was too hasty to take up positions, pitting his judgement 'against others of wider and longer experience than himself.'

It was a hard blow, and though Endicott immediately prepared a long reply to Bell, giving his version of the complaints, he sensed that perhaps there was general concern in the mission as to his fitness for returning to the work in China.[16] But James Endicott backed up his son, reminding him of a similar experience of his own thirty years earlier.[17] Since Jim was already in Vancouver with his family by this time and about to board the *Empress of Russia*, and because the West China Mission had not asked for definite disciplinary action or measures of any sort, the Endicotts headed quietly into a second term in the field.

CHAPTER THIRTEEN

Experiments in missionary work

Many times during his second term in China, from 1934 until the eve of the Pacific war between Japan and the Allied powers in 1941, Endicott felt hopelessly discouraged about his work as a missionary and about China. His main task was the teaching of English in the Gin I Middle School at Duckling Pond, a boarding school with about 180 boys between the ages of fourteen and nineteen; he had part-time teaching duties and occasional preaching assignments in the city of Chungking as well.

When he came home from the city, with its teeming, filthy streets and omnipresent beggars, he was often despondent. 'Life in this country is at such a heart-breaking level,' he once said, 'on such a vast scale that it seems hopeless. No wonder the foreign businessmen say that the kindest thing for the people here would be if the earth would open and swallow them up.' According to Mary, his thinking was evolving in an atmosphere of disillusionment and dissatisfaction; matters on which he had earlier felt confident now seemed uncertain. In his heart he felt the need for an explosion; he wanted to hack his way ruthlessly through opposition; he wanted to do big things, no matter what the cost, because in the current sorry state of the world big things needed to be done, and he was always finding himself blocked by people and circumstances beyond his control. Because he had grown up in the shadow of his father, a mighty rock, and because of his likeness to his father, a great future had always been prophesied for him. Now, in his late thirties, approaching forty, he felt his powers shrinking; perhaps he was not meant for greatness.

Outwardly he was happy and busy, always launching out further; the doubts were all below the surface. But Mary knew that her husband felt 'cribb'd, cabin'd and confined,' unable to find the key to make good his escape from the confines of his frustration. She detected in him, however, a hidden force that had not yet begun to show its real strength, and she gave him encouragement in the hope that in his forties or fifties he would find fulfilment for his particular bent, whatever it might be.[1]

Both his own experience in China to date as well as his wife's liberal theological inclinations confirmed his suspicion that little could be accomplished by evangelists proclaiming the Son of God with a loudspeaker. It was obvious to him that a lasting church could not be built, nor would the gospel be made real across a wide psychological and cultural distance, unless the evangelist-teacher somehow became more closely linked to the life of the Chinese people. And yet, within the framework of what was considered formal missionary activity, it was difficult to envisage suitable forms to accomplish this objective. His father cautioned him against rashness: 'You will go on your own way in making your contribution to the great Cause,' he wrote, 'but I should not permit for a minute, if I were you, any fundamentalist of any sort to imagine that you think your method is less Christian than his ... In other words, I wouldn't let them make a humanist of me if I were you, even though you do react from their theology at points.'[2]

As much by accident as by design, the Endicotts discovered ways to expand the boundaries of what they at least considered to be legitimate missionary work. By creating an international family within their own home, by publishing a weekly newspaper, and, finally, by accepting what seemed like a unique opportunity to do Christian work in China – an invitation to become an adviser to China's leaders, the Chiang Kai-sheks – the meaning of missionary work took on new, unusual, challenging, and sometimes controversial, dimensions. Endicott's tenuous career in China was thus prolonged, bringing satisfaction, earning him in the process the reputation of being an unconventional, maverick missionary.

The international family arose out of Mary's decision to educate her own children, at least the younger ones, at home rather than sending them away to boarding school. The Endicotts' 'schoolhouse,' which included a French boy, a White Russian girl, and the son of the Dutch consul as day pupils, was put under pressure to expand when some Chinese businessmen accompanied Endicott home for lunch one day. Impressed by what they saw, the businessmen began asking questions. After hearing an outline of Mary's educational ideas, such as letting the children plan a good deal of their work themselves and solving quarrels through family council meetings, Hwang Min-an, a member of one of the most prominent families in Chungking, said: 'I've just thought of a solution for my eight-year-old boy. I am going to throw him over into your family and you bring him up for me; he has already been expelled from three schools and his grandmother is spoiling him.'

Being cautious in action if otherwise in ideas, Mary was staggered at first when Jim proposed that the suggestion be taken seriously. To her knowledge no other missionary family had done such a thing or would consider it, and it was bound to bring down criticism from their peers; it also sounded like a lot of hard work. Gradually, however, some advantages became apparent to her: this was a natural way for her to do active missionary work while still meeting the needs of her own family; it would give the family an intimate association with Chinese friends and allow the children to think of the Chinese as 'people like ourselves, differing in tastes but not in kind'; and, incidentally, but not to be sniffed at, the boy would pay the same amount for board and tuition as their son Norman would soon be paying at the Canadian School in Chengtu.

The Hwangs had no sooner been informed that their son, who was given the English name George, could come as an experiment than the Endicotts were flooded with similar requests from many Chinese friends. It was hard to persuade them that it wasn't a real school but just an enlarged family. Within a short while two more boys, Gerald Chen and Dick Cheng, joined George in the experiment, and all three lived-in as family members for almost five years. 'To this day,' Endicott recalled thirty years later, 'these boys are almost like our own children, so that we have grandchildren in China. The experiment showed that children don't have race consciousness and will accept any environment. We didn't denationalize these boys. They studied Chinese in the afternoon and we strictly kept their Chinese culture. It was understood they were learning a foreign language, learning about a foreign culture but they were not to be de-nationalized – that's a very important distinction.'[3]

Endicott himself participated in family affairs to a degree and in a manner which allowed Mary to consider him a model father in most respects, though he occasionally lost his temper. Unlike his own experience where the distance between parent and child was clearly defined, he never treated his children as juniors but more as friends with whom he could share enthusiasms, or sort out difficulties through discussion rather than by punishment. Even when he was busiest, and especially when he was under criticism or attack from some quarter, he found relaxation and respite in collective hobbies of one kind or another. Family bridge tournaments, creating or listening to music, collecting postage stamps, feeding birds were favourites, as were outdoor activities. He enjoyed taking his sons, the Chinese boys, and their friends out camping during the summer holidays, hunting deer and wild boar on Mount Omei. Or the whole family would hike past the temples at Flying Bridges and the Elephant's Bath on paths that led through canyons of rushing mountain water, over pine-clad hills studded with wildflowers. Sometimes they would climb to the Golden Summit of Omei where the 'Buddha's glory' found reflection in the mists or the great snow mountains of Tibet could be seen if the day was fine. The following matter-of-fact letter by Norman at an early age reflects the children's appreciation of their father's role:

Chungking Sze., China
April 23, 1936

Dear Grandmother and Grandfather,
    The carpenters are at our house and they are fixing up a boat-swing for Philip and Shirley. It is between two trees. Dad made a bird house for Philip this morning and I hung it up in a tree. Dad made a big swing for Stephen, Mother and myself between two trees. Today about seven o'clock we had an earthquake and the whole house shifted.

Yours loving,
N. A. Endicott[4]

Endicott's other innovative project at this time, his first venture into journalism, began innocently enough as an effort to help raise the standard of language instruction in the middle school. Searching for new ways to stimulate his students he began producing the *Gin I English Weekly*, which he painstakingly printed by hand with special ink suitable for lithography. Presenting a mixture of poetry, short stories, fables, and international affairs, he systematically introduced new words which he defined carefully at the bottom of the page. Other schools in Szechuan and even as far away as Peking heard of the paper until its circulation reached five thousand.

As interest grew, the content became more varied, including political cartoons Endicott took from Western newspapers. To those who raised questions about the content of the paper, which to some seemed increasingly radical, Endicott explained that he was trying to teach students to believe in and to work for the kind of world where all people and every nation would organize the type of government taught by Sun Yat-sen in the Principle of Livelihood, where production would be for use and not for private profit; he was trying to show students the foolishness of all the old ideas of 'race,' 'the white man's burden,' of going to war for the 'economic possession of weak nations'; he aimed to help people understand what he considered to be the contours of a Christ-like world.

The *English Weekly*, published until 1939, spread Endicott's reputation as an educator. Among the Chinese he gained merit as one who understood their point of view. With fellow Occidentals, however, the paper landed him at the centre of acute controversies over the meaning of Christian loyalty in a contemporary world; for many Westerners, the views expressed in the paper were clearly subversive of accepted practices and cherished traditions.

One Britisher who was more congenial to the Endicotts than most was Leslie Hughes, manager of the Imperial Chemical Industries Limited. He told them that intense arguments about the political slant of the *English Weekly* and Endicott's views had become the favourite indoor sport of naval officers and other patriotic nationals at the Chungking Club. Hughes tried to ease the situation by advising Endicott to keep the *Weekly* non-political and to confine it to descriptions of inventions and scientific advances in the Western world.

Endicott appreciated the concern but characteristically rejected the advice. The students for whom the paper was intended, he replied, were nearly all of an age when they could take an intelligent interest in the events of the world and they enjoyed reading about current events as much as about inventions and hobbies or stories. 'You want me to point out to the boys what a fine thing it is that we have such wonderful modern ocean liners,' he told Hughes. 'I want to point out to the young that the men who are running the ship of state still have the idea of mediaeval pirates ... Although they have at their command all the results of scientific invention they are strewing the sea of international politics with wreckage.'[5]

When it was argued that the rulers of the British empire should be spared his criticism because they were moderates and treated the 'natives' better than any other country, Endicott was unwilling to compromise. It might be true but it was not good enough. The members of the British ruling class were exceptionally adept at rationalizing their impulses; they profited from exploiting 'the backward peoples' and at the same time believed they were giving them the boons of civilization and Christianity, a sacred process which they called the 'white man's burden.' If anyone believed that Kipling's *Recessional* was a beautiful prayer and deserved a continuing place in the hymnbook, Endicott suggested that they write out in plain, simple English what it meant. His own version began:

Oh, God of our fathers, you are the Lord of our armies; it is under your guiding hand that we have sent our soldiers in the last hundred years to rob the Indians, Africans and the peoples of the islands of the seas of their birthright of free land and liberty. It is under thy hand that we now control these lands for our own profit, denying them the privileges that we ourselves enjoy until they rise up and fight for them. It was under thy dominion that we massacred the Indians of the Punjab and shot down the Chinese students in Shanghai and in the year of grace 1927 drove the Massai from their pasture lands in Kenya Colony and gave the land over to Lord Delaware's Development Companies to exploit. They are only black men, O God, 'lesser breeds without the law' ...[6]

Such attitudes were infuriating to Endicott's British compatriots, and the German and Italian consuls officially complained to the Chinese government, demanding that Endicott be deported or at least that the *English Weekly* be stopped because of its attacks on Hitler and Mussolini. Luckily for the Canadian iconoclast, the British consul, E.W.P. Mills, rejected these complaints, but he cautioned Endicott that some of his deductions were far-fetched and indiscreet, as when he said that Hitler was under the power of the 'money-kings.' 'This may or may not be true,' said Mills, 'but possibly it is injudicious to say so.' Missionary colleagues also advised him to avoid such forthright statements in the future, although some stated that intellectually they agreed with his point of view. Endicott was aghast when a visiting senior United Church of Canada administrator, disturbed at the feeling against his junior colleague, said: 'we must be loyal to our own, you know!'

Who are 'our own'? To whom must we be loyal? The implications of these questions for universal Christian brotherhood rankled in Endicott's heart and after such confrontations he felt most dispirited. Fortunately, the same frank approach that brought down such criticisms was well appreciated by many Chinese; instead of reprimands from them he received financial donations to help continue the good work. This made it possible to go on.[7]

In the midst of such controversies came the Sian incident of December 1936, which changed the current of Chinese affairs and influenced Endicott's future as well. Chiang Kai-shek had gone to Sian in Shensi province to inspect the progress of a campaign against the Communist base area in north Shensi. His generals in charge of suppressing the Communists wanted to stop the civil war in favour of resisting Japanese encroachments into China since 1931, which now included the five northern provinces as well as Manchuria. When Chiang would not agree, the generals kidnapped him and broadcast their demand for the formation of a patriotic united front. Two weeks later, Chiang was suddenly released unharmed. When information reached Chungking that Chiang had been saved and was back in Nanking, the largest and most spontaneous celebration that Endicott had ever seen took place in the streets of the city. 'They knew that Chiang Kai-shek had come out,' he recalled, 'and they suspected with a promise to stop the civil war and fight the Japanese.'[8]

In spite of the popular rejoicing, Endicott was a bit cynical about the possibilities of a genuine united effort against Japan because there were three conflicting groups in China, the 'pure capitalists,' the 'nationalist fascist group under Chiang Kai-shek,' and the Communists, all contending for power. The first group, according to Endicott, believed that co-operation with Japan would give them enough of the spoils to make it worthwhile to set up business under Japanese occupation. He was not sure just where Chiang Kai-shek himself stood, but there was no doubt in his mind that the majority of the group in Nanking were 'out and out Fascists,' complete with German advisers, blue shirts, 'Heil Chiang' salutes, and the sudden disappearance of opponents without due process of law. The Communists, Endicott thought, consisted of students, unemployed, and the ambitious who had been left unrewarded by the other two groups, and they had the advantage of 'brilliant military leaders in Chu Teh and Mao Tse-tung.' He did not see how Chiang Kai-shek could really co-operate once more with the Communist group after his betrayal of them in 1927 and the killing of so many of their leaders, but since the Communists were reported to have modified their programme recently, perhaps a way would be found. Of one thing Endicott was certain: Chiang Kai-shek was the ablest politician in China at the moment and any movement without him would break up into opposing factions.[9]

Even after the united front of the Nationalists and Communists was consolidated in September 1937, the struggle with Japan went from bad to worse in most areas. With a million men on the mainland, the Japanese captured Nanking in 1937, all of China's seaports from the north down to Canton, as well as all the railroads of central China, forcing Chiang to abandon Hankow in central China at the end of 1938 and retreat with his government to Chungking. The Japanese, who were being supplied on a commercial basis with North American oil, scrap iron, and other strategic materials,[10] believed that the Chinese, who lacked strong allies, would have to capitulate. However, with the Communist-led guerillas, re-named the Eighth Route Army of the National government, fighting stubbornly in the north, Chiang announced that he was trading space for time in an effort to build up a new base of resistance to Japan in the vast hinterland of China.

As part of the war effort, Madame Chiang Kai-shek developed a far-flung ·system of supporting social services and morale-building activities. In Szechuan province whole-hearted co-operation in the war effort lagged, even after Chungking became the wartime national capital. It was partly because of this that Madame Chiang began looking around for the services of a missionary who knew conditions in the area. Endicott was recommended by one of her staff as a person with fluency in Chinese and high standing with both the Chinese and the foreign communities. In view of the source from which the appeal for his services came, the West China Mission executive agreed to Madame Chiang's request to lend Endicott for work in the New Life Movement at the beginning of 1939.

CHAPTER FOURTEEN

Madame Chiang's New Life Movement

The rickshaw bounced over the cobblestones one morning early in March 1939 as Jim Endicott hurried to keep an 8 a.m. appointment with Generalissimo and Madame Chiang Kai-shek, in their home at the extreme northwestern part of Chungking. Through the rising mist he could see silent junks down on the little river, while along Seven Star Ridge Street orange vendors called out their wares and noodle shops did a brisk business as people stopped for breakfast on their way to work. Seven thousand Japanese bombers would raid the city within the next two years, burning and flattening the buildings with tons of heavy explosives and incendiary bombs, driving the populace to tunnel underground, but for the moment all was serene; ramshackle structures and palatial homes perched like sparrows and hawks in haphazard fraternity upon the rocky hillsides of the city. As the time for his first private interview with China's famous leaders neared, Endicott's pulse seemed to quicken in time with the rickshaw puller's beat.

The Chiangs greeted him warmly. The generalissimo expressed pleasure in welcoming the new counsellor to the New Life Movement and said that as president of that organization he was looking forward to Endicott's reports.

'Shall I translate?' Madame Chiang interjected.

'Not necessary. I understand,' Endicott replied. The Chiangs looked at each other, smiling at his quaint Szechuanese dialect, and the interview immediately assumed an air of informality.

'I want you to make regular reports to me personally and to my wife,' Chiang continued. 'Tell us everything you see or hear or feel about the New Life Movement. If you hear of corruption or see mis-government that must be included because we are not looking for flattery. We want China to become strong enough to defeat the Japanese aggressor. We wish to build a new China according to the democratic principles of Sun Yat-sen. We know we have a hard road ahead.' Referring to Endicott's military service, the generalissimo said that he was also appointing him to be an officer instructor in the Chinese National Army; General Feng Yu-hsiang, who was in charge of recruitment and training, would be calling upon him from time to time for inspirational addresses at recruiting rallies and army camps. Chiang then added one more request: 'Madame Chiang and I wish to treat you as one of the family,' he said, 'and ask you to agree that you will never write the inside story of our affairs.' Endicott nodded in agreement, whereupon the generalissimo shook hands and briskly excused himself, leaving Madame Chiang to spend the rest of the morning with the new recruit.

'As I told you in my letter of invitation,' Madame Chiang began, 'the New Life Movement is a social movement for the amelioration of the life of the common people.' It was based, she continued, upon the principle of Christian love and the revival of the four simple Confucian virtues, Li, I, Lien, and Ch'ih – courtesy and good manners, justice and uprightness, frugality and integrity, modesty and self-respect. Its aim was to train and develop a completely new type of official who could be trusted by the people. 'The People's Anti-Opium Movement is an example,' she added. 'We are determined to sweep this hundred-year-old disgrace from our midst. We plan to create a rising tide of public indignation which will compel all minor officials to do their duty to stop the traffic. Mass meetings will be held where opium pipes will be burned in bonfires.' Endicott listened carefully as she outlined these ambitious projects, speaking with feeling and in all apparent sincerity.[1]

While emphasizing that reform remained high on the list of the movement's objectives, Madame Chiang rapidly passed on to the new priorities created by the war of resistance to Japan. They included training staff for the war orphanages, the distribution of cash bonuses to the wounded soldiers, mass education to encourage voluntary enlistment in the military services, help to organize industrial co-operatives among the million or more refugees who had fled before the Japanese.[2]

Madame Chiang then turned to what she expected of him. She explained that her staff at all levels was composed of 'one-third communists, one-third Christians and one-third from political parties.' At the highest level, the Women's Advisory Committee of the New Life Movement included such well-known personalities as the Communist women's leader, Teng Ying-chao, wife of Chou En-lai, and Madame Li Teh-chuan (a Christian who became minister of health after 1949). In Madame Chiang's view Christians acted as the leaven in the group and she needed his help on committees to assist in smoothing out difficulties among the staff; that would be his main responsibility, requiring special tact and judgement. In addition, his job was to go around and observe production departments, training classes, propaganda activities, and to send in frank reports on what he saw and thought about them. 'Don't tell me about any problems for which you have no solutions to suggest,' Madame Chiang added. On special anniversaries she also hoped he would prepare talks on China's democratic progress to be broadcast to Europe and America.[3]

'Madame is a charmer,' Endicott thought as he left the interview. 'She is doing heroic work in organizing service groups and in training the workers who form the back-bone of the staff. No wonder the Commander-in-Chief of the British Forces in the Far East has made the statement that as long as China has the Generalissimo and Madame Chiang, China cannot be conquered.' It was also true, Endicott felt, that there was a growing democratic unity among the Chinese since nearly all the advisory bodies and government service groups now included many outstanding people who at one time or another had been in jail or exiled for their political opinions. This was a new and changed China, which gave cause for optimism. He was happy to be part of a movement inspired by an open-minded fraternalism that was 'helping to complete the work of revolution which made China a republic.'[4]

Endicott was immediately preoccupied in the spring and summer of 1939 with the relief work of the New Life Movement, as a result of the commencement of Japanese terror bombings in Szechuan. During the first heavy raids on the cities of Kiating and Luchow he led a small relief squad of doctors and nurses supported by funds raised in Britain and North America. Chungking itself was hit four times in May 1939 resulting in ten thousand casualties and incredible damage. From that time on the bombing occurred almost weekly for three years. The Endicott family, that May, huddled in the basement of their home at Duckling Pond as bombs came crashing down within a range of six hundred yards; later, for greater protection, they had an underground shelter cut deep into the hillside at the back of the house.

Endicott himself was often inside the city when the raids occurred. As he helped fight the fires and responded to the screams of the unfortunates pinned under the debris of fallen buildings, he swore that he would like to take the Japanese emperor by the neck and shove him face to face with all this human misery. Nor did the Western democracies escape his condemnation for their share in China's disaster. During one of these terrible raids a Japanese bomber crashed; investigators found that it had been powered by American-made engines and was armed with machine-guns manufactured by the Birmingham Small Arms factory in Great Britain. As Endicott wrote down various serial numbers he was suspicious that 'these guns were sold to Japan about the time that our leaders in appeasement were telling us that it was necessary to sacrifice the little free democracy of Czecho-Slovakia because we didn't have enough guns to talk to Hitler in the only language he understood.[5]

Endicott's respect for Madame Chiang increased rapidly as he accompanied her from day to day and realized how hard she worked. A typical day in the hot summer of 1939 began with early morning Bible study with the generalissimo followed by a sunrise service on the banks of the river attended by two hundred girls, who were graduating and going out to war areas for service work; she told them de Maupassant's story of 'The Necklace,' emphasizing the qualities of integrity, perseverance, and hard work in the face of disaster. Endicott noted that she was as forceful and eloquent a speaker in Chinese as she was in English. After breakfast she went with a group of women secretaries of the New Life Movement to inspect a large military hospital, giving out little packages of field comforts made by her Women's War Service Clubs to each wounded soldier; the presence of gangrene made the task of visiting each soldier an agonizing one. After lunch came an interview with Rewi Alley of the Industrial Co-operatives, who wanted to know about the possibilities of buying some used cotton-spinning machinery from a factory in England; on such questions she was intense and keen, questioning every detail. After a rest she devoted the balance of the day to affairs of state – tea with the British ambassador, a French lesson in preparation for interpreting for her husband when some high French military advisers would arrive, dinner at night with a group of high government officials. It was no wonder that her husband said she was worth twenty divisions.

Although Madame Chiang shouldered heavy affairs of state and was in close personal contact with the suffering of the people, she retained a refreshing buoyancy of spirit. Occasionally Endicott had to call upon his reserves of religious thought and feeling when she was discouraged or ill, but normally she radiated confidence and enjoyed frivolity in moments of relaxation. Her fondness of hilarious party games was evident at her Christmas Eve party in 1939 when she proposed Blind Man's Buff and Musical Chairs. The more conservative shook their heads, gravely saying: 'Madame is still very American' (she had studied in the United States). When the generalissimo did not support her interpretation of one game, she playfully tossed a cushion at his head. 'Shades of Confucius on "decorum," ' thought Endicott. 'Not thus have the great men of China ever been treated by their wives.'

Endicott's admiration for Madame Chiang grew as he saw the enemies she made in the course of her work. He noticed the tension between her and men like Chen Li-fu, the minister of education, and General Ho Ying-chin, minister of war. These men, in his opinion, were afraid that because of her there was a growing democratic influence both on the generalissimo and on certain of the Kuomintang party activities that would threaten the dictatorial control exercised by themselves and the extreme right-wing cliques. Endicott classified Madame Chiang as a middle-of-the-road reformer during this period of the war effort. Her position was illustrated by the differences of political opinion within her own family: her elder sister, Madame Kung, who was married to the minister of finance, was on the right in her political sympathies, while her other sister, Soong Ching-ling, the widow of Sun Yat-sen, was on the left. For years the sisters had been politically estranged after Soong Ching-ling denounced 'the treacherous character of the counter-revolutionary Kuomintang leaders' following Chiang Kai-shek's coup d'état in 1927. In the spring of 1940 when Madame Chiang went to Hongkong for a rest cure she managed to persuade her two sisters to accompany her back to Chungking to present a united front. Endicott was standing at the top of the steps with the welcoming committee as the famous sisters were being carried up in sedan chairs, and when Madame Chiang saw him she waved her handkerchief saying: 'Hello, see what I have brought back.' She was obviously enjoying the political and other implications of this visit.[6]

During Madame Chiang's absence in Hongkong, an event in the work of the New Life Movement showed how critical her support was to stave off attacks from the reactionary wing of the Kuomintang. The New Life Movement had organized War Service Clubs in the villages to promote war production and to serve the soldiers' families by watching to see that the magistrates did not steal the rice allowance for the families. Before long the New Life secretaries who were most successful at organizing the War Service Clubs and at curbing graft were being called Communists by the magistrates. During Madame Chiang's absence about ten of these secretaries disappeared without a trace. Upon her return Endicott and a few others protested this occurrence. She took it up with the generalissimo who then gave a dinner to the senior secretaries and advisers, explaining that the missing secretaries were really key Communist personnel who had been secretly transferred elsewhere by order from the Communist party. Chiang gave his personal assurances that there was no need to worry about them.

At the time Endicott was sufficiently idealistic about the generalissimo that he accepted the story. It was not until after the war that he learned what he considered to be the true story from the associate general secretary of the New Life Movement, Yang Wu-hsin, a former YMCA secretary. Yang, having heard that Endicott by now had turned against the KMT regime, invited him to lunch. He spoke with great bitterness of how the former YMCA men had been roped into the service of what turned out to be a fascist organization. He showed Endicott the personal order from the generalissmo to carry out the arrest of those 'communist' secretaries who had disappeared five years earlier; they had been taken to the chambers of Tai Li's security service and killed after horrible torture. Yang himself died a few months after speaking to Endicott while on an airplane flight from Chengtu to Shanghai. Whether his was a natural death or whether he had talked too much, Endicott was never able to determine.[7]

In his second year of service with the New Life Movement other incidents occurred that allowed Endicott to see more clearly the growing power of entrenched privileged groups and their fascist-minded spokesmen within the Kuomintang. One morning in January 1940 a package was delivered to his front gate containing the text of a KMT resolution on 'Measures to solve the Communist Problem.' As Endicott read this remarkable document he realized that it was a plan to exterminate the Communists during the war of resistance against Japan. Especially revealing were the methods proposed for eliminating the Communists as a political and military force while camouflaging the role of the central government: 'Concerning the attitude of the various party, civil and military organizations, the Central Government must appear to be generous, the local authorities must be cautious and strict, and the lower officers and members must engage in vigorous struggle; concerning the distribution of work, the party [KMT] headquarters and members must do the fighting work, the government taking the position of mediator, while the troops are the driving force.'

If this document was genuine, then all the protestations of the generalissimo and Madame Chiang about concern for democracy and national unity to resist the Japanese invaders were a sham. And so also was his effort to act as a leaven between the Communists and the Kuomintang in the New Life Movement. What should he do? Endicott did not feel secure enough in his relationship with the Chiangs to go to them directly with a matter that called their integrity into such serious question. Instead he decided to give a copy to the British ambassador and to talk to his friend Chang Chun.

Chang Chun was a Szechuanese, a nominal Christian who had risen high in the KMT government to become foreign minister for a brief period, and who would later become prime minister. Endicott and Chang Chun had met at a missionary gathering where Chang was interested by the candid criticism this brash Canadian levelled at the minister of education for his narrow views on the teaching of English. Half joking, Chang Chun had said: 'You come and teach your system to me and perhaps someday I will witness for you.' This accidental encounter was the beginning of a long friendship between Chang and his wife and the Endicotts. The Changs would come to the Endicotts' home occasionally for a Sunday rest when they wanted to escape from the cares of office, and Endicott went to their house three mornings a week to put Chang Chun through the direct method English course. During one of these sessions Chang had revealed that he was secretary-general of the Supreme Defence Council of the National government and it was on this basis that Endicott decided to confront him with the KMT document on 'solving' the Communist problem.

'Was it true?' Endicott asked.

Chang Chun looked embarrassed, blushed a little, Endicott thought, and then said calmly: 'There was such a document discussed but the plenary session turned it down. It is not part of the official policy of the Chinese government.'

'Was it part of the *unofficial* policy of the Chinese government?'

Chang Chun would say no more.

Although Endicott was not satisfied by the reply he was at least encouraged by the inkling that Chang Chun belonged to the more moderate group which was trying to modify the influence of the extreme elements within the KMT, headed by Chen Li-fu and his cohorts, the CC clique. [8]

Endicott's friend, Earl Willmott, who had likewise received the document from some unknown source, discussed its implications in his annual letter of December 1940:

A few months ago I saw myself a secret document issued by two very high-ups in the government (with the Generalissimo's agreement? – and if so, because he was power-less to oppose?) with detailed instructions how the communists were to be liquidated. And all to be done with the appearance that the government was their friend. But they are far from being liquidated and the forces of reaction know it, and so fascist methods of suppression ... are coming into use. There are many of us who are working against these reactionary tendencies by talks to students, discussion groups, lending libraries, and at student conferences – the [Chinese] Student Christian Movement arranged that all their student conferences in June would concentrate on the topic 'Democracy and Student Life'; a committee here worked out the discussion line in which we attempted to have students think through the basic essentials of democracy, its relation to Christian religion, its enemies and what they ought to do about it. [9]

Like Willmott, Endicott was convinced that the Kuomintang would have to introduce more democratic and liberal measures if it was going to mobilize the people successfully to fight the war. As the following commentary, based upon Endicott's contacts with the Communist-held areas, shows, he did not hold out high hopes for the KMT in this respect:

A number of the boys whom I taught in the Communist prison have gone back to the 8th Route Army and through them I can get some fairly reliable information. The points under discussion with the central authorities at present seem to be as follows:

The Communist army get about $650,000 a month from the Generalissimo. They do not, however, pay their officers much better than the men and this leaves a large surplus which they use for enlarging their forces and doing party organization. They are only supposed to have three divisions whereas they actually have nine. They claim that they need nine to cover the area they now occupy. But if they were paid for nine divisions, as they wish, they would have a large surplus with which to build small arsenals, and do other industrial development which would make them much more economically independent.

The communists are doing a good deal of requisitioning of food supplies and in some cases paying with their own paper money.

They are also linking up many small bands of guerilla troops and local 'defence militia' into a rather widespread organization which reaches across to within 20 miles of Peiping.

The whole question is one of good faith. Will a promise be kept? The Communists have agreed to give up Communist practice and ideology and accept the 'Three Principles.' I believe that so far they have given evidence that they are sincere in this. I think the question is will the Kuomintang give that measure of democracy and socialism which will be acceptable. At the present time I see very little evidence that the Kuomintang are at all concerned about either the kind of 'democracy' or 'socialism' which is plainly taught by Sun Yat-sen and to which they give lip service every week ...

The present Minister of War [Ho Ying-chin] ... is greatly concerned about the fact that Colonels in the 8th Route Army only get $8 a month instead of $100. The condition of giving the 8th Army any more money is that Colonels shall get the proper $100. The argument on the other side is that they couldn't buy anything in the poverty-stricken north, even if they did get the money, and anyway, they need 100 tough guerillas more than another $100 colonel. I presume the ultimate logic of the 8th Route Army is to arm everybody in the fight against Japanese military aggression and turn the whole North into a vast armed camp. That has dangers, what happens after the war?

The Central Government view is rather to let the official army do the fighting. Let the people supply recruits, produce the needed goods and pay the taxes.

I had dinner twice last week with a former communist who is now a liaison officer from the Generalissimo's headquarters staff attached to the 8th Route. (That fact is not clearly appreciated in the West, that Central Officers go everywhere in the 8th Army area.) This man tells me that the Communists have a genius for organization with the common people. By the simplicity of their lives and the lack of class distinctions they can do wonders. At the railway bases of the Japenese they even organize the pickpockets into squads and through the light-fingered fraternity secure a steady trickle of telephone equipment, ammunition and even pistols. [10]

During the spring of 1940 there was an angry exchange between Endicott and Madame Chiang over the growing power of anti-democratic forces in the Chinese youth movement. The point at issue was the role of the San Min Chu I Youth Corps, which the generalissimo's staff had organized on the model of the Hitler Youth Corps. When the New Life girls, trained under Madame Chiang's personal supervision, were linked up with this group, Endicott protested that they were being railroaded in. Emily Hahn, who wrote a biography of the Soong sisters, recorded the encounter in her book *China to Me* (1944):

He was arguing with her. That was something worth eavesdropping on – a man, a European ... arguing with Madame, disagreeing with her! The subject was the new Youth Movement among the adolescent school children of Chungking, and Endicott maintained that they should not be called on to take an oath of allegiance en masse, or rather in the presence of all the government officials who had gathered to watch this planned ceremony. 'You are not giving them a choice,' said Endicott.
    'They aren't forced to do it,' Madame countered quickly.
    'Is any child going to refuse under such public pressure?' he asked.
    'No, perhaps not. But no child is told he must swear; no child is penalized for refusing. The question doesn't come up, anyway. They all want to take the oath.' Madame spoke sharply, but without surprise. She seemed to be used to this man's abrupt methods.
    'It's like fascism,' said Endicott. 'There's no value in it. There's no individual thought.'[11]

Endicott accepted Madame Chiang's annoyance cheerfully because he felt it represented a genuine disturbance in her own mind and he was relieved to know that the disturbance existed. He considered her to be sincere and extraordinarily clever, a person who had shown that she could rescue a situation; but he was afraid that she was giving way to pressure.

As the drift to the right continued, however, Endicott began to doubt the value of his remaining as an adviser and decided to make his position absolutely clear in a frank and constructive letter to Madame Chiang. 'When I joined the Movement,' he wrote, 'I promised you that I would report to you freely and frankly on all that I see or feel.' He reiterated his view that it was a great mistake for the New Life Movement to become part of the Kuomintang party's activities. He did not wish to belittle the achievements of the party and he realized the value of her analogy of 'the cement needed to hold the bricks together,' but in the end the party was supposed to be the mid-wife who helps to bring to birth democracy in China. 'From what I see and hear,' he said, 'there is considerable danger that the mid-wife will try to strangle the new-born baby and grab the inheritance.' Why, Endicott wanted to know, was every school teacher being forced to join the party and principals dared not hire those who did not? Why, during this time of a 'united front,' were the secret orders for the suppression of the Communists being circulated so freely? He had heard that a dozen editors of the 'Hsin Hua Newspaper' in Chungking had been secretly arrested by the security police. All these disturbing things made him feel more strongly than ever that the New Life Movement ought to remain free and independent, showing how to draw people together by the force of friendliness and the common concern for winning the war and the reconstruction of the country. One of the functions of the New Life Movement at this time, he said, 'ought to be a little healthy and helpful criticism of the Party and its doings, in order to make it aware of short-comings and spur it on to better achievements.' 'Li, I, Lien, and Ch'ih,' he concluded, could be realized more fully by the administration only in this way.

'I want you to come over and tell the G'issimo these things,' Madame Chiang said, after receiving this letter.

Endicott replied doubtfully: 'I thought that our agreement was I would work directly with you and that you would generally tell the Generalissimo.' He laughingly told her the story of the native who had six wives and got converted to Christianity; the priest said: 'Now that you have become a Christian, you have to tell all your wives, except the first one, that they have to go'; the old man looked at the missionary thoughtfully, and then said: 'You tell them.'

But Madame Chiang insisted that Endicott was the missionary and should carry the message.

During the subsequent interview with Chiang Kai-shek, Endicott spoke in his customary open manner. He said that KMT units were pushing to take complete control of the New Life Movement: the next class of women secretaries were eighty per cent KMT nominees instead of one-third from each of the three groups in the united front as previously agreed. He warned against the influence of General Kang Tseh, organizer of the Youth Corps, whose personal ambitions outweighed his loyalty to the generalissimo. Endicott suggested to Chiang that unless he took the road of Abraham Lincoln and based his policies on the needs of the Chinese people, including agrarian reform, then revolutionary forces would ultimately rise against him.

Chiang broke in to say that he was in favour of agrarian reform and that he had many plans for it. 'However,' he said, 'I cannot carry out land reform while there are so many Communists around to take advantage of it.'

'Here in Szechuan,' Endicott ventured, 'there seem not to be very many Communists. Why not try it here?'

'You are mistaken,' Chiang replied. 'There are Communists all around and I must deal with them first.'

'How do you judge whether a person is Communist or not?' Endicott asked.

Chiang answered curtly. 'Generally anyone who is in favour of land reform is a Communist!'

From Madame Chiang's flushed appearance and her increasing nervousness, Endicott sensed that the poker-faced Chiang was extremely angry. At this point, as if to relieve the tension, Colonel J.L. Huang came in and said: 'I think it would be good if you gave Mr. Endicott a picture of yourself and autograph it with some special message since he has worked all this time.' Chiang consented and then terminated the interview abruptly, excusing himself for another appointment.

About this time, Endicott was invited to fill a vacancy that had occurred in the English Department of West China Union University in Chengtu. It was an opportunity that appealed to both Mary and himself for various reasons, including the fact that the children would be able to attend the Canadian School without leaving home. Endicott told Madame Chiang of the possible move, indicating that it might be the best thing for him to do. She disagreed and wrote the mission asking it to leave him with the New Life Movement for another year.

Endicott, however, was not willing to stay on. His impression of the Kuomintang party by now was that it had little more social conscience than a cholera germ; if the New Life Movement under Madame Chiang ceased to lead in service and with goodwill that cut across party lines, then his usefulness as an adviser was finished. Also, rightly or wrongly, Endicott believed that a breach was opening between Madame Chiang and her husband in which he might be an indirect cause; he had come to the conclusion that the break would become irreparable if the strain went on much longer. Instead of becoming more democratic Chiang seemed to be turning in the opposite direction, and possibly resented the attempted pressure and domination by a woman. Endicott felt that he should withdraw from the association to avoid helping to provoke an outright split between China's two most prominent wartime leaders.

The only reservation he had about leaving was the war situation. He believed in the necessity for China to resist the Japanese military machine to the bitter end, and in that work the New Life Movement was doing useful service both in its propaganda and at the front. He would continue to help the war effort where he could, but he was not content to see the movement be so superficial. In the summer of 1940, at the age of forty-one, he returned to mission work, spending the last year of his second term as a professor of English at West China Union University and as director of the Missionary Language Training School in Chengtu.[12] One moonlit night in July 1941, together with his family, he flew high over the Japanese-held territory of China to Hongkong and set sail for home.

The Endicotts and Rev. Harold and Lal Swann (on the left), outside the Swanns' home in Chungking where the Endicotts stayed on their arrival in 1926

The Canadian missionary residence and the countryside at Duckling Pond, Chungking

Rice fields outside Chungking

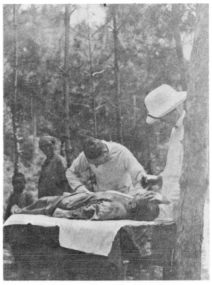

A main road through the countryside
near Chungking

Endicott gives chloroform anaesthetic
while Dr Alex Pincock removes a gangre-
nous finger, Chungchow, 1926

James Endicott, Sr, visits Shanghai during the 'Exodus Council' of the West China
Mission in 1927 and meets his first grandson, Norman

Norman Endicott held by his amah,
Chungchow, 1926

Wang Lieh-guang, pastor of Little Cross
Roads Church, Chungking, 1930

The Endicotts in Chungchow, 1926

精盂中學獎文週報

THE GINI MIDDLE SCHOOL ENGLISH WEEKLY

ITALY CONTINUES TO CIVILIZE ABYSSINIA

During the last week the Italian armies have been fighting very hard. They are afraid the League of Nations will stop them and aid. The Italian armies, with their big guns and tanks have defeated and broken two Abyssinian armies. Thousands of black men have been killed while protecting their own country and their own homes.

The Abyssinians are not finished. We shall see that they will fight on for many months yet. In the meantime (during this time) the black men all over the world are watching with interest. There is a growing feeling of hate in their hearts. (Hate = strong feeling of dislike). In the year 1936 the strong nations of the world are still as greedy and selfish as ever.

England and France only talk for several months and do very little. Americans like Mr. Hearst say they will not come into the League of Nations because they do not want to mix in Europe's quarrels. But they are ready to fight anyone who wants to stop them from selling to the quarreling nations and making a lot of money.

The people of Italy are now celebrating a great triumph at a mountain called Amba Alagi. Nearly 40 years ago, about 2000 Italian soldiers were killed here. They were going to steal the country from the Abyssinians. Now the Italians are going to steal again and this time they have killed twice as many black men. So they are feeling happy. Sometimes men are worse than monkeys!!

CIVILIZING ABYSSINIA

JAPANESE ARMY OFFICERS KILL THEMSELVES

It is reported that more than 18 of the army officers who led the soldiers into Tokyo have killed themselves. The prime minister was not killed. His brother-in-law went instead and the soldiers killed him.

An Englishman named Sampson has been taken by the Tokyo police because he was giving the people in a hotel papers which said many unfriendly things about Japan.

BRITISH AND FRENCH ARMY LEADERS HAVE STRANGE MEETING

The chiefs of the British and French armies are having a meeting to talk about how they will organize the army, navy, and air forces so that they can work together and help each other.

WELL-KNOWN AMERICAN SPEAKS TO PEIPING MEETING

A friend has sent us an interesting report of a meeting in Peiping. A well-known American was speaking about "The Future of Chinese-Japan Relations." After what happened in Tokyo he changed to "Must China Fight Japan?" Dr. Chang Mo Ling, Dr. Hu Shih and other famous Chinese were present. The general feeling was that China must fight; came can fight; because of Japan's plans no other way is possible.

Dr. Hu Shih said that now, the powerful agreement is possible. Only strong governments like those of America and England can go back after they have made a mistake. A weak government does not dare to go back because it is afraid of revolution. The Japanese is a weak government. It dare not go back. China cannot get help from England because of Italy. America is happy stirred in Asia. There seems to be no other way: China must help herself!

Endicott's weekly newspaper for language students

Foreign gunboats riding at anchor in Shanghai harbour, 1937 (British Admiralty photograph, Public Record Office, London)

The Canadian West China Mission's Gin I Middle School at Duckling Pond, Chungking

Prison for Communists in Chungking, 1932, where Endicott taught English for a year; the missionaries in the third row are, from the left, Jim Endicott, A. Ryerson, E. McCurdy, Mary Austin, H. Veals, Laura Riddell, H. Irish, and G. Rackham; prison wardens, Buddhist and YMCA teachers in back row; two Endicott boys at front left

Endicott during summer holidays on
Mount Omei, 1937

Stephen Endicott with George Huang,
Gerald Chen, and Richard Cheng, the
Chinese boys who lived with the
Endicotts, 1936–41

The Endicott family, 1936; the children,
from the left, are Stephen, Philip Michael,
Shirley, and Norman

Pilgrim on Mount Omei, 1930s (photo by Fred Owen)

Evening prayers in a Buddhist monastery on Mount Omei (photo by Fred Owen)

Famine refugees in Chungking, 1937

Woman showing result of foot binding practised in feudal China

Travelling by junk on the Yangtze, 1930s (photo by Fred Owen)

Irrigating fields in Szechuan, 1930s

Transporting cotton

Chinese army officers escorting Endicott and Rev. Fred Owen to an army base in Szechuan to speak to recruits in 1938

Endicott encourages new recruits in the struggle against the Japanese invaders after the fall of Hankow in 1938

At Chiang Kai-shek's summer residence, 1939, with Col. J.L. Huang (left), general secretary of the New Life Movement

Madame Chiang Kai-shek leaving the office of the Women's Advisory Committee of the New Life Movement

Flames approach the Canadian West China Mission's Business Agency after a Japanese bombing attack, 4 May 1939

Li Chao-ji, Endicott's former student and member of the 1940s revolutionary student group 'The Sparks,' Chengtu

Chou En-lai signs the 'ceasefire' in General Marshall's home in Chungking, while Governor Chang Chun looks on, January 1945 (UPI photo)

Endicott with Christian leader Y.T. Wu, Chengtu, 1946

CHAPTER FIFTEEN

Furlough again

Furlough was spent in a Canada at war. For Endicott it was a time of almost uninterrupted speech-making. From the autumn of 1941 until his return to China in the summer of 1944, he made over five hundred public addresses, sometimes four or five a day. From the Maritimes to British Columbia he spoke to church congregations, women's missionary societies, army camps, secondary school assemblies, university associations, Empire and Canadian clubs, Boards of Trade, Rotary, and other businessmen's clubs; he made a number of radio broadcasts, and spoke once or twice to labour unions. His name became a household word to virtually every United Church family in the country. His themes, world brotherhood through missions, China, the war and the possible foundations for a lasting peace, were constant; but his emphasis as well as his public following gradually changed during these years.

It was natural, at first, under the sponsorship of the Missionary and Maintenance Fund of the United Church, that he concentrated upon his recent missionary experiences and the missionary contribution to China's struggle for self-preservation.

One of the justifications of the missionary effort, he argued, was that Christians had a common bond of faith in the leadership that Chiang Kai-shek and Madame Chiang were giving to China. Giving the generalissimo the benefit of the doubt, Endicott described him as a moderate conservative and a Christian who could be counted upon 'to lay an enduring foundation for democracy in China.' In Churchillian words that would come back to haunt him, he told the Empire Club in Toronto in November 1941 that Chiang 'stands there in the midst of his bombed and blasted capital, a great and heroic figure, clothed with the qualities of a Lincoln ... He will not falter nor fail, and if we give him the tools, he'll finish the job for us in the Far East.' In spite of losing eighty-seven per cent of the industries and all rail communications in five years of war with Japan, Chiang, he said, stood resolute and determined to regain China's freedom and national integrity. Britain and America, who, like the priest and the Levite, had passed by on the other side and had permitted the sale of war munitions to Japan, now had a chance to make amends by coming to the aid of the Chinese people who were upholding the democratic front in the Far East.

If the request to take China seriously as a democracy came as a surprise to his listeners, Endicott said he could understand the reason; he was fully aware of some of the difficulties and dangers, both within and without the government, that cast doubt on this assertion. Nevertheless he was convinced, after living in the county, that China had been able to make substantial progress towards the democratic way of life, even in the midst of a war for which she was unprepared. His hopes for democracy in China were based not so much on her leaders, her history, and her traditions (although they were not lacking in such elements) as on the qualities of soul and character that had come out of the common people in this struggle. He described the building of the thirty thousand industrial co-operatives, the work of the New Life Movement, the care of the war orphans, the friends of the wounded, the relief of bombed cities. He gave an account of the formation of the People's Political Council, 'really the modern parliament of China,' which had a balance of people from the ruling Kuomintang, the Christians, and the Communists and was unique among Chinese institutions in having fifteen women representatives. The most important story of the common people's efforts, in Endicott's opinion, was that of the fighting guerilla bands of North China; in praise of these fearless men and women the Chinese had produced one of the most stirring of modern war songs, *The Guerilla Song*, which he thought might be considered the *Marseillaise* of modern China, and to the delight of his audiences he sang it with gusto, first in Chinese and then in English.

The Chinese people had risen to meet each crisis and each disaster in a magnificent way. 'We of the British Empire feel at Dunkirk we saw all those qualities which sanctify the human spirit when it is facing disaster'; the Chinese, he pointed out, had gone through not one but a whole series of Dunkirks, and each time they had shown that they were capable of taking their destiny into their own hands and 'moulding it for a future of freedom and justice.' The Chinese people needed our help in the form of medical supplies, Hurricanes and Spitfires, if possible with Canadian pilots; they deserved to be brought fully into international discussions on the future of the Pacific area of the world.

As for the overseas missionary enterprise, Endicott continued to present it as one of the real foundations of international co-operation. The missionary was sustained on the front lines of a Christian and humanitarian crusade by the bonds of prayer and fellowship which knew no national boundaries or racial barriers. He urged the ideal of international brotherhood, and, giving some individual instances that were real to him, he urged support for missions. In the past the missionary movement had done the best it knew how, often with better results than expected, and now, he argued, the challenge was to do something on a large scale. Apart from the pastoral care of Christians and the preaching of the gospel, he suggested that the missionary could make an important contribution to modern China by demonstrating the church's mission as the servant and advocate of the social and economic needs of humanity. Already the churches, schools, and hospitals were a splendid help to the war-ravaged country. And nothing could take the place of the individual missionary who lived with a drive that 'came from his own sense of the Church's saving purpose in the world.' There was a lot of unfinished business in China, Japan, India, Africa, 'and from Jerusalem unto the ends of the Earth.' 'Give us the means,' Endicott appealed, 'and let us get on with the job.'[1]

Mary watched with quiet rejoicing the response of his audiences; never had she seen people more deeply stirred. The dramatic interest in China's protracted war prepared the ground, but Jim himself added something that gripped people's hearts as well as stimulated their minds. She thought it was his complete naturalness of manner combined with his absorption in his subject and his clear, simple way of presenting his pictures. He had no pulpit pomp, and his style before a banquet, an auditorium audience, or a congregation differed little from his conversational way of talking.

Many people were saying that they saw the point of missions more clearly than ever before and understood China in a new light; a number of them commented on their more vivid realization of the need for social change. At one Young People's Conference the participants voted to go without their lunches for two days and sent the money to Chinese war relief; in a little western church an elderly woman brought her diamond ring to Endicott after the sermon to be sold for China. After an address in a Toronto high school an English teacher told her students that they had just listened to the finest public speech they would hear in their lifetimes, and she proceeded to use eight blackboard slates to analyse the performance.

Mary joked to a friend that the family was on the lookout to keep Jim feeling humble and reported that 'no abnormal swellings' had as yet been noticed.

The United Church headquarters was also pleased as letters began to arrive from different quarters. 'I have not attended a better missionary meeting anywhere and I have been to one or two in the Albert Hall in London, England,' wrote the organizer in Brandon; 'James Endicott, Jr, did the church a great piece of service last night ... The more men of his kind get about telling people what is being done and what is to be done, the better will be the response to the missionary tasks of the Church.' Endicott's campaign is 'fundamental and inspiring as well as informative,' wrote Dr J.H. Arnup, general secretary of the Board of Foreign Missions. 'It seems to me,' Arnup told him, 'you strike a deeper note than when you were on furlough last. You have a great mission to discharge to the home church. More power to you.'[2]

From a desperate financial situation in 1942, when the Board of Foreign Missions was finding it 'all but impossible to carry on,' the fund-raising campaigns sparked by Jim Endicott, Dr Robert McClure, and other missionary advocates had by 1944 liquidated the deficit of $1,750,000.[3]

Criticisms of Endicott's approach were not lacking, especially from some of the more theologically conservative brethren. One correspondent suggested that he was substituting socialism for the gospel, thereby not only misrepresenting Christianity but holding out false hopes to mortal beings of a heaven in this life: nothing short of immortality could satisfy the yearnings and aspirations of the human soul. This critic warned that until preachers were obedient to the heavenly vision and 'authoritatively announced the gospel of Eternal Life,' their preaching would be in vain and the churches empty.

When Victoria University, the Missionary and Maintenance Fund, and Timothy Eaton Memorial Church combined to confer an honorary doctor of divinity degree upon Endicott, he was naturally pleased; but he sensed that this decision had caused questioning and possibly opposition in more orthodox circles. In making the presentation, the principal of Emmanuel College intimated that, although theology was supreme in the church, the committee was showing its tolerance by giving this honour to a man who had distinguished himself in social service rather than in theology. The implication that the social gospel lacked a basis in theology angered Endicott. Although he felt honoured to receive the degree and made a positive speech at the convocation, he couldn't help interjecting that he had not been impressed with 'the great swing over to Karl Barth who was so sure of the transcendent omnipotence of God the Sovereign and so unsure and silent on the eternal unrighteousness of the concentration camp and the enslavement of the workers' by Nazi Germany. 'This feeling,' he added, 'is probably not one of the reasons why I am being given this degree.'[4]

After the Japanese attacked the United States at Pearl Harbor in December 1941, turning the China war into a wider Pacific war and postponing indefinitely the time when the Endicotts could return to China, Endicott volunteered to help promote the war effort in Canada. Speaking on behalf of Victory Loan campaigns and to army camps he cited heroic acts from China's valiant struggle for survival and seized upon the war aims proclaimed in President Roosevelt's Four Freedoms, the Atlantic Charter, and Churchill's inspiring oratory: 'This is no war of chieftains or of princes, of dynasties or national ambition; it is a war of peoples and of causes'; the war represented 'the forward march of the common people, in all lands, towards their just and true inheritance, and towards the broader and fuller age.' Such declarations of intent could not, of course, be relied upon to shape the post-war world; the future would be determined more by the way Canada and her allies organized themselves for victory. In order to influence this future in the direction of socialism, the Endicotts decided to join the Co-operative Commonwealth Federation.

The CCF had been badly split when war came because J.S. Woodsworth, who had struggled in vain to have Parliament take the profits out of armament-making and to prohibit the export of war materials to Japan, Germany, Italy, and Franco's Spain, had taken a pacifist position. War grew out of capitalist profit-seeking, Woodsworth believed, and the only policy for a true socialist was to oppose his country's involvement in foreign war and to fight for the social revolution at home. To this general position he attached a strong emotional bias, which resulted in dogmatic pacifism.[5]

Theoretically Endicott could be convinced that killing people in war was not consistent with the ultimate truths of Christianity, but he rejected the pacifist position as impossible because there was no practical framework in the international order in which it could be practised. In the end pacifists rested on the results of other people's sacrifices; their very right to be pacifists and to say so in public depended on someone else going to die in front of a German tank or a Japanese machine-gun. A just war, such as that of the Chinese or the people of Europe against fascism, had to be supported even while using the opportunity to change the war system and to undermine all imperialisms. For this reason Endicott approved of the CCF National Convention's view that the struggle against international fascism was 'part of the people's revolution to usher in a new era of brotherhood and security for all the peoples of the world.'[6]

In South York, where the Endicotts lived, a by-election in February 1942 resulted in the first CCF victory in Ontario when Joe Noseworthy, head of English at Vaughan Road Collegiate, decisively defeated Arthur Meighen, national leader of the Conservative party; the ruling Liberals had declined to field a candidate. It was a bitterly fought contest in which Endicott took the platform beside Noseworthy on several occasions. Meighen's plan for total war mobilization was conscription of manpower; the CCF campaigners derided this as the capitalists 'wanting to take the widow's last son to protect the millionaire's last dollar.' The CCF would agree to conscription, but only if wealth and industry were also fully mobilized. They demanded an excess profits tax, public ownership of the war industries, and a general system of social welfare to protect every citizen against the hazards of unemployment, sickness, disability, and old age. The call for conscription and the growing interest in social welfare continued to dominate Canadian politics, but it was the Liberal government of Mackenzie King which managed to side-step the conscription crisis as well as adopt half of the CCF's social programme to reap most of the political benefits.

After the South York by-election, politics in Ontario grew even more heated, especially when the CCF, under the leadership of E.B. Jolliffe, also of a Chinese missionary family, came within a few seats of forming the government of the province following the general election of August 1943. The best piece of campaign literature came from the pen of an old friend, Dave Ketchum, a satirical *Hymn to the Glory of Free Enterprise*, which Endicott rejoiced to recite from the platform on every possible occasion:

Of freedom this and freedom that the drooling leftist chatters,
But freedom for Free Enterprise is all that really matters;
   This freedom was ordained by God; upon it rest all others,
   For man's divinest impulse is to over-reach his brothers;
And so to this celestial urge we make our offering votive;
Behind all human greatness lies the noble Profit Motive.

Chorus of Bankers, Brokers, Executives and Advertising Men:
Then hail we now Free Enterprise,
   Extol and give it praise!
In it the world's salvation lies,
Without it every freedom dies;
O glorious Free Enterprise –
   The enterprise that pays![7]

The conservative, capitalist elements became seriously alarmed and began a well-financed, mendacious propaganda campaign to prove that CCF socialism was the same as Hitler's national socialism and stood for regimentation, dictatorship, and the confiscation of wealth; the choice, they told the people, was between 'free enterprise' and 'national socialism.'[8] 'Somebody is wasting a lot of money sending around pamphlets to prove that the CCF is a "menace to Canada,"' Endicott told a Toronto Board of Trade meeting in the Crystal Ballroom of the King Edward Hotel on 31 January 1944. 'I hope you are not among the political illiterates who pay for these,' he added. 'The menace to Canada is disease, ignorance, poverty, the underpaid and overworked labour of Quebec, the poverty-stricken farms of ten years ago, private greed and free grab making wasteful use of our natural resources.'

Endicott's remarks to the Toronto businessmen were highly provocative, but they listened intently because his dramatic theme was what seven thousand Japanese bombers over his head in Chungking had taught him. Democracy in China, he said, had been betrayed by the very governments in the world which should have been most interested in bringing about democracy. China's cry for help when the Japanese seized Manchuria had been a test case of the West's sincerity in upholding a new and better world order. The Western democracies had ignored China and appeased Japan, turning down the compromise proposals of the League of Nations' Lytton Commission to establish an autonomous Manchuria under Chinese sovereignty 'largely because of "red bogeys."' Western free enterprise countries, Endicott continued, showed themselves incapable of giving the leadership that the world needed because they were living by their fears and their greed: fear of social change in the enslaved colonial areas of the world; greed for the quick profits that could come from cheap and unprotected labour. 'We talk a lot about the dignity of labour,' he added, 'but Canadian labour is still the Cinderella of our society.' And a lot of people were doing their best to keep it there. Hoping to leave a trail of uneasiness behind him to justify the theme that there was 'a pulse in the conscience of the world that throbs into life at the very name Chungking,'[9] Endicott pointed his finger at his affluent crowd: 'You haven't done your duty to the men at the front when you have given them cheers or monuments,' he said. 'You have to bring about a reformed social order with economic security upon the basis of expanding welfare.' Through the efforts of Sun Yat-sen in China, Lenin in Russia, and Gandhi and Nehru in India, he claimed this had become the meaning of freedom to the common people all over the world.[10]

The speech received a mixed reaction. C.L. Burton, president of the Robert Simpson Company, was upset because he considered that Endicott had attacked the capitalist system; he therefore launched into an impromptu speech about his own personal case, how he had started out by washing windows and had risen to be head of his company, generally pointing out the finer qualities of capitalists. When the applause for Burton had died down, the chairman thanked Endicott especially warmly for his address, and, having declared that Burton had opposed him in an uncalled-for fashion, received an even stronger, overwhelming response from the audience. The ovation and the discussion that followed suggested more than politeness to a guest speaker. The radicalism of Endicott, a missionary home from the East, one of their own, as much a member of the upper crust as anyone in the room, had a disturbing yet somehow compelling effect. In imagination, perhaps, each member of the audience could visualize part of himself on a familiar trail: early Sunday School lessons about Dives and Lazarus, stories of the prophets' condemnation of the rich and the moral imperative to make things better, the sacrifices in a great war to make the world safe for democracy, images of a long-suffering and exploited people in China needing help, the remembrance of depression in a wealthy country like Canada casting reasonable doubts upon the ability of the profit incentive to meet the needs of human society in a just and adequate manner. These were the reasons why Endicott had joined the movement for a co-operative commonwealth, and they were the basis for his appeal to others to do likewise. Although Endicott spoke of oppression and condemned greed, he did not talk in terms of struggle and class conflict, alarming concepts that were still outside his way of thinking. His was the approach of an idealistic intellectual who thought in terms of good and evil, of the light and darkness that was in every person; and he believed that if people would only respond to their better nature, to their reason and their reserves of goodwill, that all the necessary changes of social organization could be brought about. Even if his audience could not accept many of the things he had to say, they went away feeling they had heard something important, perhaps worthy of further reflection.

Among many to reprove Endicott for his political campaigning was Flora McCrea Eaton, patron of his home church. Earlier Lady Eaton had warmly congratulated him on his honorary degree and had entertained the Endicott family at her estate in King City. But now she was sorely disappointed. In a letter to Endicott, she said she believed those who argued that the CCF programme and the national socialism of Hitler were similar; government controls as advocated by the CCF were wasteful, created bureaucracy, and destroyed initiative; she believed thoroughly in private enterprise and big business which, she said, did more in the last depression to relieve the misery than all the government schemes; Jolliffe and Noseworthy seemed like worthy individuals but they took orders from M.J. Coldwell, 'an outsider whose roots are not in Canada'; she did not want to see Canada torn apart by 'isms'; her forefathers did not ask the government for security, they sought that of God and builded well; it was Christianity that the world needed and nothing else would save it; if Christians would only apply Christianity there was no need of all these new political parties. She teased Endicott to 'pull your rabbits out of the hat' to make things right.

Endicott wrote a careful and conciliatory answer. He expected that she would not approve his left-wing politics but he hoped she was not taken by surprise; they were more or less implied in many of the things he had said. He related a Sunday School joke which came to mind – of the small boy who came home and announced the Golden Text as 'And Enoch walked with God and he was not what God took him for!' He 'pulled his rabbits out of the hat,' explaining the CCF programme by quoting eminent authorities including the Archbishop of Canterbury to bolster his position, and concluded that he did not see how any reasonable person who was well informed as to the philosophy, purpose, and method of fascism as it was seen in Germany, Italy, and Spain could possibly say that the CCF had anything essential in common with it – not even if the CCF programme was called 'national socialism.' It would be just as fair, he wrote, to say that the war aims of England and Germany are the same because they both believe in compulsory education and have socialized their postal services in the same way. Endicott was blunt in his characterization of fascism: Hitler, Mussolini, and Franco were 'the strong men,' the 'hired assassins and paid murderers employed by feudal landlords and monopoly capitalists' like Thyssen and Krupp to beat down all democratic progress, keep the people 'in their place,' abolish the menace of popular vote, and to break up the labour unions. Since they refused honest, internal reform, the only real programme they had left was armament for external aggression.[11] Lady Eaton never spoke to him again.

The rebukes Endicott received were more than offset by the new friends he made in the CCF. About this time David Lewis, national secretary of the party, proposed that Endicott become a full-time CCF secretary in Toronto, a proposition to which he was strongly attracted because he found himself drawn more and more to the economics of brotherhood rather than to the philanthropy of good works. However, ministerial colleagues argued that he could do much more to swing the moderate people within the church by remaining at his present task. 'The church is really a tough job,' they said, 'if it is tackled thoroughly.' Also, since he had spoken in churches across Canada for the last two years upholding the missionary effort as worthwhile, he could not very well now go into some other work. As a result he decided that he would do the movement more good by staying in the church and letting it be known that he favoured the CCF rather than by making it a direct job.[12] Meanwhile the South York CCF and some local teachers asked Mary to run for the Board of Education in York Township. To the astonishment of the family she won the election on New Year's Day 1944, the only CCF-sponsored candidate in the

Toronto area to survive the frenzied advertising campaign led by a Tory firm called Reliable Exterminators Inc. By this time the upsurge of the CCF in central Canada was over, the combined result of hostile propaganda and the platform-stealing tactics of Mackenzie King.

During his furlough several proposals were made for Endicott to be lent for work connected with the war in the Far East. One suggestion came from General Victor Odlum, Canadian ambassador in Chungking, who wrote Prime Minister Mackenzie King requesting that Endicott be sent to the embassy as 'a guide on Chinese customs and prejudices'; with his reputation in China, Odlum thought, he was the sort of man who could be taken on as a permanent member of the embassy staff.[13] However, whether because of his activities on behalf of CCF candidates or for some other reason, no request for his services was forthcoming from Mr King. On another occasion when Air Commodore Vernon Heakes told Endicott that Canada might send a couple of Canadian fighter squadrons to help China, he volunteered to go with the group as interpreter. The American War Department also sent him a request to do liaison work for the American army in China for which full expenses would be paid.[14]

The effect of these proposals, which were either stillborn or slow in maturing, was to make Endicott more restless than ever to get back to China where his special expertise could be used. It was encouraging for him to learn that this time, in contrast to the case in 1934, the West China Mission and the West China Union University were both strongly pressing for his early return to the field on the grounds of his 'experience with officials, his use of the language, his wide connections among different classes of people [and] his reputation for "understanding."'[15] The only obstacles to his return were the lack of transportation, financial problems created by inflation in China, and separation from the family.

As he waited to return to China in 1943 and through the first half of 1944, news from that country became increasingly pessimistic. Stories about the growing disunity between the Kuomintang and the Communists began leaking past the censors, accompanied by rumours of corruption and scandal surrounding the Chungking regime. A picture emerged of Chinese officials, including most of the top leaders, 'leading lives of ease and luxury' while the peasants starved, of Kuomintang leaders 'more concerned with suppressing the Communists than with any other problems in China,' and just waiting for the right psychological moment to attack them.[16] The *Ottawa Evening Citizen* of 4 April 1944 suggested pointedly that while the Canadian people gladly and gratefully sent what military and other aid they could to China, they would like some assurance that the materials 'produced by Canadian working men and women will be used against our Japanese enemies.' Then, on 1 May, *Life* magazine published a dramatic exposé by Theodore H. White, describing the Kuomintang party as a 'corrupt political clique that combines some of the worst features of Tammany Hall with the Spanish Inquisition,' more bent upon civil war with the Communists than on fighting the Japanese.

Fears about the deterioration of the Chungking regime had begun to bother Endicott early in 1943 when Madame Chiang Kai-shek was on a six-month rest cure and propaganda visit to North America. In her speech to the American Congress, she said no courageous or convincing words about the coming of democracy in China; at a critical time in the war, when the British were still being driven back on the Suez Canal and it was not certain that the Russians could hold at Stalingrad, she drove a wedge between Allied friendships by demanding that the United States turn its attention to the immediate defeat of Japan. Her line convinced Endicott that time was running out for a corrupt and reactionary government in Chungking that refused to reform, and that Madame Chiang's mission was special pleading for them; they were gambling on the defeat of Japan by the United States before their internal weaknesses caught up with them. In August 1943 Endicott predicted that 'Japan will have to be defeated in the air and on the sea, and by military campaigns in the East Indies and Burma, practically without the aid of China.'[17]

In private conversations Endicott talked quite freely about 'the powerful growth of Fascism in China,' but out of reluctance to destroy the reservoir of goodwill towards China which he had done so much to build up in Canada he refrained from speaking about it in public. A few weeks before his return to China, however, in the summer of 1944, when the Canadian Broadcasting Corporation invited him to make a national radio broadcast, he spoke out on the 'Danger Signals in the Far East.' Although the speech contained no startling new revelations, parts of his first draft were censored by the CBC as being antagonistic to Canada's Chinese ally. In the broadcast he described the wartime profiteering and speculation leading to uncontrolled inflation, and quoted from Vincent Sheean's new book, *Between the Thunder and the Sun* (1943), to the effect that never before in human history had such huge fortunes been made for such a long time in the midst of such human misery. He spoke of the fascist suppression of discussion, thought control, and secret arrests of students by the Chinese Ministry of Education. He stated as an 'established fact' that in the guerilla territories north of the Yellow River there had developed 'the best democratic life of Asia,' and he quoted Madame Sun Yat-sen on the attempts of the central government to destroy that sector by civil war. In a part that was censored he referred to *China's Destiny*, a new book purportedly written by Chiang Kai-shek which made clear that Chiang would not countenance agrarian reform and advocated an imperialist expansion programme for China that was violent in its anti-foreign sentiments; to Endicott, who still clung to the illusion of Madame Chiang's liberalizing influence, this sounded much more like the views of the feudal reactionaries in the Kuomintang than it did like Chiang Kai-shek.

In spite of the serious problems, he urged that China's allies should exercise patient understanding of her difficulties because China's war had been much longer than the West's and it had been much more disastrous for her. He still had confidence 'that the great leadership of Chiang Kai-shek' would 'overcome the chief strains and bring China safely through.'[18]

With those words of muted optimism, Endicott bade farewell to his family and set out for China in July 1944. A prolonged family separation, common in those wartime years, appeared to be inevitable. Mary, torn between going with Jim and staying home with the children – all of whom were attending high school, except Norman who was already in the air force – reluctantly accepted the mission's advice to wait in Canada until the war was over. Jim Endicott, meanwhile, would witness some of the most tumultuous years in China's modern revolutionary history; as a participant in those struggles he emerged three years later to find himself in quite unfamiliar circumstances and in many ways a profoundly changed human being.

PART THREE

CHINA IN
REVOLUTION
1944–1947

Dear Mr. Pearson:

... What Endicott says about the possibility of an agrarian revolution is worth noting. I know of no foreigner in China who is in closer touch with the common people and who has wider contacts outside of official circles. There most certainly is a rising tide of resentment in China against governmental authorities who are not only taking a terrific toll from the people to carry on civil war, but are guilty of greater corruption than has been known since the days of the warlords and the Manchus.

There is no doubt that what Endicott says about the ability of the Communists to organize this growing discontent into an effective agrarian revolution is correct. I was in interior China in 1926–27, and have seen how rapidly hatred can be whipped up into white heat by relatively few well-trained and determined organizers. That was before the Kuomintang had driven out of its ranks all effective liberals and revolutionaries. Today, these leaders are in the Chinese Communist Party, and have had twenty years of experience, and are supported by an army of trained organizers. Conditions are ripe for revolution.

I cannot share Endicott's conviction about 'a real agrarian revolution' rolling after the harvest this year. Without leadership it may take decades to gather sufficient momentum to 'roll.' If, however, Communists can 'infiltrate special corps into the areas where there are peasant revolts,' what he predicts is not impossible if he increased the time necessary from 'weeks' to 'months' or 'years' ...

Yours sincerely,
Chester Ronning
First Secretary

Mr. L.B. Pearson
Under Secretary of State for
    External Affairs
Department of External Affairs, Ottawa

Aboard the S.S. Priam

The long ocean voyage back to Asia in the summer of 1944 was a time for thinking. Jim Endicott and sixty other passengers had boarded the *S.S. Priam* in New York harbour on 6 July 1944, one month after D-Day, when the Allied armies had swept across the English Channel to open a second front in Europe. It had been a weary wait while everyone was checked by customs and immigration in preparation for the five-week journey across the South Atlantic and Indian oceans to Bombay. From there, Endicott would travel back to his mission field in Chengtu via rail to Calcutta and then by air over the Himalayan hump.

The *Priam*, a new American freighter with regular cabin space for only thirty passengers, was armed with anti-aircraft artillery and a naval gun; it carried many modern gadgets in order that enemy airplanes, submarines, and raiders could not get close without their presence being known; the life-jackets were of the latest type with a little red light on the shoulder in case the passengers were spilled into the water at night. Endicott was surprised at the number of women on board, all bound for India, some to rejoin husbands, one to be married. He shared a cabin with two other men: a Mennonite missionary on his way to India, a fundamentalist, but none the less reasonable and tolerant in Endicott's opinion; and a handsome young lad, trained as a paratrooper, who was going out on some sort of special mission to do with better relations among Allied troops in India. Other passengers who attracted Endicott's attention included a group of American army officers, all headed for General Joseph Stilwell's headquarters in Chungking, and five Chinese professors, four of whom had been to America to 'explain China,' while the fifth, Endicott concluded warily, after some conversation, was a Kuomintang secret service agent, German-educated, who had been keeping overseas Chinese students under surveillance.

His more intimate involvement with these travellers arose out of a decision by the ship's officers to organize lectures in the saloon three evenings a week, in order to help keep passengers' minds off air alarms, artillery practices, and lifeboat drills. Endicott was asked to start off on the subject, 'What seven thousand Japanese bombers taught me.' His forceful explanation of his interpretation of the origins of the Second World War, stressing the policy of appeasement and the Western powers' fear of the 'red bogey,' caused lively discussion, as did his conclusion based upon a favourite wartime quotation from Churchill: 'I cannot doubt that we have the strength to carry a good cause forward, and to break down the barriers that stand between the working man of every nation and that free and more abundant life that science is ready to afford.'

As a result of this talk several of the American officers came to ask if he would give them lessons in Chinese. Endicott readily agreed and they began working by the direct method three hours a day. In the course of these sessions the officers became friendly and talkative, especially about the sluggish pace of the Chinese contribution to the war effort against Japan.

In the face of Japan's latest offensive, codenamed Ichigo, which was directed against American air bases in central southern China, Chiang Kai-shek's armies had melted away without offering any serious resistance. Thirty-four of his divisions had been routed in Honan province, and the city of Changsha in Hunan, which had three times previously repelled Japanese assaults, fell without a fight. The lack-lustre performance of Chiang's armies disappointed his foreign allies and angered General Stilwell, American commander of the China-Burma-India theatre of war, whose outspoken manner had earned him the nickname 'Vinegar Joe.' Stilwell, who had served as military attaché at the United States legation in Peking in the 1930s and was thoroughly familiar with Chinese affairs, suspected that Chiang was not committing his best troops to battle. He also believed that Chiang and his close associates were enriching themselves personally while hoarding US-supplied arms for domestic political reasons; in the meantime, Chiang was relying upon US marines to defeat Japan via the Pacific islands. In order to avert the possibility that Chinese resistance to Japan might collapse totally, President Roosevelt had asked Chiang to place Stilwell in direct command of all China's armed forces, an unprecedented, and in some ways an insulting, request from one head of state to another. While Chiang temporized, seeking to thwart American pressure without cutting off the coveted stream of US supplies, Stilwell pressed ahead on his own to boost China's military effectiveness.

One of Stilwell's ambitions was to make better use of the Chinese Communist forces. To this end he had engineered the breakdown of Chiang Kai-shek's *de facto* blockade of the Communist-controlled regions in northern China to the extent of establishing a US military observer team at the Communist headquarters in Yenan and by forcing permission for groups of American correspondents to visit the Communist areas. Stilwell had begun planning for a landing of US troops in Japanese-occupied North China on a beachhead to be prepared by Communist-led guerilla bands.[1] Some of the American officers aboard the *S.S. Priam* expected to be involved in this scheme, and one of the more senior ones asked Endicott in confidence if he would be willing to join them for liaison work should the opportunity arise.[2]

It was an intriguing proposition. Apart from an opportunity to do some useful war service, to which the church could hardly object since it had released other missionaries for war work, he was eager to see for himself the accomplishments of the Communist regime and its philosophy at work. He had been impressed by the young revolutionaries he had taught in the Chungking prison in 1933, and, after hearing reports from Yenan in 1938, he had recommended to his own middle school students that they study seriously the reform proposals of Mao Tse-tung.[3] From Agnes Smedley, the American author who had worked with the Eighth Route Army and had visited the Endicotts at their home in Duckling Pond in 1939, Endicott had learned that the revolutionaries welcomed missionaries in their midst as long as they brought a religion that was concerned for the welfare of the people here and now; perhaps the US army proposal, if it developed, would provide a chance to investigate such a possibility on the spot.

There was another, more personal, family reason for Endicott's interest in an opportunity to go north. While he had developed an admiration for some of the achievements of the Soviet Union, especially as described by Hewlett Johnson, Dean of Canterbury, in his book, *The Socialist Sixth of the World* (1939), and perhaps had a cautious respect for Marxists, he had to confess that he really knew very little about communism. But now, his eldest son, Norman, just turned eighteen and fighting with the Royal Canadian Air Force, had declared himself 'once and for all a Communist.'[4]

Norman took his politics seriously. When leaving for overseas he had given the family a recording of Beethoven's inspiring Ninth Symphony and left instructions that if anything should happen to him his relatives were not to grieve or even to hold a service but should read more and more about Marxism. During the spring of 1944, when his home leaves coincided with his father's days free of speaking engagements, the dinner table rang with thunderous argument; Norman would quote from Lenin and criticize his father for trying to preach on the immorality of capitalism to the wealthy parishioners of Timothy Eaton Memorial Church. Such Christian socialism, as Lenin had said, Norman argued, was utopian: 'It criticized capitalist society, it condemned and damned it, it dreamed of its destruction, it indulged in fancies of a better world order and endeavoured to convince the rich of the immorality of exploitation. But utopian socialism could not point the real way out. It could not explain the laws of development nor point to the social force which is capable of becoming the creator of a new society.' In a word, Norman said, it failed to accept the reality of the 'class struggle' and the ultimate need for the 'dictatorship of the proletariat.'[5]

With the brash self-assertion and single-mindedness of the young and the newly converted, Norman was unsparing in his criticism: God and the church were established institutions which would not work for a just and classless society in an intelligent manner; the theory 'love thy neighbour as thyself' could not be applied if your neighbour was an oppressor; such a passive theory would not help the workers to organize themselves to fight for social change. How much more powerful was the cry of the Communist Manifesto: 'The proletarians have nothing to lose but their chains. They have a world to win. Working men of all countries, unite!'

Nor did Norman spare his parents' ventures into politics: the CCF's 'lust for power' would cause a strong fascist reaction, whereas the Communist Labour Progressive party's call for a broad Liberal-Labour coalition with Mackenzie King in the next election was the only correct path for post-war reconstruction; the anti-Soviet, 'anti-red' CCF crowd were traitors to the working class, 'a sort of fifth column in our midst,' who would betray the workers as the social democrats allegedly did in Germany in the 1920s, and therefore it was more important to defeat them before worrying about the enemy.[6]

Norman's cutting attacks, often brilliantly argued, did not cause a rupture in family relations because his parents, especially his mother, recognized that his passion for a cause was the same zeal that had sent his forbears to China. Also, although they rejected the maligning of the CCF party and continued to believe that the church based upon the teaching and example of Jesus could be an active force for human brotherhood, there seemed to be sufficient truth in the Marxist position to warrant further study. It was with considerable anticipation, therefore, that Endicott sent a crudely coded message to Mary en route from Capetown suggesting that if she heard he had asked for leave of absence from the mission for a special war job she would know that it 'had to do with the results of teaching the boys in that prison.'

Meanwhile, as the *S.S. Priam* churned through the waters of the South Atlantic, Endicott had to admit to himself that never looking at any Marxist-Leninist literature was not a very good way of knowing what it was all about, and he began perusing some of the pamphlets Norman had recommended. After reading the Communist Manifesto he remarked in astonishment that there was no other political document in history that was quite so up-to-date after one hundred years. Furthermore, the writing of Marx and Engels was greatly illumined when read against the background of Capetown where, during a brief stopover, Endicott saw thousands of black workers coming out of the factories; denied economic justice, educational opportunity, and parliamentary representation, they were ragged and poor and in their eyes it was easy to see and to feel a smouldering resentment against their white oppressors. He got the feeling that the communists would be bringing in the sheaves.

As applied in Canada, however, it seemed to Endicott that Marx would have favoured a people's movement such as the CCF. He could not understand why the LPP felt it could not co-operate with the CCF programme; similar parties were co-operating in other parts of the world. Was the main argument of the LPP that any attempt to bring in large measures of socialism would result in fascist reaction? Or did they feel that the CCF members were idealistic, unscientific socialists who were using the programme to get power and would not carry it out, as Ramsay MacDonald had failed to do in Britain? 'Either I don't understand the real nature of the CCF or else the comrades have made a mistake in judgement,' he wrote home. It could not be denied, he thought, that the CCF would greatly increase the economic power of the working class and would swing the farmers over to the co-operative idea and experience. While the election of T.C. Douglas as premier of Saskatchewan at the head of a CCF government in 1944 did not mean 'socialism tomorrow,' he believed it was a more important step in that direction than voting for Mackenzie King's Liberals who had already 'unwillingly and begrudgingly passed about all' the social security legislation that the free enterprise business community would allow.[7] Debates on these questions grew in profusion in the family correspondence during the next few years.

As the *Priam* made its way across the Indian Ocean the Chinese passengers also became more friendly. Once it was clear that the KMT secret service agent was properly seasick and that Endicott was aware of the dangerous political realities of life in China, Fei Hsiao-tung, a noted anthropologist,[8] and the other professors opened up and talked quite frankly about the situation in their country.

They were deeply disturbed at the prospect of an alliance of American capital with the Kuomintang for the purpose of industrializing China. Such an alliance, of foreign capital with the Kuomintang as policemen keeping 'law and order,' would lead to civil war because the leftists north of the Yellow River would never submit to such an exploiting, oppressive regime. To avoid civil war, they said, there must be a great increase of democratic rights in China, both political and economic.

The professors also gave Endicott details of China's universities. The centre of liberal thought, they said, was to be found in the Peking universities, which had taken refuge from the Japanese by moving to Kunming, the capital of Yunnan province; their democratic bias contrasted sharply with the former Shanghai universities, now located in Chungking, which were strongly pro-Kuomintang, narrowly nationalistic in outlook, and dominated by the fascist-minded KMT Youth Corps. The professors had hoped that a third centre, the Christian universities in Chengtu, would maintain independence and draw the better class of student away from the oppressive atmosphere of the party-dominated universities. However, they expressed disappointment with Christian education in China, saying that the missionaries, by their 'surrender to the inflation,' had thrown themselves onto the mercy of the most reactionary elements as well as the most corrupt people in China for their financial existence. If the church was not prepared to support the Chengtu institutions as free and independent Christian centres of thought and life, they had better close them up.[9]

Considering himself fortunate to have received this overview, Endicott told his new-found friends that he intended to test out the amount of freedom there really was on campus; if justified, he planned to ask the church to close down the Youth Corps building at West China Union University in the name of academic freedom and integrity. He related to them a previous unsuccessful attempt to block the entry of the Youth Corps onto the campus at Chengtu. When the Board of Governors met in Toronto in November 1943, his wife Mary had gone to the meeting with some friends and, after pointing out that the Youth Corps represented one of the more fascist strains in the Chinese government, she had urged the governors not only to view the situation with alarm but if possible to delay having any responsibility for conforming to the demand for a Youth Corps building, the use and control of which was out of their hands, until they could be reassured that such a course was 'either advisable or inevitable.' Since the building was already under construction it was too late to stop it. However, in view of the objections raised, the board had decided to cable that it was contrary to their principles to allow any outside organization to own and control a building on the campus; they would build the place themselves and lend it to the Youth Corps.[10]

The weakness of this compromise caused Endicott's listeners to snort in disgust. They said it confirmed their worst fears that at this critical time Christian education would become the handmaiden of Kuomintang reaction. The depth of their cynicism disturbed Endicott, but he did not believe that in general the church had sold out its possibility for independent action and influence for democracy. Whether it would be in the north with Stilwell's forces or at his usual place in Chengtu, he felt more impatient than ever to be back in China, to see for himself and to act where he could.

From the time of his return to China in 1944 until he was forced by the renewed outbreak of civil war to leave in 1947, Endicott's life was marked by conflicts and intense inner struggle, leading to his resignation from the West China Mission and the ministry as well as to the verge of nervous exhaustion. How was his break with the mission to be explained, especially since he had just spent two years preaching for the missionary cause all across Canada and had been plied with honours by a grateful church? The hypothesis of the Mission Board was that he had subconsciously made a transfer of his faith and hope from Christianity to communism.[11] Some of the things Endicott said, especially when he was angry, could be interpreted that way. But it was far too simple an explanation, erroneous in substance, a convenient way to dismiss Endicott from the conscience of the church. His new fraternal views on communism and on the relationship of Christianity to this rising secular challenge were not the result of some sudden conversion or revelation, but grew mainly out of his experience of daily life in wartime China.

He had done a lot of thinking about his political philosophy in Canada and aboard the *S.S. Priam*, but his soul-searching crisis arose in the first instance from his agreement to assist in a stepped-up, anti-Japanese, war effort, which Chiang Kai-shek was supposed to be preparing in co-operation with the Communists and under the leadership of General Stilwell. This experience resulted first in shock at the corruption and brutality of the Kuomintang camp, whose 'democratic possibilities' he had so recently been touting with extravagant praise, and, second, in the conviction that Chiang was deliberately stalling in order to save his forces for a civil war against movements for social change, Communist and otherwise, that were long overdue. At the university in Chengtu, Endicott was drawn deeper and deeper into the struggle to prevent civil war. His students found him a sympathetic listener when they discussed their difficulties with the fascist Kuomintang Youth Corps, the same group he had opposed so vigorously during his work in the New Life Movement, and he responded to their invitations to give public lectures on Sun Yat-sen's principles of democracy. They in turn included him in study groups that discussed current events, analysed modern Chinese history, and organized daring demonstrations that displeased the Kuomintang authorities. He was immensely impressed by the intelligence, integrity, courage, and dedication of these young people, some of whom he believed were secretly Communists, inspired by Mao Tse-tung, a man of whom he knew next to nothing. As a result of these experiences, he became deeply troubled by the realization that those who sacrificed most in life and were giving real leadership in China's time of crisis were not those who espoused the great cause to which he had dedicated his life but those who were despised by his missionary colleagues.

CHAPTER SEVENTEEN

Save China by democracy

When Endicott arrived back in Szechuan in September 1944, he found that Chiang Kai-shek had inaugurated a few weeks of liberalization. Smarting under domestic and foreign criticism of the Kuomintang's one-party rule, which contradicted earlier pledges for more freedom for other parties, and weakened by his inability to keep Japan at bay, the generalissimo had summoned a meeting of the People's Political Council. This body of two hundred prominent citizens, representing different areas and various political persuasions, had been created when the defence of Hankow was being prepared in 1938, but it had seldom been consulted since.[1] Council members were invited to acquaint Chiang with the grievances of the people; strong criticism would not only be tolerated, he said, but welcome.

In the surge of public opinion that followed, complaints against officials were aired and demands for a coalition government, to include the Communists and other smaller parties, as well as the Kuomintang, were put forward for the first time. It was a time of great public excitement.

Then, suddenly, having fooled the more gullible foreign diplomats and received the desired publicity abroad, especially in America, Chiang tried to clamp down. He accused those who complained about autocratic rule, corruption, and half-hearted conduct of the war of accepting the rumours and tricks of the Japanese invaders and their Chinese collaborators. Unauthorized meetings were forbidden.

The effect of this prohibition was to draw intellectuals, businessmen, liberals, radicals, and communists closer together to demand freedom of speech, press, and organization, and other democratic rights. An extraordinary meeting, held in the gymnasium of West China Union University on Saturday, 7 October 1944, by the student associations in Chengtu, reflected the mood of popular discontent. It was organized in defiance of the government's order, to hear the report of the city's delegates to the People's Political Council. Long before the appointed hour, twelve hundred students had swarmed into the hall. Pasted on the wall above the platform were huge sheets of paper with written questions submitted by the students. One row of seats at the front was reserved for foreign friends, but as far as Endicott could see he was the only one present; there was an obvious air of nervousness and student organizers seemed anxious to have some foreigners present in case there was a disturbance.

Among the formidable list of questions, which hung like a multitude of swords of Damocles above the heads of the seven PPC delegates as they filed onto the platform, were: If we keep the one-party system, how can the present problems be solved? Can a compromise be reached between the Communist insistence on democracy and the Kuomintang insistence on unity? What concrete suggestions were made by the PPC regarding price control? How will the government use the gold brought from the United States? The August regulations of the censorship of books and magazines are more rigid than before; why is this, when the PPC urged more freedom? Why is university education interfered with and restrained by the government? A pistol is now used instead of a cane, secret police instead of discipline, party government instead of self-government; is this the way of democracy? How shall we get academic freedom?

After opening speeches by Li Huang of the Youth party and Dr Wu I-fang, a Christian who was president of Ginling Women's College, the masterpiece of the afternoon was the one-hour address of delegate Chang Lan, a white-bearded scholar in his seventies, a former university president and chairman of the Democratic League. This organization, originally founded in 1941 as the League of Democratic Political Groups, was mainly composed of intellec-tuals, university professors, middle school teachers, and middle-of-the-road people who opposed the fascist tendencies of the Kuomintang. By October 1944 the league claimed a membership of twenty thousand but was unable to hold open meetings owing to the repressive policy of the government.[2]

The interest and excitement Endicott felt in Chang Lan's performance and the student response were reflected in the report he prepared, copies of which he sent to Gerald Bell, secretary of the West China Mission, to the Depart-ment of External Affairs in Ottawa, and to Annabel Jacoby and Theodore H. White, two correspondents of *Time* magazine he had met in Chungking:

Chang Lan thoroughly enjoyed himself and the great crowd of students roared approval. 'There is only one answer to all the formidable list of sixty questions with which you have confronted your delegates. There is no democracy in China. Why has the government been allowed to become so rotten and inefficient? Why has the ruling party become so despotic? Because there is no democracy.' Throughout his address Chang Lan hammered on those two themes, no democracy, and a party which has usurped despotic powers it was never intended to have. 'There are two questions facing China now. Can the government be influenced to save the situation? Can the problem of Kuomintang-Communist relations be solved? The answer is that without the full measure of democracy that we are asking, these problems cannot be solved and we will face disaster.'

The rest of the speech was a direct, fearless and extraordinarily effective attack on the Koumintang government. Chang Lan charged it with trying to build a despotism ... He was careful to give his complete allegiance to Chiang Kai-shek and insisted that Chiang wants to give China democracy. The students roared with laughter when he said 'I had two long interviews with Chairman Chiang and he was quite clear on this point of the necessity of democracy. It is the people around him who have put blinkers on him.'

Several times Chang Lan made a direct appeal to the students. 'You must talk and shout and talk and shout until you get freedom to speak. Only in this way can you help save the situation' ... He stated bluntly that most of the Chinese divisions which were supposed to have fifteen thousand men per division had only five thousand or even as low as two thousand, yet the higher ups were drawing pay for the full division. 'We must say that the rest of the men have been "eaten" (squeezed) by the high command.' Conditions are so terrible that the 'able-bodied soldiers become thin soldiers, thin soldiers become sick soldiers, sick soldiers become dead soldiers. The average Chinese soldier, if you took his gun away from him, would pass on the roadside for a beggar. These conditions are so numerous that they could not be all described in a whole day's talk. The cure is give the people democratic rights.'

He defended the Communist position as against the Kuomintang in this way. The Kuomintang insists on unity, the Communists insist on democracy first. Unless the Communists get democracy first, unity under the Kuomintang plan would mean the physical extinction of the Communists. With the Kuomintang it is a question of change; with the Communists it is a question of existence.'

Chang Lan argued that the principles of socialism as practised by the Communists and the Min Sen [Livelihood] Principle as preached by the Kuomintang have such a large measure of similarity that they ought to be brought together very easily. He put the onus of the next step on the shoulders of the Kuomintang.[3]

A few days after the meeting Endicott noticed that the government spies were out in full force. 'All discussion is watched,' he wrote, 'and plainclothesmen with revolvers are in evidence at later meetings. Thought is frozen ...'[4]

Endicott himself had a busy programme. In addition to teaching English and ethics at West China Union University, spending a good deal of time helping the provincial Ministry of Education reform the methods of English instruction, as well as doing some confidential war work, he was soon much in demand as a speaker. Chinese business groups, chambers of commerce, and student organizations, perhaps aware that he was still tutoring the provincial governor, Chang Chun, and possibly hopeful that his foreigner's status would make him immune to police harassment – and certainly intrigued by his fluency in Chinese – extended more invitations than he could accept. He was especially in demand as a guest at the weekly Monday morning memorial meetings held at every school and college in honour of Dr Sun Yat-sen.

Endicott kept the form of his speeches within the officially approved framework of the teachings of Sun Yat-sen, but at the same time he followed Chang Lan's vigorous line. Declaring his indissoluble links with China because he was born and brought up there, he urged the students to 'save China by democracy.' There was no doubt in his mind, he said, but that the founders of the Republic of China expected to see a type of responsible democratic government in China similar to that which existed in Britain and the United States. The Chinese people themselves would gradually work out a form that embodied their own culture and traditions; but, if he knew anything about the spirit and intentions of the common people, they would not cease from struggling until they had 'what everyone would recognize as a genuine democracy.'

While avoiding any direct criticism of the government, the lively examples and analogies Endicott drew from his recent experiences in Canada delighted his audiences. He described how a new, unknown, political party with very little money had gone from door to door, 'knocking until their knuckles were sore,' asking for an opportunity to talk about the real meaning of war and society. It successfully opposed the election to Parliament of the leader of the mighty Conservative party. The CCF's book, *Make this* YOUR *Canada* (Toronto 1943), showed the people how the country was really controlled by a few great companies and demonstrated how the people themselves could control the economy. The party 'organized study groups on every street, if possible, where the people met to read and discuss.' The Chinese students applauded enthusiastically when he paused and, without much subtlety, said that of course this sort of true democratic movement, 'of the people, by the people and for the people,' could not take place unless there was freedom of speech, freedom from secret police, and freedom of association.[5]

By linking the wartime sacrifices of the youth of Canada, who were 'giving their flesh and blood to destroy the virus of fascism,' with the world-wide demand for a thorough realization of democracy after the war, Endicott, as reported in the *Hsin Hua Ji Bao*, the Communist daily, roused his listeners to a high pitch of emotion with his emphatic style:

The tide of democracy is now literally spreading over the whole world and any person or country opposing it will be engulfed. For several decades, history has taught us that no country can become strong if its political, economic and social conditions are not democratic. To attain world democracy, it is necessary to mobilize the masses of the people. The most urgent and necessary task at present is to arouse the masses.

Youth of China! You should conscientiously go about this work. In this life-and-death struggle, you should have your own language, your own thoughts, your own will. Choose the right road and strive for the peace and welfare of all mankind.[6]

If democracy was the need of the hour, Endicott had also become convinced that Sun Yat-sen's third principle, people's livelihood or socialism, could not be left out, and he worked this, to him even more basic, theme into most of his talks as well. One of his most effective sermons, which he preached from the pulpit of Sze Shen Szi Church in Chengtu on one occasion when Governor Chang Chun and his wife happened to be occupying the front pew, was about 'Moses and the Principle of Livelihood.'

For the purposes of this sermon he simplified the core of the familiar story. At a time when the Jewish people were enslaved by the Egyptians, Moses, a Jewish boy, was adopted by an Egyptian princess and was brought up in comfort and luxury. One day when Moses saw an Egyptian beating a Hebrew slave he fought with the man and killed him; afterwards he was afraid and ran away to the mountains to become a shepherd. In the course of struggling with his conscience because he had left his own people in slavery, Moses had a deep religious experience. The meaning of the Bible story about a bush that was on fire but did not burn was not obvious, but the message Moses got in his heart and mind was recorded clearly: 'And God said I have surely seen the affliction of my people that are in Egypt and have heard their cry by reason of their taskmasters ... I have seen the oppression wherewith the Egyptians oppress them. Come now, therefore, and I will send thee unto the Egyptian king that thou mayest bring forth my people.'

When Moses tried to do this, Endicott commented, it must at first have seemed impossible. The economic system, which was so cruelly crushing the physical and spiritual life of the Jewish people, seemed overpowering, for it was supported by the political, economic, priestly, and military life of the whole empire; moreover, his own people seemed hopelessly ignorant and lifeless.

The story of Moses had been taught in every Christian church and Sunday school for hundreds of years, but, Endicott said, he had never seen in religious magazines any attempt to give the story its full political and economic significance; nobody ever suggested that we had only the Jewish account of Moses and not the Egyptian account:

Just suppose for a moment you could dig up in the dry sands of Egypt some ancient records showing the minutes of the Board of Directors of the Pyramid Brick Co. Or the editorials of the newspapers which were supported by the Egyptian Building Corporation. They probably sneered at his claim to have moral or religious insight in regard to economic affairs. He was denounced as a pestilential labour agitator and racketeer, in the same way as labour organizers are denounced in the American press. He was certainly on the 'black list' of the Egyptian secret police. And even after the Egyptian king and the capitalist forces of Egypt had made an agreement with Moses to let the enslaved people go, they treacherously used military force to try to crush them.[7]

In order to make some of the parallels with contemporary China even more pointed, Endicott suggested that the forms of social welfare that Moses had worked out as a result of the experience of his people in Egypt were based upon the same ideas Sun Yat-sen had made so well known to the Chinese people in the early days of the republic: the principle of equalizing ownership of the land and curtailing capital. Every seven years there was a general release of debts known as God's year of Jubilee; slaves had to be freed and given a share of the profits of the previous seven years. There were many other practical measures for curtailing human greed and selfishness, and the great Jewish religious leaders from early times down to the time of Jesus spoke of God's year of Jubilee as one of the social actions upon which good men must act. In his first recorded sermon Jesus had spoken of good news to the poor and the oppressed because of the equalization of land and curtailing of capital required by righteous observance of God's law. The justice of any social and economic system was shown by its consideration for the weak, the widows, and the hired labourers.

Moving from the ancient world to the modern world of rapid industrial development and the period of two great and destructive wars, Endicott tried to show his fellow Christians that the examples of Moses, Jesus, and Sun Yat-sen challenged the church to make itself the internal organizing force of society. If the church was too slow and too blind to work and sacrifice for an order of justice and brotherhood, then the task of organizing the Lord's year of Jubilee would be taken up by others, outside the framework of organized Christianity.

Many of Endicott's colleagues in the Szechuan synod heard his message unwillingly, and some got the impression that he no longer believed in the

Kingdom of God. 'My own belief in the Kingdom of God was hazy,' recalled Pastor Wang Chun-hsieh many years later, 'but it definitely was not a condition on earth. In my mind politics and religion were completely separate. Our favourite Bible passage was "Seek ye first His kingdom and His righteousness, and then all material needs would be added to you."'[8]

After the service Chang Chun invited Endicott to lunch. 'It was a very strong sermon,' he said. 'Are you a communist?'

'No, I am a Christian preacher,' Endicott replied, somewhat astonished.

'Some of your fellow missionaries are now saying that you are.'

'Well, I don't care what they say; but do you think that I am?'

The governor did not pursue the question any further.[9]

CHAPTER EIGHTEEN

Secret agent 'Hialeah'

The full moon drifted above the horizon, its white light and forest shadows flickering across two figures moving silently along a trail on the slopes of Mount Omei. The local peasant, out hunting a tiger that had been eating all the dogs in the vicinity, was followed by 'Hialeah,' a secret service agent of the American army. The two men were soon joined by a dozen other peasants carrying an odd assortment of weapons. After a quarter of an hour or so the men sat down, saying they wished to talk; they wanted to talk about the human tigers that were oppressing them, and they felt free to do so only where they could avoid police surveillance.

The peasants, simple, hard-working folk, incredibly patient, with a fund of good humour and practical common sense, were evidently well acquainted with 'Hialeah,' for they plied him with questions and revealed their own minds.

'Is it not true,' they asked, 'that the u.s. Army pays for all the food it uses?'

With their suspicion confirmed they told how, at a time when the Americans were building a number of large airfields around Chengtu, the district magistrate had brazenly proclaimed: 'the Americans eat wheat and potatoes; each farmer must give one bushel of potatoes and one bushel of wheat.' All the while, as the peasants had suspected, the local government was conscripting the food, selling it to the American army, and pocketing the money.

With the moon now shining clearly through the silent trees, the peasants spoke bitterly of the unjust conscription methods which had reduced the able-bodied population of the county by one-third since the beginning of the war. There were other grievances as well. Finally they told 'Hialeah' that they knew all about the regime of Mao Tse-tung and Chu Teh in Yenan; they had seen copies of the agrarian law of the liberated areas of China, brought by returning educated youth, who had also read them chapters from an anonymous book, *One Month in Yenan*.

'We now know that it is only the rich and greedy, the "long-armed grafters," who fear democratic changes in China,' they said. 'And if ever the Communists drive into this province again there are about two thousand peasants in the semi-circle of foothills between Omeihsien and the village of Chin Lung Chang who will grab whatever arms we can find and we will rush down to the plain to help them take the city of Loshan [Kiating].'[1]

'Hialeah' was Jim Endicott's codename in the Office of Strategic Services (oss), the American intelligence-gathering unit, forerunner of the Central Intelligence Agency. Endicott had become a part-time member of this organization indirectly as a result of volunteering for Allied war service in October 1944, at a time when it appeared that the Japanese army might break through and dislodge the Chinese central government from Szechuan; the Canadian West China Mission had made contingency plans with the Royal Air Force to evacuate missionary families to India,[2] but Endicott had decided to stay behind and help with the resistance if the Japanese invaded the province.

At first, with the knowledge of the Canadian Embassy, he was assigned to the United States army. His task was to ready himself to parachute into the North China coastal area as a liaison officer with General Stilwell's forces. This was the project that had been described to him on board the S. S. Priam on the way to India. The Communist general, Chu Teh, had guaranteed to Stilwell that he could produce 500,000 troops on one month's notice, to be stationed at six different centres to receive American machine-guns, grenades, and bazookas. With this force Chu Teh said he would be able to sweep the Japanese from the coast of Shantung province and even as far south as Shanghai, undertaking to maintain an area one hundred miles along the coast and extending one hundred miles inland against Japanese attacks for a period of two weeks while the United States army established a beach-head for operations against Japan. Endicott was told that the qualifications for his job were 'ability to speak Chinese and to live with and like the Chinese';[3] there was no requirement to be pro-Communist in an ideological sense.

In preparation for the colder northern climate, Endicott bought a warm, silk-lined, quilted jacket from money raised by selling twenty old *National Geographic* magazines and two chamber pots at inflated prices. With leave-of-absence from the mission and relief from his university classes arranged, he was ready to report for duty in the first half of October 1944.[4]

Then a telegram arrived from the United States command saying: 'Remain present status.'[5]

At Chiang Kai-shek's insistence, President Roosevelt had fired Stilwell from his post as commander-in-chief; the KMT leader was determined to prevent any American operations that might boost the prestige of the Chinese Communists. Endicott was alerted a second time, a few months later, when

General Albert C. Wedemeyer, Stilwell's successor, tried to revive the North China landing, but once again Chiang was able to insert his veto.[6]

Next the army assigned Endicott to help train two hundred Chinese students at a camp in Chungking as interpreters for service with US forces. This assignment was also short-lived after Endicott wrote a report to General Wedemeyer criticizing the school on both technical and political grounds; he claimed that fully half the instruction was being conducted in Chinese and was directed to training people with an eye to civil war rather than for a united war effort. Under cover of a pretence of reform in order to appease the Americans, the interpreters were being given intensive training in how to check people's movements, how to break up local organizations, and how to re-establish the Kuomintang in all re-occupied areas; students who refused to join the KMT were being trailed by the secret service.

The generalissimo's eldest son, Chiang Ching-kuo, who was director of the camp, heard of Endicott's criticisms. Changes were promised, but none materialized. After getting tipsy at a reception the younger Chiang put his arm around Endicott and said: 'Teacher Endicott, at heart you know I am really a socialist'; like his father, Chiang Ching-kuo had studied in the Soviet Union and wanted to be considered a progressive.

Endicott responded with the story of a drunken soldier who went to see the padre. 'Padre,' said the soldier, 'I want to talk religion.'

'Jock,' replied the padre, 'you ought to be ashamed of yourself, you're drunk.'

'Of course I'm drunk,' said Jock. 'If I wasn't drunk I wouldn't want to talk religion.'

Chiang laughed, without seeing any connection. Two weeks after this incident, in mid-December, Endicott resigned from this work.[7]

Meanwhile, an American missionary colleague, Clyde Sargeant, had approached him to work for the OSS. Endicott had some grave misgivings about this suggestion because of the possible, even probable, connections between the OSS and the Chinese secret intelligence organization headed by General Tai Li. Endicott regarded Tai Li as a fascist gangster of the Himmler type who operated by intimidation, blackmail, and selective assassinations. He thus told Colonel Harley Stevens, head of the OSS in Chungking, that he would only be willing to work for the OSS if he could be guaranteed that he would not be used in any way against what he called the democratic, that is, non-Kuomintang, forces in China; apparently the Allied command, including the Canadian Department of External Affairs, had similar perceptions about Tai Li,[8] so Endicott's demand created no problem. After receiving a telegram from Stevens' superior, Colonel John Coughlin, in New Delhi, promising a 'suitable contract,' Endicott was contacted once more by Sargeant.

Sargeant assigned Endicott his codename 'Hialeah' (after the Florida race-track) and informed him that his mail drop would be the American Military Hospital in Chengtu. Each month the mail drop provided comforts such as candies, DDT to kill bedbugs, a package of bullets for the automatic Colt revolver that had been supplied, $200 for travel and entertainment expenses, as well as special instructions. One amusing result of the arrangement where-by Sargeant was the only person to know the true identity of 'Hialeah' occurred when 'Hialeah' was asked by New Delhi headquarters to report on rumours that a certain Dr James Endicott of Chengtu was a communist; using his codename, Endicott replied: 'I know the gentleman in question very well. Although he is known for his outspoken ways, the rumour is quite unfounded.'9

Endicott's activities in the OSS were directly related to the basic American preoccupations in China, namely, accelerating the war effort against Japan and working to ensure that there would emerge from the war a united, modernizing China, linked if possible to the United States in foreign policy and willing to provide a friendly climate for American investments and trade. In line with these objectives Endicott's instructions were to discover the forces in Szechuan that could be mobilized for war and reform, to report on the attitude of the public towards the ruling Kuomintang, and to identify, if possible, the aims and activities of the Communist party.

His first assignment was to get information, including photographs, of Szechuan leaders, and he tackled the problem with characteristic ingenuity. Going into a photography studio on the Tung Hong Zi in Chengtu, he announced that he was interested in collecting autographs of Szechuan perso-nalities; if they had pictures he would take them to be autographed. The approach aroused no suspicion and the studio soon supplied a large number, including fifteen of the leading military men in the province. After a number of interviews, many with people he already knew, Endicott was able to piece together a picture of élite groups riddled through by jealous rivalry and opportunism, as well as serious ill-feeling between the Szechuanese forces and central government troops.

Only his old friend, Chang Chun, the governor, expressed the necessity to give unqualified support to the generalissimo. Even he, however, was willing to alter the inner core of the KMT; he would work for any kind of settlement with the other parties 'as long as it did not include the Communists.'

On the other hand, Generals Teng Hsi-hou, pacification commissioner resident in Chengtu, Pan Wen-hua, garrison commander, who headed two divisions of provincial soldiers, and Liu Wen-hui, member of the richest and most powerful of the Szechuan landlord families and currently governor of neighbouring Sikang province (whose son Endicott was tutoring), expressed their fear of the hard core of Chiang Kai-shek's forces in Chengtu; Chiang had ten thousand cadets in Chengtu trained to be fanatically loyal to the 'Supreme Leader' after the fashion of ss troops, another ten thousand airfield guards, and an unknown number of Tai Li's secret operatives. Furthermore, allegedly for purposes of economy, Chiang was demanding that the provincial forces reduce their numbers by one-third.

The Szechuanese generals, Endicott reported, were biding their time. If squeezed by Chiang Kai-shek, they would resort to the old warlord practice of financing local forces out of the lucrative opium trade, which was flourishing once again in the low hills surrounding the Chengtu plain as well as in Sikang. In the meantime they felt that they could make a better bargain with their 'old teacher,' Chang Lan, and his Democratic League.

They gave Endicott evidence, which he passed on to the oss, that Chiang Kai-shek had entered into negotiations with the Japanese and their Chinese puppets in Nanking. The Japanese proposal to Chiang was to 'withhold your military forces and allow us to make this a Japanese-u.s. war. If you do this we will not attack Chungking and [will] allow you to concentrate your strength in West China for post-war purposes.' The failure of Chiang's armies to oppose the Japanese advance in southwestern China, and then an unexpected Japanese withdrawal to the east in December 1944, taking the pressure off Chungking, seemed to indicate the existence of some such bargain. The Szechuanese generals also told Endicott that thousands of secret servicemen were being brought back from the forward areas to kill the Democratic League people and any others who tried to organize resistance movements to the Japanese or to a puppet government that was secretly being planned to collaborate with them.

As long as the United States was pressing Chiang to reform and to reorganize his government to include other parties in a coalition, the Szechuan landlords were prepared to resist his reactionary policies. 'The greatest needs of China at the present time,' General Liu Wen-hui told Endicott, 'could be expressed in three words: Democracy, Unity and Industrialization.' Liu gave it as his opinion that there could be no unity without immediate, large measures of democracy, and unless such unity was achieved soon there would be no industrial expansion 'because capital will not risk investment in long term projects until there is no danger of civil war.' Liu and his fellow landlords, Endicott knew, had the means to support their political objectives since they controlled a private army of some 100,000 men, based upon a province-wide secret society known as the Old Brotherhood Society (Ge Lao Hui). They used the society as a two-edged sword, both to resist the encroachment of the central government power and to beat down peasant unrest. At one time, when the Japanese were threatening to break into

Szechuan, the society decided to throw in its lot with the Democratic League and the Communist underground in planning a guerilla network in the counties north of Chengtu and Chungking. Endicott conducted negotiations to help this network establish unofficial contact with the United States army, and on one occasion found himself helping to teach peasants how to destroy the engines of trucks, how to throw hand-grenades and plant land mines. Later, when the great landlords realized that the United States was going to support Chiang Kai-shek fully, Endicott reported their switch in allegiance back to the Kuomintang.[10]

In December 1944 Endicott reported that the other elements in the growing resistance to the Kuomintang dictatorship in West China were more reliable and would not be so easily shaken from their purposes. The broad front of resistance, he explained, included in the first place the Communists and their sympathizers; they were to be found everywhere, 'active, alert and ready to risk their lives' for what they called the next stage of the revolution, the establishment of a united front of a progressive, democratic nature to offset the possible triumph of the existing fascist regime at the end of the war.

Another element consisted of the small shop-keepers and small manufacturers who were angry about inflation and the obvious signs of extreme corruption and favouritism. The only successful businessmen, they said, were those related to some minister or his friends, who could ensure large profits by relief from taxes, use of 'ministry credit,' and special transport privileges.

The larger 'free enterprise' capitalists, represented by Endicott's friend, Ho Beh-hen, the reconstruction commissioner, and the former Shanghai industrialists who were now bankrupt, saw no future for recovery under the Kuomintang because the latter offered them only managerial jobs under a form of bureaucratic, monopoly capitalism. Ho, who wanted to give electrical power contracts in Szechuan to Canadian companies and engineers after the war, was bitter in his denunciation of the 'family compact' of Chiang Kai-shek's in-laws, the Kungs and Soongs, in the inner Kuomintang circle. 'Everything they touch immediately becomes riddled with graft and corruption and is never done efficiently,' Ho told Endicott. 'They seed in large numbers of friends and relatives who know nothing except how to draw large salaries and muddle things up.'

In any open revolt against the Kuomintang the students of Szechuan, Endicott suggested, would also play an important role, 'almost as important as in the May 4th 1919 movement.' He knew representatives of student groups who were now travelling from centre to centre secretly setting up the framework of an organization to combat secret police oppression and KMT gangsterism in education centres.

Finally, and most fundamentally, in Endicott's assessment of discontent in

Szechuan, were the attitudes of the peasantry who made up eighty-five per cent of the population of the province. The peasants, he said, were angry to the point of desperation about the treatment of their male family members who had been conscripted into the army. In spite of criticisms raised by the People's Political Council on the handling of conscripts, harrowing stories continued to circulate of abuses of press ganging, sale of recruits, and unvarnished cruelty, of popular resistance increased by the simple lack of facilities – food, clothing, barracks – for the new batch of 300,000 recruits being raised in Szechuan. Officers were stealing the rice, selling it on the black market, and leaving their men to die of starvation.

Among his sources of information on the situation of the peasantry were the servants of the missionaries, many of whom came from villages. Endicott's reputation among the servants was greatly enhanced as a result of an incident involving the police. Dr Edward Best of the Canadian mission had accused his cook of stealing a valuable medical book and immediately turned the suspect over to the police; in retaliation the servants' association organized an angry protest at his house.

Mrs Best came running. 'Jim,' she cried, 'you must come quickly. A mob of servants has gathered, waving knives and saying terrible things to my husband. I am afraid they are going to give him a beating.'

Endicott hurried over, climbed onto a table, and began speaking. He explained that Dr Best, who was a conscientious doctor, had made a mistake because he was unfamiliar with Chinese customs; he had not realized that when he handed his cook over to the police that the latter would beat him to get a confession and then would hold him for ransom until his family was forced to pay a large sum for his release. The proper procedure, of course, was first to hand the matter over to the employees' association for settlement. Endicott stated that he was sure the association would help solve the problem of the missing article. When Dr Best acknowledged the truth of Endicott's remarks, and after Endicott offered to put up bond money immediately so that the unfortunate cook could be released on bail, the servants dispersed, satisfied, and with a strong sense of respect for this 'man of the ocean' who thought and talked as one of them.

Of the scores of cases about the conscription scandals which were reported to him, the following, told to him by an old farmer who came to visit his cook, was perhaps typical:

I have four mou [about an acre] of land and have to pay [Chinese] $3,000 for compensation to draftees. My district was supposed to send ten but twelve were taken. The head man of our hundred family system accepted a large sum of money from two of the draftees and let them go. He filled their place with two men taken at random on the roads. Nobody in our district knew them and they were shipped out to the draft pool in Chengtu before their relatives could trace them.

In the draft pool there are daily sales of draftees to districts which cannot fill their quota. The price of a 'fill-in' draftee now varies from CN$100,000 to CN$170,000. The guardians of the pool sometimes go out and grab a few on the streets and sell them at lucrative prices. In one place in our district the leading Kuomintang agent made so much money out of draftees that the local people burned his house, killed all his family and carried off his rice.[11]

Endicott's 'tiger hunt' in July 1945 on Mount Omei, taken under cover of a holiday with several friends, had been yet another opportunity to understand the real situation in the rural districts.

His intelligence-gathering operation may have had a minimal impact upon the centres of decision-making along Pennsylvania Avenue in Washington; there was, of course, a host of other 'Old China Hands' telling the same story to little effect. Upon Endicott, however, the cumulative result of going out among the people, of gaining inside information on social conditions, was to create a turmoil deep within his soul. The most important fact was his realization that the core of what the West called 'Free China' was a small leisured class of landlords and speculators, backed by their armed retainers and foreign loans, who were feeding upon a populace that was fast becoming a mass of agricultural paupers, bankrupt businessmen, and alienated intellectuals. This knowledge lay at the base of Endicott's ideological transformation from one who really believed in the saving power of missions and in the reform of individual personality to one who believed in the necessity for social revolution, a transformation that was accelerated by his attempts to understand and to report to the OSS on the aims and activities of the Chinese Communist party.

Endicott was introduced to the Communist headquarters in Chungking by an old friend, Ruth Weiss, a former teacher at the missionary Canadian School and part-time secretary at the Canadian Embassy, who was currently working as a journalist for a Western press agency. One day in January 1945 she took Endicott along to one of Chou En-lai's press conferences.

The Communist headquarters was in a large building with two courtyards located on a street overlooking the little river. Around the inner court there was a three-storey block in which the Communists had the bottom and top floors with a layer of Kuomintang police agents between them; Tung Bi-wu, a veteran Communist leader, told Endicott jokingly that it was a sandwich. Around the outside ran a balcony which was also given over to government agents. Except for a tiny secret passageway at the back, which the Communists had cut through the city wall for an emergency escape route, it was impossible for anyone to come or go without being known to Tai Li's gestapo. Chou En-lai and his staff stayed, even under this state of semi-siege, because they needed a listening post; they could publish a newspaper and distribute pamphlets to counter the propaganda of the government press; and they had a wireless transmission service to Yenan. These things were allowed as part of the original united front agreements and also because every army fighting the Japanese, including the Eighth Route Army, had its own radio station in Chungking. Perhaps most important, the Communists stayed in Chungking because they could invite foreign correspondents to press conferences in the hope of influencing Western, especially American, opinion.

The press interview, which took place in a large, bare room with whitewashed walls, on which hung large portraits of Sun Yat-sen, Stalin, Lenin, and President Chiang Kai-shek, was well underway when Chou En-lai's interpreter began having some difficulty with the correspondent of Time-Life Incorporated. Endicott could not resist the temptation and chimed in with his incisive translation. Everyone was highly amused and afterwards Chou En-lai invited him to stay behind for a long talk. It was the first of half a dozen conversations he had with Chou and with other prominent Communist leaders during the next two and a half years.

On this first occasion Endicott did most of the talking, explaining his background, his ideas, and the work he was doing in Chengtu, including reporting to the oss. Chou said he hoped Endicott would report fully to the oss on the proposals and activities of the Communist party because, he said, 'we want America to know everything about us; we have nothing to hide.' Endicott replied that as far as he knew he had no contact with any responsible party worker and he would welcome the chance for regular news. Chou nodded and said that this could be arranged. Meanwhile he wished to introduce his secretary and assistant, Kung Peng, who was in charge of the headquarters during his frequent absences, and in whom Endicott could have the completest confidence.

Many of the Communist leaders made a strong and lasting impression upon those who got to know them and Kung Peng was no exception. Daughter of a wealthy man who had worked with Sun Yat-sen, educated in Christian schools, she had turned down a chance to study abroad in favour of going to Yenan to help lead the student movement. Now a woman of twenty-seven, tall and poised, married to Chiao Kuan-hua, an editor of the *New China Daily News*, it was said that she was protected from the terrorism of Tai Li's agents by a conspiracy of admirers among the foreign correspondents; the picture of 'this tall-stemmed flower in the damp and soiled cellar' was a contrast that stuck in their minds. 'She was a beautiful woman,' wrote Eric Sevareid, the future doyen of American television commentators, 'but in her presence the male-female feeling all but disappeared, replaced by a sexless awe and admiration.' Sevareid said that in watching Kung Peng he had a feeling of uselessness, 'the crushing sense of ineffectualness that comes to the vacillating liberal ... in the presence of a truly strong, dedicated person who has accepted the perils of action, made his decision, and cast his personal life into the account as a thing of value only in terms of the future he himself will never see – the "tomorrows that sing." '[12] As it turned out, Kung Peng survived the dangers of civil war and revolution, and for fifteen years Endicott was to remain in touch with this remarkable personality, and through her with Chou En-lai after he became prime minister.

One evening in February 1945, about two weeks after returning to Chengtu from Chungking, Endicott responded to a knock on the door to find one of his students who wished to introduce a friend. The wizened, sharp-faced stranger, who wore a dusty old wide-brimmed fedora, the kind the Chinese called a 'Ph.D. hat,' turned out to be Chang Yu-yu, member of the South China Bureau of the Communist party and its leading underground organizer in the area. Chang, who was from East China and who became vice-mayor of Peking after 1949, had come to brief Endicott on Communist policies, as Chou En-lai had promised. During the next six months such briefings became a regular occurrence; sometimes Chang was accompanied by a few students, and on one or two occasions by a representative from Yenan.

'I have some information you can tell your American friends,' Chang would begin. After the factual details and analysis of current events, the discussion would often turn to more general talk about the history, character, and likely future path of the Chinese revolution. Chang and the others would explain the Communist party's thesis about a two-stage revolution, the first stage being a bourgeois, democratic revolution of a new type to achieve national freedom against imperialist domination and for social freedom against the feudal landlord system, and the second stage being a socialist revolution sometime in the future. Endicott had many questions: Why call it a bourgeois revolution and what were communists doing trying to make a revolution for capitalism? Why did Mao Tse-tung speak of 'new' democracy? How was it distinguished from 'old' democracy? Was the call for coalition government an emergency expedient for the purpose of the anti-Japanese war, a temporary demand to undermine the dictatorship of Chiang Kai-shek, or had it something to do with the Communist party's long-range strategy? What happens to the class struggle during the period of coalition government?

The answers were patient, sometimes brilliant, but the new ideas made it a painful process. 'I am gradually learning to talk with them not to them,' wrote Endicott with an unaccustomed humility that betrayed an underlying current of emotional strain. If some of the unfamiliar Marxist categories of analysis found their way into his reports to the OSS it was because the main thrust seemed right, in which case the details were not always so important.

Endicott's final report to the OSS, on 28 September 1945, summing up his conclusions after the end of the war with Japan, showed how drastically he had been forced to change his views in a single year. In his broadcast to the Canadian people of June 1944 he had said that the great leadership of Chiang Kai-shek would overcome the strains of war and bring China safely through to democracy. Now, in his opinion, Chiang Kai-shek no longer held the place he once did in the minds of the common people. Chiang was reduced to using one-third of his military budget for secret police activities to check the rising tide of democratic pressure. The whole Kuomintang government was too corrupt and inefficient to do the job that was called for in China. The central banking system was based on speculation, not on reconstruction; hoarding, speculation, and opportunism were its principles. There was 'no danger of "communism" in China in any foreseeable future,' he told the OSS, 'but the Communists are everywhere ... keen, intelligent and determined.' They had 'fanatical faith' in their own theory of social development and were honest, ruthless, in self-criticism in their own small groups; they demanded a high degree of performance and sacrifice from their members; they could not be exterminated and they would of necessity have to be given a large place of leadership in any future government of China if it was at all democratic. If they were driven underground, he believed they would organize so as to be able to take over in the next world crisis. They had learned a lot from their past mistakes and their programme was practical and met the needs of the impoverished masses of the people. If the American government wanted stability, if it wanted markets for Western goods in China, this could now only be achieved if there was a real assurance that the Chinese government was going to be honest, efficient, and democratic – a coalition government that included the Communists. In the end, the people of China would not settle for less than that.[13]

Virtually every high official in Washington paid lip-service at least to the idea that American involvement in a whirlpool of civil war in China was to be avoided. However, after President Roosevelt's death in 1945, a group centred around Ambassador Patrick Hurley, a Texas oil-man, believed that the only way to bring stability was to make Chiang Kai-shek so strong that his opponents would be forced to give up without a struggle. This group was encouraged in this view by Stalin's fateful decision, in August 1945, to conclude a treaty of friendship and alliance with the government of Chiang Kai-shek. Typical of American wishful thinking was President Harry Truman's reported remark that 'the back of the communists is broken as a result of the Russo-Chinese treaty.'[14]

Hurley proceeded to interpret the purposes of his mission and United States policy in China as being '(1) to prevent the collapse of the National Government, (2) to sustain Chiang Kai-shek as President of the Republic and Generalissimo of the Armies ...'[15]

Strengthened by such assurances of American support, the confidence of the Kuomintang increased, as did its repressive policies and its arbitrary methods against its opponents.[16] As the result of this alarming trend, Endicott found himself drawn even deeper into the currents of a growing opposition movement of students, teachers, and professors in Chengtu.

CHAPTER NINETEEN

The mice
of No 11

The study door swung open after only the faintest knock. A group of eight or nine students filed in, men and women in their early twenties: Wang Yu-guang, a student in agriculture, Li Chao-chi, Yenching school of journalism, Hsieh Tao from Nanking University, Chia Wei-yin of West China Union, Yang Tin-yin from Ginling Women's College. They were the political leaders in Chengtu of the New Democratic Youth League, an underground student organization led by the Communist party. Endicott, who knew them only as 'the Sparks (Xing Xing Tuan) of Nanking University,' made them welcome as usual with hot water for tea and a large bowl of peanuts. As the nuts were passed around, the students joked that they were 'the mice of No 11.'

No 11 on Hua Hsi Ba, the West China Union University campus, was a large, foreign-style house formerly the residence of Lewis Walmsley, princi-pal of the school for missionary children. Endicott, who occupied two rooms in the house and shared dining and kitchen facilities with other professors, had stretched out in a wicker chair, his feet on a small trunk that served as a seat in front of the fire, while he waited for his visitors to announce themselves.

The spacious ground floor study had lost the tidy precison of its former occupant. Rough planks on boxes served as tables, which bore the ordered confusion of various works in progress, including a new series of direct method English readers for the Chung Hwa Book Company. Small wooden crates, to serve as extra chairs, were stacked in one corner, while in another was the cage where Milly and Mouldy, a pair of canaries, and other birds, tiny green warblers and red-breasted finches, huddled to keep warm. Endicott had lit a candle, necessary even at the unbelievable cost of $150 apiece since electricity was available only on alternate nights, with the intention of mark-ing a pile of compositions that were stacked at his elbow.

He had often sat here looking into the fire, brooding about the low state of higher education in the Christian institutions of Chengtu. It was not merely that the majority of his students were indifferent to the learning of English; that was perhaps understandable in view of the attitude of the minister of education, Chen Li-fu, whose Confucianism and national chauvinism gave a low priority to foreign-language studies.

More disturbing was the conceited, self-seeking individualism of many students, mostly pampered children of the rich or scholarship students out for themselves, who filled the medical and dental faculties and the economics and sociology courses as a means of setting up lucrative private practices or of getting jobs in government ministries, banks, and the Kuomintang officer corps. The evidence was inescapable that successful graduates perpetuated the inequities, and were among the chief beneficiaries, of a social system that rested upon a cruel exploitation of the peasants and the urban poor. The hierarchy of the university, as well as a value system based upon a false premise that education by itself promoted equality by providing a vehicle of mobility, guaranteed the continuation of this unhappy state of affairs.

What the Christian mission in China should be producing, Endicott thought, were intellectual and spiritual partisans who would organize the people to achieve the changes they needed. But the Christian mission had no such conception of its contribution to feudal and exploited China; generally it tried to suppress any of its members who became too 'extreme.' While it was true that one of the by-products of the large educational effort of the church was a crop of genuine radicals, they were generally regarded as 'black sheep.' The so-called 'constructive approach,' dear to the middle class religionist, Endicott reflected, was really an attempt to fit the student into the old order and disturb it as little as possible, always allowing for gradual change, perhaps in a hundred years.

It was because of these melancholy feelings, and because of pressure from the government to pass a lot of Kuomintang party favourites who got as low as ten per cent on their examinations, that Endicott, while remaining a teacher, had refused to take on the responsibility of becoming head of the English Department at West China Union University.

In spite of misgivings about their excessive individualism, however, Endicott was not entirely without faith in the students of China. From his own experience during the stormy May 30th movement of 1925 and 1926 directed against British imperialism, he knew that in certain circumstances most of the students were capable of developing a keen political sense, and that they had sometimes played a leading role in the affairs of the nation. It was within this framework that he regarded the Sparks as harbingers of a new wave of public-spirited activity among students.

The Sparks had originally approached Endicott after hearing some of his outspoken sermons and speeches, saying that they needed a safe place to study certain banned texts – the classics of Western Marxism and articles that came from Yenan – which, if found in the student dormitories, made the owner subject to immediate arrest. Since he had been an adviser to Chiang Kai-shek and because he was known to be tutoring Governor Chang Chun in English, they thought that his home might offer a sanctuary. 'Could some of our study groups meet at your house?' they had asked him.

Endicott had agreed, giving them a key to his door, and sometimes he joined in their discussions. After making sure the curtains were drawn, the students would lift up a loose board in the floor and distribute the controversial reading material. As Endicott listened to them talk, he was impressed by 'the group concern for each member, the analysis of each one's ability, strength and weakness and sense of working together.'[1]

He contributed as well to several of their public projects. The first occasion had been in November 1944 when the Sparks organized a week-long demonstration against the Chengtu chief of police. The agitation arose out of an incident at a local middle school where the police had intervened, wounding several students in the process. Determined not to allow the government to hush up the affair, the Sparks asked Endicott for permission to use his rooms to prepare pamphlets and to organize a series of political activities against police terror in general.

His commitment to the students' cause was dramatically tested when the group, fearing detection, asked if he could find another missionary house where they could meet. He accompanied them to the home of his Quaker friends, Bryan and Elizabeth Harlan. Meeting there, however, proved to be a mistake since plain clothesmen were observed taking up positions outside the house. Endicott remembered a small entrance at the bottom of the garden where the gateman carried in water from the canal; he led the students out into the darkness, but when he opened the gate he was immediately challenged by a man who called out, 'Stand!'

To surrender or to act swiftly were the only choices available. He could not see if the man was armed, but he knew that there was not a moment to spare. From a course called 'Let's Get Tough,' put on by the American army, he had learned that a thrust from the shoulder with open palm under an opponent's chin was more effective than a punch. He did not hesitate. With one lunge the man was knocked senseless. The students made their escape as the stranger rolled down the canal bank. Endicott returned through the yard, past the house, and departed by the front gate where he noticed a figure fading away into the roadway.

By the end of the week, after nearly fifteen thousand students and their sympathizers had surged through the streets with slogans demanding the resignations of the mayor and the chief of police and freedom from tyranny, twelve student representatives were admitted to Chang Chun's office to present their demands. The governor treated the students courteously and informed them that the provincial government had decided to dismiss both men and to ask the central government to investigate and punish them if necessary. It was a considerable triumph for the youthful organizers.[2]

After these events, which became known as the Double Eleventh Movement since the civic officials were dismissed on 11 November 1944, secret police repression in Szechuan became even more severe. Several of the Sparks whom Endicott had come to know were caught and reported executed; a few made their way north to the areas controlled by the Eighth Route Army; others hid with friends.

Increasingly Endicott felt that the KMT secret agents were trying to get some statement which they could pin on him to prove that he was an active supporter of the Communist party. When unknown students came asking for advice on how to improve themselves, he tactfully suggested that they read Dale Carnegie's How to Win Friends and Influence People. Whenever he was invited out to Chengtu's Szechuan University, where the president was concurrently secretary-general of the Kuomintang, the question period after his speeches was always tricky. Although invited to talk on international topics such as 'The Significance of the Labour Party Victory in England,' the right-wing Youth Corps stalwarts would try to squeeze in questions about China's domestic affairs.

'If there is civil war in China, do you think there will be uprisings in the rear?' asked one.

'The answer to that is certainly better known to the Chinese gestapo than it is to a foreign friend,' Endicott replied to the roar of laughter and applause from hundreds of students.

'We Chinese think that since Marx was a foreigner his teachings are no good for China,' ventured another. 'We don't want foreign doctrine. What do you think of that?'

'As far as I know,' Endicott responded, 'nobody is trying to practise Marxism in China. Everyone is talking about the "Three Principles" which were taught by a Chinese. As for not using foreign things, if you accept that as a principle you shouldn't have electric light in your university, you shouldn't travel in an airplane and you certainly shouldn't send American tanks against the communists; you ought to go in a wheelbarrow.'[3]

One of the other political movements in which Endicott participated occurred in the autumn of 1945. This time he openly revealed his sympathies, defied the wishes of the authorities, and placed his own life in jeopardy.

It was after the American victory over Japan. The dangers for the anti-Kuomintang forces, including the Communists, had increased considerably, for, in spite of pious phrases about seeking a settlement with the Communists by negotiations, the inner circle of the Kuomintang, confident they had the unconditional support of the United States, had secretly determined to liquidate their opposition by force of arms. Rumours of all kinds had begun to spread: that General Hurley had agreed to arm and train one hundred Kuomintang divisions and to provide ten thousand trucks for the attack against the Communists; that all people suspected of leftist sympathies in the KMT areas would soon be rounded up; that when Mao Tse-tung, accompanied by General Hurley for safe passage, left his base in Yenan and came to Chungking for negotiations with Chiang Kai-shek on coalition government in August 1945, it was really a tacit admission by Mao that he had been defeated and was accepting discipline at the hands of the generalissimo.

People all over China had waited anxiously for the results of the prolonged Chungking negotiations, which lasted over forty days; this was the first time that Mao Tse-tung and Chiang Kai-shek had met face to face since the bloody coup in Shanghai eighteen years earlier when the latter had treacherously turned on his Communist allies. In the minds of many people the future of a united, peaceful China appeared to hang upon the success of this meeting. However, even as the negotiations progressed, information had spread that the American air force was flying whole Kuomintang armies eastwards and northwards over the heads of the local resistance groups and that the first pitched battles of civil war with the Communist forces had begun. The leading liberals and leftists in the KMT areas, doubtful of America's good faith as mediator and fearing Chiang Kai-shek's vengeance, were quietly taking cover in the countryside. The air was heavy with tension.[4]

After Mao flew back to Yenan on 11 October 1945, having concluded an agreement with Chiang to convene a broadly representative political consultative conference to prepare for a coalition government, Endicott's close friend, Governor Chang, who had been the chief negotiator for the central government, returned to Chengtu for a weekend rest. Following the church service on Sunday morning, he and his wife dropped around to see Endicott. It was a unique opportunity for the latter to learn from one of the most influential men in the country the inside story, and to appraise the value of the new agreement upon which so much seemed to depend. The two old friends proceeded to have a heated and at times acrimonious exchange, which Endicott recorded immediately afterwards in a letter to his family. From the attitudes revealed by Chang Chun, who was one the most liberal-minded leaders of the KMT,

Endicott was afraid that, unless popular opinion was mightily aroused, the Chungking agreement had little chance of leading to a coalition government.

'What do you think of it?' Chang Chun had asked.

'It hasn't settled any basic issues,' was Endicott's non-committal reply.

'Of course not, because the Communists won't give up their arms.'

'They can't give up their arms without being killed.'

'Oh, you've just accepted the Communist propaganda. You're hopelessly prejudiced. The Kuomintang is the legal government of China and how can it tolerate an armed party?'

After some further talk about university affairs, they returned to the central political issue of the prospects for the recent agreement.

'Coalition government as you understand it in the West is impossible in China. The opposition is armed!' Chang Chun emphasized again. 'When Chamberlain retired,' he continued, referring to British politics in 1939, 'it was the Conservative Churchill who invited the Labour Party into the government. The Communists in China are not willing to be invited in.'

'That is because the Kuomintang refuses to make the organization in any way representative,' Endicott countered. 'It, itself is the final court of appeal; the Labour Party in England could always appeal to the people. While it is true that China cannot have such an appeal,' he agreed, 'it could have a council representing every party and use that as the court of appeal instead of the one party dictatorship.'

'You foreigners make me tired with your talk of the "one party dictatorship" and the "cc Clique" etc. These are things of the past; the party is changing and developing,' Chang insisted.

'I am glad to hear that,' Endicott replied, but knowing that recently announced cabinet changes were little more than 'musical chairs' to impress the Americans, he also insisted that 'these people who are things of the past like Chen Li-fu still control education because they have seeded in their men everywhere. H.H. Kung ...'

'You can leave Kung out,' Chang interrupted, 'he is gone ...'

'Yes, but his men are still entrenched everywhere, and I have no great faith in the Soong outfit,' Endicott countered.

'You may be justified in that,' Chang admitted.

'It is altogether likely that you will get in China a compradore industrial development based on an alliance with u.s. big business and the people who have made war-fortunes and have seized the puppet and Japanese commercial and industrial set-up in China. The last thing they will want is progressive democracy. In the end, this "Agreement" that has been advertised this last week will end up in civil war,' Endicott gloomily predicted.

The governor nodded as if perhaps in partial accord. The conversation then drifted off into areas where the two men were in substantial agreement.[5] Endicott felt badly that in spite of their many years of friendship he had had to be so critical of Chang Chun's party. Therefore, when Madame Chang sent over a basket of fruit two weeks later with a note saying her husband sent regards from Chungking, Endicott was much relieved that the governor had not been too angered by their frank talk.

Meanwhile the Communists, determined not to give up their ground without fighting to the last ditch, had administered some severe defeats to the newly reinforced Kuomintang forces in North China; at the same time they reaffirmed their willingness to support Chiang Kai-shek as president of a coalition government. The coalition programme had an immense appeal to the war-weary people and once the liberals and the intellectuals saw that the Communists really could and would stand up to the Kuomintang and fight if necessary, they became more active and courageous once again in demanding reform and an end to civil war.

An anti-civil war association, established in Chungking in November 1945, issued a call to workers, students, and merchants to demonstrate their opposition to the gathering clouds of civil war. Among the first to respond had been the students in the city of Kunming where, in spite of prohibitions by the local authorities, several thousand students gathered to hear professors speak and to pass resolutions to the central government calling for the immediate cessation of hostilities on both sides, the withdrawal of the American troops from China, the formation of a coalition government, and the guarantee of elementary liberties of freedom of speech and assembly. During a hectic week of demonstrations and classroom strikes, in which an estimated thirty thousand students participated, four students were killed by the action of soldiers.[6] These students immediately became martyrs to the cause of peace and democracy, and led to Endicott's direct involvement in the struggle.

The Kuomintang tried in vain to prevent the spread of the anti-civil war agitation, the first wave of which became known as the December First Movement (1945) following the events in Kunming. The vice-minister of education flew to Chengtu and held a meeting with the foreign staff of the five Christian universities, including Endicott, urging them to keep the students quiet; he 'explained' that the fatal hand grenade in Kunming had been thrown by a hired Communist. The Chengtu Students' Self-Government Associations, still mainly under the leadership of the KMT Youth Corps, declined to organize any meeting, a task which was taken up by a hastily formed Union of Sympathizers and Supporters of the Kunming Students.

Determined, in the wake of the Kunming tragedy, to enlist the support and sympathies of the townspeople for a coalition government, these students planned a Sunday memorial service on the campus, to be followed by a march to Sao Chen Park in the city centre. Under heavy central government pressure, the organizing committee experienced difficulty in finding speakers; at the last minute one of the chief speakers, the one who was to address the climax of the rally in the park, decided not to come. Several student delegations then came to ask Endicott if he would take his place: 'certain liberal, social democrat types came by day and urged me to speak ... saying it would be a great honour as I would be the only speaker,' Endicott recalled. 'But after dark the communists came and explained that they had reliable information that Chiang Kai-shek's plainclothes police would shoot any Chinese who spoke at the mass rally. They thought that as a foreigner, missionary and former adviser to Chiang I might get away with it. They requested that I do it.'[7]

His pulse rate rose as he listened to the request. He sensed instantly that he was facing an acute moral crisis. An adverse decision would mean betrayal of his own conscience; acceptance meant confrontation with the authorities, involved treading the unfamiliar path of outright defiance, and perhaps might even lead to martyrdom. His mission colleagues, he knew, would be unsympathetic to his participation in the demonstration. Endicott took counsel with his Chinese Christian friends, T.L. Shen and Y.T. Wu; the latter was already booked to be one of the speakers at the memorial meeting on the campus. A consensus was soon reached that he ought to participate and that he should give the government some prior hint of his involvement. Since it was already noon on Saturday, Endicott sent the gateman with a note to the governor:

No. 11 Huasipa,
Chengtu
December 8, 1945

Dear Governor Chang Chun,

It is probably known to you that the students are planning a large meeting on this campus on Sunday. The purpose of the meeting seems to be, (1) to protest against the treatment of the students at Kunming, (2) to protest against the continuance of civil war.

Since Commissioner Kuo spoke to me on Wednesday I have asked my students about it and all that I can discover seems to show that the meeting will be quite peaceful and limited to the above two points.

I wish they could get some official permission to hold this meeting, if that is considered necessary but they feel that the present amount of democracy in China ought to allow such a public meeting. In order for such a meeting to do any good and not cause great harm, it is exceedingly important that no force be used to stop it and that the type of shouting bully that came in dozens and tried to stop the May 4th meeting should not be encouraged.

With good wishes for your continued success in striving for a political solution of China's most difficult problem.

Yours sincerely,

J.G. Endicott.

From this letter Chang Chun could guess Endicott's intention to participate; if told directly, however, he might have felt obliged, in his official capacity as governor, to forbid it. Endicott then drafted a brief speech. He would express support and sympathy for the Kunming students and professors who had raised a banner of peace, unity, and democracy that neither machine-guns nor hand grenades could shoot down; it was fitting that a foreign friend should express his feelings because at this critical time of history the peace of China and its democratic progress were a guarantee of the same things in the world; he would elaborate on the four freedoms of the late President Roosevelt and the lend-lease weapons policy which the great American reformer had offered those around the world who would help to promote these ideals; he would point out the corollary that if there were now, anywhere in the world, any groups who intended to deny the four freedoms to their people, they had no moral right to the use of lend-lease weapons which had been given in democratic faith and for democratic purposes; he would conclude with a call for commitment to build a democratic China on the foundations of Sun Yat-sen's three principles.

The foreboding with which Endicott viewed the morrow was reflected in the fact that he sat up after midnight writing a letter to his far-away wife. 'I have a feeling that it may happen that I go in to bat with two down and bases full,' he wrote. There was a touch of irony in his soul at the thought that in the morning there would be a church service at which a bishop would speak; *Onward Christian Soldiers* and *Faith of Our Fathers* would be sung, and a theology expounded that did not deal with the questions that had fastened on his mind and heart. He wondered whether bishops didn't become bishops because of an agility at administering the status quo and dodging the issue. He told Mary some pictures were racing through his mind: a little black squirrel in the park at Washington, Norman's first cry in the grey dawn of March, her arms thrown around his neck at midnight when he returned from that first terrible bombing in Chungking. He had not turned to the Bible, but was trying to imagine the political conditions facing Amos and Isaiah, what actual mystical experiences did they have that gave a glow to their realistic, common sense demand for plain justice and right dealing? He smiled with amusement at his wanting to read Winston Churchill, who in his opinion had become a hopeless old reactionary in the post-war period:

Come then: let us to the task,
Each to our part, each to our station.
...
Long live also
the forward march of the common people,
in all the lands
towards their just and true inheritance,
and towards the broader and fuller age.[8]

The next morning about one thousand students from the five Christian universities and Szechuan University gathered on the West China Union University campus. After a prayer for the four students killed in Kunming and some speeches, the Alumni Association of Lienta University of Kunming headed the demonstration, wearing black armbands and flying a banner reading 'The Survivors.' As the parade passed by the government news agency or groups of soldiers appropriate slogans were shouted. At the United States Information Service a student who had acted as an interpreter with the us army during the war climbed high to write 'hands off China' on the wall in impressive block letters.

When the students had all filed into Sao Chen Park a crowd of about five thousand had collected. Endicott saw that the platform was tightly surrounded by a group of thirty helmeted and uniformed police. Would they permit him through? Taken by surprise to see a foreigner approach, they let him pass, but not without one saying: 'We're going to kill this bastard foreigner!'

At first the crowd too gasped to see a Westerner, but then, according to a report that appeared the next day in a student newspaper, *Yenching News*, as the Canadian professor presented himself on the stage 'thunderous cheers arose from the audience, because they saw in him the world's sympathy for the Chinese students' fight for democracy and peace.'

Just as he started to speak one of the uniformed men rolled a hand grenade onto the platform. Endicott gambled that he had not pulled the pin. His reaction was to proceed with even more vigour than expected. The four Kunming martyrs, for whom this great meeting had come to pay homage, he said, 'were given the death penalty at the hands of brutal men for the crime of asking for peace, unity and democracy after eight years of [China] suffering at the hands of the Japanese fascists.' By the time he got to the point about

Roosevelt not intending to supply any side in China so as to start civil war, the crowd was responding enthusiastically, chanting: 'Let Roosevelt's policy be continued!'[9]

Soon after the meeting Endicott went over to Chang Chun's house and had an hour's frank and friendly talk with him. Endicott asked him directly if he resented his activities.

'I am not afraid of student demonstrations,' the governor said, 'but some of your fellow missionaries tell me that you are a Communist.'

Endicott bowed his thanks to his fellow missionaries but didn't bother to deny the charge once more. 'Do you consider that I am entitled to take part in such demonstrations?' he asked.

'I do not care to answer that question in my official capacity,' the governor replied. 'But I should like to say this: some of the Chinese say that while you are urging that foreigners should not take part in China's civil war, by your actions you are taking part in it.'

Endicott objected: 'At least I am not using tanks and marines, and anyway, I am urging the cessation, immediately, by both sides, of the civil war.'

Endicott then told him frankly how badly he felt about the Kuomintang secret police spying on students, the whole semi-fascist control of the Christian universities that had been established by Chen Li-fu. 'To sum up,' Endicott said, 'I am a foreigner, I realize, but as long as you tolerate "foreign sponsored universities," I as a foreigner will fight with all my might against this iniquitous secret police thought control, black-listing liberal students, intimidating them, arresting them and all the whole business of oppression which ought not to be. When you want me to go, you can say so and I will go.'[10]

In later years Endicott realized that Sao Chen Park symbolized a turning point in his life. The 'mice of No 11' had led him across the barrier between the viewpoint of an idealistic intellectual reformer and that of a committed revolutionary: the former might appeal to the people's better nature until the end of time but that approach alone would never end the insuperable gulf between exploiter and exploited; the latter accepted the underlying reality of struggle and class conflict, believing that this was the way in which fundamental and necessary social change took place in history, the way princes would be put down from their thrones and those of low degree exalted (Luke 1:52).

The findings of secret agent 'Hialeah' had had something to do with his transformation as well, as did his talks with Chang Chun, a fellow Christian whom he considered to be among the most enlightened of the Chinese government leaders. His contact with Chang Chun had convinced him that, even with the best of goodwill, people's attitudes are conditioned by their economic class interests. Long after the four freedoms of the Atlantic Charter – freedom from want and fear, freedom of speech and religion – had been hung in a gilt frame in the hall of liberal illusions, he was certain that the people who lived in poverty and oppression would be struggling for those freedoms with sacrifice and bloodshed, and Christian statesmen would be conniving at the killing of key political organizers in the name of law and order. It was not because they were Christians that they acted this way, but because 'the majority of them belong to the classes which either have a large share of the good things of life, or think they can get for themselves a ... large share ... by "peaceful" means, namely by getting an alliance with the owners of the instruments of production to fight the revolutionary lower classes.'[11]

In the process of adopting a revolutionary outlook and a willingness to co-operate with the despised and feared Communists, Endicott was soon to clash with his church and with the Canadian ambassador in Chungking.

CHAPTER TWENTY

The battle of the embassy

'Sitting where I am on a hill on the South Bank,' wrote the Canadian ambassador from his Chungking embassy, 'I look down to where I know the Yangtze River to be; but I cannot see it. A fog hangs over all the lower levels of the landscape; and with it a mist floats above and obscures the sun. That is just how we feel about China. We live in a fog – a mental fog – and we cannot find the sunlight.'[1]

Into this fog-bound embassy, like a stormy petrel, came Jim Endicott, as a frequent guest of Ambassador Victor Odlum. While becoming the friend of radical students on campus and working for the oss, Endicott also kept regular contact with the embassy. Although Odlum refused to accept his points of view, he could not dismiss the facts upon which they were based. 'You have had a profound influence on my thinking,' he told Endicott, '[and] have prevented me from going to extremes.'[2]

The ambassador was a tall, fit-looking, military man, who had for a time led the Second Canadian Division in the Second World War. Recently high commissioner to Australia, and in civilian life prominent in newspaper publishing and financial activities in British Columbia, the general liked to describe himself as a left-wing Liberal with strong humanitarian sympathies for 'the little people.' A man with remarkable gifts of friendliness and patronizing airs, he was a figure of considerable standing in the Canadian establishment. Prime Minister Mackenzie King had appointed him to China against the inclinations of some of the senior advisers in the Department of External Affairs, who feared that he had insufficient political judgement for successful diplomacy. Mr King apparently never had any regrets about his decision, but, when the young men at the China desk in Ottawa had to cope with Odlum's prolific writings, they observed drily that he waffled quite a bit and tended 'to confuse the uninitiate.'[3]

Initially it was Endicott's contacts and high standing among elements of the Chinese business and official community, his acquaintance through teaching English with such men as Ho Beh-hen of the Navigation Bureau, C.C. Chang of the Bank of China, Lu Tso-fu and Tung Sao-sen of the Min Sen Industrial Company, and the provincial governor, Chang Chun, that attracted Odlum's attention; a man with such connections might be useful to Canada.

As far as the ambassador was concerned, the sunlight he wished to find in Canadian-Chinese affairs required, at a minimum, the establishment of close political and personal ties with China and with those Chinese who would allow trade and commerce between the two countries to expand upon a firm basis; a united, peaceful, and modernizing China would best serve Canada's interests.

Odlum believed that China could be one of Canada's greatest natural markets, with everything in Canada's favour by way of products, proximity, and transportation. If only Canadian companies such as the Canadian Pacific Railway and E.P. Taylor's Sino-Canadian Development Corporation were prepared 'to fight every inch of the way' with their American and British rivals, and if the Canadian government would guarantee credits of $50 million, Odlum was convinced that Canada could move beyond traditional wheat sales into high value areas such as shipbuilding, supply of railway equipment, installation of hydro-electric systems, and sales of paper-making machinery. To prove his point, Odlum produced a shopping list for Canadian goods from Premier T.V. Soong, worth 270 million Canadian dollars.[4]

The conversion of shopping lists into hard cash contracts, however, depended primarily upon the political factors involved in the rehabilitation and reconstruction of China, and it was Endicott's attitudes about the line Canada should follow on political questions that caused such a stir in the embassy.

He showered Odlum with arguments and facts to show that Chiang Kai-shek and the Kuomintang were incapable of bringing about democratic, modernizing government in China. From these encounters General Odlum concluded that 'Dr. Endicott probably presents the case against the Government as strongly as anyone can do it.' Endicott also argued, with all the skill he could muster, that the Communists and the Democratic League would have to be included in any genuinely popular post-war government that could provide the stability and economic development necessary for sound trading, and therefore be worthy of Canada's friendship and support.

The ambassador, on the other hand, had his own simple formula to describe his job: if you wish to discover where the car is going, get behind the mind of the man at the wheel. The key to the whole problem of China, he thought, was to discover Chiang Kai-shek's intentions. Odlum soon developed a close rapport with the generalissimo and as a result he was invited to frequent audiences with the Chinese leader.

'The big question is,' Odlum wrote Endicott, 'does this man intend to lead his people towards a democracy built to promote the standard of life and comfort and freedom of the little man or does he not?'

Odlum believed that Chiang did. 'His eyes, so delightfully animated, with such keen perception and such an instantaneous signal of each perceptive act, intrigue me.'

With a mysticism worthy of a disciple of Mackenzie King, the ambassador added: 'They are direct, steady eyes. I instinctively trust him.'

The ambassador was prepared to admit the unfortunate truth that the inner circle surrounding the generalissimo was composed of 'bankers, and land-lords and big merchants,' and that 'the little people' were far away, 'inarticu-late and dispersed.' He thought this could be changed.

Even after Wong Wen-hao, the minister of economic affairs, in a moment of rare candour, told him that the generalissimo 'was not a dynamic leader trying to infuse democratic principles into the Kuomintang policy, but rather a static figure who has surrounded himself with the reactionary elements in Chinese life,' the Canadian diplomat remained stubbornly committed to his day-dream that Chiang Kai-shek intended to lead China into Western democracy.

'We, he and I, talk of those little people; and he knows I think he can never become a great man ... unless he places himself as the leader and protector of those little people. I know what he says he will do, and I trust his word.' 'The Generalissimo's eyes, and his words, tell me where his heart is.' It was almost as if the Chinese general had a moral duty to his great white friend.

General Odlum was also prepared to concede that the 'financial success,' as he politely called it, of the small group at the top of the Kuomintang was disconcerting.

'The democratic world does not like the over rich,' remarked Odlum, himself a wealthy man, 'especially when they are not clever enough to make a good case for themselves or to screen the evidence of their wealth. Nor does it like those caught lying ...'

Perhaps in China it was different. Odlum believed corruption to be normal in China, something that had to be accepted, like the 'lack of sanitation, unpleasant smells, curious, impertinent crowds, indifference to time and widespread dishonesty.' The latter was exemplified by the barber who tried to charge Odlum and the military attaché, Brigadier Orville Kay, $100 each for haircuts and finally settled at two for $80; Odlum was incensed at this attempt to cheat. As for Chiang and his ministers, he declared that in spite of their wealth he had been unable to discover anyone who knew of 'a single action that could be classified as dishonest.'[5]

Ambassador Odlum was always courteous, often genuinely impressed, when Endicott turned up at the embassy or wrote a letter to present his case. 'Come to Chungking as often as you can so that the little David that is in me may talk with the big David that is in you,' he told Endicott. 'When I write to Ottawa and make any comments about my conversations with you, I always admit that you have had a wider experience here than have I and that your knowledge of the language gives you access to doors that are denied to me ... There is no one in China with whom I would rather talk.'

In spite of his willingness to listen, Odlum was never convinced. He told the Department of External Affairs that Endicott made him 'think furiously,' but the missionary's humanity had led him into depths of emotion which prevented him from seeing things fairly; as a preacher and 'propagandist,' Odlum thought, Endicott was bound to indulge in exaggerated language when criticizing Chiang Kai-shek or when praising the Communists.[6]

Endicott rejected the notion that a preacher must necessarily lack sound judgement; nor did he attach much importance to the fact that he could speak Chinese: this ability might enable him to get some information a little more quickly, to extract a bit more meaning from an emphasis here and there, and to establish a certain naturalness in conversation, but these things were relatively unimportant.

'What really matters,' he told Odlum, 'is the general framework that is in one's mind, plus the desires and convictions regarding what is either right or necessary for human progress.'

The general framework in Endicott's mind, which he talked about to Odlum, described the Kuomintang as the party of the past and the Communists as the party of the future; the party of the present would have to be a compromise containing liberal and semi-liberal elements in the Kuomintang, the smaller forces represented by the Democratic League, and a vigorous measure of Communists who would do a much better job of honest administration and productive industrialization than anyone else.

'I think you will realize from this analysis,' he told Odlum, 'that I have completely abandoned the "hero" theory of history.' Individuals do not alter the course of events, he argued, except in very special circumstances and for a brief time. A man remained a 'leader' only as long as he expressed the will of the group that supported him. Chiang Kai-shek, in whom Odlum continued to have such faith, was put into power by the big landlords and monopoly capitalists in alliance with the gangsters, some of the worst elements in Chinese society, and his chief basis of support had remained there.

There was a period in 1937, after Chiang had been kidnapped and forced to change, when he symbolized the will of the people in their fight against Japanese imperialism; this challenge had brought out certain elements of nobility in him for a few years. But it was now quite obvious that Chiang was reverting steadily to his former anti-democratic position.

'I certainly once felt as you do,' Endicott admitted to General Odlum; as late as 1943 'I continued to hope and give him every benefit of the doubt. It is only since I have been making a study of the actual social forces that are locked in the struggle in China that I have come to realize that he not only does not, but cannot want democracy and stay at the head of his group.'

In its most essential features the Kuomintang inner circle, Endicott argued, was quite similar to the regime that had recently been put on trial in Nuremberg: its police system was vicious, corrupt, and oppressive; its administration of the army, especially its policy of conscription, was scandalous; the huge fortunes made in hoarding, speculation, and gambling showed a real lack of intention to 'industrialize'; its county administration was rotten and was extorting payments from the peasants until they were getting nearer and nearer to the point of revolution; its 'farcical facades of elections' in the cities fooled no one except a few foreigners who wanted to be fooled.

This state of affairs, which Endicott could and did document, chapter and verse, was ample proof that Chiang Kai-shek and the Kuomintang were discredited in the eyes of their own people, and would be overthrown if they allowed any real freedom of expression. The future of China was not a question of the debatable morality of a few individuals; as long as the economic and political structures were under the control of a feudal-minded landlord bureaucracy, a unified, democratic, industrialized China could never be realized. The more the Kuomintang's power became threatened, Endicott suggested, the more Chiang Kai-shek would resort to treachery, insincerity, and blocking tactics against any democratic alternatives. It was not possible that Odlum's hopeful estimate of Chiang could be realized or that the latter would 'go down in history as the man who gave democracy to China and who commenced to raise the standard of life of the average people.' Instead, Endicott predicted in May 1945, Chiang Kai-shek 'will end up by being propped up by foreign bayonets.' Even with plenty of American help, the Kuomintang would be forced out of power in the next five years.

The party of the future, the Communist party, Endicott thought, would control all of China within ten to twenty years:

It is thoroughly Marxian socialist in its outlook and education. It is rooted in the people and has come up the hard way, having its members killed by the hundreds of thousands by the Kuomintang and its subsidiary feudal warlords. It contains the most intelligent students of the social needs of China ... The Communist Party does not fear the people ... It trains them how to organize themselves in order to achieve sufficient political power in local self-government so that they can improve their own lot. It is strictly non-paternalistic; sternly disciplined; all its members, especially the younger ones, believe in its principles and purposes with passionate conviction and sacrificial devotion ... In the matter of military strength, the Communist Party is determined to achieve military equality with the so-called National Army, which is really the private political army of the counter-revolutionary party. The only way that the Communists can hope to stay alive and active is by some sort of military equality with their opponents. This must be accepted as one of the central facts of the situation in China. The Communists are quite sincere in saying that with a democratic government in China they will merge their army into a national army. At the same time, they are quite clear and determined about the nature of this 'democratic government' and they are sure that the KMT will do everything in its power to keep its own military strength and force the Communists to give up theirs in the name of political unity and facade democracy.

Between the fall of the party of the past and the rise of the party of the future was the party needed for the present. This loose coalition of the Communists, the Democratic League, and some elements of the Kuomintang should include Chiang Kai-shek and a large number of free enterprise capitalists. Not included would be the Chen brothers, Ho Ying-chin, and others who represented the reactionary sectors of the Kuomintang. Also excluded, Endicott thought, would be T.V. Soong, a favourite of Mr King's, who symbolized a fourth group which the Chinese called the 'compradore capitalists': local capitalists who co-operated with Western capital for the exploitation of the Chinese people and who squeezed out the smaller, free enterprise businessmen. Increasingly, Endicott believed, T.V. Soong's group would serve American interests and help in every possible way to check the spread of the kind of democracy the Communist party was trying to bring about in China. The great value of the Democratic League, Endicott felt, was that it would force the more impatient of the Communists to go slowly. Eventually, however, as the social crisis in China developed and the tempo increased, the Democratic League would gradually dissolve, its liberal and more leftist members going over to the Communists, the right-wing elements joining the counter-revolution and trying to stem the tide of socialism in China.[7]

Flattering pleasantries aside, General Odlum completely rejected Endicott's 'general framework' with a variety of arguments. Why, he wanted to know, did the Communists clamour for a coalition if the Kuomintang was so rotten? How could you coalesce with the devil? 'I just don't get it,' he fumed at Endicott. 'It does not make sense. It sounds like elbowing into power.' 'They deny ideology!'

Odlum seized upon the idea that, since the Kuomintang was the *de facto* government of China, it could only be replaced 'when by some constitutional means' another party proved to have more general support from the people. The central government of China should not be expected to tolerate an armed opposition party. Admittedly, the Kuomintang itself had come to power by armed revolution, and, admittedly, it was not reassuring, in fact it was downright mortifying, to discover a clause in the new electoral laws which stipulated that, if it was proved that 'the number of voters who have been bribed has exceeded one-third of the total number of voters registered,' an election would be considered null and void. Nevertheless, Odlum doggedly maintained that the Kuomintang had the right to represent the majority of Chinese until an election was held.

From the former missionary, United States congressman Walter Judd, Odlum picked up another argument to reject the Communists: the Chinese Communists were not Chinese at all, but stemmed from 'the Russian Communist world revolution'; the Yenan leaders were more concerned with the future welfare of Russia than that of China. Although Odlum had met Mao Tse-tung, had often talked with Chou En-lai, and was greatly impressed with their ability and sincerity as individuals, after a visit to the generalissimo at Kuling he said angrily to Endicott: 'the Communists are a Russian party and ought to be eliminated.' Since Odlum freely admitted that there was no evidence that Moscow ever provided any supplies or munitions to Yenan, it was clearly the implications of their common Marxist ideology which he found so upsetting.

Odlum further argued against any pressure on the Kuomintang to negotiate a settlement with the Communists by saying that the latter were no better than their rivals at making officials honest and efficient; the exactions of the one and the corruptions of the other were, according to Odlum, 'a robbery of the people to serve the purposes or desire of the few.' 'In essence they are really the same,' he maintained, apparently without examining some impressive evidence to the contrary produced within his own embassy by Ralph Collins.[8]

Odlum's arguments, when reported to Ottawa, elicited such adjectives as 'ridiculous' or 'amazing' from the political analysts at the China desk at External Affairs. They were, however, secondary to, and dependent upon, General Odlum's more central perceptions of the global strategy of the Western world. He foresaw that a United States' bid for hegemony, 'Pax-Americana,' was about to be set up, 'by force if necessary.' He considered that this would 'be good for the world.' Although he prided himself on having a strong sense of Canadianism, and although he showed considerable scorn for the Henry Luce type of American, 'heady for the moment with power' and 'intoxicated with full pocketbooks,' he believed that Canada's role would have to be that of a friendly supporter of major American policy. General Odlum, too, had his 'general framework.'[9]

In this struggle for world power Odlum expected that there would be war with Russia. Since this was the case, he saw no sense in trying to achieve peace and unity in China by giving recognition to the Communists; such a policy would only weaken 'the hands of those who must eventually make the first stand in the coming struggle with Russia – the National Government of China.' Odlum was convinced that the Chinese Communist forces were 'a phantom army,' lacking ammunition and incapable of decisive action, an army which could be defeated in a comparatively short time by the militarily superior Kuomintang–central government forces. A short, decisive, all-out civil war, supported by the Western democracies, would achieve the desired purpose of saving China as a base in the future struggle with the Soviet Union.[10]

These views on global strategy for the 'free enterprise world,' which were shared by the United States ambassador, Major-General Patrick Hurley, General Albert C. Wedemeyer, and US chargé d'affaires Walter Robertson, and later by many Western planners of high policy, were held 'top secret' by Odlum, since, as the Australian ambassador, Dr Douglas Copland, told Endicott, it was important to make it appear that 'the Chinese Communists are responsible for the refusal to have a settlement.'[11]

Within Odlum's world view, his romantic presentation of Chiang Kai-shek's sincerity apparently made political sense: this alone would justify asking the North American public to support a regime whose reputation was becoming increasingly sullied; the generalissimo had to be seen as the brightest hope for democracy and free elections in China since the fall of the Manchu dynasty. The senior officials of the Department of External Affairs were highly sceptical of this course of action, but they were overruled by Prime Minister King, who saw the value of this line and encouraged Odlum: 'I read with greatest interest your highly appreciative references to the Generalissimo ... The important thing to believe, as you and General Hurley so firmly do, is that his fundamental purpose is to bring real democracy to his people.'[12]

At the time, Endicott, who was told little of Odlum's 'general framework,' suspected that Odlum had fallen under the spell of that 'war-whooping oil magnate,' Ambassador Hurley, and 'the global war strategy' of General Wedemeyer. When in March 1946 he received from Chinese friends what he felt sure was a reliable report on talks which Hurley's successor, General George Marshall, had with the generalissimo, Endicott tried to get some reaction from the Canadian ambassador about American policy: 'The conclusion I come to from reports,' Endicott told Odlum, 'is that the u.s. believes in the necessity of a war with Russia and is preparing for it. It believes in the necessity of gaining an ally of China for this conflict. In order to have an effective ally the u.s. wants a reasonably democratic China so that immediate civil war can be avoided, and also, so that industrialization can be begun ... Marshall has reassured Chiang that the Communists will not be allowed to gain military strength and that with future u.s. help in forming a new army, Chiang will be in a position to defeat them.'[13]

This was an exact and succinct statement of General Odlum's own understanding of American policy, but the ambassador, regarding Endicott as a 'fiery evangelist' whom the Communist leaders considered 'one of their great foreign friends,' carefully refrained from commenting on this sensitive area.[14] In a letter to his family, Endicott was outspoken in his criticism of United States policy: 'It is now quite apparent,' he wrote, 'that Marshall's policy re China is the same old Hurley-Wedemeyer policy only he knows how to wear kid gloves instead of mailed fists ... the u.s. basic wish in China [is] a market both for the investment of surplus capital and for the export of u.s. luxury goods as well as goods needed by the Chinese; a subservient government which will assist the u.s. to build up a striking force of about 5 million Chinese troops to attack Russia.'[15]

Later, when Douglas Copland, a professor of economics as well as ambassador, invited Endicott to lunch, he was confirmed in his interpretation of this policy. A good part of American policy in China could only be explained, according to Copland, by supposing that the United States was definitely planning a war against Russia in the Far East; it was not possible to explain this policy from the point of view of the best interests of the Chinese people. Washington, he continued, had long ago decided on all-out support to the Chiang regime, while 'trying to prove that the Communists are responsible for the refusal to have a settlement.' Whether General Marshall liked it or not, 'he was in an insincere position.' The Australian ambassador rather startled Endicott by expressing almost complete disagreement with the interpretations of General Odlum on the situation in China: in his opinion, the Chiang regime was hopelessly corrupt and inefficient and would rapidly ruin China; moreover, he said emphatically that all the best intellectual and moral leadership in China was going over to the Communists.

When Endicott's summary of this conversation, along with his own plea to the Canadian government not to support the Chiang regime as Ambassador Odlum was urging, reached Ottawa, it received a warm reception. Arthur

Menzies, of the China desk, circulated it widely through the Canadian diplomatic service, and Lester Pearson, under-secretary of state for external affairs, wrote to Endicott saying his letter had 'been read with a good deal of interest ... I hope you will continue to send us reports.' 'Whatever allowance should be made either in modifying or reinforcing Dr. Endicott's judgments on the significance of events,' another member of the department had written, 'I have invariably found his reporting on events and on statements which he quotes to be thoroughly objective and reliable.'[16]

The enthusiasm at External Affairs for Endicott's analysis was not based upon any pronounced admiration for the Chinese Communists, but rather upon an already formed conviction that the unity of China could not be brought about by civil war because the two groups were too nearly equal in strength; even if the United States backed the Kuomintang, the Communists would remain entrenched in the countryside as they had all during the Japanese occupation, only now they were much stronger. The department saw no evidence that the Chinese Communists were interested in the further-ance of the Soviet Union's power, nor did it see any evidence that the Kuomintang had any genuine desire to proceed towards some semblance of democratic government. The internal problems of China were so complex that the department ignored Odlum's advice and proposed that Canada should follow a policy of 'hands off.'[17]

The Canadian cabinet, however, slighted the advice of its External Affairs Department. Early in 1946 the Canadian government decided to aid the Chiang Kai-shek regime in its civil war with the Communists. Motivated partly by the desire to dispose of surplus Second World War stocks, which were sold to China at ten cents on the dollar, and partly by the hope of future trade with China, a $60 million credit to help finance the purchase of Cana-dian-made munitions and civilian goods was announced by Finance Minister J.L. Ilsley on 11 February 1946. It was the first post-war loan given to China by any country. Beginning in 1947 ships loaded with munitions began to sail for China from Vancouver and Montreal, and, by 1948, 150 of Canada's plywood Mosquito bombers were being used to strafe and bomb the villages and towns of North China.

The Chinese Communists, who had taken General Odlum's pretense of friendliness both to themselves and to 'the little people' at face value, and who as a result had tried to interest him in providing some war relief to the International Peace Hospitals founded in their areas by the famous Canadian surgeon, Dr Norman Bethune, were sorely disappointed at the turn in Cana-da's attitude. 'Your country's ambassador,' Chou En-lai told Endicott coolly, 'is a diplomatic trickster.'[18]

Against this background of the 'battle of the embassy,' as he called it, which was a battle to convince Canadians to accept the new forces that were rising up to revolutionize China, as well as his increasingly obvious attempts to help those new forces achieve success, Endicott's relationship with his church and with his fellow missionaries grew more tense. Although his colleagues were not fully aware of all his activities, his involvement within the confines of the West China Union University itself was sufficient to create serious friction and eventually to prompt demands for his resignation.

CHAPTER TWENTY-ONE

Resignation

At the beginning of his final term in China in 1944, Endicott's relations with his fellow missionaries were warm and friendly. Everyone seemed to feel that his presence would be a source of strength to the West China Mission and to the English Department of the university. It was even proposed that he should become acting secretary of the mission during the absence of the secretary, Rev. Gerald Bell. Endicott himself found genuine pleasure in his colleagues and enjoyed their good fellowship; he participated in the play readings of the Saturday Club and other sociable activities, and often felt an aching void when members of the community left on furlough.

Soon after his arrival, however, there grew up an undercurrent of resentments. Missionary administrators, especially, were displeased with the effect upon the young people of Endicott's outspoken preaching on social and political questions; he, in turn, became impatient with what he considered to be the narrow, business-as-usual, safety-first outlook of the administrators. A major source of contention was the activity of the KMT Youth Corps on the Chengtu campus.

After watching the Youth Corps for some time at close quarters, Endicott went to Dr Ashley Lindsay, vice-chancellor of the university, with evidence to suggest that some of its members were paid by the government to act as spies, bullies, and informers on their fellow students; they threatened liberal-minded students, suppressed any free discussions, and used gangster methods to break up meetings; they were a blackmailing outfit, extorting money from wealthy parents of children who expressed 'radical thoughts' and were there-fore liable to secret arrest; some of these gangsters mysteriously graduated from his classes without having passed any of his examinations. He wanted the Youth Corps building shut down, an action which the university was legally entitled to take.

The vice-chancellor made no effort to refute the charges, but neither did he act to curb attacks on the principles of freedom and human dignity, which were usually considered fundamental to Christian education. Endicott was met with a cold stare and a question: 'How do you know?'

Students who were thus disciplined, Lindsay told Endicott, were 'just a bunch of Communists.' 'We have disturbing elements in our midst,' he said, but their demonstrations are 'planned merely to stimulate dissatisfaction and not because of any real need to agitate.'

The president of the university, S.H. Fong, joined Lindsay in denying that there was any evidence that the Youth Corps building had ever been used by the secret police. 'Jim Endicott's charge is definitely a false one,' Fong asserted, adding that since Endicott was known in Chengtu 'as one with extreme Leftist views, it is natural that he should see things in a biased way.' In Toronto, Dr Jesse Arnup, moderator of the Canadian church, later admitted in private that the question of the Youth Corps was 'a tangled skein,' but he also declined to take any action.[1]

While Endicott chafed at these reactions, he continued with his preaching and public speaking, only to find some of the mission brethren suggesting that the day of preaching was over in China and should be replaced by 'corporate worship' emphasizing ritual. Was it a sign of the times, Endicott wondered, that, when political repression became more severe on the campus, the Christian groups began holding evangelistic services stressing personal salvation, with posters warning students that dancing and card-playing would lead to spiritual death? 'Funny,' he thought, 'but there seems to be a direct connection between reactionary imperialism and fundamentalist religion'; it had been the same while circuit-riding in Saskatchewan twenty years earlier, when the fundamentalist preachers did their best to turn the farmers' minds away from trying to organize the wheat pool. The great social issues confronting China, he believed, did not call for puritanical moral strictures or for 'more candles on the altar and commissions on the proper robing of the clergy.' Too much 'worship' and too little challenging preaching meant running away from the question of ethical conduct in an age that required reform and fundamental change.

Through sleepless nights and a distraught frame of mind Endicott lost thirty pounds over three or four months in late 1944 and early 1945. There were not only doubts about the necessity of sacraments, but he also began to lose faith that the Christian church would stand for justice and decency in the political struggle in China, and he feared it would become the spokesman of a tyranny that was daily getting worse.

As far as needed social and economic reforms were concerned, Christianity, in his opinion, 'ought to be 100% on the side of the communists,' but instead of that it was largely on the side of those 'who preach law and order and protect property, as against human need.' At its best now, Christianity was 'handing out charity in a cruel, exploiting world, without any real convictions about changing it.' The Christian leaders, both Chinese and foreign, were by and large sitting on the fence, 'a comfortable well-fed, well-warmed fence,' and when obvious lies were spread against the Communist forces by the Kuomintang they didn't struggle against them, they didn't say 'well how do we know?' but they swallowed everything against the Communists without question. The spirit of truth, the ability to think straight, the compassion for the poor and passion for justice, were largely absent.[2]

He wakened out of a fitful sleep one night in February 1945 to write out his resignation from the West China Mission and from the ministry of the United Church of Canada. The painful decision came to him on an impulse as the result of an emotional confrontation over starving conscripts a few days previously. The scene passed through his mind again in the form of a parable he called 'The Christian Good Samaritan Passes By on the Other Side,' which he later wrote out and sent to Rev. David MacLennan, pastor of his home church in Toronto:

In a certain city in West China there were five 'Christian' universities. They were much advertised in America and England as symbolizing the heroic spirit of resistance of the Chinese people against the Japanese fascists. They had a large and well-kept campus.

In the province in which they lived, several million young men, peasants from the farms, were conscripted for the army. The system of conscription was wickedly unjust and corrupt. After these young peasants were conscripted they were shut into camps and ill-fed because their officers stole their rations. At one time a few hundred of these miserable conscripts were brought onto the campus to drill. They were divided into three groups; first those who could still do marching drill; second, those who could only do light rifle drill, but no marching because of malnutrition; and third, those who were in an advanced state of malnutrition and were allowed to hobble to one corner of the campus and sit down, with armed guards to watch.

This spectacle was presented there day after day for the Christian eyes to look upon, but while all deplored it, they shook their heads and passed by on the other side. One small group of Good Samaritans tried to interest the students in the desperate plight of the conscripts and to do two things: take them some hot tea and biscuits, and start discussions on the necessity of large scale democratic reforms as the only cure for this inhuman treatment. This group was attacked by the Christian Educationalists as being 'Communist motivated' and the students were warned against any activity which would embarrass the government in war-time.

The poor ignorant women on the stalls in the street were more intelligent than the students on the matter: once or twice they took butcher knives and forced the guards to release the poor conscripts, saying, 'if you can't treat them better than that, then let them go home.'

Now it happened that there was one Missionary there who was teaching the Governor of the province some English and could see him informally and frequently. And in the course of time the starving conscripts who could not walk, did not walk to the toilets but went behind the trees of the campus and by the ditches. This raised a question of 'public health' in the minds of the more enlightened and scientific of the Christians who believe that disease may be from germs and is not necessarily an act of God.

The Missionary was asked to suggest to the Governor that it would be more convenient if the soldiers did not come to the campus.

The Missionary proposed a petition to the government about the needs of the starving soldiers but this was thought to be 'just so-and-so trying to inject socialism into every question.'

In the course of time the soldiers were stopped from coming. The 'public health' was saved, the 'framework of the church' was not even jarred and none of the saints wrapped in cellophane got themselves soiled by worldly or political matters.

In the years 1940–45 nearly 3,000,000 helpless recruits died of starvation or disease induced by malnutrition. At the same time 'never before have such fortunes been made in the midst of such great misery.' But the Christian campuses were loaded with spies, informers and gestapo agents to prevent the students from having 'wrong thoughts' or meetings to discuss the reasons why so many men died of starvation; reasons which were political only, because there was lots of food in the country. But most of the 'unpolitical' missionaries were still talking about those Russians who died of famine in the Ukraine in 1922.[3]

Endicott's impulse to resign found its first expression in purely theological terms, in a desire to be free of the unscientific trappings of his faith, trappings which co-religionists often employed to blur the social issues and to take the edge off action

In the past Endicott had reacted emotionally to his wife's scientific questioning of religion. Subconsciously, too, he had been afraid he might have to admit something he didn't want to admit because of emotional ties to his father or for fear of upsetting the security he enjoyed in the church. A decade earlier his father had successfully curbed his impatience with gospel evangelists who went around with a loud speaker. Now, however, Endicott had the feeling that his evasion in matters of belief was a reflection of a fundamental weakness of character which gave rise to irresponsibility in his life. He reflected that this irresponsibility was shown by the way he had buried himself in the preparation of textbooks and readers for so much of his time instead of facing and working through the difficulties of his evangelistic mission. 'The plain truth,' he wrote Mary, 'is that I don't like myself.'

Within the context of the vast social upheaval occurring in China, was it worth fighting any longer to keep those parts of his faith which had been a burden to him intellectually and spiritually? Somehow, Endicott felt, he must be free. From his experience in teaching Chinese students he knew that the 'cloak of supernaturalism' and the non-rational 'claims for revelation' of the New Testament detracted from the 'supreme importance' of the life and teaching of Jesus of Galilee, which Albert Schweitzer had so clearly delineated. The necessity of working as an ordained minister of a credal church now seemed unimportant; he would take his religious convictions and his 'ordination' from the same place that Amos and Moses took them. He realized that this was a fairly dangerous and perhaps boastful thing to say, but that was the way he felt. 'When you are in an organization, or an institution,' he wrote, 'you are always made to feel that you must be "loyal to your own" and I want to feel free if necessary and to say also, without these everlasting discussions about the fundamentals of the faith, "Is thy heart as my heart, then give me your hand."' He wanted to extend his hand and to join forces with anyone – including the Communists – who might not be saying 'Lord, Lord ...' but was in fact working sincerely for the 'Lord's year of Jubilee.'

His resignation and an accompanying letter to Dr Arnup were sent off to Mary, with instructions to hold them and not to tell anyone about them until he wrote or cabled for them to be released. Since he had served the mission well for twenty years, it did not matter whether he dropped out this year or the next. He would let the matter simmer rather than do anything in a hurry; the immediate necessity to lift whatever it was that was eating away at his 'innards' was to write out his resignation. In the uncertainty of wartime mail delivery, it would be two months before he received a reaction from Toronto.[4]

During this time of Endicott's public witness against the crushing of social reform by the Kuomintang, and his inward disillusionment and nervous strain, two people were of special support to him.

One was Hilde Jiang, a lecturer in French and German at Yenching University who had fled Germany to escape Hitler's persecution of the Jews in the 1930s. Hilde, who had been married to a Chinese medical student studying in Berlin, made searching criticisms of the missionary effort and had a sophisticated knowledge of Marxism. Her talks with Endicott led to an emotional involvement, and over the course of eight months, until Hilde got a visa to join her mother in Chicago, they had a quiet but renewing love affair.

The relationship was not without strains. Jim had no thought of breaking with Mary, but he was troubled by the possible interpretation that might be placed upon his behaviour. It was a worry he need not have carried if he could have known that Mary, in her loneliness, was having a similar experience in Toronto.

In some respects, also, Hilde was hard on his self-assurance. 'I am surprised to find how pleasant you can be, personally, to those you like,' she said, 'and how unfeeling, and even hostile, to those you do not take to.' She also expressed the opinion after the meeting of a discussion group that he was not interested in learning anything new or in getting the views of others. 'Unless you can "star,"' she complained, 'you prefer to retire into the blackout of your own thoughts.'

At a moment in his life when he desperately needed some warm, human fellowship, this assault on his inner defences, even if partially justified, was hard to take. He began to feel that his outward appearance of self-sufficiency was a façade to cover something in the nature of an inner defeat, which he traced back to childhood frustrations and fears of not measuring up to his father's expectations. 'I know this now,' he wrote Mary, 'but it doesn't help much ... I'm having a difficult time as you can see.'[5]

The other person who had a special influence upon Endicott was the Chinese Christian scholar, Wu Yao-tsung, who was a war refugee from Shanghai. For twenty-odd years Wu had been secretary of the Student Christian Movement or of the YMCA, a prolific writer on Christian praxis, who later became one of the most controversial figures in the history of Christianity in China following the establishment of the People's Republic in 1949 because of his positive attitude about possibilities for Christian witness in the new political regime.

Y.T., as he was called, was also discouraged about the immediate prospect for Christianity, but he strengthened Endicott's ability to retain his faith. He argued that there was something radically wrong with Endicott's desire to resign from the ministry; instead he should stay within the church and strengthen his grasp of the objective reality of the universe which was God. Y.T. pointed out that in the Judaeo-Christian tradition people's understanding of God had changed in the past and would likely continue to progress. The main thing, he argued, was to see both attributes of God which traditional theology expounds, God's transcendence and God's immanence, in their dialectical unity. Jesus had said: 'None is good, save one, that is, God' (Luke 18:19). This was a judgement made from the plane of the transcendence of God. But Jesus also said: 'Be ye therefore perfect, even as your Father which is in heaven is perfect' (Matthew 5:48). Here was revealed a faith in the potentiality of man which comes from faith in God who is indwelling in man.

For more than a thousand years, Y.T. suggested, the main currents of theological thinking had dwelt on God in his transcendence to the neglect or underestimation of the doctrine of God's immanence. 'If we see God only in his transcendence, we are bound to arrive at a pessimistic view of man ... According to this one-sided emphasis, man is sinful, miserable and utterly depraved; God and man are separated from each other by an absolute chasm ... The "salvation of the soul" takes the place of interest in social change since genuine social uplift is impossible with man's heart "at fault" ... Thus we arrive at the "above politics" mentality par excellence.' 'Unfortunately,' Y.T. mused, 'this is not "above politics" but a service to reactionary politics!'

But if God is seen also as immanent in the processes of nature and society, then there is no ground for pessimism. Prayer consists no longer of requesting God for protection, favours, and comfort; it becomes receptiveness to and search for the will of God and reliance on His love and obedience to His truth. 'The religious person is consequently full of joy and confidence. In realizing that his vocation is to co-operate with God in the working out of His will in history, he finds his place in God's economy for the recreation of the world.'

These concepts of theology were not new to Endicott, but it was inspiring and refreshing to hear Y.T.'s brilliant exposition. The effect was reassuring, steadying.

Even more important to Endicott at this stage, however, was Y.T.'s belief that Marxism and Christianity, as he interpreted them, were not in conflict. The two did part company, but both were travelling in the same direction, Christianity going beyond the Marxist goal.

After Wu, who was ill with tuberculosis, was evicted from his house in order to make way for some American army officers, Endicott invited him to share his quarters and they spent many of their spare hours discussing the relation of Christianity and communism with a small group of friends. With unusual humility, Endicott was quick to realize that Y.T. was the intellectual leader of the group.

The tentative conclusion of the study group was that Marxism was primarily a philosophy and a method of social change and as such confined its emphasis to one period of history, namely, the period of transition from the capitalistic to the socialistic social order. Christianity, on the other hand, was a faith that governed all phases of human life and had for its scope the whole sweep of cosmic history from 'the Creation' to 'the Life Everlasting.' Christianity had no difficulty in accepting the dialectical materialist view of the world as an attempt to describe the way in which God works, just as it had no difficulty in accepting the theory of evolution for the same reason.

In the dialectical materialist view everything is relative; in the Christian view things are both relative and absolute. For the former there is the danger of making an absolute of the relative, resulting in lack of humility and intolerance; for the latter there is the danger of over-emphasizing the absolute, resulting in sentimentalism, escape, and other-worldliness.

With regard to the problem of social change, the group concluded that, as to goal, Christians believed in the classless society no less than the Communists did, because such a society better expressed the spirit and teaching of Jesus. There was only this difference: the Communists regarded the classless society as the epitome of social revolution, whereas the Christians would regard it only as one step forward, the Kingdom of God still being far away because of human imperfection.

As to method, violence was not an issue, for Christians, no less than Communists, accepted the reality of violence; there was only a handful of pacifists among the Christians. The theme advanced by Reinhold Niebuhr, in *Moral Man and Immoral Society* and other writings, that power corrupts and that those in power will not give up until they are compelled to, did not differ essentially from the Marxist view; the amount of violence needed to bring social change would vary, of course, with the political experience and tradition of a people and the general national and international situation at a particular time.

The group, which based its study upon the classical European texts of Marxism, at a time when the writings of Mao Tse-tung on the need for continuing revolution and personal transformation were either still not well known or not fully formulated, concluded, in summary, that there were ample grounds for contact between Christians and Marxists; at the same time, they believed that Christianity offered something more by venturing into territory which the Communists seemed to find irrelevant. Ironically, for Endicott, the United Church of Canada reached a similar conclusion twenty years later at its twenty-first general council meeting in 1964.[6]

From several letters that had preceded the one bringing his resignation in February 1945, Mary knew that her husband was discouraged and that he had an inner sense of defeat about much of his life's work. Nevertheless, when the draft resignation reached her hands it was a profound shock. She felt she would burst unless she talked to someone. The logical person was Dr Arnup, and in spite of Endicott's injunction not to tell anyone, she went to their mutual old friend, who was by now moderator of the church, and bound him to secrecy.

Arnup listened to Mary and then did his best to dissuade Endicott from resignation. He wrote that he had watched the careers of a number of ministers who had resigned to join with other forces; the only one who had gained access to freedom and power without personal deterioration and dismal failure 'was Jim Woodsworth whose lofty character made him a national figure.' After disparaging the Communists for 'their totalitarian system,' the moderator suggested that if Jim joined forces with them he might have a temporary increase of power but he would eventually lose his freedom at their hands. The weaknesses of the church, on the other hand, in Arnup's opinion, seemed more apparent because the church was 'always measured against her own impossible ideal'; but that ideal brought a power of renewal into her life. 'Keep smiling,' he said, 'we're all pulling for you.'[7]

When Mary received a copy of Arnup's letter she felt that he had read into Jim's letter more than was intended in so far as any relationship or plans for working with the Communists were concerned. She was also dismayed for fear that through wartime censorship Arnup's assumptions might prove harmful to Jim. She regretted her indiscretion in talking to Arnup. A fait accompli, however, could not be undone.

Mary spared no emotion in telling Jim the reaction of herself and the children: 'It was almost as if we saw you struggling in dark waters that might bear you down.' She was also critical of his defeatism. The curtness of his resignation letter was painful evidence that all he wanted was to have it over and done with, and forgotten by the church and by himself. For as big a person as he was to simply slam the door and say 'I don't like your game any more,' just wasn't good enough, Mary wrote. It wasn't even the truth. 'You do yourself an injustice to let it go at that.' Moreover, it was an injustice to herself, who had to bear the onus of anything he did, and it was unfair to his father, to the Mission Board, and to Dr Arnup in particular. If he was to go out of the picture, he must go out for some great purpose; he must lift the church in his going, not slip out unobtrusively as if it didn't matter if one of her sons, whom she had honoured, had found that he could no longer conscientiously be in her company. If his resignation was sincere, and if it was to be an emancipation of his soul from the bondage of childhood fetters forged by parental love and religious upbringing, it should be as dignified and noble an act as he had ever committed.

'Maybe you think that sounds dramatic,' Mary continued, 'like taking your place in the church too seriously.' If so, she felt that such a position might well be false modesty, and perhaps, hardest of all for her to say, 'a form of cowardice.' Or perhaps his statement of resignation said nothing real because he felt the church would understand no more than Pilate or the high priests understood the position of Jesus. 'That is a possibility,' Mary conceded, but she believed there was more nobility in the church than that, faltering and complacent as it was. 'There will be some people touched by the courage and pain of what you do, if you let them see the purpose.' If he did not make clear some new purpose, the church would merely shake her head sadly and in pity over a resigning minister who had 'lost his faith,' as they would put it.

Although Mary had often criticized aspects of Endicott's inherited theology, in the present circumstances she saw clearly that strivings for theological purity were poor grounds on which to fight a battle for men's hearts. Such grounds would only add fuel to the smouldering fires of academic pedants. Therefore she suggested that before resigning he should first put the mission to a test by asking for some new kind of appointment that would allow him to do the work he had his heart set upon; by this she meant working in the Communist-held areas of North China. This would be straightforward and would be no stranger than some missionaries asking to do agricultural work or others requesting to work in the area inhabited by minority nationalities. If the mission refused, then would be the time to consider another stand.[8]

In contrast to Mary's dynamic concepts on strategy and tactics, Endicott's reactions at this stage appeared limpid and defensive. 'It is desperately difficult for me to get the time and rest I need to think out all the implications of my own experiences of these last months and to your reactions to them,' he wrote. 'You know how slowly I write. I have lost a lot of sleep.' As for Mary's idea about considering work in the Communist areas, Y.T. Wu had already raised that proposition at a conference of Christians, both missionaries and converts, in Chengtu, and it had been turned down. Mary's criticism that he was just shutting the door abruptly was true to some extent, he admitted, but under the prevailing oppressive conditions of Kuomintang China he did not see any other way of doing it. Although making his resignation on purely theological grounds still appealed strongly, he sensed the strength of Mary's powerful argument. He had no clear alternative path in mind. He did not wish to put the mission to any test. Therefore, until transportation became available for him to return to Canada or for her to come out to China to talk things over, he would continue working as his conscience dictated.[9]

Unfortunately for Endicott's intentions neither time nor the Chinese revolution stood still, and neither could his social conscience. His participation in the nation-wide student movement of December 1945, especially his appearance as a speaker in Sao Chen Park, brought strong reactions from church and state.

Through William P. Fenn, representative of the Associated Boards for Christian Colleges in China, the Chinese Ministry of Education, which by now had moved back to Nanking, notified the United Church of Canada and the West China Mission in December 1945 that unless Endicott was out of

China within one month he would be deported and barred from re-entry as an undesirable alien.

The Christian universities were extremely anxious to prevent such action from taking place, since they were afraid that Endicott's deportation would trigger more embarrassing student demonstrations. Dr Leslie Kilborn and Dr Ashley Lindsay of the West China Mission tried to settle the problem quietly by getting the help of the Canadian Embassy to find some way of ushering him out of the country without his knowledge of the threatened deportation. General Odlum co-operated by having Lu Tso-fu of the Min Sen Company request Endicott to join a business trip to Canada. Endicott considered the request and was sorely tempted in order to see Mary, but innocently turned it down because he had recently started a special class for middle school teachers, at the request of the same Ministry of Education, to train them in his direct methods.

The deportation threat turned out to be a bluff. Perhaps General Odlum told the Kuomintang that Endicott would do them more damage in Canada than he could do in China. Possibly the government also feared student demonstrations. But, more probably, Endicott was protected by his friend, Governor Chang Chun, who was himself under attack by the reactionary 'CC Clique' as a 'traitor to the party' and a 'bloodsucking parasite on the body politic' for his part in the peace negotiations with General George Marshall.

Instead of deportation, Endicott was made the subject of harassment by groups of students who were being urged by the 'CC Clique' to 'deal directly' with the 'unpatriotic.' In the newspaper of the Youth party, a small group allied to the KMT, he was attacked as a 'British traitor' and a 'Soviet spy,' along with his friend Y.T. Wu, who was also made the target of a huge notice outside the gate of the university administration building that read: 'Y.T. Wu's Lord's prayer – Our father Stalin, who art in Moscow, thy will be done in China, as it is in Russia ...' This was all part of an anti-Soviet campaign directed at the left, stirred up as the result of Soviet economic claims in Manchuria and Sinkiang.[10]

In the meantime, Rev. Gerald Bell, who was acting secretary of the Board of Foreign Missions in Toronto, consulted Dr Arnup about the case and then wrote an 'unofficial' letter to Endicott, dated 23 January 1946, saying that by his rabble-rousing opposition to the national government at the student demonstrations he was 'jeopardizing the influence of the whole Christian movement': 'It seems to many of us that active participation in political controversy is contrary to the rules which should govern us as aliens in China ... No one would willingly take any step to separate you from your Mission connection, but it seems to me that you should face the situation frankly and make a choice between two lines of action. First, retain your present position, but use your abilities and talents in giving constructive leadership to the young people within the accepted framework of the Mission and Church, or else cease that connection and seek to achieve your aims in a wider and less restricted sphere.'[11]

Bell's letter made Endicott fighting mad. He immediately invited a number of the leading missionaries, including Leslie Kilborn, Ashley Lindsay, George Sparling, Howard Veals, and Annie Thexton, as well as Y.T. Wu and T.L. Shen, for an evening meal at which they had discussions that lasted several hours.

Endicott read out Bell's letter, analysed the questions it raised, and stated his case. First there were the general propositions made by the letter from Toronto: that it was not the business of missionaries to criticize the government, that the church should keep out of politics, that missionaries were guests in China, and, finally, that the church had some generally accepted framework within which everyone should operate.

Endicott tried to place the discussion within an historical perspective. The missionaries, he said, had never been guests of the Chinese: a guest was one who was invited; all of the foreigners in the room, including himself, had been sent by the home church. And who could forget that the Good Samaritan, in the immortal parable of Jesus, was a foreigner? However, even supposing missionaries were considered as guests, did that mean they had no right to condemn evil acts? Was there some geographical limit on the Lord's commandment to practise brotherhood? The question of whether missionaries should take part in political activity was more complicated, but when it was realized that most of the so-called political issues were also moral questions, then it must be clear that the church could not stand aside. When an older generation of China missionaries had campaigned against the opium traffic, they too had been involved in political controversy. Now, when millions of peasants in Szechuan were suffering from a corrupt system of conscription and from unjust burdens of rents and taxes, and when students were being harassed by a ruthless secret police, the government and political parties responsible for such oppressive practices could not be exempt from judgement by Christians, unless it was maintained that there was an 'accepted framework of the church' which required that criticism be limited to purely individual acts of immorality. Was there anyone present who would advance such an idea? Criticism of temporal powers could be embarrassing and even dangerous, but an injunction to avoid politics such as that contained in Bell's letter could not be justified by the example of the Hebrew prophets or the life of Jesus who consistently championed the poor and the oppressed.

On the specific issue of 'jeopardizing the influence of the whole Christian movement' by his participation in the meeting at the park on 9 December, Endicott pointed out that this meeting had been legally organized, having been passed by the student councils of those universities that actively supported it. All the slogans and songs protesting civil war and expressing sympathy with the Kunming students who had been brutally beaten by police were first discussed and passed on in open meetings; he had been invited by the committee of student council chairmen to make the speech, the contents of which he had cleared with them in advance. Moreover, he had been in touch with the provincial governor both before and after the meeting and the latter did not make any protest. Endicott reported that he had told the governor quite frankly what he felt about the gestapo's activities among the students and how he would continue to oppose them. In these circumstances, did his colleagues feel that he had endangered the church or the missionaries?

There followed an awkward and disjointed discussion. Endicott had thrown out a formidable challenge from a well-fortified position. Some tried to insist that Bell's letter was unofficial, did not represent the attitude of the church, and that no notice should be taken of it. Dr Lindsay especially, Endicott thought, 'pussyfooted like nobody's business and hedged and hawed.' One missionary said Christians should preach the social gospel and hope that it would be practised, but not take an active part in political activity. George Sparling surprised everyone by saying he thought there should be room in the church for a revolutionary.

In the end Y.T. Wu spoke out strongly in support of Endicott. Too many missionaries, he said, did not understand what was happening on the campus; the students were not just an irresponsible rabble. 'Most of you,' he charged, 'can't even read the slogans they've put up.' 'What is the use of all this devotional study if in the end you don't know the difference between right and wrong? I wish the missionaries would learn that you can't preach the gospel in a vacuum.' They had no answer.[12]

After Endicott's request that the local mission executive define Bell's conception of the 'accepted framework of the church,' a resolution was passed a few days later, not unanimously or easily, which did not condemn his activities, as Arnup and Bell had done, but held that: 'members of that fellowship [the church] should be willing to lead in all movements for the uplift of the people, especially of the oppressed and underprivileged ... In pursuit of these ends we realize that members ... may often find themselves in opposition to entrenched and selfish interests. The form this opposition may take and the methods used to accomplish our purposes must be left under God's guidance to each individual member ... Resolved that we inform Dr Endicott that as long as he is in harmony with the aims and purposes of this fellowship we wish him God's blessing on any activity that he may undertake, and that we can say no more.'

When Howard Veals wrote to Toronto explaining the executive resolution, he said: 'We need men of the prophet type ... There is grave danger of our church and Christians here becoming too deeply involved in the same methods of money making and corruption that we all so much deplore in certain officials ... too much concerned about security and official position.' If only the prophets could have 'a little better judgement,' he lamented.[13]

Endicott was happy to have the vote of confidence from his missionary colleagues, whose statement he considered fair and generous. But he did not heed the advice of Y.T. Wu and other friends to stay in the mission. When Chou En-lai, who had been educated in Christian schools, heard of Endicott's resignation, he said to him: 'Why not stay in it and solve the problem of making a living? The Church does not stand for anything real that you are not working for anyway.'

But Endicott believed that any tackling of the problems with which he was concerned would bring the mission into danger and even lead to persecution by the government. Indeed the mission was most anxious to avoid such a fate. Therefore he felt that the continuance of his activities, in serving what he was convinced was 'the "social gospel" of our time,' could only lead to increasing resentment against him by the majority of mission members. The point of hatred had already been reached on the part of some. Although some of the younger missionaries would be sorry to see him leave, he did not feel that they looked to him for leadership. 'They give me tolerance but not support,' he said. It would be better, he felt, to 'be on the outside, offering the right hand of fellowship,' than on the inside doing what so many felt was 'unwise,' 'not the business of the Mission,' and 'unbecoming in a church member.'

The normal alternative to serving in the mission, of course, would be to return to Canada to seek a position as the minister of a local church. In his current mood this prospect had no appeal. Therefore, ignoring Y.T. Wu's discussion on the need for a more mature, dialectical view of the possibilities of continuing his work in the church, he decided to abandon a position of potential power and social influence by resigning from the ministry as well as from the mission, while continuing as a lay member of the church. He redrafted his statement of resignation to the Toronto Conference; harking back to his early doubts about the position of ordained Christians, as well as referring to the controversy surrounding his recent activities, the letter was brief and written in a spirit of goodwill:

Chengtu, China
May 5, 1946

Secretary, Toronto Conference
United Church of Canada

Dear Sir:

I regret very much that I feel it is now necessary for me to resign from the ministry of the United Church of Canada. I will not attempt to go into any detailed explanation of how I have gradually arrived at the necessity for making this decision. It has come after long and painful deliberation and travail of spirit. It is due primarily, of course, to a change in my own experience, understanding and explanation in regard to such matters as creeds, sacraments, especially 'orders and ordination.' It is also due to the fact that I now feel called to take an active part in the struggle for human betterment in the field of social and political movements, areas of life that are considered unsuitable for ministers to be active in unless possibly they happen to be on the 'right' side. I hope it will be possible for my resignation to take place without any undue publicity especially of such a nature as would discourage people in their support of the overseas work of the church. It is not necessary for me to assure you that this decision on my part has been arrived at only after long and painful deliberation.

Yours very sincerely,
James G. Endicott

In a separate letter of the same date to Dr Arnup, secretary of the Board of Overseas Missions as well as moderator, communicating his decision to resign from the mission field, Endicott again stressed that he did not want his leaving to cause any embarrassment in the matter of giving to missionary work, and he expressed the hope that he would be returning home soon to consult as to the best way of making public the announcement.

His resignations were accepted in Toronto, with expressions of regret, in June 1946.

His farewell message to his missionary colleagues in Chengtu contained a stronger note of criticism, but he did not cut all ties. 'I would like my brethren to be assured,' he wrote, 'that I still have a "personal and living faith in God." I believe quite sincerely that according to my light I am working for the Kingdom of God.'

As soon as Endicott's capitalist friends among the Chinese heard of his resignation, they approached him to work for them. He was offered a partnership in a press and publishing company, he could be part of a three-man industrial planning board to develop Szechuan industries with Canadian capital, he was offered the position of English secretary to the provincial ministry of industry. 'In five years, what with gifts from contract-hungry builders, commissions and delicately managed bribes, I could be a rich man,' he chuckled. 'With "enlightened self-interest," think of all the good I could do with the money! Memorial chapels, libraries, honorary degrees to the well-known philanthropist, etc. The only trouble is that I would choke.'

As Endicott prepared to leave Chengtu, he burned many of his files, told 'old Vesuvius,' the cook, to sell the furniture, including the piano, for whatever he could get, and packed Mary's most precious belongings in one trunk with the hope that it might reach Canada when communications improved. The contents of the trunk were all that was left of the boatload of Charles Austin's 'wedding loot,' which the Endicotts had so painstakingly nursed up the Yangtze River twenty years earlier. This was no time for regrets. 'I am feeling profoundly content after sending in my resignation,' he wrote to Mary. 'I feel free for the first time in my life. It's rather late but we will try to make the best of it.' He was now in his forty-eighth year.

On the eve of his departure there were many farewells from friends and colleagues, but the most memorable was from the surviving members of the Sparks, 'the mice of No 11.' They invited him to a dinner at the Yen Pin Lou restaurant, along with Wu Yao-tsung and Shen Ti-lan, to 'express our hearty gratitude for the joyful days we have shared with you in the past.' 'You have mingled your sweat with our sweat and offered your blood with ours.'

With unforgettable memories of the young Chinese revolutionaries lodged in his mind, their keen, youthful faces, their integrity of character, honesty of purpose, and their simplicity of life, Endicott set off once more on the long voyage down the Yangtze, thinking that he was headed for Toronto and an uncertain future.[14]

CHAPTER TWENTY-TWO

The
Shanghai
Newsletter

On his way to Shanghai in May 1946, Endicott received a message that one of the Communist leaders, Chou En-lai, wished to see him when he passed through Nanking. Chou, under the protection of General George Marshall, had recently established a headquarters in the newly restored Kuomintang capital in order to participate in the United States-sponsored negotiations to bring about a truce in the sputtering civil war between the Kuomintang and the Communist party.

Endicott had never seen the Communists so perturbed and anxious as when, during the course of a long interview, Chou En-lai, Tung Bi-wu, Li Hsien-nien, and one or two other leaders explained the complexities and the urgency of the political situation. Local disputes, they said, were now being turned into all-out civil war. The situation was critical. The United States government, in spite of official denials and misleading stories in the 'free press,' was covertly helping the civil war instigators, transporting troops, guarding and repairing ports and railways, training Chinese personnel to use US aircraft and tanks. Without American aid, Chou said, the reactionary clique in the Kuomintang could not last three months; with such support a bitter struggle could last for years. Democracy could not be defeated in China, Chou maintained firmly, but neither could it win without great difficulty against these odds. It was a life-and-death struggle and much therefore depended upon the way in which the case was presented to the outside world. This was where Endicott's help could be vitally important; with his skills and knowledge of both China and the West, he could help to strengthen the friendly bonds between the North American and Chinese peoples and thereby stop the transfer of arms and ammunition to aggravate civil war. 'Will you postpone your return to Canada and help us with publicity work?' Chou En-lai asked.[1]

Chou said he would like Endicott to locate himself in KMT-controlled Shanghai and start a newsletter. He warned that this would not be an easy task, not only because resources available for the project were limited but also, and more importantly, because the KMT would certainly try to suppress it. The circulation would have to be organized in clandestine fashion and Endicott would have to exercise the utmost care to prevent the authorities from discovering that he was the editor; otherwise he would likely be deported. In spite of these difficulties, Chou stressed the value of the project since it would allow an important readership both in China and abroad to have a clearer knowledge of the real situation and of the position of the liberation forces. The liberal intellectuals of the Democratic League in Shanghai, Chou thought, would also probably support him. As for the future, Chou said he planned to start an academy to train diplomats, possibly in Kalgan in the liberated areas, where he hoped Endicott might be available to teach – a hope that was never fulfilled.

When Chou was through speaking, Endicott could easily understand why General Marshall had said that Chou was the ablest advocate he had ever had to deal with. His approach was calm and reasonable, and he had a thorough grasp of factual details and a sincerity that were impossible to deny. At Marshall's headquarters in Nanking, Endicott found confirmation of Chou's estimate of American policy when Colonel J. Hart Caughey, Marshall's chief of staff, told him: 'We've made Chiang Kai-shek so strong that he will wipe out your friends in six months.'[2]

Endicott decided to start the newsletter. 'I cannot justify myself in leaving now,' he wrote Mary. 'How soon can you come over,' he asked, 'even if only for a short time? You can be excessively useful in writing. And anyway, I've just got to see you and soon.'[3] They had been separated for two years.

Endicott was glad to be back in Shanghai, even though it meant being under the watchful eye of the KMT secret police while living a double life, so to speak, 'a white one and a red one.' He felt nearer to Toronto than in Chengtu and, as he wrote to Mary, it was an interesting, if discouraging, city: 'It will yet be called the great eastern stench. Everything is deteriorating, the public services, the sewage system ... It is a place for quick profits, graft, crooks and luxury goods for the tourists of wealthy lands. Western businessmen, except for the United States importers, are sure that they cannot do business for long under things as they are ... it is amusing to see the look of incredulity when the said Westerners hear "respectable" Chinese businessmen say quite frankly that they would rather take a chance on the Communist regime than on the present gang in power ...'[4]

Endicott found temporary lodgings with the family of his former student,

Li Chao-chi, on the rue Albert in the French Concession. It was a strange experience to live with this semi-foreignized, middle class, Shanghai family. He found it hard to believe that Chao-chi, coming from this environment, had gone off to join the guerilla bands in North China before coming to Chengtu to continue his university studies. The younger brothers and sister, capable and bright, were completely 'amahized,' leaving things anywhere and everywhere for the amah (nursemaid) to collect and almost calling for her to wash their faces. All the family wash was done in the bathroom, a very small place, so that one had to play hide-and-seek with the amah to get in when the place was not occupied. Hot water had to be bought from the shop at the corner, which had a well. The amah kept a watchful eye on Endicott at bath time and if he passed up one day she asked 'Are you taking a bath?' in the tone of an ultimatum. When he washed a pair of socks one evening, he received a gentle reminder that amah was the official sock-washer.

In another part of the city, where he would lead his 'white' life, a spacious office for revising the English-language readers was made available to him by his old friend and publisher, Milton Hsu, manager of the Chung Hwa Book Company; Hsu, Endicott reported, like many businessmen, was 'entirely anti-Kuomintang.' To earn his living, Endicott found a temporary job teaching at Medhurst College, run by British missionaries, and, ironically, at the most prestigious and conservative Christian institution of higher learning in China, St John's University; when offering him a contract, the president of St John's had said that since the name Wen Yiu-chang 'has become a sort of legend among the students of China,' his stay at the university was conditional upon keeping clear of any student political activities.[5]

The first edition of the underground *Shanghai Newsletter*, which appeared on 19 June 1946, announced its credo in terms of Jeffersonian democracy, saying that 'no king, no tyrant, no dictator can govern people as well as they can govern for themselves'; it dedicated itself to 'the struggle for a peaceful, progressive and united China.' Anyone who wished to judge the pros and cons of the present troubles in China, the paper said, would have to remember that the central problems were those of the Chinese farmers who constituted over eighty per cent of the population and were struggling with poverty. A reduction of rent on the land they farmed and a reduction of interest on loans would be what the peasants wanted, if they could govern for themselves. The basic question to ask, therefore, was: 'what are the forces working for these things and what are the forces opposing them?' The underlying message was that all foreign governments should keep out of the Chinese struggle and let the Chinese people settle their own affairs in their own way; Western democracy was on trial in China and now was the time for the true friends of China and democracy 'to make their voices to be heard and their influence to be felt' for a 'hands off China' policy. From the fluent and vigorous style, it was not difficult for the Canadian ambassador, Victor Odlum,[6] and perhaps the Kuomintang as well, to guess the editorship.

Anything was possible in the Shanghai of those days, if one had some connections. The newsletter, which appeared once a week for the next year, was produced on a press owned by Vic Schnierson, a member of the large White Russian community in Shanghai; and through an old friend from Chatham, Harold Brown, who was back in China working for the United Nations Relief and Rehabilitation Administration, Endicott was able to mail the paper without having to pass the KMT censor. With the help of other friends he developed a growing mailing list of politicians, journalists, church leaders, diplomats, trade unionists, university professors, and special friends in China and throughout the English-speaking world.

Material was collected from every possible and widely differing sources. These included Tao Hung-chi, educational director of the Democratic League, Ma Yin-chu, a noted economist, and two long-time American residents of Shanghai, Telitha Gerlach of the China Welfare Institute and John W. Powell, editor and publisher of the liberal *China Weekly Review*. After her return from interviewing Mao Tse-tung in Yenan, Endicott also had talks with Anna Louise Strong, the famous American socialist writer, who impressed him as a 'strong and level-headed person.'[7]

On Friday evenings, while many of the Britishers were over at the Shanghai Club drinking pink gins and weeping over the days of the past, Endicott met one of Chou En-lai's staff, usually Chiao Kuan-hua, to review and analyse the current situation and to decide upon the main points to be made in the newsletter. Chiao would 'lose his tail' by chatting with idlers in a nearby tea-house and then, when the agent of the secret police wasn't looking, he would slip over to the room on the rue Albert.

At times, Endicott became carried away in his response to events and used uncompromising and polemical language. Following the assassinations of Professors Li Kung-po and Wen I-do of the Democratic League, when his indignation knew no bounds, he called the KMT government 'the finest collection of thugs, murderers and gangsters left unhanged after World War II.' After such outbursts his Communist friends cautioned him against sounding too far left, politely suggesting that such overly positive and definite language could lead to unnecessary sacrifices and weaken the newsletter's effectiveness in being able to reach uncommitted people. 'Bu yao tai hung' ('Don't be too red'), said Li Hsien-nien.[8]

The deep-seated, anti-communist sentiment that was growing stronger in the Western world was a formidable obstacle to understanding the truth of China as Endicott saw it. When Randall Gould, the editor of the *Shanghai Evening Post and Mercury*, an American daily newspaper, irately denounced the *Shanghai Newsletter* as 'a communist sheet of unknown origin,' Endicott at least had the satisfaction of knowing that his journalistic efforts were reaching some targets.

The archives of the Canadian government reveal that the *Newsletter* was read in Ottawa with interest, but without noticeable effect upon policy. Justice T.C. Davis, Mackenzie King's choice to succeed General Odlum as ambassador to China, continued to advocate that it was 'the duty of every person and every nation to make every possible contribution towards the defeat of communism in China.'[9] It was an opinion shared by many other Western diplomats who felt, along with Davis, that war with Russia was inevitable and that 'the showdown may as well come now as later.'[10] But Davis also believed that all-out aid to the floundering Kuomintang government could be given only if the onus of the continuation of hostilities could be placed 'squarely and beyond doubt upon the shoulders of the Communists.'[11] The role of the *Newsletter*, then, was to prevent Western governments from convincing public opinion of this hoax by supplying firsthand information about the struggle in China to such groups as the Committee for a Democratic Far Eastern Policy in New York, or the Committee on Principles for Canadian Aid to China in Toronto, who in turn mobilized influential people to put pressure on their governments to suspend credit and arms until the threat of civil war in China was over.[12]

When asked many years later about the contribution of Endicott's newsletter, Chiao Kuan-hua, by now foreign minister of China, replied that 'it was immensely valuable to us. Its circulation was not large but it put us into contact with many influential quarters and won us many new foreign friends. Those were very difficult days in Shanghai – we had no foreknowledge that the Chiang regime would collapse so rapidly and therefore we needed all the sympathy and support which we could get in order to frustrate the attempt by Chiang to involve the Americans more deeply in his civil war against us. Jim was our comrade-in-arms in this struggle.'[13]

Endicott was in Shanghai six months before Mary managed to secure transportation across the Pacific, and even then it took some help from her old friend, Mike Pearson, at the Canadian Embassy in Washington to acquire a steamship ticket and a Chinese visa. At first the Canadian government tried to have Mary use its channels to send a cipher message to persuade Endicott to return to Canada; the reasons given were the need for moderation in China and the advantage of coming home for a rest. However, when Mary explained his frame of mind and sense of duty, and asked, 'What could you cable a man like that?' Pearson said he understood and would continue trying to get passage. This was eventually secured aboard the *S.S. Marine Lynx* sailing from San Francisco, on which the Canadian government already had places for Mrs Chester Ronning and her four children. To overcome Mary's lack of priority because she was not diplomatic personnel, Pearson arranged to advance payment for her passage, describing her as a nursemaid helping to care for the Ronning children.[14] A final hurdle was a longshoreman's strike on the west coast which delayed the sailing from October until December 1946.

Once Mary arrived in Shanghai, with a thousand and one lonely days and nights to make up for, it seemed as if the Endicotts could not get enough of just being together. Jim had found an apartment in a St John's University staff residence that had remained vacant and in disrepair since the Japanese invasion; with the help of a coal-oil heater the Endicotts managed to keep one room at a liveable temperature. When one of the women on the campus apologized for not having been to call on Mary, Jim replied: 'Well, to tell you the truth, we haven't minded whether anybody came or not. We've been too busy calling on each other.'

The joy of reunion was tempered by the accumulated strains of a long separation, which revealed some severe and unexpected tensions in their relationship. The pent-up thoughts and emotions, the changes only vaguely referred to through two and a half years of censored wartime correspondence, were almost too overwhelming for Jim to handle. As they reviewed the years they had spent together, recalling some of the high spots and some of the mistakes, and discovering some of the reasons they behaved as they did, their roles were reversed. Mary, whose years of work on the Board of Education in York and on various committees of the church had given her poise and self-assurance, was now the confident one, while Jim found himself plunged into depression and for several days on the verge of a nervous breakdown.

In trying to understand what was happening to him, Endicott spoke of all his failings and the mistakes he had made: of his worship and fear of his father from an early age, that had something to do with his going into the church and defending an orthodox theology with which he did not entirely agree, thus preventing him from being his real self in many ways; of the crisis caused by his difficulty in reconciling the new form of knowledge revealed by Marxism with the existing role of the church in society; of his childhood anxieties about his mental and physical capabilities, stemming from bitter incidents at the Chungking school, which led to exaggerated traits of self-reliance, a desire to 'get back' at people or to prove that he was successful or right.

Most of all he was worried and depressed by a sense of failure in his marriage.

'As you know,' he wrote to his son Stephen, after the most acute days of crisis were over, hoping that someday the next generation might take comfort from the ghosts of old lovers, 'after I had been away a long, long time there came to Mary a man "with love in his eyes" as she herself reports it and she accepted him.' 'When Mary began to tell me,' he continued, 'her voice was so steady and heart so true that I had to accept it. (As a matter of fact as soon as I really held her in my arms I knew that she had had a very satisfactory experience of some other kind and that it had freed her from all her feelings of inferiority which were my fault.) When Mary looked at me so trustingly and said, "It was good for me, he loved me for myself," it was as if I had been stabbed.'

He related how he had found some notes that Mary once made of her thoughts in Chungking where she had written that 'there are times when Jim is a stranger to me and I think he does not love anybody but himself.' More recently, when Mary passed through Chicago to visit Hilde Jiang, the latter had ended up a résumé of his character by saying to Mary: 'Jim doesn't love anybody but himself.' The identical words from two different women who knew him well were more than a coincidence; they made him despair of his egocentricity, which had partly spoiled his intimate life with Mary because she never felt really secure in his love.

During one of the worst phases of his black mood, Dr Fritz Kobler, a refugee psychiatrist from Vienna whom he had befriended in Chengtu, came to spend a weekend and helped the Endicotts discuss their difficulties; his greatest assistance was in making an interpretation of Mary's personality after she had related to him some recent dreams. According to Kobler, she had an Elektra complex, or father fixation, that had affected almost every side of her life and was responsible for part of Jim's conflict. Mary was convinced by the truth of this analysis and thus was able to relieve Jim of some of his feelings of guilt and remorse.[15] With the balancing of responsibility for their emotional turmoil, Jim's spirit rose; in spite of the 'affairs,' the happiness of their marriage was renewed and grew stronger thereafter.

Endicott's well-being was further increased by Mary's eagerness to participate side by side with him in the political and social life of Shanghai. She toured textile and silk factories to get a firsthand impression of conditions and she helped with the newsletter; she was uncomplaining about the personal discomforts resulting from the crowded, poor housing on St John's campus and the soaring cost of living. In spite of the painful crisis he had been through, Endicott felt that asking Mary to come out to Shanghai to be with him and to feel the new pulse of China was the wisest decision he had ever made and that it would ensure their mutual understanding and contentment no matter where they went in the future.

Mary, for her part, was relieved to find that Jim had not lost his fire and zeal for a good cause. The question as to whether his influence in China had waned since he had taken a stand with the Communists, the Democratic League, and the other groups opposing civil war was answered for her by the calibre of his personal friends, by the warm response given him by intellectual leaders, and the widespread reputation he had even among workers who did not know him, and among students who looked to him as a leader in the peace demonstrations that came to a climax in the spring of 1947.

At conservative St John's, student pressure was such that the president of the university was forced to release Endicott from his undertaking to refrain from speaking publicly. As a result, one morning in May 1947 after a large student rally the Endicotts awoke to find that the Youth Corps had paid them a retaliatory visit during the night; their house was plastered with slogans in English and Chinese, saying 'James Endicott is a running dog of the Comintern' and 'Scram, You Anti-God!' On another occasion when Lo Lung-chi, vice-chairman of the Democratic League and one of the liberal intellectual leaders in Shanghai, met Endicott, he said: 'Give me your hand. It is a pleasure to meet you; you qualify for assassination.'[16]

One of the memorable times for Mary, which showed the genuine love and trust which Jim's new friends had for him, was an invitation to visit the Communist liaison office in Shanghai in the first week of March 1947. The Communists wanted to propose that Jim take their library because they thought that an open break was coming with the Kuomintang and they did not wish to have it destroyed. While the Endicotts were having dinner at the office with Teng Ying-chao, wife of Chou En-lai and a member of the Communist liaison team in Shanghai, and Tung Bi-wu, one of the twelve founding members of the Communist party, the latter was called to the telephone. When he returned he said: 'General Marshall has told me that as from tomorrow morning the civil war is on; all negotiations are off and we are ordered to take Marshall's airplane tomorrow morning to return to Yenan.'[17]

This news did not seem to disturb the dinner hosts unduly and the talk continued. 'We have watched you through the last two or three years,' said Tung to Endicott, 'and we admire the way you have thrown in your lot with the Chinese people. Perhaps after we have gone you may be able to continue some reporting here and we may even manage to get you some accurate information.'[18]

Tung Bi-wu then took out a large-scale military map and told Endicott he wanted to give him an overview of the situation and of what was likely to happen in the course of the next year. One of Chiang Kai-shek's armies, he said, had moved away up to the northwest, where for prestige reasons it was going to attack the Chinese Communist headquarters; this army was now bogged down and could neither get in any further nor out. A second army was stationed along the railways of East China, while the third and best army was in a strategically unsound position far up in Manchuria. This left the whole centre of China open, an area teeming with guerilla activity, and sooner or later Liu Po-cheng, 'the one-eyed dragon,' Chen Yi, and the other liberation army commanders would sweep into the plains of northern and central China, isolating the great cities. Tung explained that for reasons of prestige and looting Chiang's armies would seek to attack or hold 150 of the larger population centres. 'When you hear that he has captured 120 of them you will know he has lost the war,' said Tung, 'because we will highjack the communications, the cities will be surrounded, the Kuomintang cannot give good government and the populace will become hostile to them.' It was this strategic outline of the future of China's civil war that Endicott would use to predict the course and outcome of the struggle in a lecture tour across Canada later in the year.

As the sounds of gunfire began to intensify across the plains of North China, the Endicotts' stay in Shanghai came to an end. One morning when Endicott was working at the Chung Hwa Book Company, he received a telephone call from Chang Chu, a former friend and secretary in the New Life Movement who was working in the generalissimo's headquarters in Shanghai. The friend invited him for lunch, saying: 'I will send a car at twelve o'clock.'

Endicott thought he was going to be arrested and called Mary to say that, if he failed to return, she was to notify the Canadian trade commissioner and set some wheels in motion.

He was taken to headquarters in a large bullet-proof Buick with two armed guards. After a pleasant luncheon where several others were present, Chang took him aside and said bluntly: 'What are you going to do in the future?'

'Well,' Endicott replied, 'I will either go back to Canada or if I stay here I think I will throw in my lot with the revolution. You know how I feel about it in general.'

'Jim,' said the official, 'you are either a fool or a genius.' Then, looking at him solemnly, and straight in the eye, he added: 'I think you had better go back to Canada as soon as possible.'[19]

When Endicott told his friends of this encounter they became alarmed for his safety. In consultation with his contacts in the revolutionary underground, it was decided that it would be impossible for him to carry on much longer in Shanghai and that he should return to Canada where he could do much to win sympathy for China's struggle. Since the Endicotts had some months earlier placed their names on a waiting list, passage was soon arranged. While the announcement of their departure was sudden, it did not take place before a large public reception was organized by their friends and students. 'It is a matter of regret,' Endicott told the assembled throng, 'that I have to leave while the struggle for democracy is still at its most critical stage. While I feel a deep sense of grief for the thousands of fine young men and women who are facing torture and misery in the concentration camps of the Kuomintang Party and the Military Affairs Committee, I also have a strong feeling of optimism that the struggle will not be very long now and that this time the forces that are struggling for the liberation of the Chinese people are going to win ... You and I, as we part,' he concluded, 'can be of good cheer and high courage because we know that the youth of China are awake and marching forward, the peasants are being loosed from the chains of the past and everywhere the masses are being given the opportunity to start on the great task of building an independent, democratic and industrially progressive China.'[20]

The Endicotts sailed out of Shanghai harbour after dark on 19 June 1947. It was their wedding anniversary. As the lights of the city disappeared they reminisced about their twenty-two years in China, taking pleasure in remembering the past by recalling all the different houses they had lived in. The circumstances were not conducive to much celebration, however, because the S.S. *General Meigs* was a troopship, with men and women segregated into different sections and assigned to three-decker bunks; in addition the boat was crowded to capacity, mainly with Jewish refugees who had received visas to settle in the United States. The next day, when the swells of the Pacific Ocean began to roll, Jim, as usual, spent much of the time lying on his bunk trying to fend off the feelings of seasickness.

CHAPTER TWENTY-THREE

The 'Endicott controversy'

On 19 July 1947, when the Endicotts reached Toronto, they were interviewed immediately upon arrival by the *Toronto Star*. In the front-page story that resulted, the former Canadian adviser to Madame Chiang Kai-shek predicted that by the New Year the Chinese president would be deposed and either shot, imprisoned, or a refugee in the United States. Endicott condemned the increasingly dictatorial and oppressive character of the Nanking government, and praised instead the 'united people's campaign' to overthrow Chiang Kai-shek, declaring that it deserved the approval of progressive, decent, and democratic people everywhere. Moreover, Endicott asserted, the opinion that the Chiang administration would be knocked out by the end of the year was shared by most businessmen and diplomatic representatives of foreign governments in China.[1] These sensational views came as a shock to the public accustomed to hearing news of Chiang Kai-shek's victories.

The question of China's civil war might have remained little more than an academic question in Canada except for the government's decision in February 1946 to allow Chiang Kai-shek to buy Canadian surplus war material on credit for his struggle against the Chinese Communists. When government spokesmen solemnly declared in September 1947 that Canada had no thought of 'taking sides' in the civil strife in China and yet justified the shipment of arms to Chiang, saying that the programme of mutual aid was simply a 'hangover,' the 'continuation of a deal begun in happier days,'[2] Endicott determined to stir the moral conscience of Canadians against this policy.

A hectic, year-long round of public speaking took him from coast to coast, along trails familiar and unfamiliar, during which he spoke about the nature and purpose of the Chinese revolution. At first it was difficult to find sponsors for his meetings because many considered him to be the prisoner of an ideology and treated him as an object of suspicion. One minister telephoned

Endicott long-distance, collect, to say that before he could speak to his church he needed a guarantee that he was still a Christian, proof that he was not being sponsored by anyone, and a promise that he would not expect to receive any of the collection; Endicott gave the necessary assurances, joking that he was now sponsored by God and the prophets, and that even Elijah had to be fed by the ravens.

In one city some friends had a fine line-up of meetings arranged, including the Canadian Institute of International Affairs and other highly respectable groups. All went well until a Ukrainian-Canadian organization known to be sympathetic to the Soviet Union wanted to sponsor a public meeting for him; the liberal academics and Christians then threw up their hands and said, if 'they' had him, then he would not do for themselves.

On another occasion, company agents at a logging camp on Vancouver Island, where he had been invited by the labour union, insisted that he leave and dumped him in the country miles from town on a frosty night.

Before long, however, more and more people came forward demanding a 'hands off China' policy. After a series of meetings in Montreal at which Endicott spoke, about one hundred students from McGill University joined him on a picket line to protest the loading of the Canadian ship, the *S.S. Cliffside*, with arms for China. 'Not bullets but bread for China,' they chanted, in words that echoed around the world as far as Shanghai and Peking. Efforts to involve students at the University of Toronto were less successful owing to the tighter control of the administration over the Students' Administrative Council,[3] but several ministers in Toronto, including Gordon Domm and Laval Smith, circulated petitions protesting the sailing of arms ships, collecting hundreds of names among their congregations.

On the initiative of some members of Parliament in Ottawa, Endicott was invited to address the local chapter of the Empire Parliamentary Association. During this visit to the capital he also met members of the Department of External Affairs and had a good hearing from M.J. Coldwell, leader of the CCF. Coldwell did not invite Endicott to rejoin the party, but subsequently wrote party organizers saying that even though Endicott had been labelled subversive because of his willingness to work with various groups in opposition to the Chiang Kai-shek government, he personally did not believe that Dr Endicott was a communist and felt that his story of China was well worth hearing, 'whether it is entirely acceptable or not.'[4]

Although initial reports from friends in western Canada were that 'people don't seem to trust Jim any more,' this assessment changed after he began his tour. The retired manager of Imperial Chemical Industries, Shanghai office, an old friend of the Endicotts with conservative political views, left the St

John's United Church forum in Vancouver feeling that he had 'seldom heard so inspiring or so earnest or so courageous an address, and in so restrained language in the light of Jim's own feelings and the attitude of his critics.'[5]

'It was a great experience,' was the comment of Dr Bruce Collier, a former colleague of the Endicotts in China, then living in Saskatoon, who helped arrange meetings at the Canadian Club, the United Nations Association, the University of Saskatchewan, and in a United Church in that city. In Regina, Tommy Douglas, premier of Saskatchewan, invited him to speak to members of the legislature, an encouraging sign, Endicott thought, that the CCF group in western Canada was not so filled with 'anti-red hysteria as some.' Perhaps most moving was the strong sense of kinship for the struggling peasants of China shown by the striking coal miners in the Drumheller Valley, who raised $47 to support his tour. 'They are "my gang,"' he wrote home.[6]

Through Ontario and the West, then in Quebec and the Maritimes, thousands of citizens listened with obvious sympathy and respect for the integrity of Endicott's message.

Bearing in mind the old Chinese proverb that 'one seeing is worth a hundred tellings,' the Endicotts began in January 1948 to publish a monthly bulletin, the *Canadian Far Eastern Newsletter*. This continuation of the *Shanghai Newsletter* appeared without interruption for more than thirty years as a personal interpretation of the revolutionary changes taking place in Asia. Jack Kellerman, Bill Ackerman, and other interested professional and business people in Toronto provided the paper, postage, and a mimeograph machine, as well as the volunteer labour required for an initial distribution of five thousand copies to clergymen, editors, politicians, labour and farm organizations in Canada and the United States. Soon the *Newsletter* had over two thousand paid subscriptions.

A large part of Endicott's energies were spent in urging the Christian community to reconsider its attitude towards the revolutionary developments in Asia. That the Protestant churches were deeply concerned about this issue was shown by the results of their meeting in Amsterdam in 1948 at which the World Council of Churches was formed. After heated debates between representatives from East and West, a stalemate was reached, the ideologies of both capitalism and communism being rejected. Returning American delegates emphasized that the church council 'was aware of the dangers of communism' but omitted the other fact that capitalism had been equally condemned. Endicott was grateful, therefore, for the statement of the Anglican Bishop of Toronto, R.J. Renison, who said that 'by making common cause with anti-Communist forces, the Church might have some success, but such a short term policy would prove in the end to be disastrous to the Church, both in the East and in the West.'[7] Endicott's own reflections on the tension between Marxist ideas and liberal ideals and upon the dangers of dwelling on the 'Red menace' were set down in a draft chapter of a book about his experiences in China, which he began in 1948 but never completed:

Underlying all the tensions in our modern world is the one question: should non-Communists of any faith or outlook co-operate with Communists on any practical program? All sincere religious bodies and all liberals and socialists are troubled by this question. Only the outright reactionaries – those pulling us back to the past – have an untroubled answer. They are sure we should absolutely shun such co-operation; more, that we should destroy not only the Communists but everything which they touch. To them it is tainted, with some fantastic touch of evil about which they build up legends from slender bases and the most biased sources. There is no use discussing the point with these people. They can learn only by the hard way, a way which will mean intolerable suffering for all ...

To others, to all those who really long for the evolution of a more humanitarian social organization, the end of that road of suffering will bring the opening of a new era, a day in which their dreams will be realized beyond their expectations. This is what is happening in China today, beyond a doubt. The liberals, the socialists of all varieties and the humanitarians of any faith are seeing the transformation begun. In the Liberated Areas, in proportion to the time in which the new forces have been operating, and also at a snowballing rate of success, the pall of bankruptcy, starvation and oppression is being lifted. More than that, the age-long tradition of corruption on all levels – which even the best Chinese have often declared is inherent, ingrained, inseparable from Chinese life – is being replaced by a conscious emphasis on the necessity for exploiting no one, not even in the smallest trifle, as indicated by one of the orders to the occupation forces of the Liberation Army that they were not to take a needle or a spool of thread from anyone without paying for it. Many foreign observers have written of the amazement of the Chinese people with whom the victorious troops are billeted. The American wife of a Chinese engineer in Tientsin writes: 'There's no stealing, no quarrelling and brawling and what's so amazing in an army, no liquor and no "Wimmen"! Any soldier caught going into a house of prostitution would be shot. I heard an American say it was the first chaste army he'd ever seen, and it got him down!' She compared these troops to the disciplined troops of Cromwell's army as described by Macaulay, and added her own comment. 'They all seem kind and courteous and good-natured ...'

One could spend a great deal of time citing such examples from China, but the point to be discussed here is the fact that all this is happening under the leadership of the Communist Party of China. Can it be denied by rational people that this transformation is a good thing? To say, 'I cannot distinguish between right and wrong unless I am sure that Communists are not involved in the situation,' is to destroy one's moral judgement ...

Endicott then commented that since returning to Canada he had noted how the Western press generally suppressed news favourable to Russia, distorted many items, and stressed two points of view continually: that there was an 'iron curtain' and therefore favourable reports were to be discounted because 'we cannot see for ourselves,' and, secondly, that in spite of the 'iron curtain' the Western press knew all about tens of millions of slaves in Siberia. It was his guess that a similar press phenomenon would soon appear on the subject of China. As China proceeded on the road to socialism and as Western-sponsored, anti-socialist movements and counter-revolutionary elements were suppressed, the press in North America would compensate by pretend-ing that nothing was really knowable about what went on behind the 'iron curtain.'

Before that happens it is well to remind ourselves that there has been no iron curtain in China. Up till the present there have been about eight thousand foreign missionaries in every nook and corner of the country. Western travellers and journalists have been relatively free to go everywhere. The inhuman factory conditions in China's coastal cities, the slave labour and cruelty to childhood in the southeast tin mines, the high incidence of TB in the buffalo drivers of the salt well district of West China, the greed and brutality of the feudal landlords and their warlord armies, all these and a host of other evils have been openly displayed for all to see. At the end of the Japanese War the 'quintessence of corruption' that was the Chiang regime, was plainly revealed in the hoarding, black-marketing and starving of the soldiers. Was there any general empha-sis of these evil things in the reports? Did the western observers create an impression that the ruling powers ought to be overthrown, as they think the regime in Russia ought to be overthrown? They certainly did not.

The middle class religionists of my acquaintance in China nearly all believed that such conditions [slave labour and starvation] existed in Russia. They all read the 'Reader's Digest,' and these conditions, far away behind the iron curtain, were a matter of concern and conscience to them, especially in any discussion of socialism. But when in China these conditions, in reality, were there before their very eyes, they defended the ruling powers, or else they ignored these conditions, claiming for the Gospel a spiritual realm which did not meddle in politics. The same people who would express hope that the Russian people would revolt, condemned those who revolted in China.

There was no iron curtain hung between thousands of western observers and one of the greatest revolutions in all human history, certainly the greatest in China's history. They were there to see for themselves, but having eyes they saw not. They neither understood it in its social implications nor sympathized with it. They flooded the world with atrocity stories and spent endless hours arguing whether or not it was 'Russian dominated' and how many secret advisers Stalin had in Yenan.[8]

Unable to find time to complete his book, Endicott nevertheless moved beyond the narrow question of 'Should we send arms to China?' and took up the wider issues in his short articles and speeches. He was convinced that a general explanation of the nature of the Chinese revolution and of the possibilities of a Christian contribution to revolutionary Asia was necessary because dangerous ideas were getting established which would be used by capitalist America to justify plans to overthrow the revolution in China. The news media and the government of Canada, following the lead of men like John Foster Dulles, were systematically spreading the notion that the Chinese Communists were simply an outward and visible sign of 'internal Russian aggression,' an alien element that was attempting to impose its system on China by force of arms. Persecution of Christians was alleged to have reached a 'new and horrifying level.' According to this way of thinking, material aid to Chiang Kai-shek was justified fully.[9]

In explaining the upheaval in the East, Endicott tried to present the case in historical terms meaningful to the West. He emphasized that the revolution unfolding in China had been going on for a hundred years, before the Communist Manifesto had ever been heard of. It began with the Taiping Rebellion in 1850; it had outbursts in 1900, 1911, and 1927. The long view of history would show that this movement marked the break-up of feudalism and could therefore be regarded as the Chinese equivalent of those great landmarks of the past such as the English revolution of Cromwell's time, the French revolution of 1789, or the American revolution led by George Washington.

The changes in China were partly forced upon the country by the impact of the industrial revolution of the West. Faced with the loss of supplementary income from their handicraft industries through the advent of cheap machine-made goods, carried in modern steamships, the agricultural population of China sank to the level of semi-starvation. To make a living by farming the population needed two things: in the first place, land reform, which would remove high rent, high interest, oppressive taxation, and the continuous conscription of peasant labour by both the government and the landlord; and, secondly, a programme of industrialization, which would both absorb the surplus rural population and protect China from foreign exploitation. In times past, each attempt by the Chinese people to bring about these reforms was stopped or set back by Western or Japanese armed intervention. Armed interference was followed by indirect intervention, which consisted of arming and financing a small reactionary group to stop reforms and give foreign patrons the economic advantages they demanded. The present anti-American feeling, rising like a tide in China, was not the work of agitators, but represented a deep fear on the part of the great majority that the United States was planning to continue the old policies that impoverished and divided China.

Against this historical background Endicott made his devastating criticisms of the Kuomintang government. Since there was no machinery for general elections in China, the only alternative was a coalition of all parties; this was the present-day Chinese equivalent of an election, Endicott argued, and the sooner it came, the sooner the political situation would be stabilized.

Although Chiang Kai-shek had managed to survive into 1948, owing to massive United States aid, an appraisal of the military situation showed that he had lost 90 per cent of Manchuria, 70 per cent of China north of the Yellow River, and 20 per cent between the Yellow River and the Yangtze. Chiang could not last much longer.

In watching the success of the revolutionary forces in China, some Westerners were apt to conclude that the Communist armies were receiving aid from the Soviet Union. This was emphatically not the case, Endicott asserted: there was no evidence of Russian help; the revolutionary forces were winning because they were giving eighty per cent of the people what they wanted, namely, honest government, local democracy, light taxes, enough to eat and wear for everyone. Since V-J Day, sixty million poverty-stricken peasants in North China had routed the landlords and had received property in the greatest land distribution of all history. If the Western democracies would let things take their natural course, without prolonging the struggle by supporting Chiang Kai-shek, Endicott maintained that China would get a progressive government including part of the Kuomintang, a large element of middle-of-the-road influence, and the Communists; such a government would allow opportunities for religious and social service work and would be willing to trade with the West on a basis profitable to both sides. 'The longer we keep Chiang in power,' Endicott declared, 'the stronger will the left wing become.'[10]

One source of authority in Endicott's presentation of the case for trusting the good faith of the Communists was that he spoke from personal experience and knowledge of the Chinese revolutionaries. He described how, after he had come to know Chou En-lai and other Communist party leaders, he had had to open his mind to the fact that 'in such things as simplicity of life, integrity of character and honesty of purpose, they were far superior to the government group.' He had found that this extraordinary group of men and women combined an intelligent analysis of the forces of history with courageous action and organization of the oppressed to struggle against their oppressors. Since the Chinese Communist party was on record as favouring freedom of religious belief, and had allowed missionaries to continue working in the areas it controlled, Endicott urged that the possibilities for Christian work in co-operation with Communists should be honestly and fully considered by the church.[11] A common concern for social justice made it possible for Marxists and Christians to find fellowship, and furthermore, he suggested, if the Western church wished to justify its claim to moral leadership, it would have to come to terms with the reality that communism in China was practically important for the economics of brotherhood and not theoretically dreadful from a Christian point of view.

Heavy pressure for an official church statement to counteract Endicott's viewpoints began to arise, especially from the wealthy churches in the larger cities. They found the situation 'fraught with embarrassing possibilities' and feared that unless he was disowned the United Church might be thought of as 'lending itself to "subversive elements."'[12]

With only one dissenting voice in the executive, that of Rev. I.G. Perkins, Dr Jesse Arnup, as moderator, set forth the church's position in February 1948, in a document entitled 'Dr. J.G. Endicott and the Board of Foreign Missions.' Prefacing his remarks by the statement that he would not forget the fact that Dr Endicott was a former colleague and a friend of many years standing, Arnup accepted much of what Endicott said about China. He had, however, several important reservations. He did not believe that Chiang Kai-shek had degenerated so far 'since having fallen out with Dr. Endicott'; Chiang was not the monster he was made out to be. Arnup also could not believe that communism, whether in Russia or China, was a 'liberator' of the people; witness the stream of refugees travelling south. The church in Nationalist China was not hopelessly reactionary since it had openly criticized the government more than once; in Communist areas, according to Arnup, the church was unable to carry on. Missionaries in China were aliens; it was not their business to take part in struggles either for or against the government. The university where Dr Endicott 'failed to find his vocation' was carrying on with nearly two thousand students, training leaders for China. The missionaries, said Arnup, who was their chief exponent and official guardian, were exercising a powerful influence for good.

Arnup followed up this statement with public addresses and an extensive private correspondence in which he suggested that Endicott had transferred his faith from Christianity to communism. In Arnup's view the two were incompatible. By its atheism, its opposition to religion, its subordination of individualism to a collective mode, its ruthless methods in dealing with opponents, communism, according to Arnup, destroyed the basis of human morality and the Christian concept of human freedom. Not a few United Church ministers and laymen, as well as the *Toronto Telegram*, joined Arnup in believing that the way out of a difficult problem would be to prove or to have Endicott admit that he was a communist, or at least a 'fellow traveller.' That would 'do more than anything else to clear the atmosphere,' wrote the former missionary, Rev. A.C. Hoffman, to Arnup.[13]

The Endicotts were upset by what they considered to be the less than generous attitude in Arnup's interpretations of Endicott's motives; however, under Mary's restraining influence, Jim wrote a conciliatory reply to clear up certain ambiguities and point out omissions.

Endicott thought that Arnup ought to have acknowledged the initiative taken by Dr G.S. Bell, acting secretary of the Board of Overseas Missions, in sending the letter of January 1946 which had requested Endicott to change his ways or else cease his connection with the church. He also wished to reiterate that in resigning he had assured his brethren that he still had a 'personal and living faith in God.' Finally, he was at a loss to know why it was urgent for Arnup to warn the church against his 'campaign'; many who had heard the type of educational lecture he was giving had agreed that it should not be harmful to the support of missions. 'I have only stated my conviction that the Chinese people are entitled to have a revolution to meet their needs, if they are denied other channels,' Endicott wrote, 'and that in that revolution the Communist Party is getting a following largely because it is putting into practice Sun Yat-sen's land reform.' He criticized Arnup for making unwarranted propaganda about refugees since there were also refugees fleeing the Nationalists, as was inevitable in a civil war.[14]

Following publication of the exchange of letters between Arnup and Endicott in the *United Church Observer* and the *Toronto Star*, Arnup remarked that he had never received so wide a response from any communication; in the heat of the battle he claimed that the mail was strongly in his favour, but the archives suggest that opinion was more evenly divided.

The smaller, less wealthy churches and the younger missionaries tended to be more supportive of Endicott, feeling that in spite of his earlier extravagant praise of Chiang Kai-shek during the Second World War, he was expressing a mature judgement upon a changing situation in China. 'I am greatly heartened to realize that the Board of Foreign Missions had once in its service as able and noble a person as Dr. Jas. Endicott,' wrote a minister from rural Ontario.[15]

Some of the ministers wanted to circulate a proposal for Endicott's reinstatement by raising the matter officially through their presbyteries. He declined their offers, however, and did not wish to have any case made. He had made it clear that he resigned from the mission and the ministry basically because of personal doctrinal reasons. All he was concerned to do now was to show those who had wanted his resignation, for what he thought were wrong and unjustifiable reasons, the error of their ways so that Christianity in China would not be put on the wrong path.

Endicott estimated that about one-third of the younger ministers were receptive to his viewpoints. In addition, a heartening number of the giants of an older generation in the church also offered him encouragement and support. In congratulating him on the newsletter, the famous preacher Salem Bland offered the prophecy that the Chinese were going to be 'the great human instrument for introducing the world to a reasonable, practical, brotherly and scientific Christianity which we have never yet had on a large scale.' The former chancellor of Victoria College, R.P. Bowles, also sent a message assuring Endicott of his unbroken sense of fellowship with him in his trying task, and of his own move to the left: 'I am always a little behind but thank God I think always coming on,' he wrote. 'Had I to lecture in Homiletics again,' he added, 'it certainly would not be the old lectures. In other words, Endicott, I have risen in grace to become an unblushing socialist. It was a slow and at times a hard ascent.' In a friendly gesture Professor C.B. Sissons told Endicott that if he was being called a communist he was in good company, because the first man to be termed such in Ontario was Egerton Ryerson; Bishop John Strachan had tried to apply this 'kiss of death' upon his Methodist rival because the latter was proposing free education for all children under the age of twelve years and because he wanted to substitute the pedagogue for the priest in the schools.[16]

Perhaps the greatest personal joy to Endicott at this time was the unexpected attitude of his father to the 'Endicott controversy.' He had been afraid his father would be sorely disappointed over his recent activities. In addition, during the previous half-decade relations between the two men had been severely strained over the proper interpretation of world events; when Endicott had attempted to assign responsibility for the appeasement of Hitler in the 1930s, his father had interjected angrily: 'I refuse to believe that the British Empire is governed by a bunch of scoundrels.'

Another time, at the Endicott cottage in Muskoka, when Jim passed a favourable comment on a novel about the Soviet Union by the leftist American writer, Anna Louise Strong, his father wanted to know if he considered the Soviet Union to be a democracy.

'In many fundamental respects, yes,' was Jim's reply. 'Through the workings of the Five-Year Plans the worker has meaningful participation in the determination of questions which vitally affect his life.'

After some further exchanges, Endicott, Sr, thinking that Jim was justifying a slave labour camp system, was unable to contain himself and in an emotional outburst declared that he never wanted to have anything to do with him again. As the family looked on in horror, the eighty-year-old man, eyes blazing, rose hastily from the table, caught his chair on the uneven floor and tipped over onto the verandah in a backwards somersault. Before anyone could move, the old man was back on his feet, brushing himself off, and departed the scene without a further word.

No one can remember how that particular crisis was overcome. However, when Jim and Mary returned from Shanghai in 1947, they went right away to Muskoka. 'After the tenseness of the first five minutes I knew it was going to be all right,' Mary recalled. 'They talked for hours and Father was simply thrilled over Jim's thorough knowledge and handling of his subject ... he realized it was not emotional propaganda but a careful covering of the situation, and documents to back what he said.'[17]

Rumours began to circulate in the church that Endicott had broken his old father's heart. When Endicott, Sr, read in the press that only the respect they had for him had kept the church silent on the subject of Jim's resignation, he began to boil. 'So they're going to hide behind me!' he roared. 'Perhaps I ought to make a statement.'[18]

Emerging from eight years of retirement, he appeared before the Toronto Ministerial Association in January 1948, and confirmed once more his reputation as one of the most powerful platform speakers in the church. After assuring the brethren that he was not broken hearted, he made a spirited defence of Jim's political involvement on the larger moral and social issues, showing how it was within the best traditions of missiology. He followed this with an impassioned plea for the church to realign its mission policy in keeping with the situation in China:

We are now at the greatest crisis I know anything about in Chinese missions. A tremendous movement is on foot. The Chinese peasants are fighting a war for self-preservation, the most justifiable war that has ever been fought ...

I believe that the present government of Chiang Kai-shek has betrayed its friends; I believe they repudiated their principles; I believe it is not any more a democratic movement; I believe that on the morals of the question, the weight is heavily on the side of the so-called Communists.

I say that the peasant farmers of China are far more entitled to the land upon which they have worked than are the legal owners. They have paid for it over and over again in the exorbitant rents and interests. They would be far better off than they are now if there were justice in the land and they could take their cause to the courts of free government, but that course is not open to them ...

By sending ammunition to China to destroy the people ... we are being manœuvred in the wrong direction ... It is not Christ who is driving us in that direction. We learn nothing from Christ which says we shall hate one group and love another, or serve one group and not serve another. I am suggesting that we should remain free to take whatever course that seems necessary over the years but not forsake those who have been exploited more than any other people in the whole history of China.

We should curb those blood-suckers, who are collecting high rents, imposing iniquitous rates of interest, compelling hundreds of millions to live in debt and die in debt, where the only legacy they leave their children is a burden of unpaid debts. It is disgraceful, to my mind.[19]

Such impassioned pleas passed like wind in a horse's ear, making little visible impression upon Dr Arnup and his executive board.

Two years later, however, after the triumph of the revolutionary forces in China, Arnup began to change his attitude. His change of heart was as impressive as his eloquence, which suggests that he, too, was one of the great orators of the church: 'We live at the end of an age. While in Canada life goes on in a state of apparent unawareness, in Asia there is in progress one of the greatest revolutions in the history of the human race. In that continent 1000 million people have struck their tents and are upon the march. Where they are going may be a matter of opinion but for good or evil half the population of the world have cast off their moorings and are upon their way ... the East has announced that it will no longer be dominated by the West.'

After reviewing reports coming from the mission field, Arnup declared early in 1950 that 'it is not for nothing that the Communist forces are welcomed almost everywhere as the army of liberation.' He urged Canadian recognition of the new government of China, which, he was persuaded, was temporarily at least a great improvement over the old. 'All in all,' he said, 'our China Mission is a going concern. We do not expect to pull out.'

Deeply satisfied with this outcome of the debate over Canadian missionary policy, and with the weakening of a dangerous source of propaganda against the new China, Endicott reprinted Arnup's 'conversion' and circulated thousands of copies through the *Newsletter*.[20] This happy state of affairs, unfortunately, lasted less than six months; it was shattered as a consequence of a civil war in Korea that in June 1950 assumed international significance.

PART FOUR

THE PEACE
MOVEMENT
1948–1971

CONTRADICTIONS

They shall beat their swords into plowshares
   and their spears into pruninghooks:
   nation shall not lift up sword against nation,
   neither shall they learn war any more.

                         Micah 4:3

Proclaim ye this among the nations;
   prepare war: stir up the mighty men ...
   Beat your plowshares into swords,
   and your pruninghooks into spears:
   let the weak say, I am strong.

                       Joel 3:9,10

Contradictions are the moving force behind the development of all things.
This was true in the past, it is true today, and it will continue to be true
tomorrow.

Once the principal contradiction is grasped, all problems can be readily
solved.

                   Mao Tse-tung 1966, 1937

CHAPTER TWENTY-FOUR

Founding the peace movement

Almost fifty, an unemployed missionary, what were the prospects for the future? The summer of 1948 offered few clues. After a year of speaking to alert the public to the seriousness of the situation in China, ending with a week of lectures in Alberta on 'The Bible as a Guide in a Revolutionary World,' Jim and Mary Endicott retired to their property on Beaver Lake, in the northeastern Kawarthas of Ontario, for a period of rest and reflection; there, on a small piece of land, Jim made improvements to the log cabin he and the family had built during the previous summer. But there was little escape from the feeling that the world was passing through dangerous and explosive times.

Of more immediate concern, he contemplated his own bleak financial prospects: he had spent most of his pension savings, returned to him by the church without interest, and now his sole means of support, apart from occasional remuneration for writing and speaking about China, was a modest income from property given to Mary by her father.

Mary tried to reassure him that something would turn up, reminding him of the first speech he had made in Shanghai, twenty-two years earlier, when his text had been: 'By faith Abraham went out, not knowing whither he went. By faith he sojourned in the land of promise, for he looked for a city which hath foundations, whose builder and maker is God' (see Hebrews 11:8-10). The memory stirred optimism. They both agreed that if the way opened up for them to return to China, perhaps to teach English in the liberated areas as Chou En-lai had suggested, their financial problems would be solved.

The period of uncertainty came to an end soon, in the autumn of 1948, with an unexpected invitation to help organize a peace movement in Canada. The invitation grew out of an appeal by the famous American social gospel leader, Dr Harry Ward, professor emeritus of Christian Ethics at Union Theological Seminary in New York City. On his way home from his summer cottage in

Ontario, Dr Ward gathered together former students and friends in Toronto to voice his alarm at the drift of United States policy. 'The generals in high positions are outnumbered only by investment bankers,'[1] he declared, and that combination was behind all the growing war propaganda against socialist Russia; the result of this propaganda was the growth of a dangerous war psychosis in the West, based upon false premises: the Soviet presence in Eastern Europe following the defeat of fascism, the growth of strong Communist parties in Western Europe, the struggle of colonial peoples for self-determination, the decline of the British empire, and the victories of the Chinese People's Liberation Army, were all being blamed on an expansive 'Red imperialism,' operating from the Kremlin behind 'an iron curtain.'

But the reality of Soviet activity, Dr Ward maintained, was quite different. He advanced the point of view, later acknowledged to be sound by many Western scholars, that the Soviet leaders at this time were preoccupied by the reconstruction of their own war-devastated country, and, fortified by the Marxist belief that capitalism contained the seeds of its own destruction, they had no intention of trying to forward their cause by sending their armed forces across frontiers.[2] The extension of Soviet influence in Eastern Europe seemed to him to be not aggression, but a legitimate attempt on the part of the Russians to defend themselves against another invasion from the west and a desire to re-establish their own western frontier at the line drawn by Lord Curzon on ethnic grounds after the First World War.

Dr Ward developed his case by reviewing the origins of the Cold War. It had begun, he recalled, with Sir Winston Churchill's speech at Fulton, Missouri, in 1946, when the former British prime minister spoke of an 'iron curtain' descending upon Europe and called for an alliance of the English-speaking peoples for a show-down with 'Red Russia.' The American president followed in 1947 with the Truman Doctrine, which forbade revolution anywhere in the world and established the United States as the world's policeman to defend the Western social order, including its dying colonial empires.[3] After the recent confrontation over the status of Berlin, Dr Ward was convinced that President Truman had decided to mobilize the Western world to destroy the Soviet Union and was prepared to use the atomic bomb for this purpose. He thought it was the duty of all men of goodwill to counterpoise something to this folly and related how he had been prompted to action as a result of reading about a 'World Conference of Intellectuals for Peace' being held on the initiative of French and Polish peace committees in Wroclaw, Poland.

Following Dr Ward's appeal, Rev. I.G. Perkins of Donlands United Church in Toronto approached Endicott and proposed that they become co-chairmen and organizers of a committee to establish a peace movement in Canada.[4]

At first Endicott was hesitant. For one thing, he had little firsthand experience to qualify him as a spokesman for a peace movement that would likely be centred on Europe where many people seemed to believe the tensions were most acute. Also he sensed a divergence between the interests of Asia and Europe: how could the stability required for the peaceful coexistence of different social systems in Europe be made to fit with the instability caused by the anti-colonial, national liberation movements in Asia? There was no clear answer to this dilemma, which would persist, and grow painfully acute at times, during the next twenty-three years of his active leadership in the peace movement. The common link between the two areas, and with the situation in North America itself, he concluded, was the expansive drive of American monopolies to establish control and domination of economic life on a global scale. After reflecting on these issues, Endicott decided to take on the task, and thus in late 1948 he began his long career as an advocate of world peace.

According to his analysis at this stage, the new American imperialism, which had effectively replaced that of the British and was being so widely popularized by *Time*, *Life*, and *Fortune* magazines as 'the American century,' was geared to fight on three main battlefronts. First, there was the attempt to regiment and control the vital democratic forces among the American people; the opening campaign in this regard was the passing of the Taft-Hartley Bill restricting the rights of labour in the United States. The second battleground was the struggle between American capitalism and other surviving capitalist groups, namely Great Britain, France, Holland, and the lesser lights, a contest usually spoken of in American magazines as 'the coming fight for world markets.' The third great battlefield took the form of an 'anti-communist crusade,' but it was in reality a struggle for control of the colonial world; when the peoples of Asia declared that they were no longer willing to be 'rickshaw-pullers' for the high standard of living of America and Western Europe, Endicott observed, the American secretary of state, Dean Acheson, accused them of succumbing to outside communist domination.

In spite of the fact that the North Atlantic Treaty Organization, being created by Acheson, Lester Pearson, and Britain's Ernest Bevin, was ostensibly directed to a threat stemming from the Soviet Union, Endicott was firmly convinced that the main danger of a new war lay in Asia: already major combat units of such NATO countries as France, Holland, and Britain were on active service in Vietnam, Indonesia, and Malaya; the United States itself was still heavily involved in China's civil war, and Canada, as late as May 1949, was still shipping arms to Chiang Kai-shek. From the perspective of Asia,

Endicott declared, the North Atlantic pact, far from promising freedom, peace, and democracy, spelt war, a military instrument for economic enslavement, a white man's club for preserving colonies, in which the atomic bomb could be used for blackmail.[5]

From small beginnings at peace assemblies in Vancouver and Toronto in 1948, the peace movement grew rapidly.[6] A national conference held at Bathurst Street United Church in Toronto, 6-8 May 1949, attended by three hundred delegates, founded the Canadian Peace Congress with Jim Endicott as chairman, Mrs Eva Sanderson of Toronto as vice-chairman, and Mary Jennison of Hamilton as executive secretary. At a second national gathering in Toronto one year later, there were 1706 registered and paid delegates; by this time there had been hundreds of meetings in towns and cities across the country, four assemblies in Massey Hall in Toronto, a rally of twelve thousand people at the Maple Leaf Gardens, and, perhaps most astonishing of all, 200,000 names gathered for a petition to 'Ban the Bomb.'

The daily newspaper editors, who without exception attacked the peace movement, tried to find hidden or sinister explanations for this outburst of public expression. 'The Canadian Peace Congress, of which Dr. James Endicott is chairman,' wrote the *Montreal Gazette* in 1951, 'is one of the most remarkable examples of sure-footed innocence this country is likely to see.' If Endicott and his associates were 'merely foolish, as some say, or merely erratic, as others suggest,' they would have shown themselves to be less astute in their consistency. 'But their utterances continue to be so cleverly plausible,' declared the *Gazette*, 'their omissions so studied, their propaganda methods so typical, and their financial resources so considerable that more than innocence seems to inspire their actions.' As if to prove that the Peace Congress was laying snares for the gullible, it was pointed out that the only political party in Canada officially favouring Endicott's movement was the Labour Progressive Party, 'that is to say, the Communists.' The press in general encouraged the public to label peace workers as 'fellow travellers,' and to dismiss the peace movement as a 'communist front.'[7]

Such attempts at intimidation did not sit well with Endicott. 'Just because Joe Stalin says that two and two are four,' he said, 'I am not going to stop saying the same thing. The fact that my findings in Asia please the Communists should be seen in the same light.'[8] Furthermore, he refused to concede that because the peace movement did not exclude anyone, right, left, or centre, it would therefore necessarily be dominated by the left. In his keynote addresses he took pains to underline the ideal of openness in the movement and stressed that no peace worker would be asked to surrender privately held opinions or to give way on matters of conscience. The peace movement, he said, was organized around the simple conviction that disagreements between nations which threatened world peace should be settled through the United Nations. It was not the purpose of the peace movement to support or defend the foreign policy of the Soviet Union; neither was it its purpose to attack it – the proper place for that too was in the United Nations. 'But the people of the West might as well make up their minds,' he suggested, 'that the Soviet Union and its economic system are here to stay, and if the Russian people want it that way, they are entitled to have it that way'; if it did not suit them, it was their responsibility to change it, and they did not need the West's assistance by way of war. To those who cursed and reviled the peace movement, he replied: 'If you are not planning war, you have no need to fear a peace movement! If you are planning and working for peace, there will be no need for military alliances and vast schemes of re-armament.'[9]

Often accused by pacifists of being inconsistent when he worked for peace and at the same time supported the cause of the People's Liberation Army in China, Endicott replied: 'The Chinese people, including the Communists, asked for peace, and Chiang Kai-shek, with American and Canadian weapons assassinated them. Chiang and his American and Canadian friends elected to have a war of extermination. His regime was degenerate and corrupt. Therefore, as a religious man I thank God for the quick and overwhelming victory of the Chinese People's Liberation Army. It is the only way that the Chinese people can get peace and reform ... As time goes on an increasing number of the Chinese Christian forces will take the same position. This is the answer to the critics of inconsistency.'[10] His premise was the time-honoured right of the people to rise up and overthrow, by force if necessary, a government they found to be corrupt.

The success of the peace movement in touching the deepest feelings of many of the Canadian people, in giving expression to their authentic fears about the atomic bomb, about the rearmament of Germany and talk of war against Soviet Russia, about the suppression of colonial liberation movements, could not be explained by a theory of conspiracy and subversion. Government officials in Ottawa admitted privately that the peace propagandists were able to arouse doubt and disagreement with government policies by appealing to much that was truly liberal in Western thought. 'Even in our own terms,' ran a memorandum of the External Affairs Department in 1950, 'our governments are condemned by their support of reactionary regimes.' Further testimony to the success of the peace movement was provided by the American consul in Montreal, who reported to his government that 'it is obvious from the reception given to Dr. Endicott that the so-called "Movement for Peace" is receiving a considerable amount of support from people in different walks of life.'[11]

Endicott and the other peace workers in Canada were greatly encouraged and inspired by the international gatherings for peace that were held in Poland in 1948, and in New York, Paris, and Mexico City in 1949. Endicott attended the meetings in Paris and Mexico on behalf of the Canadian movement.

The great boulevards of Paris, garlanded in April by the candle-like blossoms of the majestic horse-chestnut trees, created an impression of serenity, a reminder of life's continual rebirths. To the representatives from seventy-two countries who crowded into La Salle Pleyel, near the Arc de Triomphe, the Paris Congress of the Partisans of Peace was a mighty refusal of war, a culmination of all the bitter years of bloodshed and misery since the outbreak of the Great War in August 1914. After listening to the dignity and sanity of the opening address by the famous French atomic scientist, Frédéric Joliot-Curie, son-in-law of Madame Curie, after hearing the volcanic Soviet writer, Ilya Ehrenburg, and after meeting many delegates from the colonial areas, Endicott felt at home, as if at an international missionary gathering. Ehrenburg's use of the story of Solomon and the two quarrelling mothers to argue for a united world, not two worlds, was impressive. 'The mother who really loved the child,' he said, 'was unwilling to see it divided.'

In his address to the plenary session, Endicott promised an unceasing struggle for peace in Canada.[12] He told his audience that this was the second time he had had the honour of coming to France. The first time, as a reinforcement for the Canadian Corps, he had observed at first hand the terrible and bloody battles of the summer of 1918, when at Amiens, Cambrai, and the Canal du Nord the Canadian Corps had had fifty thousand casualties; he recalled that since that time many thousands more Canadians had died, all along the road from Normandy to Holland.

In coming to France now to take part in a world-wide struggle for peace, he had a profound conviction that he was honouring the memory of his fallen Canadian comrades; there was no meaning to their sacrifices unless it came to pass that democracy, peace, and brotherhood became the bonds that linked the races of man together.

As for the future, he predicted that the struggle for peace and disarmament on the North American continent was going to be tough and bitter. The Canadian ruling group, he said, had, in their own minds at least, already committed the country to any war the United States saw fit to start; that was his interpretation of the statement of Canada's new prime minister, Louis St Laurent, to the Quebec Bar Association in October 1948, that 'Canada cannot remain out of a third world war even if 11,999,999 of her twelve million people wanted to remain neutral.' Using truthful words, which the *Ottawa Journal* later complained were 'perilously near treason,' Endicott told the international gathering that the northern Canadian territories, where the

American army had extraterritorial rights, were quietly and effectively being prepared as a base for long-range, atomic bomb attacks on the Soviet Union.[13]

Perhaps the most memorable international peace meeting Endicott attended during this period was in Stockholm in March 1950. There, as a member of a committee of five, he helped to draft the wording of the famous Stockholm Appeal.[14] This appeal, directed to all governments, was made after the Soviet Union had joined the nuclear club and after the World Council of Churches had condemned the hydrogen bomb as a sin against God and called for a 'gigantic new effort for peace'; the appeal asked that atomic weapons be outlawed and that members of the first government to use them be declared war criminals.

Based on a strategy of mobilizing public opinion against atomic weapons, the appeal resulted, as some of its enemies admitted, in a surprisingly vigorous and sustained effort that was dangerous to dismiss as 'mere propaganda.'[15] Within a few months – a prodigious effort by local peace committees – hundreds of millions of signatures were collected on petitions in different parts of the world, mainly in the Soviet Union, China, and other countries of Eastern Europe and Asia, and world attention was focused for the first time upon the horror of the weapon of mass extermination around which America's strategy was built. In Canada, where 300,000 signatures were collected, members of the peace movement went door to door, marched in peace demonstrations, spoke at street corner meetings, and young people sang: 'I'm going to put my name down, brother; where do I sign?'[16]

At no time was the impact of the international movement more dramatically expressed in North America than in two visits of the Very Reverend Hewlett Johnson, dean of Canterbury Cathedral, in 1948 and 1950. The 'Red Dean,' Endicott soon discovered, was one of the more unusual and colourful figures of modern history. Appointed to his position by King George v in 1931, he had worked for social causes most of his public life, and his books, translated into more than twenty languages, were read widely; he held a Bachelor of Science degree in engineering and was, as well, a Doctor of Divinity. Now in his mid-seventies, he was an unusually rugged man, over six feet tall, with a fringe of curly white hair surrounding his genial face. He wore bishop's gaiters buttoned around his long legs and a traditional black frock coat; around his neck was a chain from which hung a gold and diamond crucifix, which had been given to him by Patriarch Alexei, head of the Russian Orthodox Church, in the Soviet Union in 1945, during one of the dean's many visits to that country.

The response of the people of North America to Dr Johnson's meetings was far beyond expectations: five thousand gathered in Winnipeg, twenty thousand in New York's Madison Square Gardens in 1948, and five thousand were turned away from an overflow meeting of almost three thousand in Toronto's Massey Hall. His reception reflected the concern felt among the people about the growing danger of war and their desire for leadership towards peace.

'Everything points to the Soviet Union wanting peace,' he told his audiences. Having suffered the whole or partial destruction of 1700 cities, 70,000 villages, and with two-thirds of her industrial capacity destroyed in the recent war, it was no wonder, he said, that 'they talk peace, think peace and work for peace.' He dealt in detail with the points of disagreement between the West and Russia – atomic energy control, the Berlin blockade, Soviet influence in Eastern Europe – and suggested that Stalin had repeatedly shown he was willing to talk peace but the Western powers had spurned his offers.

Even more controversially, the dean spoke of the differing concepts of liberty in the East and the West, saying that each had much to learn from the other. He expressed his view that some of Russia's questionable or disturbing methods were temporary expedients. 'There is an example of a temporary expedient in British history,' he recalled, 'when Parliament cut off the head of Charles I. Now, I don't like cutting off the heads of kings, and I feel that the Stuarts had many splendid qualities, but they stood in the way of liberties – the Western liberties we enjoy ... We in the West have our traditional liberties of freedom of speech, press and association, which are of infinite value. They, in the East, are putting into practice another set of liberties – the right to work, the right to adequate pay for work, the right to rest after work, the right to health, to education, to full security for all, regardless of sex, religion, or race. These liberties are complementary to ours. They are not antagonistic. Such liberties are singularly in accord with the standards by which we Christians expect one day to be judged.'

By his serenity and his steadfast conviction of the truth of his message, Dr Johnson made an impression such that his listeners would never forget. And when he said that the alternative to peace was a type of war more terrible than any the world had yet known, atomic and possibly bacteriological wars of mass extermination, they tended to believe him.

The authorities in the United States and Canada did not suffer the dean's presence willingly. An attempt to refuse him a visa to the United States was overcome only by the formation of a broad committee headed by professors of Harvard University. In the Canadian Parliament a Tory MP called the dean 'a hairy old goat'; rowdies and hoodlums were organized to disrupt his meetings. An organization calling itself the Russian Freedom League telephoned threats against Endicott in Toronto, proposing to castrate him if he continued to accompany the dean. In Hamilton, a large rock was hurled through a window of the meeting hall, showering glass splinters over the audience, followed by firecrackers.

Although denounced and insulted, and represented unfairly in the press, the dean did not say a bitter word in retaliation and the people responded warmly to his friendliness. When the Endicotts drove him down to see Niagara Falls, crowds rubber-necked and besieged him for pictures and autographs. At the end of his 1950 tour, when the gaitered engineer walked into Maple Leaf Gardens in Toronto with the suggestion that if the common man refused to be cannon fodder there would not be another war, ten thousand people rose to their feet to give him a standing ovation. 'Blessed are the peacemakers, and thanks be to God for such a man as Dr. Hewlett Johnson, Dean of Canterbury, in such a time as this,' was Endicott's benediction on the dean's visit.[17]

As the peace movement gained momentum, those who were opposed to it inevitably grew more vocal. Church people who believed that there were theological reasons why Christians should not work with atheists, or who feared that advocating peaceful coexistence with 'godless' Russia and China implied an endorsation of those regimes, doubted the wisdom of associating with the Canadian Peace Congress because it contained 'known Communists' and perhaps even 'unknown Communists.' Their fears were strengthened by the militant campaign of the Canadian Chamber of Commerce, which drew attention to anti-religious propaganda in Russia and warned about 'crypto-Communists.'[18]

A sizeable number of Christians, however, rejected this approach, saying that there were no Christian principles upon which a person could not co-operate with professed atheists; the great enemy that had obstructed the march of the Kingdom of God in all ages had not been atheism, they said, 'but too much religion of the wrong kind,' especially the worship of Mammon and Mars.[19] In spite of heavy pressure from conservatives in the church, therefore, defiant clergy were to be found on committees at every level of the peace movement, and over one hundred ministers of many denominations signed the Stockholm Appeal in Canada.

A similar debate took place within the ranks of the social democratic Co-operative Commonwealth Federation. Like the church, the CCF was divided about Endicott; some were suspicious or hostile while others desired to have his voice heard with theirs. His application to renew his membership in the South York CCF in 1948, when he was lecturing about China and before he became involved in the peace movement, was not accepted – because he had good words to say about communists, he suspected.[20]

As a leading figure in the peace movement he became an even more controversial figure. The majority on the CCF national council, including its national leaders, M.J. Coldwell, Angus MacInnis, David Lewis, and Donald MacDonald, basically agreed with the Liberals and Conservatives that the United States was the leader of the 'free world' and that the Soviet Union and communist conspiracies were mainly responsible for the Cold War; it followed that they had no sympathy with a peace movement that included communists.

When Endicott asked Coldwell to sign the 'Ban the Bomb' petition, Coldwell refused angrily, saying that the petition was 'an instrument of Russian policy' which would undermine the defences of democracy.[21] The national office of the CCF warned its members to have nothing to do with the peace movement. Endicott was denounced in the CCF organ, *Across Canada*, for offering 'no word about Soviet aggression in Eastern Europe' and for uttering 'fantastic and typically communist fabrication.'[22] When he replied, explaining why the peace movement did not exclude the communists as 'morally untouchable,' and offering an alternative interpretation of events in Czechoslovakia based largely upon the views of Rev. Josef L. Hromadka, the theologian who had left a post at Princeton University to return to his native Prague, the leaders of 'democratic socialism' in Canada did not allow him to state his case in their paper.[23]

In spite of Coldwell and Lewis, however, large sections of the party refused to endorse the North Atlantic pact or to support the rearmament of Germany; hundreds of members read the *Canadian Far Eastern Newsletter* and circulated the 'Ban the Bomb' petition. William Irvine of Alberta and Eva Sanderson and Mrs Rae Luckock of Ontario were among a number of prominent CCF members who took an active part in the councils of the peace movement. T.C. Douglas also refused to follow the United States' lead in world affairs blindfolded; in the troubled 1950s the doughty Saskatchewan premier and members of his cabinet regularly gave the peace movement a hearing and offered their encouragement and support. Douglas had faith in Endicott's integrity, describing him as 'one of my favourite people'[24] – the feeling was mutual.

The fact remained, however, that the only political party which officially and openly supported the peace movement in Canada was the communist party, then called the Labour Progressive party. As a result of this support, there was considerable speculation by friends, in the press, and by hostile critics about Endicott's relation to the party. Since several of Endicott's children were party members, it was sometimes assumed that he was also a member but that for tactical reasons he did not admit it. This was not the case. There were no barriers of principle to prevent him joining the party since he agreed with Y.T. Wu's estimation that Marxism and Christianity, properly understood, were travelling in a parallel direction, that Christianity had no difficulty in accepting the dialectical materialist view of the world as an attempt to describe the way in which God works. At one time he and Mary considered joining and for a short while they attended meetings of one of the party's professional groups. The experience, for Mary at least, was not a compelling one. 'Neither of us feel that we want to go into the LPP,' she wrote to a friend, 'although we are not afraid of it. It seems more like joining a sect than a political party,' she added, 'and, having just emerged from such a close fellowship, we do not want to get involved in another.'[25]

For Endicott, a decision to join the party or not was largely a matter of how he could be most effective in the struggle for social justice. Many of his impulses and instincts pushed him to make a declaration of political affiliation: it would be the kind of clear-cut action that appealed to him. But he held back because of the feeling that it might be an empty gesture. With his background, training, and missionary experience, he felt that he could never become a representative or leader of the working class, which such a declaration of communist affiliation would imply. Moreover, he would cut himself off from his natural constituency, the middle class Christian community, which he believed ought to become more involved in the peace movement. In China he had ignored the advice of Y.T. Wu and Chou En-lai to remain in the active ministry of the church. Now, although he did not regret that decision, he realized that to be effective he would have to work as an independent without any party affiliation. It was a difficult road to follow, requiring calm nerves and toughmindedness, since it involved being stigmatized as a 'fellow traveller' and being faced with the accusatory question of his middle class friends: 'Are you a communist; and, if not, why not?' – in the circumstances of the anti-communist Cold War of the 1940s and 1950s such a question was like asking a woman of seventeenth-century Salem, Massachusetts: 'Are you a witch?'[26]

Fortunately, Endicott soon developed a personal relationship with the leaders of the Canadian party, much as he had done with Chou En-lai, which allowed him to overcome feelings of isolation and permitted him to be in touch with their thinking and them with his. He first met Tim Buck, Leslie Morris, Stanley Ryerson, and William Kashtan when he invited them to his house in the summer of 1947 to hear his account of the Chinese revolution. The communist leaders were fascinated by his enthusiasm and his detailed grasp of the situation but more than a little sceptical about his optimistic forecast of the imminent success of the revolution. After the peace movement was established, Leslie Morris, then editor of the party paper, the *Canadian*

Tribune, was assigned by the LPP to be responsible for liaison with the peace movement; this articulate Welsh-Canadian was highly intelligent, with a warm and genial personality, and a lasting friendship soon developed between the two men. After some experiences in trying to organize peace committees where local communists occasionally played a vociferous role, Endicott suggested to Buck and Morris that, in cases of differences over policy statements, his judgement and that of his colleagues in the peace executive must take precedence; otherwise no coalition of peace forces could be built. He added that if the party ever lost confidence in his leadership of the peace movement, then he wished them to come and tell him so, and he would act in whatever way seemed appropriate. The party leaders listened sympathetically and accepted his proposal in the spirit of a working agreement, which, according to Endicott's understanding, was communicated to local party committees. It was not until near the end of the first decade of the peace movement, following the Hungarian crisis of 1956, that he had any serious problem in his relations with the party.[27]

The communist parties of the world, as Endicott soon discovered, had their own difficulties in relating to a peace movement. Some members, remembering Lenin's famous thesis that war was inevitable as long as capitalist imperialism existed, were slow to accept any rationale for peaceful coexistence and were reluctant to engage in peace work because it seemed futile. Eventually Stalin brought his immense prestige into the debate, saying that Lenin's teaching on the inevitability of wars between capitalist states still held, but that war between capitalism and socialism could be averted if 'the people take the cause of preserving peace into their own hands and defend it to the end.'[28]

Because Endicott allegedly never differed from the communists and never criticized the Soviet Union, one of the favourite methods of attack on him took the form of calling him a 'dupe' or a 'tool' of the communists. This charge was false and foolish, but inevitable in the political climate created by US Senator Joseph McCarthy. Although Endicott did occasionally express criticisms of Soviet or Chinese policy when interviewed by newspapermen,[29] in his public speeches he was, in principle, unwilling to say anything that would provide aid and comfort to the 'preventive war' zealots.

Within the peace movement, however, both in Canada and abroad, he was prepared to be quite blunt in order to make the movement more effective. He criticized publications of the world peace movement for being overly positive about the merits of the Soviet Union and Eastern Europe and too pessimistic about the forces for peace in the United States and Canada; he maintained that too much effort was spent trying to direct and educate the communists to work for peace, not enough to reach middle-of-the-road people; he held, without much success, that the peace movement should not take sides in intra-party disputes such as the one between Stalin and Marshal Tito of Yugoslavia.[30]

The first major confrontation between the peace movement and the Canadian government occurred in the spring of 1950 with a series of well-publicized exchanges between Endicott and members of the cabinet. It began with a request for an interview to present the 'Ban the Bomb' petition to the government; Prime Minister Louis St Laurent replied in the negative, suggesting, rather contemptuously, that if the Canadian Peace Congress wished to help world peace it should knock instead on the door of the Soviet Union.[31]

The peace movement was not to be so easily dismissed. Quite by coincidence, St Laurent's suggestion was made possible through an invitation from the World Partisans of Peace, which had been established in Paris in 1949 and was called the World Council of Peace after 1950. This group asked that a Canadian participate in an international delegation to present to the Supreme Soviet the world peace movement's request for simultaneous reduction of conventional armaments and the outlawing of nuclear weapons; such delegations were being sent to parliaments in a number of countries.

Thus the invitation resulted in Endicott's first visit to Moscow, where he stayed for a week. His excitement with this fascinating and unfamiliar city was reflected in long and detailed letters home, in which he described visits to Red Square and the Kremlin, a reception in the marble St George's Hall where he sat at the same table as the great Soviet composer Dmitri Shostakovich and his wife, tours of the city, a visit to a collective farm, a long talk at the Canadian Embassy, and an evening at the Bolshoi theatre. During intermission at the Bolshoi, the stars of the ballet came to greet the peace delegation, which occupied the czar's royal box. One woman introduced herself as Ulanova.

'Oh,' said Endicott, 'and what do you do?'

'I dance,' was the short reply.

He was not alone in his lamentable unfamiliarity with the Soviet Union. The previous evening the British foreign secretary, Ernest Bevin, who was also visiting Moscow, had attended the performance at the Bolshoi; he told John Platts-Mills, MP, a British member of the peace delegation, about looking out over the ground floor from the royal box. 'I have seen freedom,' said Bevin sarcastically. 'There they were sitting all stiff and formal. The people don't dare talk to each other.' The next night when Platts-Mills was seated in the same place of honour, the ballerina, Madame Plisetskaya, came over to him and said: 'We were so excited last night because Mr. Molotov brought Mr. Bevin and the whole ground floor was filled with members of the diplomatic corps!'[32]

When Endicott's turn came to address the representatives of the Supreme Soviet, he spoke briefly and with restraint. He emphasized the desire of the Canadian people for friendship and peace with their Soviet neighbours across the North Pole and complimented the Russians for the absence of war-mongering in their press. He also referred to the fact that Prime Minister St Laurent had refused to meet the Canadian Peace Congress and suggested, therefore, that if the Soviet Union gave positive support to the proposals of the peace delegation it would greatly strengthen the work for peace in Canada.

Later, at a well-attended press conference, he became involved in a debate which made headlines and drew a sharp rebuke from Lester Pearson for allegedly maligning his country.

The controversy arose because his colleague on the peace delegation, John Rogge, a former assistant attorney-general in the Roosevelt administration and now a civil rights lawyer, took the opportunity of the press conference to deliver a twenty-minute discourse to the Russians on the virtues of Jefferso-nian democracy. As Endicott listened to Rogge give the impression that freedom to 'go where you like, think what you like, say what you like and do what you like' was actually practised in the America of Congressman McCar-thy's witch-hunts and loyalty oaths, he grew increasingly agitated. Such a picture, he felt, was neither fair nor honest, and he believed intuitively that any attempt to contrast Western ideals, as distinct from Western practices, with Soviet practices, was not a sound basis upon which to try to build peace with the Russians.

On an impulse, therefore, he asked for the floor.

Sensing that he was going to give the middle-of-the-road Americans a jolt, the young woman who translated brought a fire and vigour into her interpret-ing. The result, as Endicott happily recounted, was that he came across in grandstand style, to the huge delight of the Russians and to the discomfort of most of the foreign correspondents present.

He first drew laughter by producing the contents of his briefcase as evi-dence of 'Our Vanishing Civil Liberties,' which was the title of a book by Rogge: from a report in the *Ottawa Citizen* about eleven thousand Canadian citizens being listed as subversive, he told how the United States FBI con-ducted espionage on Canadians; he spoke of the case of Glen Shortliffe, the Queen's University professor who had been barred from the United States for driving the dean of Canterbury from Malton Airport to Hamilton; and he described the workings of the Padlock Law in Quebec, which allowed the government, without reference to the courts, to place a lock on the door of any institution or house where meetings were held or where literature was found which it deemed to be 'communist.' Without qualifying his remarks, and thus leaving himself open to attack, he cited these examples as illustrations of the state of democracy in Canada. 'It cannot be denied,' he stated, 'that on the North American continent a police state is in the process of forming and the battle for peace has become a battle for civil rights.' In this battle, he added, 'John Rogge is a notable and valiant fighter.'[33]

The reports of Endicott's activities in Moscow irritated and angered the Canadian government. Under a caption, 'Endicott's Soviet Trip Toughens Ottawa Policy,' the *Financial Post* on 6 May reported that from now on the government would not remain silent but was 'going to try to cut the ground from under him.' In a speech to civil servants in Ottawa, Lester Pearson, minister for external affairs, warned that 'we should be on guard against ... the individual who ... wearing the mantle of the Peace Congress has knowingly or unknowingly sold his soul to Moscow.' After reading garbled accounts in the Soviet press of what Endicott had said at the Moscow press conference about restrictions on civil liberties in Canada (the Soviet press either wilfully or unwittingly having given the impression that the Quebec Padlock Law applied throughout the country), Pearson went further and stated that 'a man who, professing honest motives and high ideals, goes among strangers and maligns his country with this kind of falsehood is beneath contempt.' Pearson's attack on the peace movement and upon Endicott personally was typical of the government's new approach to what it called 'the Communist problem.' Based on an assumption of America's moral leadership in world affairs, this outlook justified the defence of freedom through a military alliance outside the United Nations on the grounds, as Pearson put it, of 'fear of the aggressive and subversive policies of Communism'; in such a world view, it was a Russian-controlled conspiracy that was responsible for, or was taking advantage of, social unrest in various parts of the globe to upset social order and to threaten world peace.[34]

When Endicott returned to Canada in April 1950, amid considerable publicity, preparations for the second national gathering of the Canadian Peace Congress were at a fever pitch. Almost two thousand delegates from coast to coast were expected to converge on Toronto in the first week in May. Sensing the drama of the moment and realizing the asset they had in the powerful debating ability of their chairman, the executive decided to invite the minister for external affairs to address the congress in person. Pearson declined but, in line with the government's decision to try to counteract the peace movement, said he would send a written message outlining the government's views on foreign policy; Prime Minister St Laurent followed with a message to say that he had appointed Pearson to receive a delegation from the congress which could present the Stockholm Appeal petition to the government.[35]

As arranged, Pearson's letter was read to the plenary session but in the meantime Endicott had led a small delegation to see the foreign minister in Ottawa. Perhaps in an effort to relieve personal tensions, Pearson did not renew his 'beneath contempt' charges during the interview. When the question of the right of the new government of China to be seated in the United Nations arose, he nodded, smiling, and said to Endicott: 'I have read your reports [from China] with pleasure.'

And Endicott, while not ready to concede that the things he had said in Moscow were exaggerated, nevertheless agreed that they might not have been in the best interests of winning everyone to the position of the peace movement. 'Don't take what I said too seriously,' he commented as they parted, 'I always did talk a lot.'[36]

Beneath surface courtesies, however, there lay a deep divergence of views between the two men and between the forces they represented. The essence of Pearson's position on war and peace, according to Endicott, was that the desire for peace was the sole possession of the Western powers, that the Liberal party, which formed the government of Canada, made no serious mistakes that endangered world peace (one or two minor mistakes were conceded), and that anyone who challenged its policy had base and ulterior motives and was seditious. In dealing with pressing world problems, he maintained, the minister for external affairs had not advocated 'the slightest compromise on any important issue.' Pearson favoured banning the bomb but only by a rigid adherence to the US Baruch Plan, a plan which Walter Lippmann, the respected American columnist, had publicly dismissed as unworkable and which General A.G.L. McNaughton, Canada's representative at the United Nations, privately regarded as 'insincerity from beginning to end':[37] the plan called for the control of all atomic raw materials by a UN commission whose work would not be subject to veto and whose control would have to be established before existing stockpiles of atomic bombs would be destroyed. To Endicott's question 'Would you favour branding as a war criminal the first government to use the atomic bomb?' Pearson made no answer, except to say that Canada would not be involved in aggressive warfare.[38]

Most North American politicians, in Endicott's view, gave the impression that they were discussing only the question of dropping bombs on the Soviet Union, whereas his first concern was to prohibit Soviet bombs from dropping on North America. This selfish objective, he told the national rally in Toronto in May 1950, had been the real purpose of his visit to Moscow. He reported that during his stay in the Soviet capital he had been encouraged by the government's endorsation of the peace movement's efforts and by the Soviet peace committee's agreement to conduct a nation-wide canvass to petition their government to sign, in the United Nations, an agreement that it would not be the first to use the atomic bomb; he warned that it would be a dangerous illusion to think that the Soviet Union was using the peace petition merely to make up for a shortage of atomic bombs.

Peace, he insisted, was not the preserve of political parties; it was properly the people's business, the business of those who would have to do the dying should atomic bombers penetrate the skies over their country. The people of all countries needed an assurance from their political leaders that, come what may, the atomic annihilation of civilian populations would not take place. Therefore it would be a sad day if at any time in the future the aims of the peace movement, or the desire of a single person for world understanding, were dismissed or suppressed as 'subversive.' To the cheers of his audience he promised a more vigorous and effective peace campaign. 'Far from being put off by evasive remarks and challenges of sincerities,' he declared, 'we will continue our work and step it up ten-fold.'[39]

The climax for the peace workers came when their rally at Maple Leaf Gardens on 7 May 1950 was attended by twelve thousand people. There could be little doubt that the Endicott-Pearson exchanges had strengthened, rather than weakened, the peace movement. Such public support, in spite of a hostile press, was an indication that in the minds of many people the Canadian Peace Congress was a necessary forum for the expression of alternatives in foreign policy.

The rally came none too soon. Shortly thereafter, following the outbreak of war in Korea, the peace movement was confronted by severe new tests; as the flames of war spread and threatened a wider conflict in the Far East, its leader would be attacked and pilloried in parliament, press, and pulpit, and singled out as 'public enemy number one.'

CHAPTER TWENTY-FIVE

War in Korea

Scheduled to address a rally of the Manitoba Peace Council, Endicott was in Winnipeg on the weekend of 24-25 June 1950. In spite of preoccupations with the overflowing Red River, which resulted in one of the worst floods in Manitoba's history, Winnipegers packed the Dominion Theatre that Sunday night. Their interest, uneasiness, or curiosity had been heightened by reports of an outbreak of fighting between North and South Korea. Radio stations had been broadcasting bulletins throughout the day, suggesting with increasing frequency that the Soviet Union was behind the conflict.

By late afternoon of the 25th it was reported that the North Korean forces had advanced several miles into the South. Finally, an announcement came from New York, where the United Nations Security Council was meeting in emergency session. In the absence of the Soviet Union and China, North Korea, a member of the socialist bloc, had been declared guilty of unprovoked aggression. Sanctions were being prepared, led by the United States.

Endicott was gloomy as he prepared to face his audience. Prior to the meeting a local leader of the communist party had suggested that he be non-committal; right-wingers, believing that he would not dare say anything until he had received the 'authentic line' from Moscow, had come to see him squirm; middle-of-the-roaders hoped he would have a twinge of conscience and begin spreading the blame for the world's ills more evenly; while some leftists wanted to hear him cheer a rapid advance by the Northerners. The majority, who were supporters of the peace movement, came to the meeting because they were confused and deeply disturbed by the apparent turn of events in Asia.

He decided to rely upon his intuition. He sketched in the background of the crisis for his audience. He stressed that there was a civil war in Korea: clashes had been taking place for several years at the 38th parallel, the border between

North and South Korea, which had been established in 1945 along the line where Soviet and American troops had met during the final stages of the war against Japan. The real trouble in Korea, he said, was that the Western powers and Russia had divided arbitrarily a nation that wished to remain united. Abolition of the 38th parallel as a political boundary was an objective to which every politically minded Korean was dedicated, whether he or she lived north or south. North Korea, he suggested, had carried out a thorough land reform, winning the support of the peasantry, and thus had a solid base of support; its government, led by communists, was a coalition of forces, as in the case of China; the vice-president and secretary were both Christians, educated in American missionary schools. South Korea, on the other hand, was headed by Syngman Rhee, who had returned to Korea after living for thirty years in the United States. He had brought back to power many of the pro-Japanese elements which had ruled Korea as a Japanese colony from 1910 to 1945. Owing to his failure to solve the land problem, Rhee had faced uprisings in 1946 and 1949, which he suppressed with great brutality, killing, according to some sources, over ninety thousand people in four years.[1]

In the last three weeks, Endicott reminded his listeners, President Rhee had lost in elections to the National Assembly, his party winning but 48 seats out of 210. He labelled the South Korean president 'an out-right fascist' who ran a police state and speculated that Rhee might have provoked the latest troubles in a desperate bid to stay in power.

On the subject of Soviet involvement, Endicott was categoric. 'There is no shred of evidence,' he declared, 'for terming the Korean outbreaks as manifestations of "Russian Communist imperialism."' He was more inclined to believe that American imperialism was involved, reminding his audience that John Foster Dulles, the prominent Republican whom President Truman had appointed as a special consultant to the US State Department, had visited Korea a few days earlier and had spoken of the need for positive action in Asia, even at the risk of war. 'A series of disasters can be prevented,' Dulles had said, 'if at some doubtful point we quickly take a dramatic and strong stand that shows our confidence and resolution.' Endicott described how the main aim of the United States, with its military bases in Japan, Okinawa, Taiwan, and south to French Indo-China and the Philippines, was to prevent the spread of revolution in Asia and, if possible, to cause the downfall of the new government of China headed by Mao Tse-tung. He spoke feelingly from his own experience in the Far East and pointed out how, in line with its aims, the United States had stopped the People's Republic of China from taking its seat in the United Nations. He agreed that the Korean question be given to the United Nations, 'but not to any committee on which the United States has a majority or which includes any nations receiving funds from either United States or Russia.' The press was clamouring for a show-down with Russia, he said, but that issue was not involved. 'Our first care should be to look behind the headlines, avoid the slanted propaganda of the front page and the editorials.'[2]

It was an impressive effort. Those who came to heckle found it difficult; those who came in support left encouraged.

Within a few hours the sweeping nature of American plans was revealed when President Truman not only announced us armed intervention in Korea but also ordered the navy to station itself around Taiwan and authorized support to the French colonial war in Indo-China. Through a chain of events, in which the flair for intrigue of General Douglas MacArthur, us supreme commander in the Far East, played a not inconsiderable role, an existing civil war in Korea was transformed into a confrontation between the great powers. Events moved so rapidly that it was difficult for those on the outside to discern what was happening; the only thing that was clear was that the world was heading into a major crisis.

In spite of having reason to feel satisfied with his general analysis, Endicott became increasingly aware of the importance of establishing the truth about the origins of the particular flare-up at the 38th parallel on June 25th. Public opinion on that question was of decisive importance in determining whether such countries as Canada would send armed forces into the conflict.

The first clue, from Western sources, that the South may have provoked the incident came to Endicott when he picked up the early edition of the morning paper on the way back to his Winnipeg hotel at midnight. His eye immediately fell upon a small item datelined 25 June: 'This morning, according to the South Korean Office of Public Information, South Korean troops pushing northward captured Haeju, capital of Wranghoe province, which is a mile north of the border.'[3]

Next morning, in later editions of the paper, the item was missing, an omission that aroused Endicott's suspicions.

A few days later while in Saskatchewan, after receiving a letter from H.G. Rhodes, an amateur radio buff in Regina and a reader of the *Newsletter*, Endicott became convinced that there was an attempt to cover up the origins of the fighting on the 25th. Rhodes had made notes of a number of news items on that historic Sunday; one of them, a broadcast at 0600 Greenwich Mean Time, 25 June, of a report recorded earlier by a Western correspondent, Charles Sims, included this statement: 'American Armed Forces Radio Service, Voice of Information and Education, Seoul, June 25, 1950: The origin of the fighting appears confused – at some points South Korean troops are operating north of the 38th parallel. One South Korean unit advanced and found themselves in possession of the town of Haeju.' In sending this item to Endicott, Rhodes added: 'The map shows Haeju 6 to 8 miles north of the 38th parallel on the main road to Pyongyang. How do you "find yourself in possession of a town"? Particularly with personnel map-trained under efficient American officers?'

When Endicott read these statements to a meeting in Saskatchewan he was challenged by a man in the audience who said that he had been in the Associated Press office in Winnipeg when that broadcast came through and that later an AP service telegram arrived cancelling the dispatch.

'You may judge for yourself,' Endicott replied, 'whether or not this "correction" was part of the conspiracy of silence due to the policy which the US immediately began urging the United Nations to adopt, in line with action the US had already taken.'[4]

Later it would be argued by some friends that to ask who fired the first shot was in the nature of legalistic quibbling, and was of less importance than understanding that 25 June was simply an escalation of a continuing civil war. He did not entirely agree. In view of the extensive propaganda over allegations about North Korea's guilt, which subsequently became the starting point for all Western accounts of the war, the origin of the fighting on 25 June could not be dismissed as irrelevant. His strong desire to see the war brought to an end was therefore matched by a militant and equally strong wish to fix historical and moral responsibility for its outbreak and for the subsequent death of over two million innocent people.

A major doubt in people's minds was that, if the North had not taken the initiative, how was it possible that after a few days they managed to capture Seoul, the capital of South Korea?

According to Endicott's reconstruction of the events, Dulles and MacArthur gave Syngman Rhee the nod to go ahead and the South Korean forces attacked on 25 June advancing six miles; mass risings of partisans in their rear, he speculated, spread panic in the South Korean army, and when they were hit by the northern forces they collapsed. The Americans found themselves 'holding the bag,' with a small force of Japanese-trained professional soldiers, and had to order a hasty retreat.[5]

The concrete evidence for Endicott's thesis about the origins of the war was sparse. However, documents captured at Seoul by the North Korean army in the summer of 1950, and filed at the United Nations, provided him with ample evidence of Rhee's plans to attack the North with promises of help from the United States. The validity of these documents, which spoke of 'large scale preparations ... for the campaign against the North,' were never disputed by the United States.[6]

In addition, he was greatly influenced by the opinion of Sir John Pratt, a

British Foreign Office expert on the Far East, whom he knew personally, who came out of retirement in an attempt to establish the truth in terms of international law. From his files, Pratt prepared a case showing that there was 'not a scrap of evidence' for the resolution, proposed by the United States and adopted by the UN Security Council on 25 June 1950, which declared that North Korea was the guilty party. The telegram from the UN Commission in Korea to the Security Council on 25 June (s/1496) reported only that the North accused the South of aggression; the South denied and made a counter-accusation of aggression. The UN Commission in Korea placed no blame and made no judgement. In spite of this, Dean Acheson, US secretary of state, declared that the Security Council had passed its resolution 'after hearing the report of the United Nation's Commission labelling the Communist action as an unprovoked act of aggression.' All the other countries on the Security Council, except Yugoslavia, followed the lead of the United States. Acheson's statement 'was a deliberate lie,' said Pratt.

'Such things do not happen unless there is something to be hushed up,' the veteran British diplomat added, 'and the fact which they were hushing up was that it was the South Koreans who started the war, having been encouraged to do so by the Americans because they wanted an excuse to seize Formosa – on the way back into China.'

Pratt's analysis in *Korea: The Lie That Led to War* (1951) has rarely been confronted. When the threat of civil war in Korea loomed again in 1973, Endicott had Pratt's pamphlet reprinted and sent to every member of the Canadian Parliament as a warning; he hoped also to remind the Canadian government of past errors.[7]

In the memoirs of Lester Pearson there is a vivid description of the late Prime Minister Mackenzie King's struggle to prevent Canada from becoming a 'cat's paw' of United States policy in South Korea in late 1947 and early 1948; this struggle very nearly resulted in the resignation of King and the collapse of the Canadian cabinet. After King departed the scene in the summer of 1948, there was no one, in Pearson's account, who would speak out so frankly 'to prevent Canada being dragged along dangerous paths by Washington.' When the crisis arose in 1950, Pearson himself, and the new prime minister, St Laurent, favoured a 'forward' foreign policy in co-operation with the United States against what Acheson called the 'naked aggression of the communists.'[8]

Endicott was determined to challenge the legitimacy of any action to send Canadian forces to Korea.[9] Canada's proposed military expedition, he thought, could not be shielded under the tattered umbrella of the United Nations, since that organization had been led to betray its own charter; the mission of the United Nations – to preserve peace by recognizing the necessity of negotiation and the unity of the great powers – was made null and void, he pointed out, by a decision taken in the absence of both the Soviet Union and the People's Republic of China. Moreover, the decision was to wage war, without negotiation and without ever hearing the case of the accused in the Security Council, thereby violating Article 32, which said: 'any state which is not a Member of the United Nations, if it is a party to a dispute under consideration by the Security Council, shall be invited to participate, without vote, in the discussion relating to the dispute.' The war in Korea, Endicott said, was 'a violent intervention in the internal affairs of a proud, long-suffering and heroic people who were promised the right to run their own affairs after liberation from forty years of Japanese colonial oppression.' As leader of the peace movement he wished to reverse, if possible, a course that he believed was unworthy of Canada's own best traditions and unfair to democracy in Asia.

Endicott's first action was to lead a delegation of peace workers who converged on Ottawa from all over Ontario and Quebec to lobby members of Parliament. According to press reports, following 'a fighting pep talk by their leader, Dr. J.G. Endicott,' two hundred members of the Canadian Peace Congress 'swarmed over Parliament Hill with orders to press every Member of Parliament with demands for an end to the Korean War.' Several delegates were promptly taken into custody by Ottawa city police and most were barred from entering the Centre Block. Inside the House, party leaders George Drew and M.J. Coldwell denounced the peace delegates for 'repeating the despicable Communist line' and for being 'either very ignorant or misled' – a decidedly discouraging reception.[10]

By the end of September 1950, after General MacArthur had raised an armed force of a quarter of a million men, mostly from the United States but later including forces from Great Britain, Australia, New Zealand, and a battalion from Canada, the South Koreans were back on the 38th parallel. Without waiting for United Nations approval, MacArthur's armies continued northward until they began to approach the border of China at the Yalu River. In spite of repeated warnings from China that it would not stand idly by if its frontiers were threatened, MacArthur pressed onward. On the very day that a Chinese general arrived at the United Nations in New York to present China's proposals for settling the conflicts in Asia, MacArthur launched a campaign to 'end the war by Christmas.' His offensive ran into a force of up to sixty thousand Chinese soldiers, named the Chinese People's Volunteers, which had crossed the Yalu into North Korea. In this mountainous region, the seasoned Chinese fighters administered a punishing blow to the UN forces, which then quickly retreated south of the 38th parallel. MacArthur claimed his armies had been overwhelmed by 'hordes' of Chinese.

From this time on, according to Pearson, the 'main Canadian objective was to bring the hostilities in Korea to an end.'[11] But when the United Nations, under strong American pressure, branded China as an aggressor, Canada joined in, thus 'missing the bus for peace and making at the last minute an undignified scramble onto the Truman war chariot,'[12] as Endicott put it. There was, nevertheless, some sense of relief in that the United Nations refused MacArthur's wishes to blockade China, to bomb its mainland, and to use Chiang Kai-shek's army in Korea.

During the next two years of acrimonious armistice talks, from 1951 until 1953, Endicott became well known abroad as the spokesman of the Canadian Peace Congress through attending meetings organized by the World Council of Peace in such Eastern European capitals as Warsaw, Berlin, Vienna, and Budapest. In Canada, as a result of numerous national speaking tours and half a dozen rallies in Massey Hall, his name became a virtual household word. Analysts in intelligence agencies of the United States, who monitored his activities, described him as 'persuasive,' 'a dynamic speaker,' 'a dangerous Communist propagandist,' and found it 'difficult to understand why the Canadian public will flock to hear this "spell-binder."' One US agent in Canada noted that, 'although he meets opposition here and there, a great many of his listeners are not Communists or radicals. Many are devout church people, many are curiosity seekers and no doubt many attend his meetings to see him squirm under heckling and booing.'[13] His fighting speeches, spiced with humour, combining much from his rich religious heritage with his keen sense of what was important in the passing scene, generally fired the enthusiasm of his audiences.

A favourite target was General MacArthur, whom Endicott described as a 'dangerous military dictator' with racist ideas. 'The Pacific has become an Anglo-Saxon lake,' MacArthur had said in 1949. The man Truman was calling in 1950 the great 'soldier-statesman of the Far East' outlined his plan for an easy victory in Asia with small loss of American lives by having Asians fight Asians: rearm and finance Chiang Kai-shek and look forward to the day when he would reinvade the mainland with American help; meanwhile, use Taiwan as an American base to control the Pacific.[14] A wealthy man, who had married into the J.P. Morgan family and owned profitable breweries and gold mine shares in the Philippines, MacArthur would, Endicott predicted, act according to his military and millionaire's outlook; the general's answer to social reform and independence in Asia, he said, was to crush it. 'We must down with him!' Endicott would roar to cheering crowds, the veins in his head appearing at the bursting point.[15]

With Truman and Acheson threatening to use atomic bombs in Korea,

Pearson responded to the possibility of nuclear annihilation by saying: 'a victim is just as dead whether he is killed by a bayonet or an atom bomb.'[16] This was not acceptable to the peace movement. Endicott continued to press the importance of signing the Stockholm Appeal, for it offered the restraint of affirming that the first to use the bomb in the future would be considered a war criminal. In Warsaw in November 1950, where he attended the second world peace congress, a definition of aggression was adopted as a standard by which to measure international conduct: '*The aggressor is that State which first uses armed force, under any pretext, against another State; no political, economic or strategic considerations, no pretext based on the internal situation of a State, can justify armed intervention.*' This was followed by a new world-wide petition campaign for a 'Pact of Peace among the Five Great Powers,' open to all countries, which entailed recognition of the People's Republic of China by other governments and her reception into the United Nations. The peace movement called upon people 'whatever may be their view of the causes that have brought about the danger of a world war' to join forces in demanding negotiations to bring an end to the Cold War and to the killing in Korea.[17]

For two years Endicott had travelled freely to and from Europe, to represent Canada at international peace meetings, without hindrance from the Canadian government. Then one day in the spring of 1951, when he was returning from a World Council of Peace meeting in East Berlin, he was detained at Montreal's Dorval Airport by customs and immigration officials. They turned him over to plainclothes RCMP constables. In a small room he was made to undress and hand over all his clothes and effects, which they examined at their leisure in another room; presumably they hoped to find something they could consider incriminating. When he asked what was their authority for doing this, they said: 'We have authority,' but they refused to answer any further questions and kept his documents.

'I realized when I was being held in this room how helpless I was,' Endicott recalled. 'Democracy is one thing when you talk about it in polling booths, but it is the dictatorship of the capitalist class when they wish it to be. There I was, absolutely helpless. They could put material in and declare that I brought it in. Anytime they had really wanted to destroy me and put me in jail they could have done it quite easily.'

Several weeks later, without notice, an unidentified carton arrived on the Endicott's verandah in Toronto. Since there had already been an incident of a bomb exploding at a hall where Jim was advertised to speak, and on another occasion a fire bomb had been placed inside the door of their home, Mary was alarmed at the sudden appearance of this large, loosely done-up, box. Some friends volunteered to take it by open truck out into the country to open it. After elaborate precautions to 'explode' it with long fishing poles, everyone was relieved to find the contents were the documents of the peace meeting returned from the RCMP.

When Endicott protested to the minister of justice about the whole procedure carried out by the police, he was curtly informed that he was being searched according to the appropriate sections of the Customs Act. This treatment continued, off and on, for eight years, except that afterwards confiscated documents were returned to him by registered mail. Under the regimes of Justice Minister Stuart Garson and his successor, Davie Fulton, Endicott observed drily, the clause 'reasonable grounds of suspicion' in the Customs Act was 'an elastic term.'[18]

Endicott decided that his experience was a reflection of the fact that the peace movement was winning wider public support for its criticism of government policy, and that, as a result, the government was undertaking an even more concerted campaign of counter-measures. Lester Pearson, especially, brought his considerable reputation to bear against the Canadian Peace Congress. He told the Canadian people that the world was divided between freedom and slavery and warned that the wrong side had the initiative. The 'battle of attrition,' he said, needed dual tactics, military and civil, 'the rifle and the plough of our forefathers in their struggles with any savages lurking in the woods.' While suggesting that foreign affairs were now the 'business of every Canadian family and the responsibility of every Canadian citizen,' he made an exception in the case of the Peace Congress and its supporters, denouncing the congress as an 'agent of a foreign aggressive imperialism.' He argued that it was confusing many well-meaning people, and called upon Canadians to frustrate its propaganda. In this connection he singled out for praise the action of fifty engineering students who swamped the annual meeting of the University of Toronto peace council and took over the organization. 'If more Canadians were to show something of this same high-spirited crusading zeal,' said Pearson, 'we would very soon hear little of the Canadian Peace Council and its works. We would simply take it over.'[19]

Where Pearson led, others followed. The minister of citizenship and immigration, Walter E. Harris, warned his sister-in-law, Mrs Rae Luckock, a member of the peace executive, to get out of the Peace Congress. 'If you knew what we have planned for those people,' he said, as Mrs Luckock reported to Endicott, 'you would not stay one minute longer.'[20] Soon groups of anti-communist toughs, mainly displaced persons and recent immigrants from Europe, were organized by forces unknown to attend, harass, and break up peace meetings by strictly un-parliamentary methods.[21]

Possibly even more threatening were the amendments which the minister of justice, Stuart Garson, introduced into the criminal code in the summer of 1951. These amendments, grouped into Bill H-8, went a long way in attempting to restrict traditional civil rights, threatening the right to strike, the right to picket, and freedom of speech, but they did not go as far as George Drew and the other leaders of the Tory party demanded. From that time on, anyone who criticized the RCMP or foreign troops stationed on Canadian soil was liable to punishment by five years' imprisonment. Furthermore, with the case of Korea and the Chinese People's Volunteers clearly in mind, it would be treasonous, punishable by death, if, while in or out of Canada, a person said or did anything which could be considered as helping any armed forces against which Canadian forces were engaged in hostilities, whether or not a state of war existed (Section 74). It was a draconian law. Of this amendment, John Diefenbaker, MP, said at the time: 'The objective of this clause is laudable, but its implications are very dangerous! ... I know of no case in four or five hundred years' interpretation of the law of treason that goes as far as this amendment.'[22]

The RCMP also took a more direct hand in promoting lies and distortions about the Canadian Peace Congress. On one occasion an unscrupulous forgery looked suspiciously like the work of the Special Branch of that organization. In a manner that foreshadowed acts of wrongdoing which came to light in official commissions of enquiry into the RCMP in the 1970s, letters were distributed to people who were collecting signatures to the world peace appeal by an unknown organization calling itself the 'Canadian Youth Peace Movement.' The letters stated that the objective of the peace movement was to promote a major communist party in Canada; recipients were summoned to attend a meeting of 'this great modern organization' on pain of having their names turned over to the RCMP along with foolproof evidence that they were active members of the communist party if they failed to show up. The *Montreal Gazette* and other papers across Canada picked up the forged document in order to accuse the Peace Congress of blackmail as well as of complete identification with the communist party.[23]

Another common method of disrupting the peace movement was the use of secret police agents. One of these agents, who later boasted publicly about his work, made wildly provocative and revolutionary sounding speeches, shouting that capitalism must be overthrown before there could be peace, and then reported to the RCMP that the Peace Congress was subversive by using his own speeches as evidence. It was contemptible and anti-democratic, Endicott protested, for the RCMP to plant someone who acted in ways to discredit an organization: 'They did not need under-cover agents ... Our meetings were open to all, our documents public property.'[24]

The government's curtailment of civil liberties was not without its effect on the peace forces of the 1950s. Endicott recalled that many people who wished to participate and sincerely wanted peace were frightened, fired from jobs, visited by the RCMP, warned, and otherwise driven into silence.

The subservient free press in Canada, as Endicott considered it, also worked overtime in assisting the government in its campaign. When distinguished men and women around the world adhered to the peace movement – Soong Ching-ling, Bertolt Brecht, Jean-Paul Sartre, Georg Lukács, Ilya Ehrenburg, Pablo Picasso, Joseph Hromadka, Nazim Hikmet, Pablo Neruda, Salvador Allende, W.E.B. DuBois, Paul Robeson, and many others – the press seemed to respond only with strenuous denunciations. Canadian public figures were pressed in editorials to withdraw their signatures from the Stockholm Appeal; they were subjected to red-baiting attacks, called fellow travellers or dupes, if they joined a delegation or took part in conferences attended by representatives of the Eastern countries.

In these circumstances, those in positions of public responsibility who held to their convictions in the face of unrelenting pressure won a special place in Endicott's heart. Among these, once again, was the Hon. T.C. Douglas: in the most difficult days of the Korean War he refused to be stampeded into labelling as 'communist or subversive' everyone who failed to fall in behind the Americans in forcing 'sawdust Caesars' (as he called them) like Chiang Kai-shek and Syngman Rhee upon people who did not want them.

There were many others who stood firm, including Dr E. Crossley Hunter, the pastor of Endicott's church; when approached by the *Toronto Daily Star* to withdraw his signature from the Stockholm Appeal as others had done, Hunter replied that he would make a statement on condition it was printed as given: 'The Stockholm Appeal, I carefully read and willingly signed. I see no reason why any Christian should not sign it.'[25]

These responses were a heartening omen as Endicott headed into his next major battle: the storm that broke after he stated his conviction that American forces were secretly experimenting with germ warfare on the people of Korea and China.

CHAPTER TWENTY-SIX

Charges of germ warfare

In the first week of February 1952 the Endicotts were high in the clear sky over the vast forests and frozen rivers of Siberia. After touching down briefly in Ulan Bator, they flew on across the Gobi Desert towards China. Looking down on the endless sand, they saw camels, here and there, plodding their way between oases; further off, great ranges of brown, white-capped mountains twisted like 'writhing silver serpents,'[1] guarding the walled towns and patchwork of brown fields on the plains beyond. Distances requiring weeks to cover by ancient caravans were now traversed in a few hours, in the comfort of modern, four-engined aircraft. Soon they were over northern China, approaching Peking.

Suddenly, below them, lay the great city, hazy from the wind-blown sand of the desert. One could see the yellow-glazed tiles on the roof of the Summer Palace, the ancient home of the Manchu emperors, and the frozen lake with its arched bridges; the curved roofs of the old imperial tea-houses and a great pagoda were silhouetted amongst the leafless trees on the hills. Of all the directions from which to approach China, Mary remarked to her husband, the route through Peking was the most romantic and historic. Waiting at the airport were Kuo Mo-jo, vice-premier of China and chairman of the Chinese peace movement, and three of his children, who rushed forward with large bouquets of flowers; there, also, among the welcoming group, was Li Teh-chuan, an old friend, former YWCA secretary, widow of the famous 'Christian general' Feng Yu-hsiang, and now minister of health.

The Endicotts were about to begin the first of three visits to China in the 1950s at the invitation of the Chinese Committee for World Peace. Mary concentrated on collecting material for a book, while Jim, who had lost none of his ability in the Chinese language in five years' absence, was able to converse freely with the people. In the next two months he talked to peasant farmers and addressed learned groups; he preached in the Christian churches of various cities to packed congregations; he was introduced at meetings by the presidents of China's greatest universities, where students gave him a tumultuous welcome. He was heartened and inspired by the signs of reconstruction which he saw, and he in turn tried to encourage and strengthen the Chinese people in their difficult task of remoulding and rebuilding their country.

In the midst of their tour, in Shanghai, before they had a chance to travel back to Szechuan as planned, they received a telephone call from Kung Peng, Premier Chou En-lai's secretary, about an ominous turn of events in the war in Korea.

'As you may have seen in our press,' said Kung Peng, 'since you have come to China the American forces have begun field experiments in biological warfare in Korea and Northeast China. When you return to North America you will be asked about this. Do you wish to go to the Northeast to make an investigation for yourself?'[2] There was no pressure; only an invitation.

The Endicotts talked it over, fully aware that the charge that the Americans were practising germ warfare would seem like incredible propaganda to all well-meaning people in the West. They consulted their old friends, Y.T. Wu and K.H. and Sui May Ting, who were with them at the time. In encouraging acceptance of the invitation, their Chinese friends pointed out that the Christian community in China had already made its own appeal to Christians in the United States, requesting immediate action 'to check the American aggressive war and all its crimes.'[3] Endicott also spoke to his American friends, Bill and Sylvia Powell, who were still producing the *China Monthly Review* in Shanghai and had published reports about the germ warfare in their paper. After making up their minds, the Endicotts flew back to Peking, where Mary stayed, while Jim proceeded north to Shenyang, then called Mukden, in the Northeast in order to make his personal investigations in the area.

Endicott, of course, had no medical or scientific training; he would have to rely upon the expertise of others and upon his general observations.

On the way north he was made immediately aware of a massive public health campaign in progress – the stopping of southbound trains for disinfectant spraying, the blocking off of certain areas and rapid quarantine measures, the wholesale inoculation of the population for cholera, typhoid, and other diseases, for which he also was immunized. There was no sense of panic as tens of thousands prepared to face a new and hidden enemy. The same people who had gathered the peasants together to explain the principles of the recently completed land reform were now explaining the principles of hygiene and the benefits of inoculation, for the land reform had provided the Chinese government with an apparatus of organization and education never before known in China. Endicott saw no evidence of neglect or incompetence on the part of the Chinese authorities, though later the United States alleged that these were the reasons for any epidemics that occurred in China.

In the Northeast Endicott visited a number of rural areas and was able to question peasants who had been eye-witnesses to air-attacks; they had collected various insects, chicken feathers, and dried leaves, which they claimed had appeared in large quantities after raids, as well as voles that had apparently been dropped in containers with small parachutes attached. He examined other bomb-like containers of the type normally used by the Americans for dropping propaganda leaflets, took down serial numbers from the casings, and handled the remains of smaller procelain-type bombs in which it was claimed infected insects and bacteria had also been delivered.

In Mukden he went to hospitals and laboratories. In one of these he was shown reports and results of autopsies which revealed thirteen cases of encephalitis occurring in ten days, a disease, he was told, which had never been known before in Manchuria. Medical workers also told him that the American aircraft were spraying airborne viruses mixed with dust and gelatine; in some cases the germ turned out to be a deadly toxin causing botulism. The Chinese military censors required an agreement of silence on the number of casualties, since they did not wish the American command to get details about the effectiveness of their bacteriological warfare. In one case, however, Endicott reported that he had been told of 44,000 casualties in three weeks in one small area as a result of aerosol spraying.[4]

Endicott was also able to meet several Chinese scientists of international repute. Dr Li Pei-lin, a graduate of London University and a member of the Pathological Society of Great Britain and Ireland, Dr C.M. Chu, formerly of Cambridge University, and others, showed him, step by step, how they had used one test after another to detect the presence of bacteria on the insects and other materials that had been collected, and explained the probabilities and abnormalities of the various cases. They said they could come to no other conclusion but that China and Korea were experiencing large-scale field trials of bacteriological warfare waged by the Americans; to them the evidence was unquestionable and overwhelming.[5]

After a week in the Northeast, Endicott wired an interim report to Lester Pearson, Canadian minister of external affairs: PERSONAL INVESTIGATIONS REVEAL UNDENIABLE EVIDENCE LARGE SCALE CONTINUING AMERICAN GERM WARFARE ON CHINESE MAINLAND URGE YOU PROTEST SHAMEFUL VIOLATION UNITED NATIONS AGREEMENTS. Perhaps not really expecting a reply, Endicott repeated the cable to the Canadian Press service and to the Canadian Council of Churches, hoping to inform the public of his findings. Then he continued his investigation.

At times it seemed impossible to him that the United States, which had sent so many missionaries to China, could do so great an evil. And yet he also felt that no nation on earth was more open to the charge of waging wars of mass extermination by means of brutal, scientific weapons. It was Americans who had experimented with the atomic bomb on two great Japanese cities, claiming the lives of up to 200,000 civilian victims. And in Korea, where they had used seven million gallons of napalm jellied gasoline, the destruction of civilian life was the worst in the history of modern warfare.

The indiscriminate bombing of non-military targets, low-level strafing that blotted out whole villages, the use of sophisticated modern weapons against a nation of lightly armed peasants,[6] all these had been freely reported by the Western news media. 'The napalm bomb hit the village,' reported the *New York Times*: 'The inhabitants ... were caught and killed and kept the exact postures they held when the napalm struck – a man about to get on his bicycle, 50 boys and girls playing in an orphanage, a housewife strangely unmarked holding in her hand a page torn from a catalogue ...'[7] In another account René Cutforth, Korean correspondent for the British Broadcasting Corporation, had described the victim of a napalm attack: 'In front of us a curious figure was standing, a little crouched, legs straddled, arms held out from his sides. He had no eyes and his whole body, nearly all of which was visible through tatters of burnt rags, was covered with a hard black crust speckled with yellow pus ... He had to stand because he was no longer covered with a skin but with a crust like crackling which broke easily.'[8] After that, was anything implausible?

To those who could so use napalm, Endicott believed, germ warfare would seem merely a natural, logical, and in some ways more attractive, extension of existing weaponry. Germs were relatively inexpensive to produce; their production could be camouflaged under the guise of legitimate medical research; it would be difficult for the victims to determine whether an outbreak of disease among men, animals, or plants was the work of nature or of man; and their use would make possible the defeat of an enemy without destroying his factories or economy. He was aware also that there were powerful political and military voices in the United States that were advocating the use of bacteriological warfare as a means of saving the lives of American soldiers. In addition, the United States and Japan were the only two major powers that had refused to bind themselves by the moral and legal restraints of the Geneva Protocol of 1925, which prohibited the use of toxic weapons.[9]

He shrank from believing that human beings could do such a thing – and he knew others would also – but he could not escape the evidence that had been presented to him. He did not wish to be a martyr, and for that reason he had avoided going to Korea because of the greater possibility that the Garson amendments to the criminal code could be used to lay a charge of treason against him.

Following a press conference in Mukden on 10 April, he broadcast his findings to the world over the international service of Radio Peking. He told how he had been to the villages of the Northeast and had talked to the peasants and heard their testimony. He had been shown germ-laden insects: 'In fact, I have caught some myself.' Cholera, typhoid, typhus, acute infectious encephalitis, anthrax, were some of the germs that Chinese scientists, trained in America and Great Britain, had demonstrated under the microscope for him. 'I will not give any detailed and specific account of many things I saw because I do not wish to make available to the American germ war criminals any useful facts,' he said. Without wishing to minimize the awfulness of this type of warfare, he expressed confidence that the newly liberated and aroused people of China were quite capable of overcoming this criminal attack upon them. 'The Chinese,' he said in conclusion, 'are waiting to hear whether Christians in the West will take a just stand on this latest crime against humanity.'[10]

Some of the reporters at the Mukden press conference showed him printed material from the West which seemed to condone the use of germ warfare. An article from the Reader's Digest of January 1951, for instance, had described germ war preparations in Canada at Suffield, Alberta. And in the Standard, a Montreal newspaper, of 15 October 1949, Dr O.M. Solandt, head of the Canadian Defence Research Board, had been interviewed by Gerald Waring in an article entitled 'The Next War Will Be Different'; the first paragraph read: 'Omond McKillop Solandt, a quiet, soft-spoken man, knows more ways of killing people than anybody else in Canada, and he says that the future of death on a mass scale is very bright.'

In response to a question from Chinese newsmen as to whether Canada was involved in United States' germ warfare, Endicott replied that he had no personal knowledge of Suffield or of any complicity on the part of Canada in the supplying of infected insects. He speculated, however, that it might be possible that Canada was involved in some way in view of the existence of defence-sharing agreements between the two countries and because the colder climate of Canada would be suitable for breeding bacteria-carrying, cold-resistant insects.[11] He denounced the remarks attributed to Solandt and stated that on his return to Canada he would make public the results of his investigation in hopes of rallying the people 'to oppose this criminal germ war.'

Reports of the Mukden press conference were broadcast over Radio Moscow. In Canada, newspaper editorials and prominent politicians spoke of treason and sedition, charging Endicott with demoralizing the public and undermining Canadian participation in the war in Korea; they demanded that action be taken to have him muzzled and quarantined. Terming his reported remarks 'damnable,' John Diefenbaker, a future prime minister, said that 'a large body of Canadians' were demanding to know why such a person could go abroad and make remarks that were 'far and beyond those that constitute expressions of free speech.' Another Conservative member of Parliament, Gordon Graydon, an old college friend, denounced Endicott as a 'so-called Canadian' and proposed that his citizenship be revoked to prevent him from returning to Canada.[12]

Spurred by this outcry, Justice Minister Garson announced that his law officers were studying the statutes for possible methods of prosecution, while External Affairs Minister Pearson declared that his department was planning to question Endicott and would consider impounding his passport. Apparently having some doubts that Endicott could be convicted, Pearson added lamely: 'if he has broken the law of Canada I should think he will suffer the consequences.'[13]

Unaware of this furore, the Endicotts began their return journey to Canada via Moscow, Prague, and London. Even if he had known that the Canadian government was now monitoring his every statement, Endicott would probably have continued as he did, giving press conferences and making speeches along the way. In London on 21 April he was met by several reporters who questioned him about the germ war charges. Canadian Press asked for a signed statement, which seemed a little unusual. Unsatisfied with that, CP later telephoned from Montreal to ask if he had told the Chinese newsmen at Mukden that infected insects were being bred in Canada for use by the United States forces in Korea and northeastern China. Endicott replied that he had not said that Canada was participating in the germ warfare in China: newsmen in Mukden had asked him about a story on Canadian bacteriological experiments which had been published in a Montreal newspaper and he had said it was 'probably correct'; 'But I made no statement I had knowledge the insects were bred in Canada.'[14]

Then, at three o'clock in the morning of 23 April, the night porter in the old-fashioned Royal Hotel near Russell Square, where the Endicotts were staying, knocked on their bedroom door.

'Telephone call for you – trunk call, sir.' 'Sorry to disturb you, sir,' he added apologetically, 'it's from Canada.' There's been a death in the family, thought Mary, as she followed Jim down to the hotel lobby.

It was Bruce Mickleburgh, publicity director of the Canadian Peace Congress, calling from an emergency meeting of the executive (at 10 p.m. their time) to urge an early flight home. Mary heard snatches of the conversation: 'I can't leave tomorrow; I preach in two churches here. But I will try for passage on Monday ... Yes, I've been interviewed by some London papers and by the Canadian Press ... I gathered there was considerable stew brewing but ... No, I didn't say anything about Korea, only China ... Oh, the Maple Leaf Gardens? Do they think there is that much interest? Well, our thanks to the executive for their faith in me. We'll cable flight arrival. Good night.'

When they had returned to their room, Jim filled in the details of the great storm that had broken, of the alarming headlines as to the fate of the unsuspecting travellers: 'Endicott Faces Jail.' The peace executive had decided to meet the attack by a mass rally on 11 May in the hockey stadium in Toronto, where Endicott would make his report; they had no idea what he would say, but they had confidence in him and wanted him home as quickly as possible to prepare for the rally and to stop rumours that he was hiding from the government.[15]

Without losing any sleep from worry, Endicott decided to honour his speaking engagements in London. He also sent another cable to Lester Pearson requesting an interview or a hearing with the External Affairs Committe of the House of Commons before giving his report to the Canadian people.

On 4 May the Endicotts endured a long transatlantic flight to Montreal, not knowing what to expect upon arrival; it was no surprise, however, that all Endicott's papers were seized by three plainclothes policemen at Dorval Airport. Upon returning to Toronto, Endicott learned that the External Affairs Committee had turned down his request in favour of hearing O.M. Solandt;[16] Pearson also would not grant an interview, sending instead a questionnaire demanding that Endicott confirm or deny statements he had made in China.

Endicott refused to take part in this cat-and-mouse procedure. 'I have been unable to trace any authority possessed by your department which gives the right to question Canadian citizens in such a way,' he replied. 'Nor is the purpose of the questions clear to me. Until I receive some clarification on this point I must decline to submit to cross-examination from your officials.' He added that he would be speaking in Toronto and would repeat what he had said abroad about the use of germ warfare by the United States forces against the Chinese people.

The night of the rally, his opponents arrived at Maple Leaf Gardens with eggs, tomatoes, firecrackers, stink-bombs, and placards. 'The meeting had all the elements of explosiveness,' wrote the *Toronto Telegram*,[17] which had sent three staff reporters and a battery of photographers to record the expected débâcle. The Peace Congress was also well prepared: as the crowd of ten thousand streamed into the building, the regular ushers were supplemented by five hundred peace supporters, seamen, auto-workers, steel and electrical workers, miners from Sudbury, and other trade unionists who had volunteered to help in case of trouble. Except for some minor skirmishes, the disrupters held fire until it was too late.

For a great cheer arose, indicating the sentiment of the meeting, as Endicott, his father, now a little shaky on his feet, and the other platform guests mounted to the stage. Only W.E.B. DuBois, the venerable American black scholar, was missing; he had been refused entry to address the meeting by immigration officials at Toronto international airport. James Endicott, Sr, who had asked for the privilege of introducing his son, stepped forward, stood straight as a ramrod, his face almost as white as his hair. Then, for fifteen minutes, without a note as in days of old, the eighty-seven-year-old former moderator of the United Church held the undivided attention of the vast audience. After a whimsical beginning, he went on to explain what it was in his son's childhood surroundings, early training, and later experiences that had led him to become 'public enemy number one' in the eyes of the press. 'They've been after Jim for years,' declared his father, 'because he dared to see what was there to be seen and to tell what he had seen. And he has proven himself, up to date, a true prophet of how things would happen and what would turn out in China ... in spite of them all, I'm as proud of him as though they had sent out a ticker-tape welcome for him when he came back to Toronto.'

It was a superb effort, 'a wonderful and most moving document,' declared Gregory Vlastos, professor at Queen's University;[18] it set the tone for the whole meeting in a way that stirred deep emotions in the collective consciousness of Canadians, Christian and Jew, believer and non-believer, alike.

Jim Endicott followed with his report on China, outlining optimistically the new developments in that country. It was a fighting speech, lasting over an hour, in which he attacked American policy, warning that if it were not checked a wider war in Asia would be the result; the West could not win such a war. He reiterated his charge that the 'lawless American militarists' in Korea were using germ warfare against the Chinese people, and he gave a detailed account of his personal investigations. In spite of the 'homicidal maniacs,' he believed that the world peace movement, 'the greatest, most universal, most effective movement of the people of the world' that had so far appeared in all of history, could be a decisive instrument to prevent the outbreak of a general war. To this end he urged his audience to support the various proposals of the peace pledge that was being circulated by the Canadian Peace Congress. He did not ask for agreement with his findings on germ war as a basis for action, only that all governments be asked to sign the Geneva Protocol promising never to use that kind of weapon.

As for attacks on his character and loyalty, made during the previous weeks in the House of Commons Standing Committee on External Affairs and by certain members of Parliament such as Diefenbaker and Graydon, sheltered behind parliamentary immunity, Endicott told how he had telegraphed asking permission to appear before his accusers and had been refused: 'Once I am here where they can charge me or hear me they beat a hasty retreat; their charges came in like a lion and went out like a lamb.'

He also needled the Canadian newspaper editors for the way they had handled his case. 'They have tried me in absence, condemned me unheard and sentenced me to their own satisfaction. They have all said the same thing, from Halifax to Vancouver.' It was a bad case of 'parrot fever,' he said, pointing to the press table: 'not one original idea among the whole lot of them.'

He denied that he had done anything while abroad to harm the prestige of Canada. Operating, no doubt, on the principle that the best defence is to take the offensive, he charged that it was the authorities in Ottawa who were not properly informed of what it was that raised or lowered the prestige of Canada in the Far East; statements such as those of Dr Solandt on the possibilities of germ warfare, or those of the prime minister headlined 'Canada Atom Weapons Able to Ruin Crops for Generations,'[19] were not helpful.

Canada's prestige was actually fairly high in China, he stated, 'because of the great work of Dr. Norman Bethune, who gave his life helping the Chinese to defeat the Japanese imperialists.' More recently, Canada's prestige had risen when the minister of external affairs had gone to New York and 'told his American friends that Canada does not want to be dragged into a war with China.' Endicott approved of this gesture and wished to dispel any impression that he had a deep or implacable quarrel with Lester Pearson. It was common knowledge that Pearson had been in favour of recognizing the new government of China: he could continue to represent majority opinion in Canada by advocating that common sense course in diplomatic circles and by voting to seat China in the Security Council of the United Nations where she belonged; such actions, in addition, would help reduce international tension by undermining 'the determination of certain American militarists to extend the war to China.'[20]

When Endicott completed his lengthy address, perhaps the most crucial of his whole career, he was given a standing ovation. Even the most bitter, right-wing enemies of the peace movement reported that 'both Endicotts conveyed a sense of sincerity as well as of supreme confidence in the righteousness of their cause.'[21] Moreover, the meeting was a financial success: the *Telegram* noted sardonically that the Peace Congress collected over $5000 in buckets and 'promptly had it hauled away by Brinks Express armoured trucks.'[22]

The following day, when Pearson rose in the House of Commons to reply, it was clear that the government had backed away from any idea of prosecuting him in the courts. While Pearson denounced the germ warfare charge as a 'subversive campaign,' a 'clumsy hoax,' false and fantastic 'Soviet communist propaganda,' he was careful to avoid saying that any Canadian law had been broken. Claiming concern for freedom and for the preservation of human rights, he indicated that the government was going to be careful not to make a martyr of anyone 'in a way which would only make them more dangerous.'[23]

The leader of the opposition, George Drew, like most of the newspaper editors, was not satisfied with the government's position. He demanded some kind of punishment or restraining action on people like Endicott and Mrs Nora Rodd of Windsor, who had participated in an international women's delegation to North Korea, stating that when he had voted for the government's amendments to the criminal code respecting the law of treason it was precisely this kind of situation he had in mind.[24]

'What is treason, if Endicott is not guilty of it?' cried the *Owen Sound Sun-Times* on 26 June. Was it not treason when a Canadian described Canada's American allies, the United Nations authorities, and Canada's own government leaders as 'war criminals'? 'The Reds,' complained the paper, 'are now in the happy position of being able to relay to their Communist colleagues in China and elsewhere that the great Canadian Christian missionary Endicott carried his charges of germ warfare back home, repeated them there, and even the Government dared not prosecute him ... the only dupes yet revealed in the Endicott case are in Ottawa.'

The government, however, refused to budge. Like Ben Gunn in *Treasure Island*, it 'had its reasons.' Some of them were contradictory: while dropping hints that it might be difficult to get a jury to convict, the government also suggested that the promoters of the Peace Congress were having very little effect on public opinion. After considerable procrastination the government announced that it would be unwise to conduct a prosecution even though legal grounds existed; the advantages, it had decided, were more than offset by the disadvantages. The minister of justice asked those who were pressing for prosecution to accept his opinion that a conviction could add little to the discredit that Endicott, a 'dupe and tool' of 'the communist conspiracy,' had already brought upon himself by 'allying himself with the forces of oppression, terror and atheism.'[25]

Without full access to government files, which after nearly thirty years remain partially closed in this case, some aspects of the cabinet's thinking are necessarily obscure. However, from such cabinet papers as have been made public, the general outline is clear: the government could not push the usual 'communist conspiracy' theme too far because the RCMP had plainly told it that there was no evidence, overt or otherwise, that Endicott was a member of the party. Furthermore, the RCMP, which was trailing him everywhere, was finding it difficult to pin anything on him; a confidential biographical note, based upon RCMP reports, stated: 'He is very skillful and avoids with great dexterity any remark that might get him into trouble.'[26]

There were other, even more compelling, reasons for not staging a treason trial involving one of Canada's most knowledgeable citizens on East Asia. The Canadian government itself, and especially Lester Pearson, had serious concern about United States conduct in the Far East; a trial of Jim Endicott might have turned into a trial of the whole American foreign policy in which Canada was deeply and uncomfortably enmeshed.

The majority of Canadians, Pearson privately admitted in April 1951, watched the development of American policy in the Far East with 'anxiety and hesitation'; the strong public response to any criticism of the United States, he told Hume Wrong, the Canadian ambassador in Washington, showed 'how easy it would be to work up a strong anti-American feeling in this country at this time.'[27] Cabinet papers reveal that Pearson and his top advisers believed that the tactics of their American allies were 'disingenuous and inconsistent' and based upon the hope of overthrowing the government in Peking; they feared that the United States was prolonging the armistice talks in Korea in the hope that a breakdown of negotiations, if it could be blamed on the Chinese, might result in a mounting public demand in America for the extension of the war to China. Canadian government experts also felt that the American delegates at the Korean armistice talks were trying to draft terms that would 'protect the United Nations [read, United States] position in South Korea indefinitely'; this stand had been adopted because some members of the US State Department (as well as many high-ranking Canadian officials) suspected that if Korea were unified and independent, the communists would likely win overall control by peaceful means.[28] With all these uncertainties and hesitations in mind, the government apparently decided that it would be unwise to try to convict a man for saying he believed the Americans were guilty of the crime of bacteriological warfare. Thus a stalemate had been reached.

Endicott, of course, knew little about the thinking of the government at the time. While Pearson was himself raising some questions through diplomatic channels,[29] publicly he continued to criticize Endicott's character and called his loyalty into question.[30]

As well, the government relied upon three prominent Canadian entomologists, C.E. Atwood, A.W. Baker, and W.H. Brittain, who worked closely with the Department of External Affairs to produce a hurried refutation of the charges; their statement, declared by Justice Minister Garson to be the result of the initiative of 'free men in a free society,' totally independent of the government, was deemed suitable for the government to use 'in case need for it should arise during the Estimates' debate.'[31] The scientists did not have firsthand access to the evidence. Nor did they qualify their conclusions pending the findings of a well-publicized International Scientific Commission including distinguished scientists such as Dr Joseph Needham of Cambridge University, which conducted on-the-spot investigations in China and Korea and published a massive report in the summer of 1952 concluding that germ warfare experiments had in fact occurred.[32] In spite of the fact that the Canadian scientists did not review this substantial body of scientific evidence, their report, widely distributed by the Department of External Affairs, was subsequently used by a number of scholars to prove that Endicott's charges lacked credibility.[33]

The government was not alone in its attempts to discredit and muzzle Endicott. The president of the University of Alberta in Edmonton banned him from speaking on the campus, and the chief of police in Calgary informed proprietors of public halls that police protection could not be guaranteed if he spoke. In a front-page, open letter in his newspaper, the editor of the *Winnipeg Tribune* called him a 'renegade' and hoped that this would be the last time he would ever have to foul his paper with Endicott's name, until 'We may happily announce that you have departed the world you betrayed to join the Prince of Lies.'

Not to be outdone in demonstrations of loyalty, and wishing to prove that the church was not harbouring a subversive element, some delegates to the fifteenth General Council of the United Church of Canada, meeting in Hamilton in September 1952, introduced resolutions denouncing Endicott. One resolution declared that 'Dr. Endicott does not speak for, or in any way officially represent the church' and that the church had not been and was not now in any way associated with the Canadian Peace Congress; it passed by a vote of four hundred in favour to three against. A few delegates even wanted to have him formally expelled from the church.

In most cases these acts of anger, fear, abuse, and hatred turned into their opposites.

Many students and staff members at the University of Alberta rallied to the banner of free speech, condemning the position of their president and of the board of governors of the university.[34]

In Winnipeg, at least, there was no problem of police protection: as

Endicott walked into the Playhouse Theatre to deliver his germ warfare speech, a plainclothes detective stepped up and whispered in his ear: 'General Kay sends his greetings.' Endicott grinned broadly, for the message was from Orville Kay, former military attaché of the Canadian Embassy in Chungking, now the local chief of police.

And after the editor of the *Winnipeg Tribune* had written his open letter, several staff members, led by the assistant editor, Eric Wells, altered the final wording slightly and sent in their resignations; after an enquiry, the paper's board of directors fired the editor and appointed Wells in his place.[35]

Even the efforts of the church members who wanted to have him expelled from the church backfired. The secretary of the General Council, Dr Gordon Sisco, defended him at the meeting in Hamilton, explaining that although Endicott was no longer a minister of a particular denomination, the United Church, this did not mean he had been unfrocked: he was still a minister of the universal Church of God into which he had been ordained in 1925; despite his chairmanship of the Peace Congress and his opinions on communist China, Endicott had not contravened any church laws, but had merely exercised his right of free speech. Sisco told the press that there were no church records that could prove anything undesirable against James Endicott.

As Endicott sat in the gallery of the church auditorium in Hamilton, watching the proceedings of the highest court of his church, he experienced another moment of triumph. After several preachers had proved to their satisfaction that Marxist-Leninist, materialist, Godless communism was indeed the chief menace to world peace, one mild-mannered brother got up and said: 'It is easy to make peace with our friends, we must learn to make peace with our enemies.' The General Council then proceeded to pass a resolution advocating recognition of the People's Republic of China. When this resolution was adopted, Dr A.J. Wilson, editor of the *United Church Observer*, who was sitting in the front row, looked up at Endicott in the gallery and held up his thumb; Endicott returned the greeting to general laughter. Rev. Simon Edwards, who had been the pastor at Park Street United in Chatham, where Mary had grown up, and had always been friendly to the Endicotts, came over to offer congratulations: 'You and your Newsletter spearheaded this.'[36] Unfortunately, it would be almost twenty years before the resolution of the church council became the law of the land.

At the end of 1952 Endicott was in Vienna as part of the Canadian delegation at the 'Congress of the Peoples for Peace.' This congress, which brought together over two thousand representatives from eighty countries, was a profoundly moving experience for the participants, strengthening their will to continue. It met in the wake of the latest American offensive in Korea which occurred after the Americans walked out of the truce tent at Panmunjon in October with a take-it-or-leave-it proposal: the top of Sangkumryung Ridge had then been lowered six feet by the barrage of us heavy artillery, leaving behind 24,000 casualties, all of which failed to produce any gain.

Endicott was asked by the Chinese delegation to make a simultaneous translation into English as Kuo Mo-jo, with great clarity and dignity, presented the Chinese case for an immediate ceasefire and a negotiated settlement. He also served as chairman of the commission on 'How to end the wars now going on,' where some interesting exchanges took place, especially between the Chinese and Saifuddin Kitchlew, representing India's Congress party of Prime Minister Jawaharlal Nehru, and between the Vietnamese and the French representatives.

One of those attending the congress was Jean-Paul Sartre, the famous French writer and philosopher, who declared: 'I have had three such experiences since I reached the status of manhood, three experiences which rudely awakened hope in me – the Popular Front of '36, the Liberation and the Vienna Congress.'[37]

For Endicott, one of the most moving moments came with the meeting of a Korean mother and a French-Canadian veteran of the Korean War, Yvan Ducharme, who spoke in his native tongue: 'I am only 20 and I have seen things in Korea that no human being should ever see – the effects of napalm bombs. I am only 20, my life is ahead of me, and I have returned with a permanent disability. I appeal to all people to stop the war in Korea so that all the boys may come home.' At the Catholic school he attended in Montreal, he had learned of the struggle of his ancestors for the right to their own language, their own traditions, their own religion: 'I have therefore been able to understand why the Koreans fight so ardently for their national independence.' At the conclusion of his address, on an impulse, Mrs Kim Yen-song of the Korean delegation rushed forward and embraced him. Their meeting was greeted by a standing ovation that lasted ten minutes.[38] The moment signified that when the nations gathered face to face there could be light and understanding.

CHAPTER TWENTY-SEVEN

The Stalin Peace Prize

One crisp, sunny, December afternoon in 1952 a Canadian Pacific delivery boy cycled up to the Endicotts' front door in Toronto and asked Mary to sign for a telegram. It was from Moscow, four pages long, and in Russian; the only easily recognizable word, appearing three times, was 'Stalin.'

After a flurry of excitement finding a translator, Mary discovered that her husband had been awarded the Stalin Peace Prize. 'Highly esteemed Dr. Endicott,' the message began, 'I have the honour to inform you that the Committee for International Stalin Prizes, which consists of representatives of the democratic societies of various countries, has decided to award you, for your outstanding contribution to the cause of the struggle for the preservation of world peace, the International Stalin Prize for Strengthening Peace between Nations.' The telegram stated that the award, to be announced officially in the press and over Radio Moscow on 21 December, consisted of a diploma, a gold medal, and a monetary sum of 100,000 roubles or the equivalent value of any other currency; it was signed by Dimitri Skobeltsyn, professor, member of the Academy of Sciences, and chairman of the Committee of Stalin Prizes of the Soviet Union. At the time the award was announced, shortly after the Peoples' Congress for Peace in Vienna, Endicott was visiting Budapest at the invitation of the Hungarian peace committee and Protestant churches.

When Mary recovered from her astonishment she recalled that the International Stalin Peace Prize, the Soviet equivalent of the Nobel Peace Prize, had been instituted in 1949 by a decree of the praesidium of the Supreme Soviet in honour of Stalin's seventieth birthday. It was awarded annually to seven or eight citizens of the world. Since Jim had not yet returned from Europe, she began to prepare herself mentally for an onslaught of calls from the press.

Comments ranged from sarcastic belittlement to indignation. 'Home town boy makes good,' said one local radio station. 'Paid in full,' was the heading in *Time* on 5 January 1953. The Toronto columnist J.V. McAree recalled the ancient Greek philosopher who, when interrupted by applause from the populace, paused, and then asked: 'What foolish thing have I said, now?' Most Canadians, McAree maintained, would ask themselves what horrible thing they had done if they happened to receive a word of approval from Stalin: he thought it would be otherwise with Mr Endicott who had received a large sum of money for his efforts on behalf of peace, 'Soviet model'; 'Nobody who knows him need expect him to reject [the prize] with indignation.'[1] McAree was correct in his speculation.

In view of the considerable interest expressed by friends and opponents alike as to what they would do with the $25,000, which did seem to be a staggering sum of money, the Endicotts issued a press release following Jim's return to Toronto later in the month. It was not intended, they said, to use the money in any way to take the place of funds raised all across the country for the maintenance of the Peace Congress or for the promotion of its activities; to make such use of the money would quickly dissipate its effect. Rather, the prize money would be used for some extras which the peace movement ordinarily would never feel free to afford, but which would make it more effective – a house to be used as a headquarters, an electric typewriter, and a car for transportation.[2]

In announcing the awards on Stalin's seventy-third birthday, which was to be his last, *Pravda*, the organ of the Soviet Communist party, greeted the new winners including the American singer Paul Robeson and the Soviet writer Ilya Ehrenburg with words of praise. The Rev. James Endicott, as 'strong and upright as the great trees of his native Canada,' was described as an 'ardent champion of peace' whose voice resounded around the world, calling upon 'all upright people ... to struggle actively for peace.'[3]

By the time Endicott went to Moscow to receive his award officially, in March 1953, Stalin had been dead for three weeks. The atmosphere was solemn, the funeral orations still fresh in people's minds. So far there was no hint of the explosion of denunciations that Stalin's survivors would heap upon his head three years later. In the West there was even an attempt, from the most unlikely of quarters, to give some objective understanding of Stalin's importance: the European correspondent of the conservative Hearst papers, Howard K. Smith, wrote that 'Stalin did more to change the world in the first half of this century than any other man who lived in it'; in leading Russia to become a world power and the world's first socialist state, Smith said, Stalin had 'altered the West's whole attitude to the workingman': the New Deal in America, the welfare state in Great Britain, were responses to the Soviet five-year plans, a form of competition to stave off revolution.[4]

The awarding of international Stalin prizes was a function of no little importance in Moscow. It was a formal ceremony, held in the great hall of the Kremlin, attended by some five hundred guests, representing groups such as trade unions, scientists, writers, and artists; the chairman was always the head of the Academy of Sciences.

The main speech of welcome in 1953 was given by the patriarch of the Russian Orthodox Church, Metropolitan Nikolai. Endicott had preached in several Baptist churches during previous visits to Moscow, and on this occasion the head of the Russian church appeared to gain satisfaction from the opportunity to proclaim him as a Christian brother whose faith led to works of peace.

Endicott's acceptance speech combined a keen sense of historical context with an optimism about the future. He began with suitable acknowledgement of the honour of the award by referring to the list of previous Stalin Peace Prize winners such as Frédéric Joliot-Curie, president of the World Council of Peace, and Madame Sun Yat-sen of China. After paying a brief tribute to Stalin as the 'great leader and teacher' of the Soviet Union, he dwelt on the sacrifices of the Soviet people in overthrowing the evil forces of Nazism. 'For us in the British Commonwealth,' he said, 'the sword presented in honour of Stalingrad by His Majesty King George VI will always be a symbol of our respect and admiration for your valorous people.' Such people, he continued, could be relied upon now to 'take the cause of peace into their own hands and defend it just as valiantly.'

He spoke also of his impressions of the Soviet Union, formed while paying visits on behalf of the peace movement each year since 1950. He had witnessed an intensive education for peace and 'a magnificent faith in peace,' which had led the Soviet people to undertake vast projects of construction for the future.

The major part of his address was devoted to the problems of Asia. In speaking of the deadlock in the negotiations to end the war in Korea, he put forward the view of the Canadian Peace Congress that only one point should be emphasized – the need for an immediate ceasefire – and thereby suggested the Soviets withdraw some of their demands at the United Nations. This request was ignored by the Western press which always accused the Canadian Peace Congress of slavishly following the Soviet Union, but it was duly noted by his hosts who said: 'any proposition can be reconsidered.'

The emotional impact of his presentation was greatest when he emphasized, in the best biblical tradition, that there could be no peace in the world without justice. Perhaps to the surprise of his Kremlin audience, this Stalin prize winner spoke of the peace movement as an extension of his Christian missionary experience in China. Then, as now, he said, he had sought to help establish a practical basis for universal brotherhood: 'According to my faith and my understanding of the nature of the religion of Jesus, I would expect Christian missionaries to be widely represented in the lists of those receiving peace prizes.' He pointed out that the international missionary movement, which operated exclusively in the colonial and semi-colonial areas of the world, claimed to be a movement for the weak, the poor, and the oppressed. A few years earlier there had been a time of testing in Asia; now there was a great struggle looming in Africa. Anyone who wished to practise the principles of religious living as they were revealed in the Bible would find no difficulty in taking the side of the liberation of the people from their oppressors. Any person desiring to pray for peace would also have to work for freedom, equality, and independence of all people, especially those who now suffered from colonial oppression. 'By the teaching of Jesus,' he recalled, 'you must first establish right relationships with your brother before you "bring your gift to the altar."'

'The work that I am doing in the peace movement is, therefore, a necessary and vital part of my religious life,' Endicott continued. 'The peace movement is the most universal and effective movement of the people that has appeared so far in history. It crosses all national boundaries and is now so well organized that it can be the decisive instrument to prevent the outbreak of a general war. It is, for our day, the best expression of many of the noblest aspirations and the most morally praiseworthy desires of all humanity. For me, a Christian and a missionary, it is an act of faith to take part in this movement with all my heart and soul.'

The honour he had received, he said in conclusion, really belonged to the thousands who worked in the peace movement across Canada. In accepting it on their behalf, he expressed the hope that the Soviet people and their government would have their faith in the possibility of peace fully justified.[5]

The Kremlin audience responded warmly to his address. According to *Pravda* there was 'stormy, prolonged applause,' and its editors saw fit to print most of the text.

When the time came to re-evaluate the history of 'the Stalin era,' some of Endicott's friends were surprised and pained by his refusal to join those who wished to destroy Stalin's reputation. Endicott was shocked by the revelations of Stalin's misdeeds made by Nikita Khrushchev in a report to the twentieth congress of the Communist party of the Soviet Union in 1956, three years after Stalin's death. And yet he could not agree with Khrushchev's method of pouring all the blame for failures upon one man; nor could he accept Khrushchev's theory of 'the cult of personality' as a satisfactory or truthful explanation of the difficulties of building socialism in the Soviet Union.

Compared with his knowledge of China, Endicott had little direct information about the Soviet Union, but attacks by Khrushchev and other Soviet leaders on Stalin as a 'murderer,' 'criminal,' 'bandit,' 'gambler,' 'despot of the type of Ivan the Terrible,' 'the greatest dictator in Russian history,' 'a fool,' 'an idiot,' appeared to be demagogic and self-serving caricatures. It was a dishonest way of evading their own responsibilities. Furthermore, the fact that Khrushchev's report, given in a secret session and never officially published by the Soviet Union, had been released by United States intelligence sources, did not increase his confidence in its complete authenticity.[6]

Endicott made up his mind not to join the chorus of lamentations. He had never met Stalin, but during half a dozen trips to the Soviet Union he had talked to many people who were sincere and intelligent supporters of the Soviet regime. As a result, he believed that a great and generally good transformation was taking place. The rumours about atrocities committed in prisons and concentration camps disturbed him greatly, and they could not be proved or disproved to his satisfaction; but he rationalized in the end that it was not necessarily his duty to give the Soviet system his approval. He believed that most of the earlier tales of horror about the Soviet Union, about millions of people dying of starvation in camps, had been spread largely to justify making war upon that country; even if they were true, he could not see that the situation would be improved by a conflict the only result of which would be the killing of more people.

Like all groups, the peace movement was guided by certain convictions, and thus an important distinction was made: the Soviets under Stalin's misrule treated their own people badly; the Americans, at war in Asia, were using their weapons of modern warfare against other peoples. In neither case was the cause of justice being served, but the peace movement's first responsibility was to concentrate on stopping wars and the threat of wars between states.

Endicott shared this perspective. It was not the situation in the Soviet Union, in his opinion, but rather the actions and war propaganda of the United States, its threats to use nuclear weapons, and the determination of its leaders to overthrow the government of China, that created the danger of war and therefore deserved the closest attention.

It could be argued that, as is usually the case, there was good and bad on both sides, and it was not the purpose of the peace movement to take upon itself the support or condemnation of the internal political system of any country. 'It is doubtful to me,' Endicott wrote the Rev. E. Crossley Hunter in 1953, 'if the present capitalist system can claim to be more religious or more conducive to the bringing into being of a Christ-like world than the various socialist systems that are struggling to be born.' He had been profoundly shocked by the Methodist preachers in the United States who had said they would prefer a war with hydrogen bombs to allowing the world to 'go communist.'[7]

There remained a final episode in the Stalin Peace Prize drama. In later years the Soviet peace committee requested all Stalin Prize winners to return their diplomas and medals in exchange for untarnished Lenin Peace Prizes. Endicott refused to co-operate. If there was to be a new prize, it would have more integrity, he thought, if named the Soviet People's International Peace Prize, and he told the Russians so. If he was recalcitrant, he said to his friends, it was not so much because he was an admirer of Stalin as the fact that he thought the Soviets should not try to mock history by rewriting it. He would keep his prize. Someday he would deposit it in the Public Archives of Canada and let history be the judge of its worth.[8]

Endicott, chairman, and Eva Sanderson, vice-chairman, of the Canadian Peace Congress, signing the Stockholm Appeal to ban nuclear weapons in 1950

Endicott welcomes American black leader and singer Paul Robeson to a Toronto rally of the peace movement, c. 1949

Founding meeting of the Canadian Peace Congress, Bathurst Street United Church, Toronto, 1949

Endicott with Rev. Hewlett Johnson, Dean of Canterbury, on platform of Maple Leaf Gardens, Toronto, for rally demanding abolition of atomic weapons, 1950

'Discrimination,' *Toronto Telegram*'s depiction of the 'Red Dean,' Hewlett Johnson, and Endicott when the latter's Stalin Peace Prize was announced, 26 December 1952

'Peace! It's Wonderful!' *Canadian Forum*, June 1952, satirizing the peace movement

Mural for the second British Columbia Peace Conference, held in the Marine and Boilermakers Union Hall, Vancouver, 1950 (artist, Frazer Wilson)

American folksinger, Pete Seeger, with members of the national council of the Canadian Peace Congress, Massey Hall, Toronto, 1953

Endicott meets Chinese decontamination workers near Mukden while investigating claim that the United States was conducting germ warfare experiments in northeastern China, March 1952

Endicott, in Mukden, examines compartmentalized bomb casing of the type normally used for distributing propaganda leaflets

'Get dressed for School, young man ... and stop saying "get Dr. Endicott" ...'
Vancouver Sun, 23 June 1952

Vice-premier Kuo Mo-jo welcomes
Endicott to Peking in 1952

J.W. (Bill) and Sylvia Powell, publishers
of the *China Monthly Review* in Shanghai until 1953. The Powells were
charged with sedition by the US government for publicizing germ war reports;
the charges were dropped in 1961.

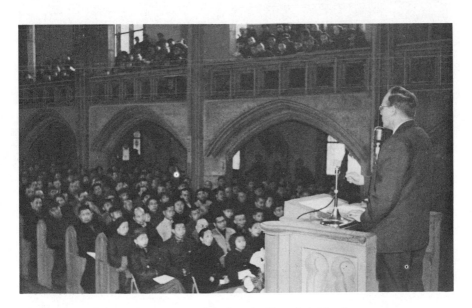

Endicott preaching in Moore Memorial Church, Shanghai, March 1952

The Endicotts entertained at dinner by Soong Ching-ling (Madame Sun Yat-sen), Shanghai, 1952

Endicott and Y.T. Wu (left) in the Peking National Library, 1956

Endicott visits St John's University, Shanghai, 1952

The Endicotts in Peking, 1956, with Richard Cheng (on the left), George Huang, and their families, twenty years after the two boys came to live with them in Chungking

Students assembled on the sports ground of the former Gin I Middle School (renamed No 11 Middle School), Chungking, to hear Endicott speak in 1956

Endicott speaking to a meeting of Hungarian Protestant church leaders, Budapest,
1957

Jim and Mary Endicott in local costume
with host during a visit to Tashkent in the
Soviet Union, 1952

Endicott at a reception of the Hungarian
peace council, Budapest, 1953; Hungarian writer Georg Lukács is at left

Prime Minister Cheddi Jagan and Endicott in Georgetown, British Guiana, 1962

Mary Endicott, at the publication of her book, *Five Stars over China*, 1953

Jim Endicott in Stockholm, 1958

Mao Tse-tung received a delegation of the World Council of Peace in October 1959; Endicott is third from the left in the back row, Mary Endicott is on the left at the front

Prime Minister Chou En-lai greets Endicott in Peking, December 1972

A world conference for peace and international co-operation, calling for a total ban on all atomic arms, New Delhi, November 1964, addressed by Indian Prime Minister Lal Bahadur Shastri; on the left Krishna Menon, on the right Jim Endicott

Peace marchers from Hiroshima, August 1958, are joined by others from Tokyo; among the foreign guests are the Endicotts in the sixth row

A seaside peace festival in Kamakura, Japan, 1958; Mary Endicott responds to the welcome as foreign friends are introduced to a crowd of thirty thousand

Vancouver city hall, Remembrance Day, 1963; Endicott urges two hundred supporters to call for a non-aggression pact between NATO and Warsaw Pact countries (photo by Carl Erickson)

Demonstration against the United States war in Vietnam, Parliament Hill, Ottawa, c. 1967: left to right, Stanley Knowles, MP, T.C. Douglas, leader of the New Democratic Party, and Jim Endicott, chairman of the Canadian Peace Congress

In 1975 Endicott visited the house where he was born and found it being used as a kindergarten

Kampuchean ambassador to the United Nations, Thiounn Prasith, with Endicott in Montreal, April 1979, to protest Vietnamese invasion of Kampuchea (*Montreal Star*)

Jim and Ella Endicott at their home in Toronto, 1980

CHAPTER TWENTY-EIGHT

Return
to China

During the tumultuous 1950s the Endicotts visited China three times at the invitation of the Chinese Committee for World Peace. Each trip was an adventure. Each time they saw more clearly the contrasts between the new and the old China. And on each occasion their admiration increased. Their central impression was simple: this truly was a people's China; the new government was the most representative, most democratic, most progressive China had ever had. It deserved the recognition and friendship of other countries of the world.[1]

The first trip, in 1952, had been cut short by the invitation to investigate charges of American bacteriological warfare in northeastern China. The second and third visits, in comparison, were leisurely: three months in 1956 travelling only with a guide and six weeks in 1959 as part of a delegation from the World Council of Peace invited to help celebrate the tenth anniversary of the People's Republic. Both visits began with national day celebrations on 1 October in Peking, where they met Mao Tse-tung; then came thousands of miles of travel, by train, air, automobile, and steamer, to new places and to familiar haunts to meet old friends.

In 1956 they went for the first time to the northwestern province of Kansu to see the new industrial development there. And on a strenuous side-trip, in which they drove across 250 miles of the Little Gobi Desert, around the end of the Great Wall, through the Yumen oil fields, and to several oases where large-scale farming had begun, they visited one of the world's greatest treasure houses of ancient art, the Caves of the Thousand Buddhas at Tunhuang, the eastern end of what was once the 'silk road' to Central Asia. 'That place has all the exotic atmosphere of a Shangri-La,' Endicott exclaimed, 'it is an artist's dream.'[2] The travellers were impressed by the scientific work being done to restore the cave murals, to explain them, and to make reproductions available.

In 1959 they visited the Three Gate Gorge in Honan province to see the worksite of the Yellow River dam; three hundred feet high and half a mile long, this dam was the key link in the government's determination to control and harness 'China's sorrow,' the river that had brought little good and much disaster in the three thousand years of its recorded history. And they travelled on the newly completed railway from Sian to Szechuan over the high Tsinling mountains. 'It is one series of bridges and tunnels,' Endicott remarked, 'probably more difficult of construction than the Canadian Pacific Railway from Calgary to Vancouver via the Kicking Horse Pass.' After each of their visits to Szechuan the Endicotts sailed once again down the mighty Yangtze, eager to see how the river, especially the Kung Ling rapids where they had been wrecked twenty-three years earlier, had been made safer by the blasting out of many rocks and by the use of white and red painted buoys to mark the passage.

At times the pace was almost too much for them. 'This business of travelling, viewing the "construction works of socialism" and trying to find time to write is a problem not yet solved,' Endicott wrote to one of his children from Loyang in 1959. 'What do you do when you are over sixty and come to the end of your energy?' he asked. For Mary it was even more difficult: she had developed angina the previous year and standing or walking any distance brought pain. 'Maybe you heard that I couldn't make the walk across the border in the time allowed and so we missed the Hongkong train,' she wrote back to their hosts in Canton in 1959. 'For a moment we felt forlorn but we found there was another in an hour so we sat in the filthy, fly-ridden restaurant – so like the old China that the contrast was startling ... Perhaps,' she added, 'it is good for visitors to spend an hour at the border!'

Back in Canada the Endicotts reported their findings and opinions in dozens of speeches and newsletters. Mary wrote a book, *Five Stars over China*. Although no Canadian publisher was interested, the book was published privately, was translated into Chinese, Japanese, and German, and remains an illuminating documentary account of the early stages of China's rebirth. Favourable reviews in farm, labour, and several church papers, as well as in liberal American journals such as *The Nation*, resulted in the sale of ten thousand copies in Canada and the United States.

The daily press accounts of their meetings, and the academics who reviewed the book, roundly criticized the Endicotts' reporting. They were called starry-eyed, naïve, uncritical, soft-headed. Why didn't they write of the costs of the revolution? Were they blind to the inevitable suffering, injustices, errors, and confusions that accompany violent upheavals?[3]

Endicott's characteristic reply was that he did not make any claim to be impartial. While agreeing that there was room for scholarly studies, he felt that there was already too much morbid concentration by the Western press on China's difficulties, both real and imagined. The black reports on the new China, he thought, should be placed in proper perspective, and he recalled the example of the British civil war of the seventeenth century; Macaulay, in an essay on Milton, had written that the violence in the war was proportionate to the oppression and degradation under which the people had been accustomed to live: 'It is the character of such revolutions that we always see the worst of them first ... It is just at this point that its enemies love to exhibit it, [but] if men are to wait for liberty till they become wise and good in slavery they may indeed wait forever.'[4]

Particularly disturbing for Endicott was the fact that hostile and false reporting on China was being used as justification for a war of intervention. He believed that the biases of former missionary colleagues such as Walter Judd in the United States and Stewart Allen and Leslie Kilborn in Canada were serving to bolster the American policy, which was to keep alive a constant threat of military action against China in the hope that at some time there would be an internal breakdown. Apart from its threat to world peace, this policy discouraged Canada and other countries from normalizing relations and trade with China, even though, as Prime Minister Louis St Laurent had said in March 1954, 'we are going to have to admit the government of China is the government the people want.'[5]

The best way to overcome America's madness and Canada's timidity, Endicott believed, was to tell the truth about New China's astonishing progress, and refute false rumours. To these tasks he and Mary lent their experience and talents. There would be time to sum up the experience of the revolution after its right to exist had been secured.

The Endicotts had felt warmly welcomed wherever they went in China. They were introduced as Canadians with 'a fervent love for China' who had 'supported the democratic movement of the Chinese people with enthusiasm.'[6] In 1956, Jim was deeply moved to learn that the workers at the annual flower show in Chengtu had voted to work through the night to advance the opening by one day for the visit of 'our good friend who helped us in our revolution.'

On this first visit to the city after an absence of ten years – fifteen for Mary – the Endicotts were amazed by the changes they saw. Chengtu still looked 'more genteel, less in a hurry to get somewhere,' than Chungking, but several wide thoroughfares had been cut through the city and were flanked by tall, modern buildings. Sao Chen Park, where Jim had spoken against the renewal of civil war in 1946, was hardly recognizable with its new trees, gardens, and exhibits of birds and animals; the house where he had grown up, still 'clean and orderly,' was now the headquarters of the Szechuan branch of the Church of Christ in China, while the nearby mission printing house, which his father had once supervised, had been nationalized and greatly expanded.

Greatest of all the changes were those at the West China Union University, which had been transformed into the Szechuan Medical University with two hundred graduates a year and a goal of one thousand. It was difficult not to feel a certain melancholy as they stood where the West China Mission had made such heroic efforts to build and maintain an institution, and reflected on the bitterness on both sides with which the attempt had ended. It was plain that foreigners were no longer needed. 'One must see it as an era in history leading out of the past and into a new day not quickly understood,' Mary wrote. 'There seems only good feeling here now for those who came and gave their years: the first schools and hospitals were opened and the fruit of their labour is seen in the generation now in leading posts.'

During their visits to China in the 1950s the Endicotts concentrated on studying changes in three groups with which they had been familiar before the revolution: the peasants, the former wealthy capitalists, and the Christian community.

Undoubtedly the foremost achievement of the Chinese revolution in their minds was the ending of the power of the landlords and money-lenders, and the substitution of a co-operative society benefiting the poor and formerly landless peasants. In repeated visits to rural areas in the Yangtze River basin and the North China plain they saw the progress of rural reconstruction. At one large co-operative farm on the fertile plain outside Chengtu in 1956, a former poor peasant, now a leader, beamed at them with a ruddy, weather-beaten face: 'It's a new time for us peasants. I'm a member of the National People's Congress. I went to Peking and met Mao Tse-tung. He talked with us about our problems. Who ever heard of such a thing!' The speaker, Endicott observed, was alert, vigorous, and self-confident as he explained efforts to mechanize production and introduce two crops of rice a year.

'Things are different now, Teacher Wen,' shouted the cargo carriers when Endicott returned to the river bank in Chungking in 1956. Some of the older ones still recognized him and vied to tell of the changes: 'When we get sick we have a hospital managed by our union. We have dormitories to sleep in and when we are too old to work we have retirement homes. Our children can go to school now ...' In the past Endicott had been carried up the 150 steps from the river bank to the city gate in a chair slung between two bamboo poles and carried by three men; now passengers rode up in a cable car.

The carriers still shouldered heavy loads, however, and Endicott reflected on how Western visitors often were shocked at the sight of men and women carrying or pulling heavy burdens: 'The uninformed or strongly prejudiced blame this on "socialism" or a totalitarian regime which forces "blue ants" to work hard. We who have lived there know that they always did carry heavy loads. There was no mechanized transport in most places. Under the socialist regime women were encouraged to work and transport was the easiest way to get work. Some naïve people, hearing how the people's life was much better, with enough to eat and enough to wear, seemed to have expected "instant socialism" in all areas. Such critics do not realize that after socialism is established in a backward country you still carry heavy loads on your back for many years. China is being boycotted by the capitalist bloc; Canada has refused to sell one thousand Ford trucks due to pressure from Washington.'

Chungking, laid waste by the Japanese bombing, was physically even more changed than Chengtu. 'I could not find my way around,' Jim wrote to the Willmotts in 1956, describing the 'great wide, winding streets, electric trolley buses and new buildings.' The Endicotts' hotel was attached to the new Assembly Hall, an enlarged version of the Temple of Heaven with enormous red pillars, white balustrades, carved roofs in the Ming style, and hundreds of steps leading up from the street through beautiful gardens. 'It's like having the Arabian Nights come true,' Jim enthused, 'all red and blue and gold.' 'One can hardly say it is beautiful,' Mary demurred, 'but it is gorgeous, in a sort of overdressed fashion'; she saw the huge palace as an expression of the suddenly expanding vitality and confidence of China.

Over on the south bank, at Duckling Pond, the two missionary residences where they had lived at one time or another had been turned into a fifty-bed district hospital – a good use, but since the buildings were badly in need of paint the overall effect was a little depressing. The former Gin I Middle School for boys, which used to have an enrolment of 200, had been made co-educational and now 1400 students attended it in two shifts; seventy per cent were children of peasants. 'Formerly,' Endicott noted, 'we had less than two per cent of these.' He addressed the pupils on the sports field.

The third visit, in 1959, coincided with a sweeping change in peasant life – the Great Leap Forward, a mass movement intended to promote the industrialization of China by emphasizing small, local, industrial enterprises, including 'back-yard iron and steel furnaces.' It also coincided with the first year of the People's Communes, which introduced a larger unit of administration in the countryside to improve marketing, social services, and capital construction such as reservoirs and defence structures; this involved a three-tier system of teams, brigades, and communes in place of the former producers' co-operatives.[7]

These developments were connected at least in part with the growing tensions between the Soviet and Chinese Communist parties. For several years Soviet experts had been working under contract in China, promoting an élitist, technological approach to the building of industry. Their programme tended to concentrate industrial development in the cities and encouraged the growth of a large managerial and technological bureaucracy; it also stimulated a spirit of careerism and special privilege within the Communist party. This ran counter to Mao's 'mass line' of mobilizing all the people. He feared it would create a luxury-oriented, consumerism type of socialism, one for 'urban lords,' and to prevent this he put forward the alternative strategy embodied in the Great Leap Forward.

In the West, the changes were assailed. The communes were called 'agricultural labour camps' in which family life was abolished, men and women segregated in separate barracks, and no one allowed to eat at home 'in the old bourgeois way.'[8] The Endicotts set out to return to familiar places to see for themselves what had happened.

At Yellow Earth Ridge, a brigade of the China-Hungary Friendship Commune in Hopei province near Peking, they found that the former producers' co-operative was now one of thirteen brigades in a commune with 6000 families comprising 26,000 people living on about 9000 acres of land. Nowhere did they see 'barracks' for men and women. Here, as in all other communes they visited or heard of, there was a free supply of food: people could eat in the canteen or take their food home to eat if they lived close by. The commune had 14,000 pigs and 24,000 chickens; each family privately owned the number it could care for.

In most communes, the people lived exactly where they had when the commune was organized; new homes retained the traditional three-generation family unit. The leading women of several communes knew of Western propaganda about the separation of men and women, but when Endicott asked about it they most often replied: 'How can the American people be so stupid as to believe such lies?' In the old days women often carried their babies on their backs while they dug and pulled implements in the fields; now there were crèches and nurseries, which freed the women to work as equals with the men and gave children better care and education.

At Yellow Earth Ridge the commune had scarcely completed its organization when the area was hit by natural disaster. Drought had been mastered through irrigation, but during the planting of the autumn crop the rains had come. Not in a hundred years did the farmers remember such downpours; five times in July and August the crop was washed out, and each time the commune mobilized its production brigades, 12,000 strong, to drain, pump, and replant. Despite the deluge the crop, and its surplus, proved greater than the year before. The members sang in collective triumph: 'This year not a single family had to borrow from the collective for any purpose whatever.' Beyond social benefits, the commune had proved its worth in production.

The peasants seemed equally enthusiastic about the new commune-run industrial units, which made farm implements, insecticides, and building materials, and processed some farm products. About seventy per cent of the production was consumed locally and the rest was exchanged for other commodities. The advantages of small rural industry were explained as the Endicotts toured the shops. Only a small amount of initial capital was required; plants could be designed and built quickly with local equipment and benefits yielded equally quickly; the programme helped to train technical forces and provided a more balanced economic development. Because the output was extremely varied, moreover, factories could easily switch from one product to another. The closeness of rural industry to raw material sources and to the market added further flexibility. Manpower was used rationally because the worker-peasants could engage in industry when farm work was slack.

Endicott was told by his hosts that commune-run industry in 1959 accounted for ten per cent of China's total value of industrial output; when he commented that according to Western newspapers steel produced in the 'back-yard furnaces' was useless, they replied: 'Well, we don't read those papers and we did not know it was useless, so we used it. We made hoes, sickles and many tools which the peasants needed.'

Endicott found that the Great Leap Forward had spread talent across the country, helped balance regional development, and created regional self-reliance and self-sufficiency, especially in the financing of local projects and local defence. 'The government has learned,' he thought, 'that the more you decentralize, the more initiative you get and the quicker and better the results.' In spite of the inevitable confusions, waste, and exaggerations of the surging mass movements, he felt that there was enthusiastic support for central government projects and plans. 'The people seem a little tired, but happy,' he wrote in 1959.

The remark that stuck most clearly in his mind was made by Yin Wei-tai, a former poor peasant, now director of Yellow Earth Ridge and a member of the National People's Congress elected by the commune: 'Our answer to all imperialist criticism,' said Yin, 'is this. Formerly for half the year we ate husks and wild herbs; now we eat grain all the year and plenty of it.'

Life had changed equally drastically for the capitalists the Endicotts had known before. The success of the new order in persuading this class to give up its old ideology and join in building a socialist society impressed both the Canadians deeply. The transformation had been accomplished without civil war. But it had involved a period of intense struggle – the Movement against Five Evils: bribery, theft of government property, tax frauds, cheating on government contracts, and theft of economic information for private speculation – which was in full swing when the Endicotts paid their visit in 1952.[9] The businessmen had set up their own schools to study how they could contribute to the new society, and Endicott learned that they also had a political party, the China Democratic National Construction Association, which took part in the National People's Congress.

During trips to Szechuan province in 1956 and 1959, the Endicotts were able to meet a number of their capitalist friends. They had several talks with the Hwangs and the Chens, relatives of the Chinese boys who had been members of their own family for some years, and found them, almost without exception, adjusted to the new social conditions. One of the Hwangs had not at first co-operated; he had tried to bribe the new government inspector and had falsified inventories – and had been sentenced to five years at reform through labour. The Endicotts were permitted to go and see him in prison. The warden arranged a small table in the middle of the exercise field so that they could be private, and, as he said, 'speak frankly.' They sat and drank tea:

My friend did not seem embarrassed. He greeted me with, 'Well, my old friend, I do not need to tell you that I did the things for which I have been imprisoned. You know me well enough to know I did.'

He then spoke simply of how he learned to carry bricks and how his guards carried his load for him when he was too tired. He read newspapers regularly and knew a good deal about my activities in the world peace movement which were often reported in the Chinese press. He said several times how much the Hwang family's friendship with us had meant to him and how the memory of it helped him through the difficult times when he was 'being struggled against' and coming painfully to understand. The prison conditions were strict and rather severe but it was clear to us, after talks with our friend and with the warden, that the objective was to change the mental and spiritual outlook of those who had done wrong, not only to punish them. Chairman Mao had spoken of the need 'to wash away the stains of the old society.'

We saw our friend again in 1959 in Chungking. He was out of prison and a changed man. He then had a responsible position in the coal-mining bureau of Szechuan Province and was using his former practical experience to organize the supply of pit props for the mines.

From visits to several friends in prison and from talking to their families, the Endicotts concluded that the picture drawn in the Western press of people being terrified by a ruthless police system was essentially false. The atmosphere was more like that of an old-fashioned Methodist class meeting, where people were persuaded to confess their faults and receive forgiveness. For the crimes of stealing, graft, or wilful or spiteful harming of public property, those who made a full public confession and said they were sorry were not given any sentence but were put on probation. The attitude was not one of police threat but of 'Come, brother, repent and reform.' 'There is so much here to make a Christian rejoice,' Endicott wrote in 1956, 'that I cannot understand why so many missionaries do not see it.'[10]

This was not to say that the Chinese legal system was without serious problems, especially in trying to establish some independence and responsibility for the judiciary. Endicott talked about this aspect with Shih Liang, the minister of justice, whom he had known in 1940 when he was working with Madame Chiang Kai-shek in the New Life Movement. She outlined how, after the abrogation of the old laws of the Kuomintang, a whole new system had had to be prepared. Because of pressure, some of the laws were experimental, hastily contrived to meet special conditions. During 1955–56, for example, when 190,000 counter-revolutionaries had given themselves up voluntarily, the courts had been burdened with problems of parole and with demands for sentences of death. At the National People's Congress in 1956 it had been decreed that no death sentence could be carried out before review by the Supreme Court. 'Before that,' said Shih Liang, 'some executions had undoubtedly been too hasty.' It seemed clear to the Endicotts, however, even from what Shih Liang had said, that future efforts to remould society would continue to rely more upon arousing public opinion through mass movements than upon due process of law.

Each of these mass movements had its narrow targets, sometimes within the Communist party, sometimes in other segments of society: 'die-hard capitalist roaders,' a 'counter-revolutionary clique,' 'an enemy agent,' 'rightists,' or other 'bad elements.' The lines dividing good from bad, friend from foe, however, were often ambiguous and elusive. This was especially so because of the continuing influence of the Confucian concept of crime and punishment, which dictated that when a person was disgraced his entire family should suffer. After one particularly bitter struggle Chen Wei-hsi (Gerald), one of the three boys who had lived with the Endicotts, explained what could happen when someone was subjected to criticism and put under surveillance: 'It could mean that his son loses a very suitable job, his fiancee, or his right to receive a university education. His troubled wife, who, one should think, has enough problems on her hands as a result of the evil fate befalling her husband and son, also finds herself a target of discrimination: she loses the political confidence she normally enjoys, she is asked to move to a smaller place to live.

The chain reaction goes on and comes back again in a circle until one realizes that by Confucian canons, the whole family has indeed suffered!'[11]

The average Chinese, Chen continued, seemed to know his constitutional rights, but more often than not he guided himself by policies formulated by Mao and the Communist party, many of them of long standing but not necessarily written into law. These included: 'all counter-revolutionaries should be exposed, but if the verdict is wrong, then it must be corrected'; 'what one thinks cannot be taken as grounds for indictment without witnesses and material evidence'; 'to obtain evidence by compulsion and then give such evidence credence is forbidden'; 'a person should not be judged by a single mistake he or she committed, but by his or her performance all along'; 'treat the disease in order to save the patient.'

In China, in short, it was to policy rather than to law that a citizen turned for security in times of stress and unrest, for protection when threatened by persecution, and for redress when justice had miscarried. Unfortunately, policies could be upheld and boldly applied or they could be distorted and ignored, depending upon the political leadership of the time and the locality. Eternal struggle and vigilance were still necessary for liberty. Endicott was immensely encouraged, however, by the fact that, led by Mao in unpublished but informally circulated speeches, the Chinese people knew of, and were discussing widely, such problems. 'The Mao era,' Endicott predicted in 1957, 'is going to be easier to live with than the Stalin era.'[12]

As former missionaries the Endicotts were naturally interested in the fate of the Christian community in the new China. How would their Christian friends adjust to the loss of overseas funding? How would the church formulate its message in a society that was aiming to substitute the collective values of socialism for the individualism of capitalism preached by the missionaries? If Chinese Christians could make the necessary adjustments, win support among the people, and propagate the gospel of Jesus effectively under such changed conditions, the Endicotts believed, the example would revitalize the Christian hope everywhere in the world.

Endicott's old friend Y.T. Wu was in good health and leading the Christian Reform Movement of the Protestant churches. From long talks with Y.T. and meetings with many other friends, and from visits to preach in churches as far apart as Peking, Chengtu, and Shanghai, he was able to form a comprehensive picture of the Chinese church in the 1950s. He found considerable vitality. Chinese citizens engaged in religious work travelled freely about the country; they published and sold religious books and magazines, and organized themselves into congregations for worship and fellowship. The importance of denominational differences had begun to disappear as soon as the Western missionaries left in 1952; by 1958, after many conferences on how to accommodate diverse rituals and traditions, all the Protestant denominations had merged into one body.

While the Communists did not believe in religion, the government took the stand that if religious organizations served the people and were not against the Common Programme of 1949, they should not be discriminated against and should be regarded as full members of the united front in building the new China. Premier Chou En-lai said that religion could not be abolished by order for, 'as religion is in the heart, if religion has value it will survive.'[13]

The principle of religious liberty was outlined in the new constitution of 1954. But the government did more than recognize religious freedom; it helped the churches carry on. It exempted their buildings from land tax, and considered all vacant missionary buildings as church property for which it paid rent. 'The higher you go in government authority,' said Y.T. Wu, 'the more tolerance and understanding you find for the church.'

Protection by the government did not necessarily mean acceptance at the local level. Sometimes religious activities were hindered on the pretext that they interfered with production; in some villages local officials used threats to prevent believers from making offerings; in other areas officials borrowed church buildings, prohibited the building of new churches, or so crudely attacked religious believers as non-progressive that people doubted the reality of religious freedom. Y.T. Wu explained these shortcomings by past use of the church by imperialists, the present weakness of the church itself, and insufficient knowledge of the government's policy towards religion. He felt these problems would gradually be solved, especially because more and more Christians were becoming deputies of people's congresses and members of the political consultative conferences from the village level up to the central government.

The reform movement led by Y.T. Wu was aiming to make a truly national church through 'self-government, self-finance and self-propagation.' These were the same objectives proposed by the 'Exodus Council' of the West China Mission back in 1927, which Endicott had attended as a young missionary and about which so little had been done.

In a report written in 1952, Endicott predicted that reformed Christians in China would write a new history of the missionary movement and it would not be complimentary. It would expose and stress the racist attitudes and personal egoism of the missionaries, their support for the militarism of their own governments, and their open backing of unpopular regimes like those of Chiang Kai-shek and Syngman Rhee. 'Missionaries would be pained and angered by these charges,' Endicott wrote. 'But we will do the Church better service if we are willing to undertake serious and deep self-criticism to see what truth lies in the claims of our Chinese brethren.'[14]

The resentment of the Chinese Christians was not only for harm done in the past. The Chinese, he learned, were indignant about the fact that the World Council of Churches, the American churches, and most of the missionaries had opposed the abolition of the atomic bomb and had denounced the Stockholm Appeal as 'a communist trick.' But it was the Korean War particularly, Endicott believed, that finally convinced the average Chinese Christian of the inherent imperialism of the missionary and his church. With few exceptions the missionaries, many of whom continued to live and work in China until 1952, accepted the American State Department's version of the war without much question. When the Chinese volunteers went to the defence of their own border on the Yalu River, the missionaries declared it was 'Chinese imperialism'; they quoted the United Nations resolutions as proof of China's wrongdoing and America's righteousness. Any remaining trust in America and its missionaries ceased, Endicott concluded, when Warren Austin, us representative at the United Nations, stated in November 1950 that the Chinese would understand American actions in Korea because the United States had acted in the same philanthropical way in China in the past.

The last of the missionaries left in 1953, except for a relatively small number detained for several years by the Chinese government on charges of spying and other misdemeanours. Gradually thereafter Christians consolidated their position in Chinese society as citizens taking a full share in the efforts towards national reconstruction. This meant taking the road to socialism. During the Great Leap Forward all religious workers, pastors included, did one day of voluntary labour weekly, in factories or on farms. According to Bishop K.H. Ting of Nanking, 'everybody who can, works, and they find this way of living is good for society, for health and for their mental outlook.'[15]

Most of the Chinese Christians Endicott talked to seemed to feel that their future depended fundamentally on themselves, on how effectively they bore testimony to the power of love, and on how their lives demonstrated the sacrificial spirit of the cross.

Ours 'will be a Church,' Y.T. Wu had written in 1951, 'in which love for their religion will be combined with love for their country, in which Chinese Christians, free from the trammels of imperialism, will dig into the riches of the Christian gospel and let themselves become the medium through which this gospel will shine in love and service to the people.'[16] Some of these objectives were now going to be easier, Wu thought, free from corrupt government and ruinous inflation, strengthened by improved transportation and land reform.

Endicott found that the Chinese Christian leaders were concerned, beyond politics and economics, with the theological implications of their reform movement. Once again, Y.T. Wu was helping to lead the way. The Endicotts spent an evening at his home while Y.T. developed further the thoughts he had first discussed with Endicott in the 1940s and had recently presented to a group of theological students and Christian workers in Shanghai. He reviewed some of the theological systems that had been moulded in the soil of feudalism and capitalism over the previous thousand years. Could it be doubted, he asked, that during these great epochs of human history Christian theology had taken on ideological taints peculiar to the age and environment of the builders of great theological systems? Could it be doubted that, with few exceptions, the outstanding theological trend running through the centuries had been the over-emphasis of the transcendence of God and the helplessness of mankind, rather than the dialectical unity of God's transcendence and His immanence and the possibilities of mankind when released from social enslavement?

Y.T. wondered whether the preoccupation with the perennial sinfulness of human nature was not due, at least in part, 'to the fact of social injustice and unrest which exist in every epoch in history.' If this suspicion was confirmed, then one had the right to conclude that a true social emancipation would be followed by a true spiritual uplift, which simply meant 'a profounder realization of God's immanence in history, informed and conditioned by His transcendental perfection.'

If a new theological system was emerging, Y.T. offered some suggestions as to what its components might be:

We must restore and re-establish the Christian conception of God as both transcendent and immanent ... and apply it fruitfully in the present world situation.

We need to recognize the universality of God's revelation. We need to realize that God's purpose is worked out through all sorts of means. Even those who do not confess His name may be channels through which His truth is revealed. The one great cause for the difficulties some Christians in China are facing is their inability to appreciate the true meaning of God's omnipresence. They are bewildered because they refuse to see God's light which comes through unexpected channels. We must break down the wall of this sectarianism; and must not divide people up into camps of 'Christians' and 'non-Christians,' 'theists' and 'atheists,' with the assumption that only 'Christians' and 'theists' can know the truth.

We should look at nature and society as areas of the working of God and the sciences of nature and society and the laws governing their changes and processes as ways in which God works. The secular and the religious, the social and the spiritual aspects of our life are not divided and shut up in water-tight compartments.

We should gain a new confidence in man. God works in man. Man is the temple of

God and therefore, a being capable of great things. This is an optimistic view of man but it is not blind optimism ... We appeal for a new appreciation of man's powers, not because man is faultless, but because such an appreciation will remove the inhibition inherent in an over-critical attitude and will serve as a force for emancipation.

We should not conceive of the Kingdom of God as something in the distant future, for which we can just wait. The Kingdom begins here and now for all who waken to its reality. The Niebuhrian school takes pride in using the absolute criterion of the transcendent God in judging the 'relativity' of the method and goal of communism. This 'perfectionism' is only a means by which the privileged class discounts and puts to nought the revolutionary movements.

What are we Christians to do? First, we must repent. In the past, wittingly or unwittingly, we have been blindfolded and utilized by forces which are at bottom selfish ... and we have rebelled against Christ. We have twisted His teachings. We have not only failed to help liberate our people but have become a tool for binding them. Today we should repent and become brave fighters for Christ.

Then, we must learn from the Communist Party. The Communists are genuinely working for the people and have great lessons to teach us Christians. Many of us who say 'Lord, Lord' have in reality betrayed Christ and crucified Him anew. God is using those who are actually practising His will to serve His purpose. I do not mean to make this statement for Communists to hear because it sounds like a mean attempt to Christianize Communism or to claim for Christianity the truth which Communism represents. But to Christians ourselves, it is right to assert that the Communists are fulfilling the purpose of God in a way which we Christians need to learn ...

In the final analysis, our future is in our own hands, not in the hands of the Communist Party or the philosophy of Marxism-Leninism. It depends on how much we identify ourselves with the life of the people in the struggle for socialism and peace. If we witness truly, no matter what obstructions, the future of the Church is bright and glorious.[17]

Endicott thought that it would be difficult to find such faith in those countries that worried most about the destruction of the church in China. Later he wrote to Y.T.: 'Mary and I have talked a great deal of the evening we spent discussing our Christian faith and I think that you will help greatly in giving me a rational ground for the faith that is really quite deep in my heart and mind and from which I cannot depart without doing violence to my nature.'[18]

During visits to China the Endicotts enjoyed meeting with the brilliant and good-natured Chou En-lai. In 1952, Chou and his wife Teng Ying-chao organized an informal evening at their home in Peking to which they invited many of Jim's old friends from Chungking – Wang Bin-nan, Kung Peng,

Chen Chia-kang, Chang Han-fu, and others. They were reminded of the simplicity of living and manner of the Chinese leaders, of their humour and scholarly appreciation of the best in their traditions, and of their confidence and determination about the future.

In 1952 also, Chou invited Endicott to speak about Canada to a group of foreign affairs officials. In 1956, he asked him to speak at a rally in Peking commemorating the ninetieth anniversary of Sun Yat-sen's birth; he shared the platform with a son of Dr James Cantlie, an Englishman who had been Sun's teacher at medical school in Hongkong, and with the American, Morris 'Two Gun' Cohen, who had been the revolutionary leader's body-guard. Endicott, who paid tribute to Dr Sun as a Christian, added a Canadian touch, recalling that on more than one occasion Sun had visited Canada to rouse the overseas Chinese and collect money for his work. 'There are people still living in Niagara Falls,' he said, 'who remember him walking in the park and eagerly discussing his plans with the roar of the great waterfall in his ears and the thunder of the revolution in his heart.'[19]

Chou En-lai showed his appreciation for the friendship of foreigners in many ways. In 1956, conversation inevitably touched on Bill and Sylvia Powell and Julian Schuman, who were on trial for sedition in the United States over charges of American use of germ warfare in Korea; Chou worried lest the three Americans had not been specially invited to stay on in China as an alternative to returning home to face prosecution. 'Now,' he said, 'they remind us of a Chinese saying: only when winter comes and the other trees have lost their leaves do we fully realize the nature of the pine and cedar.'

The changes that were taking place in China, the Endicotts believed, as did other observers, might well come to be regarded as amongst the most conse-quential in all recorded history. China's national rebirth had occurred on a high tide of revolution which, twenty years earlier, Mao Tse-tung had pre-dicted would come 'like a ship far out at sea whose mast-head can already be seen from the shore; it is like the morning sun in the east whose shimmering rays are visible from a high mountain top; it is like a child about to be born moving restlessly in its mother's womb.'[20] If it was inevitable, it was also earth-shaking. Great movements swept over the country like waves, advanc-ing, receding, then advancing again. It was a time of turmoil and confusion, of love and hate, of criticism and thought-reform, of letting 'one hundred flowers bloom' and then uprooting poisonous weeds, of great engineering projects and 'walking on two legs' by uniting traditional and modern methods through revolutionary practice.

In the course of a single decade Mao Tse-tung, Chou En-lai, and their comrades had led the world's most heavily populated country, by trial and error, through successive stages of social transformation: land reform and reconstruction of the cities, the socialization of agriculture and industry, and, finally, the Great Leap Forward to achieve modernization while building socialism. The continuing revolution had raised the social and economic conditions of China's teeming millions; it had also deeply influenced their moral and spiritual standards. The strange and puzzling thing to the Endicotts, as well as to other friends of China, was that in the West there was 'a stubborn reluctance to seek out the facts'; it even seemed important to cultivate blindness to what was really happening in China.[21]

CHAPTER TWENTY-NINE

One divides into two

When the foreign ministers of the great powers, including for the first time the People's Republic of China, met in Switzerland in the summer of 1954 to attempt to bring about the end of the French colonial war in Indo-China, many people breathed a sigh of relief. The 'spirit of Geneva' – the fact that the nations in conflict were willing to sit down around a table and talk to each other – was expected to bring an end to the tensions of the Cold War. After five years of continuous alarms and mobilizations, of wars in Korea and Indo-China, of quarrels about the status of Berlin, and of confrontations across the Taiwan Strait, peace workers, especially those in the West, were more than content with the prospect of being able to spend some of their evenings at home in front of the latest invention of modern technology, the television set. The days of peace petitions and mass rallies, it seemed, were over.

Even in this more favourable environment, Jim Endicott continued to fear the minority he felt were planning a military show-down. China's exclusion from the United Nations and the refusal by major powers to recognize her government, small colonial wars in Africa and Asia, the rearmament of West Germany, the air-poisoning tests of powerful nuclear weapons, all seemed to suggest that the dangers of the Cold War would linger on.

Thus Endicott opposed the retrenchment of the Canadian Peace Congress, and instead attempted to keep its members alert and enthusiastic by pointing to church groups, service clubs, boards of trade, and other organizations which, for various reasons, were becoming more active in working for peace. 'We will try to establish friendly relations with them,' he proposed, 'without any "I told you so" attitude and without any suggestion of pushing into their affairs, but simply as fellow human beings interested in living in a constantly improving world.' For him, as a Christian, it continued to be an act of faith to take part in a peace movement that touched people at such levels and was at the same time world-wide, but the effort was often discouraging. As he toured Canada people everywhere seemed to be saying: 'We are tired; it's the same old crowd always being asked for the same old dollar.'[1]

Events in 1956 were particularly hard on the morale of the peace workers. Following Nikita Khrushchev's revelations about the Stalin era in February, a number of disillusioned communists withdrew from activity altogether, and local peace committees in some places ceased to function. Then, in October and November, came the Suez Canal crisis and the Soviet intervention in Hungary.

The Peace Congress felt able to make a straightforward and vigorous denunciation of the armed attack on Egypt by Britain, France, and Israel; it seemed a clear case of neo-colonialism. In this case the congress gave full support to the peace-keeping initiatives Lester Pearson was conducting through the United Nations. Events in Hungary, however, were more difficult. The Soviet Union, a strong supporter of the peace movement, was involved, but so were thousands of people (among them sincere socialists) whose uprising had been put down by Soviet troops stationed in Hungary by agreement of the two countries.

Endicott was troubled. In his view the Hungarian crisis was less significant for the maintenance of world peace than the three-power attack on Egypt and the concurrent French 'rape of Algeria,' which was 'fifty times worse' and ignored by the same Western propagandists who were deploring the loss of human rights in Hungary.[2] Nevertheless, he was certain that the Soviet action in Hungary did not accord with the principles stated by the Second World Congress of the Defenders of Peace held in Warsaw in November 1950, that 'no political, economic or strategic considerations, no pretext based on the internal situation of a State, can justify armed intervention.'[3]

Basing its statement on these principles, the executive of the Canadian Peace Congress declared that in common with most Canadians it did not support the use of foreign troops in the affairs of any country: 'No matter what reasons may be put forward to justify such action, we believe this holds true in Egypt, Hungary or any of the other countries of the world where foreign troops are stationed.'[4]

Endicott was in agreement with this position, though he was in China at the time of the Hungarian crisis. In his absence, Bruce Mickleburgh, executive secretary of the Peace Congress, flew to Helsinki to present Canadian views to an emergency session of the executive of the World Council of Peace, calling for 'the earliest possible withdrawal of foreign troops from Egypt and Hungary and a general withdrawal of the forces of all countries to their own boundaries.'[5]

At first the world body was unable to agree on an evaluation of the situation in Hungary, for the Soviet delegates opposed mention of the incident in any statement. Eventually, however, a consensus was reached on 'the withdrawal of Soviet troops in accordance with the terms of an agreement between Hungary and the U.S.S.R. [and] the full exercise of Hungarian sovereignty.'[6] It was an ambiguous statement, but it was better than nothing because it reaffirmed an important principle. More importantly, it rebuffed the heavy pressure that would have reduced the World Council of Peace to being a pliant instrument of Soviet policy.

When Endicott passed through Moscow on his way back from China, the Soviet peace committee requested him to stay over for a day. He was met by Ilya Ehrenburg, the well-known Soviet writer, who took him out to his house in the country. There, surrounded by Ehrenburg's priceless collection of French impressionist and cubist paintings, the two men talked over the state of the world and especially the events in Hungary. Ehrenburg readily admitted that the latter had tarnished the image of socialism. After apportioning the blame, partly to American policy which had fostered years of hate and distrust during the Cold War, and partly to the faults of the former Hungarian administration, he referred briefly to what he considered to be the well-intentioned but sometimes misguided advice of the Soviet Union – advice that had resulted in too rapid collectivization of the farms in Hungary and too slow a rise in the standard of living in the cities. Ehrenburg pointed out that the Soviets had bowed at Helsinki to the pressure of Canadian and other Western delegates. 'But I want to warn you, comrade Endicott,' he said, 'do not expect us to make any further concessions. That is as far as we will go. As long as Europe remains an armed camp we cannot relax our guard.'

Endicott appreciated the candour and responded by saying that he hoped the need for further Soviet concessions would not arise. 'Quite frankly though,' he added, 'many of the peace fighters in the West have ceased, for the time being, to trust Soviet leadership in some matters.'[7]

Later, during a speaking tour of western Canada, Endicott found that many members of the peace committees did not understand or accept his position on Hungary: they split two ways, some believing that he was not sincere when he failed to condemn in outright terms the Soviet action in Hungary in exactly the same way as he did the British, French, and Israeli action in Egypt; others, the majority, feeling that he ought to have insisted that what happened in Hungary was a counter-revolution promoted by the Americans.

During a stopover in Saskatchewan, Endicott became involved in an intense debate over the wording of a brief that was to be taken to the provincial legislature. After an exhausting evening in which he finally persuaded the local peace council to include a point re-emphasizing Hungary's right to sovereignty, he went off to bed, leaving a small committee to cut the stencils and run off the submission for presentation the following day.

When the delegation was assembled in the cabinet committee room the next morning, Premier T.C. Douglas invited Endicott to make an oral introduction. Douglas, who had been leafing through the brief during the speech, said he was glad that Endicott had mentioned the right of sovereign independence, because he was amazed to see nothing of that nature in the brief itself! Endicott was greatly embarrassed and inwardly furious: after he had gone to bed the local leaders had decided to leave out the section that might be interpreted as obliquely critical of the Soviet Union;[8] the sectarians of the left, it seemed, were more pro-Soviet than the Soviets, more 'Marxist-Leninist' than Lenin, and felt it their duty to defend every mistake of the Soviet Union.

About this time a rumour spread that Endicott had resigned from the peace movement and was planning to return to church work. The Vancouver dailies phoned and the *Toronto Star* rushed a reporter up to the house to take pictures. 'Alas for wishful thinking,' Endicott told them. 'There is no fact therein. I am sticking to the peace fight.'[9]

In the future the fight would have to be conducted with more modest means. During its heyday the Canadian Peace Congress had an extensive network: peace correspondents in several centres in the Maritimes, and peace committees in Quebec City, Montreal, various Ontario cities such as Ottawa, Hamilton, London, Windsor, Sudbury, and the Lakehead, in the main centres of the prairies, out to the west coast where the British Columbia peace council had its own full-time organizer. The co-ordinating centre was in a solid, red brick house, which had been purchased with the Stalin Peace Prize money, at 25 Cumberland Avenue in the busy but not yet fashionable Bloor-Yonge district of Toronto. Here for almost five years Mary Jennison, Bruce Mickleburgh, Jean Stewart, Olga Veloff, and Jim Endicott worked on a full-time paid basis; they planned the conferences, lobbies and fund-raising campaigns, wrote press releases and bulletins, and organized the work for scores of volunteers who came during evenings and weekends for committee meetings or to make posters, address envelopes, or do the countless other things that were required in a movement that was thriving. By the end of 1956, the British Columbia peace council was no longer able to sustain Ray Gardner as its paid organizer, and by 1957 the five full-time workers in Toronto had been reduced to Endicott and Jacqueline Dineen, who served as part-time secretary. The peace house on Cumberland Avenue was sold and the office moved into the basement of Endicott's home in the borough of York, where it stayed for the fourteen remaining years of his leadership.

As the fortunes of the Canadian Peace Congress declined, some of its members dispersed to older, long-established, peace organizations such as the pacifist Society of Friends, the Fellowship of Reconciliation, and the Women's International League. Others turned their attention to the Campaign for Nuclear Disarmament, the Voice of Women, the Student Union for Peace Action, and other pressure groups which began to proliferate under separate banners in the late 1950s and early 1960s. Not until the mid-sixties and the trauma of the war in Vietnam did a mass peace movement emerge briefly once again. Meanwhile,throughout these years, the Peace Congress managed to remain active. According to one chronicler, whatever the Peace Congress lacked in tact and impartiality, it could be 'credited with stirring Canada's conscience at a time when the parliamentary political parties and the bulk of public opinion were uncritically following an ever-increasing commitment to a growing arms race.'[10] The Peace Congress continued to have a loyal body of supporters and workers; it had its affiliation with the World Council of Peace; and, perhaps not least in importance, it had Jim Endicott as a spokesman at home and on the world stage.

By the middle 1950s Endicott was a well-known world figure, a circuit-rider for peace to many countries. He went mainly by air, sometimes alone, usually as the invited guest of some national peace movement, and other times as a member of a small delegation to promote the work of the World Council of Peace. Once in 1949, en route to a conference in Mexico City, he was stopped at the Canadian-American border and told that his name was on a list of people prohibited from entering the United States; under the lingering influences of McCarthyism the ban continued in force for thirty years. But Endicott travelled to all the continents of the world, speaking at peace rallies, giving press interviews, and on occasion meeting with heads of state to seek their endorsement for some plan of action.

Because of his deep concern about the dangers of atomic war he was frequently invited to Japan on the anniversary of the bombing of Hiroshima. There, according to Yoshitaro Hirano, president of the national peace council, he helped to strengthen the Japanese peace movement by his presence and the political judgement displayed in his speeches as well as 'by his outgoing personality which allowed him to make immediate contact with the common people without any pride of an intellectual.' After meeting Mary, who accompanied her husband on one visit, Hirano added: 'behind this perhaps his wife contributed.'[11] On another visit to Japan, during a birth control campaign, Endicott had the novel experience of being presented to an audience as a fine example of man who had had a vasectomy yet maintained his virility; at the time, no Japanese males would consider taking such a step.

Other peace workers spoke highly of their Canadian colleague. 'He made us feel warm-hearted, confident and hopeful,' recalled Professor Goro Hani, also of Japan, who appreciated 'his sense of humour, something rare in people of high society.' Mrs Sandra Ranghet, general-secretary of the Romanian peace committee, spoke of warm affection for a person 'who was determined and did not vacillate or lose his bearings because of some momentary situation. His views were always clear and precise and he expressed his ideas frankly. We got to know him well and admired him.' A British colleague, Roy Gore, appreciated Endicott's tolerance and pervading sense of calm when chairing a difficult meeting, qualities he attributed to Endicott's background as a missionary and his habit of taking a nap each afternoon.[12]

A central feature of Endicott's position in the international peace movement was that for much of the time he possessed the confidence of both the Russians and the Chinese. With their support, he was added to the bureau of the World Council of Peace, was elected to the executive in 1955, and became vice-president two years later.

In 1957 he was also chosen first president of the International Institute for Peace, a position he occupied until 1971. The headquarters of the institute, an arm of the World Council of Peace, was located in Vienna, where Endicott had an office and temporary living space on the Mollwaldplatz, a small square in the southeastern part of the city; ironically, the building faced the spacious grounds of an eighteenth-century military academy founded by Maria Theresa, archduchess of Austria, queen of Hungary and Bohemia. The Soviet Red Army had taken over the premises at the end of the Second World War, and, in the absence of their Jewish owners who had disappeared during the Hitler regime, the buildings were paid for according to Austrian law and owned by Soviet commercial interests. Although the large elegant rooms with high ceilings and polished hardwood floors made ideal reception halls and offices, providing ample accommodation for the sixty secretarial workers, the World Council of Peace was not entirely happy with the arrangement because Vienna itself was far removed from the important political centres of Europe. In earlier years the World Council of Peace had been more favourably located in Paris, but when the French government refused entry permits to representatives of the Eastern bloc, the secretariat had been forced eastwards. By 1957, under external pressure from opponents determined to deprive the World Council of a Western address, the Austrian government decreed that its presence in Vienna was contrary to the neutrality clauses of the Austrian peace treaty. Endicott was able to help the movement establish a new, legal organization to own the facilities; thus the Mollwaldplatz complex was transformed into the International Institute for Peace with Endicott as president and an Austrian physician, Dr Friedrich Scholl, as vice-president. The new institute, which both sides recognized was in part a legal fiction, was duly registered with the Ministry of the Interior as a non-political organization whose tasks were to serve as a centre for international discussion on questions of world peace and to promote peace research on disarmament and the exchange of information; its officers were required to file an annual report to the Austrian government. While the institute conducted a minimal, independent programme, it served mainly as an umbrella under which the World Council of Peace was able to continue its campaigns for a decade without serious obstruction from the Austrian authorities.[13]

In other ways, too, the period from 1957 to 1962 was one of mounting strains within the world peace movement. For a time little was known of these difficulties outside; as Kuo Mo-jo, the Chinese representative, said, the organization was 'maintaining common ground while reserving differences.'[14] However, at the 1957 session of the World Council of Peace, where he was elected vice-president, Endicott became acutely aware of the depth of feelings on matters of policy and direction. Meeting in Colombo, in Asia, and in the environment of colonialism for the first time, the council felt the full force of opinions from the millions of the 'third world.'

'If I had to put the difficulty in one sentence,' Endicott wrote to peace workers in Canada, 'I would say it is a question of what the peace movement does and says about the question of colonialism, and to a lesser degree, what it says about the new American imperialism – a phrase not used in Western peace movements, but common in China, India, Latin America and now in Africa.'[15] National liberation meant armed struggle, peaceful coexistence was based on disarmament, yet the two were closely related; in Endicott's opinion they had to be handled differently, even separately, and ought never to be counterpoised to each other as opposites.

The physical arrangement of his own house in Toronto reflected the practical way he tried to deal with these complicated issues: down in the basement he worked with Jacqueline Dineen to produce the *Peace Letter*, which hammered on the necessity for banning atomic weapons, for disarmament, and for peaceful coexistence among the industrialized nations; upstairs he worked with Mary to publish the *Canadian Far Eastern Newsletter*, which exposed the workings of imperialism in the Third World and publicized the struggles of oppressed peoples to be free.

The avoidance of an atomic holocaust was obviously crucial for the survival of mankind, and yet there would be no lasting peace without national and social justice. Thus Endicott rejected the pacifist position, the demand to abolish the use of all armed force as an instrument of policy, as untimely. 'As long as the struggle for general and complete disarmament does not achieve success,' he wrote in 1963, 'the people of all oppressed areas are forced to take up arms and fight.'[16] Since he hoped that the peace movement would act as a leaven and would tip the balance for change without world war, it was therefore the greatest of disappointments to perceive a hardening of positions along two distinct lines within the World Council of Peace, a split that ultimately destroyed the unity and the effectiveness of the peace movement.

The situation came to a head at Colombo when the French peace leaders, known to be generally in close touch with Soviet thinking, recognized the fact of colonial revolt, but would not within the council support direct action for national independence. The opening message, sent by the ailing president of the council, Frédéric Joliot-Curie, referred to the dangers for world peace in Africa, Asia, and the Middle East: 'we do not claim to offer ready-made solutions to these problems,' he added, 'but we do know that these solutions, whatever they may be, must exclude the use of force.'[17] Although Joliot-Curie may have been thinking only of the use of force by colonial powers, the victims of colonial war, especially those in Algeria, resented the implications of this statement.

In even more uncompromising terms, Joliot-Curie's personal representative at Colombo, Emmanuel d'Astier de la Vigerie, stressed the peace movement's Euro-centric orientation and its original objectives, namely the abolition of nuclear tests, disarmament, and ways and means to peaceful coexistence: 'The continuance of colonialism and the developments of new doctrines which lead ... to political or military tutelage, these things contain within themselves the seeds of war ... Our duty is to proclaim this aloud ... But let us not forget that when it comes to such questions as national independence and the right of self-determination, we friends of peace must seek only peaceful solutions through negotiations, not through war. We are a movement for peace, we are not a movement for national liberation ...'[18]

Sharp indignation and opposition to this approach arose from the African, Asian, and Latin American delegates, and debates became heated. As some Latin American delegates told Endicott: 'The problems of fall-out and hydrogen bombs are remote for us. Our people are so poor they want economic change, and this is what a peace program must mean for them.' An African delegate declared: 'If an atomic bomb blows away our mud house, we can build another, we are not worried about the big cities and running water like you are.' Other representatives, especially those from Japan and China, believed that the United States would no longer dare to use atomic weapons; therefore the people should press forward for changes without fear of massive retaliation.[19]

The differences within the World Council of Peace became so severe that after the death of Joliot-Curie in 1958 it was impossible to reach agreement on the choice of a new president. After much delay and bargaining the council went to the extraordinary length of electing twenty-four presidents! This committee, of which Endicott was a member, then chose Professor J.D. Bernal of Great Britain as chairman and selected three permanent secretaries, one each from France, the Soviet Union, and China.

Owing to Endicott's long years of friendly association with the Chinese revolutionaries, a few of them came to him at Colombo in June 1957 to tell him that China was going to spearhead a 'diametrically opposed line' in the struggle for the prevention of war. The vice-chairman of the Chinese peace committee, Liao Cheng-chih, nicknamed 'Fatty Liao' by Western newsmen, invited Endicott to return once more to China to live and work with them.

The main content of Liao's argument, as Endicott understood it, was that the military-industrial complex of the United States and its related monopoly capitalist groups in other countries had no intention of agreeing to disarmament. Indeed they were feverishly arming. They intended to blackmail and, if possible, to frighten the Soviet Union into a nuclear stalemate of immobility, meanwhile intensifying their own exploitation and aggression against the peoples of Asia, Africa, and Latin America. They were acting through subversion, through political, economic, and cultural penetration, and, where necessary, through military intervention with 'special forces,' using an arsenal of napalm, phosphorous bombs, secret assassinations, and other terrorist weapons. In view of these policies, Liao argued, it was time to change the struggle for peace into a defensive alliance of all who were victims of United States imperialism and other colonial empires. The world balance of forces was such that imperialism could be defeated: 'the east wind prevails over the west wind.' 'In China's opinion,' said Liao, 'the forces making for war must be offered every reasonable proposal for peace and at the same time they must be faced with massive and fearless resistance.'

As far as the oppressed nations were concerned, whether it was Laos, Algeria, Angola, the Cameroons, or others, Liao suggested that the most important issue was clearly not disarmament. What little armaments they now had should be strengthened to build up their own forces in order to defend themselves. The peace movement should give its warm sympathy and active support to all those who gave the American aggressors 'tit-for-tat' blows all round the world.

'Does this mean the abandonment of the principle of peaceful coexistence?' Endicott interjected.

'No,' replied Liao Cheng-chih. 'China is for peaceful coexistence between countries with differing social systems provided it is clearly defined as at the

Bandung Conference of 1955 and means absolute respect for territorial integrity and non-aggression.' Peaceful coexistence could not be agreed to if it meant accepting an unjust situation imposed by external force or aggression, such as the American occupation of Taiwan, where, Liao added, Matador guided missiles had recently been installed by the United States. Peaceful coexistence could not be accepted if it meant acquiescence in the victimization of another country.

In response to further questions, Liao told Endicott that China favoured a campaign for general and complete disarmament, especially in the countries which had the bulk of the world's armaments, provided the peace movement informed the people 'honestly' that the United States was the most ferocious enemy of peace. Otherwise, China believed that the kind of 'détente' that was being established between the Soviet Union and the United States with a programme of cultural exchanges would lead to a betrayal of the colonial peoples.[20]

The moral problem of the peace movement, stated so clearly by his Chinese friend, was not an easy one. Endicott felt reasonably certain that the Chinese analysis of us intentions was not mistaken. The invitation to work in China, therefore, was not only a welcome sign of their faith in him, but attractive because the issues seemed to him to be so clearly and sharply defined. Such a move, however, was out of the question. He was now too deeply committed to participation in the potentially more complex struggle for peace in Canada and the West where the level of awakening to the dangers of war was still relatively low.

In view of the twin poles of disarmament and national liberation, Endicott was enthusiastic about a suggestion by Valentine Sorokin, the Soviet secretary, that for the time being at any rate the peace movement should cease attempting to establish global priorities and seek instead a regional basis of operations. The northern hemisphere could concentrate on curbing the arms race while the southern hemisphere combatted the old and new forms of colonialism, which, by general agreement, contained the seeds of war. When this approach was discussed at the headquarters of the World Council of Peace in Vienna following the Colombo meeting, there seemed to be general agreement by all the key figures. Sorokin compared the World Council to a 'general staff for peace,' which, like a military general staff, would operate in different ways on different fronts.

Unfortunately, from Endicott's point of view, Sorokin was shortly recalled by the Soviet peace committee. His replacement was a bushy eyebrowed professor of law, Victor Chkhikvadse, who had entirely different ideas. During one notable debate in Stockholm in 1961 when Endicott was presiding, Chkhikvadse pressed for concentration on the 'general disarmament' objectives of Soviet policy, declaring that 'without the prohibition of nuclear weapons the national liberation movement will be a movement for dead people'; upon hearing the translation that 'the national liberation movement is a movement for corpses,' the Chinese delegation rose from their places, banged on the table, and walked out of the room.[21] This explosive incident stripped away the trappings of the doctrine and dogma, revealing the real core of the conflict.

In the face of multiplying incidents of this kind, Endicott tried to steer a middle course. In the company of doctrinaire Marxist-Leninists and the practitioners of the thought of Mao Tse-tung, this was a difficult, if not impossible, posture. The laws of revolutionary dialectics had their own inexorable logic: one divides into two. 'Whatever happens, there is no doubt at all that at every stage in the development of a process,' Mao had written, 'there is only one principal contradiction which plays the leading role.'[22] At any given moment there must be one key link, not two, Lenin had said, one main contradiction playing the leading and decisive part, the identification of which was vital to the success of all else. Was the principal contradiction that between the capitalist and socialist systems – was the United States seeking a show-down with the Soviet Union – as the Russians claimed; or was the prime contradiction that between the capitalist system and its colonial areas of exploitation, as the Chinese maintained?[23] The correct strategy for preventing global war could come only from attempting to find answers to the right question.

Untrained in the theory of dialectical reasoning and reluctant to take sides, Endicott was often distressed by the subjectivity and partisanship of the contestants; their attitudes made rational discussion virtually impossible. He realized that underlying many of the arguments there was a third contradiction, between two different and competing brands of socialism. During the heat of one debate over the Chinese and Soviet positions, he startled his colleagues by joking that he was in the position of Mark Twain at a dinner party where the conversation turned to the question of heaven and hell, eternal life and future punishment; Twain said nothing until a lady finally turned to him and demanded to know his opinion. 'Madame,' he said gravely, 'I am silent of necessity; I have friends in both places.'

In the privacy of his letters to Mary in Toronto, Endicott revealed how embattled and emotionally drained he sometimes felt:

I am a bit dazed and confused and seem somehow unwittingly to have pleased both sides. The Presiding Committee rather lost control and certain 'accepted procedures,' practices and principles were abandoned. For the last eight hours of a stormy plenary session I was asked to chair, I played by ear, broke Roberts' Rules of Order once or twice, stopped the Soviet-led bloc from shouting down the irregular Chinese speaker and generally acted as a rather over-busy referee at a general scrimmage.

However, the Chinese were pleased, said I was fair and invited us to visit China on the occasion of the 15th Anniversary. The Soviet friends said they were pleased, that we got the best result that could be obtained.[24]

As a mark of appreciation, and perhaps in the hope of influencing Endicott to take over the post of chairman from the ailing J.D. Bernal who had announced his intention to retire, the secretariat of the World Council of Peace in 1965 awarded him its highest honour, the Frédéric Joliot-Curie Gold Medal. Endicott accepted the award but declined the office. Since he was not known for shirking either responsibility or the limelight, his refusal caused surprise and some disappointment, especially among his Soviet friends.

His reasons, however, were both political and personal. Given the balance of forces in the World Council of Peace, he sensed that as chairman of the executive he would inevitably be pressured into acceptance of the Soviet analysis of every world crisis. From past experience, he was uneasy about this prospect. By temperament and background he also felt that he had little patience or talent for administrative work, preferring instead the role of propagandist and peace evangelist. An additional reason for declining, the one he stressed in order to avoid argument, was Mary's poor health and the fact that at the age of sixty-eight she had no wish to move to Europe, far from family and close friends. Keeping Canada and Toronto as home base, therefore, he agreed to take part in the field-work and the executive committee of the World Council of Peace as often as possible.

As Endicott criss-crossed oceans and continents, speaking, preaching (on one occasion in Canterbury Cathedral), and writing on behalf of the peace movement, he was often trailed by American intelligence agents who considered him to be a subversive element. His travels took him to such Third World countries as Colombia, Venezuela, Nigeria, Kenya, Egypt, Syria, Iraq, India, and Burma. A few episodes help to explain why it was that the 'peace pilgrim,' as Mary used to call him, began to give more and more emphasis to an open criticism of US imperialism, thus bringing him closer to the Chinese position within the peace movement.

During the week of 13–20 February 1962, while in Georgetown, British Guiana, trying to raise interest in a world congress for disarmament to be held in Moscow, Endicott experienced at first hand the comparative irrelevance of a movement for peaceful coexistence and disarmament in colonial and semi-colonial territories.

His visit to the British colony coincided with an unsuccessful attempt to oust the government of Prime Minister Cheddi Jagan. A popular, American-educated dentist, Jagan defined himself as a believer in 'the economic theories of scientific socialism'; since 1953 his People's Progressive party had been elected to office three times. Under the then existing system of limited internal self-rule, the British government tried, however, to use its power to transfer political control to a domestic ruling class that would keep the country securely within the capitalist system. In its attempt to have Jagan out of power before granting full independence (which occurred in 1966 when the country was renamed Guyana) Britain had the support of the United States government: with funds channelled through the secretariat of the International Confederation of Free Trade Unions in Brussels, the CIA was stirring up racial conflict between the blacks and East Indians and was subsidizing a group of local trade union leaders to create trouble for Jagan.[25]

On 16 February, Endicott, as a house guest of the prime minister and his wife Janet, found himself in an awkward, if not perilous, situation in the middle of 'a deep and well-organized plot, treasonable and evil, to overthrow the government by force, violence and mob action.'[26] After several days of peaceful demonstrations against a new budget, Jagan had withdrawn some of the controversial proposals only to find that the attacks on him increased. Well-organized demonstrators went on a rampage of rioting, arson, and looting in which the centre of Georgetown was burned, government buildings attacked, and several people killed. Jagan's appeals to the British governor to use the army to 'preserve the Queen's peace' fell on deaf ears.

'I stood on the verandah of the Premier's home and saw a mob being egged on by members of the business community of Georgetown,' Endicott told the press later; 'soon stones were whistling by my head and there were shouts of "kill him." They held up a black paper coffin.'

Convinced that the insurgents were preparing an assault with intent to kill the prime minister and some of his ministers in his official residence, Jagan's aides began distributing the few available weapons. Endicott, who had more military training than the others, volunteered to take part in the defence and was stationed at an attic window with a rifle. If the attackers began breaking in, his instructions were to shoot two of the ringleaders who were hiding behind some bushes on the grounds of the bishop's residence nearby. It was an unusual assignment for a world peace leader; although nervous, Endicott felt no qualms in the circumstances.

At the last moment, the governor intervened. With remarkable speed, the forces of law and order appeared from around a corner and the rioters were dispersed. Having allowed the situation to deteriorate into violence as a matter of policy, Endicott believed, either to force Jagan's resignation or to prove that there could not yet be independence, the governor announced that British troops would restore order and that the constitution would not be suspended.

Impressed by the courage, perseverance, and integrity of the Guyanese leadership on this 'Black Friday,' Endicott decided that he should do all he could to help them. After hearing about the economic difficulties, rising unemployment, and need for markets for surplus rice, lumber, and minerals, he suggested that the Jagans come to Canada to seek trade and aid. As secretary-general of the party and former minister of labour, health, and housing, Janet Jagan followed up this suggestion without notable results. While in Toronto, however, Endicott introduced her to an enthusiastic disarmament rally at Massey Hall as a representative of the forces that were pioneering fundamental reforms for the welfare of the people of British Guiana. Later, at the disarmament congress in Moscow, Endicott requested an interview with Anastas Mikoyan, the minister of trade, to ask for help.

'I'm very surprised, comrade Endicott,' Mikoyan began cheerily, 'I thought you were a much older man.'

Endicott, who was now sixty-three, returned the compliment to the last of the old Bolsheviks, and then told the story of British Guiana. Mikoyan shook his head doubtfully: 'It's not possible for us to give financial aid to a British colony,' he said. 'Even a numbered Swiss account would be no use. The British secret intelligence know about every account in the Geneva banks.' Then, after a pause, Mikoyan added: 'Tell Jagan that the u.s.s.r. will buy all the surplus rice; we will provide a guaranteed market at world prices.'[27]

Endicott was also witness to dramatic events in Cuba in the 1960s. One memorable evening in December 1960, he and Mary found themselves seated at a long head table on the parade ground of the old Columbia fortress in Havana, the spot from which former dictator General Fulgencio Batista had fled by plane to Florida two years previously. The new chief of state, Premier Fidel Castro, was presiding over a New Year's Eve reception honouring ten thousand school teachers who were about to inaugurate 1961 as the Year of Education, and in a long, impassioned speech he warned them of the dangers of counter-revolution. During this visit, Endicott was invited to appear on Cuban television, and he used the opportunity to declare the 'absolute solidarity and support' of the Canadian and world peace movements for the struggles of the Cuban people against United States intervention.[28]

During a visit to Cuba in 1964 Endicott wrote: 'On the twenty-first storey of the Hotel Havana Libre I sit under the watchful eye of an American imperialist cruiser on the horizon.'[29]

From the time of the revolution, the United States had maintained its surveillance of the island and worked to overthrow the Castro government. In the face of US actions such as the Bay of Pigs,[30] it was not surprising that the Cubans looked to their friends for something stronger than nostrums for disarmament and peaceful coexistence. Thus negotiations between the World Council of Peace and the Cuban peace committee and government members were sometimes difficult, delicate, and protracted. The Cubans had no wish to be in the middle of Sino-Soviet disputes, and they rebuffed efforts to draw them into an anti-Chinese position. At the time, too, they were less than satisfied with the Soviet stand on their behalf: they believed that during the 'missile crisis' of 1962 the Soviet Union should have declared that any attack on Cuba would mean war. 'This point must be firm and clear,' Castro told Endicott in 1964. 'The only real defence of Cuba is nuclear weapons.'[31] Endicott duly forwarded a strong message to the World Council of Peace giving the Cuban viewpoint.

From his experiences in the country, Endicott became convinced that Cuba was a critical front, a test case of the right of an underdeveloped nation to free itself from colonial exploitation. Though more successful than most, the struggles of the Cubans were being duplicated in many other parts of the world. Using its superiority in nuclear weapons as blackmail, Endicott believed, the United States was fighting local actions at places and on terms of its own choosing, shifting to the other side the risk of initiating all-out war. In these circumstances, it was inevitable that the focus of the world peace movement would have to change. Peaceful coexistence seemed, increasingly, an illusion.

After seven years of debate following the Colombo meeting in 1957, and after American attacks had begun against the Democratic Republic of Vietnam in 1964, Endicott and others begun to see more clearly the logic of the Chinese position. The decisive turning point in this process, a painful one for Endicott, came in November 1964 at a small international conference in Hanoi to which he had been invited by the Vietnam peace committee as a representative from Canada. A large banner greeted the 150 delegates: 'International Conference for Solidarity with the People of Vietnam against U.S. Imperialist Aggression and for the Defence of World Peace.'

The Vietnamese hosts, treading delicately like cats over snow-covered ground, carefully avoided any direct reference to the opposing factions in the peace movement. People couldn't help noticing, however, that they had invited three times more Chinese than Soviet participants, and a Chinese television crew as well. Endicott felt the tension when, spotting several old friends among the Chinese, he walked over to exchange greetings. 'We are going to attack you,' they said curtly, and turned away.

As expected, Endicott's speech supporting the general position of the World Council of Peace – peaceful coexistence and disarmament as well as national liberation – was hissed. The French delegate was met with boos and jeers when he made a defiant plea for peaceful coexistence. The Soviet delegates remained as inconspicuous as possible.

As the conference progressed, the undercurrents became more evident. The Vietnamese, from both the north and the south, were determined to drive the United States forces from their soil by force, even though they claimed that the toll of dead, wounded, and burned had passed one million. President Ho Chi Minh's militant address, predicting 'complete victory' for the 'sacred struggle' for national reunification,[32] emphasized further that the purpose of the gathering was to help Vietnam stiffen its resistance by isolating those within Vietnam and elsewhere who might favour a compromise solution by negotiation with the Americans.

Outside the conference hall Hanoi was a city preparing to defend itself. The streets were torn open by brick-lined trenches. Old people and children had been evacuated to the country; schools had been closed since August. Food was being distributed at dispersed markets to avoid massive destruction in case of bombardment. In the factories the workers' militia were carrying out constant defence training; their rifles leaned up against their machines during working hours. Anti-aircraft defences were in place. Among the people there was a determination to resist aggression totally; there was a hatred of the American government, and gratitude for official and popular international support after the 5 August attack by US forces in the Gulf of Tonkin. One theme recurred constantly: the Americans must get out of Vietnam.

The Vietnamese were disappointed with the peace movement and with the failure of the Soviet Union, as one of the co-chairmen of the Geneva Conference on Indo-China, to support their cause firmly. In talks with Endicott, and especially in a private meeting with Isabelle Blume, one of the other council presidents, they made it clear why they, as well as the Chinese, Korean, and Japanese members, had refused to stand in tribute to the memory of President Kennedy and had voted against the general line of the World Council of Peace at its last meeting in Warsaw.[33] To speak vaguely of 'military extremists in the United States' and of 'vestiges of colonialism' was unacceptable. In reality, they said, the undeclared war in Vietnam had been directed by Kennedy himself, and after his death by Lyndon Johnson; it was a new kind of colonial warfare planned by the Pentagon, fully endorsed by the White House, and fought with puppet armies. How could the peace movement continue to favour policies of co-operation and peaceful coexistence with the leaders of such a nation?

'Don't you worry about our casualties,' Premier Pham Van Dong said to Endicott during one of the receptions at the conference in Hanoi. 'All we ask from you and the peace forces is a campaign of explanation and struggle to oblige the United States Government to agree to the Geneva Agreements of 1954 on Indochina,[34] and to force the withdrawal of u.s. troops and an end to u.s. intervention. Is this not the very minimum that the American people demand for themselves – the right to settle their own affairs without the presence of foreign troops on their soil?'[35]

It was a request for solidarity which Endicott felt no reasonable person could deny, and one to which he was eager to respond. The Vietnamese clearly resented the unmistakable pressure coming from the Soviet Union to force them into negotiations and acceptance of a division of the country, as in Korea. Following Madame Blume's report on Vietnam, the World Council of Peace began openly to identify United States imperialism as a target of the peace movement in its official resolutions.[36] After the United States had landed half a million soldiers in South-East Asia, the World Council of Peace declared opposition to American imperialism as the fundamental basis of its activity, and central to the struggle for world peace. By this time also, however, Vietnam had aroused the anti-war energies of a younger generation of North Americans and Europeans. The upsurge of youth tended to push long-established movements such as the World Council of Peace and its affiliates into a secondary, supportive role. For many old-timers, including Endicott, who had by this time settled the principal contradiction in his own mind, it was mainly a welcome, and long over-due, development.

CHAPTER THIRTY

A time of decision

The world peace movement that took shape in the years 1948–50 from various peace congresses and assemblies was based on the idea, expressed in an early slogan, that 'war is not a natural calamity like a tempest or an earthquake; war is man-made and man can prevent it.' It was conceived as an all-inclusive movement of the world's people: throughout history mankind had been the passive object of warring rulers and conquerors; now, with the horrors of a world-wide holocaust still fresh in memory, the opportunity had arisen for people from all countries and all walks of life to organize themselves to take the cause of preventing war into their own hands.

The World Council of Peace considered itself to be an organizing centre for these sentiments. According to its founding document, 'any people, any group, any body inspired by peace-loving ideas, willing to work for the realization of one or other of the proposals for peace drawn up by the World Congress,' had a place in the organization and could send its representatives to the World Council. There was no orthodoxy to which peace groups must conform; even individuals could participate in its activities, with the right to speak and to vote. The premise of the council was that all who wished to uphold peace would be encouraged to play as great a part as they were willing to assume.[1]

A second, largely unspoken premise common to most members of the World Council of Peace was that the drives towards aggression, war-mongering, and the colonial subjection of other peoples stemmed from certain powerful forces within countries that were organized according to the capitalist, acquisitive, form of political economy; the history of the last hundred years seemed to prove that it was the expanding, industrial, private enterprise societies that had been the mainspring of aggressive war. On the other hand, those nations that had adopted the newer, socialist form of organization were believed by these same people, including Jim Endicott, to be immune from such offensive compulsions because of the non-competitive character of their economies; upon this assumption rested the comfortable feeling that the united, peace-loving, socialist camp was a reliable bulwark of the peace movement.

The growing friction beginning in the late 1950s between China and the Soviet Union, the two giants of the socialist 'peace camp,' was therefore difficult and disturbing. Beginning with differing views on how best to carry on the struggle against capitalism, their quarrels about the practical steps for building socialism and over the ultimate nature of socialist society eventually led to serious armed clashes over minor boundary disputes. How could such conflict occur between socialist neighbours? The talk on each side was of 'revisionism' and 'petty-bourgeois fanaticism,' but there was little factual or fundamental theoretical analysis to explain the turn of events.

Following the open schism in 1963, Endicott, according to his own account, sided mainly with the Soviet Union because of his preoccupations with the problems of disarmament. In the inner recesses of his mind, however, he always felt that the Chinese, who finally left the World Council of Peace in 1966, had stated their case well. His insistence on discussing and reporting the Chinese viewpoint in the *Canadian Far Eastern Newsletter* irritated the Soviet leaders, and annoyed as well the pro-Soviet Communist party of Canada, which gradually put pressure on him either to cease publication of his *Newsletter* or else to resign as chairman of the Canadian Peace Congress and as representative to the World Council of Peace.

Endicott's ultimate decision in 1971 to break with the peace movement and with the Soviet Union was the result of a prolonged and reluctant process. He had none of the feeling of 'a God that failed' which haunted some earlier admirers of the world's first socialist republic; perhaps his religious background never allowed him to expect perfection, since, as he often remarked, 'all men sin and fall short of the glory of God.' When he came to recognize that the Soviets were using their preponderant position within the World Council of Peace to turn that organization into an arm of their diplomatic manœuvres, it was like seeing an inexplicable switch in the behaviour of a trusted member in a close-knit family. As the Soviet leaders became less fearful of American military power and more confident of their own, this process accelerated. Gradually, the Soviet Union began to emerge in Endicott's eyes as a new imperialist superpower aggressively contending for domination and spheres of influence with the older American imperialism.

One of Endicott's early clashes with Soviet policy was over the India-China border war, in 1962. The Soviet Union had quietly abandoned its socialist ally, China, and sided with India. After studying the facts closely Endicott felt impelled to challenge the Indian position. His was a lonely voice at the time in declaring Nehru '100% the aggressor.'[2]

He also became disturbed by the cynicism with which the Soviets conducted their debates with China. The Russians, for example, had disguised the authorship of an article entitled 'Against Falsification' attacking the Chinese position on the nuclear test ban treaty of 1963. They attributed it to the International Institute for Peace, of which Endicott was president, and under this cover gave it rapid world-wide publicity. Dr Friedrich Scholl, vice-president of the institute, immediately took strong objection to the fact that the executive had not been consulted. Instead of admitting and correcting their error, however, the Soviet peace leaders hurriedly invited Endicott, who was on vacation at his cottage on Beaver Lake, to come to Moscow and asked him, in his capacity as president, to say that he had been consulted about the article prior to its publication. 'Since we are "against falsification,"' he replied sarcastically, 'I cannot very well say that I was consulted.' However, out of deference to their difficulty and a desire to avoid further splits, in the end he agreed to refrain from saying anything publicly.[3]

Meanwhile, the Chinese began to lose patience with Endicott's hope for a workable co-operation between the two socialist giants. They abruptly terminated the Endicotts as North American distributors of the magazine *China Reconstructs*; a tersely worded notice from the China Publications Centre in Peking in early 1965 informed them that the North American franchise had been transferred and asked Mary to send all subscription and other records to the new person responsible in Vancouver.

Tears of disbelief and hurt ran down Mary's cheeks as she read the letter. There was no explanation, no sign of appreciation for her fifteen years of hard work outwitting the FBI and the CIA to build a network of readers, especially in the United States where publications coming directly from the People's Republic were illegal and banned from the mails. The cancellation was, moreover, a blow to the *Canadian Far Eastern Newsletter*, since the arrangement with the China Publications Centre had helped to pay the overhead and had made it possible to have a part-time office secretary. The Endicotts accepted Peking's decision without outward complaint,[4] feeling, perhaps, that a friend should bear a friend's infirmities. With the support of family and close friends they decided to carry on the *Newsletter*, since the original reasons for which it had been started, to gain friendship and support for the diplomatic recognition of the People's Republic by Canada and the United States, had not yet been achieved.

Shortly afterward, Mary's health seriously weakened. At the end of a long and debilitating illness, she died in Toronto in August 1967 at the age of seventy. At a simple memorial service, the *Golden Sonata* of Chungking days was played by Jim's nieces, Joyce and Carolyn Gundy; intimate portrayals of her life were drawn by Rev. Omar Walmsley, and by Lukin Robinson of the Peace Congress executive, giving glimpses of the splendid things she had done; and readings of her finest poems were given by Rev. John Morgan. Letters and telegrams, warm words of friendship, brought comfort.[5] Still, Jim faced the reality: 'My good companion of forty years is gone.'

Both the Endicotts had believed that the best of all answers to death is the whole-hearted and continuing affirmation of life. Yet the parting weighed heavily. 'There are times,' Endicott wrote some months later, 'when I feel like retreating from it all and I give way to deep feelings of loneliness and grief.'[6]

His spirits were not improved by the reports of chaos and confusion that had been emanating from China since 1966. News stories seemed to call into question the understanding of China's purpose and achievements which he and Mary had striven so long to build. China, some said, had gone mad. Her foes in the Soviet Union and the West were decrying the Great Proletarian Cultural Revolution as a manifestation of 'political criminal insanity.' As the Red Guards and the revolutionary storms swept across the country, toppling well-known figures from power and closing down schools, it was indeed difficult to gain an objective and comprehensive understanding of what was happening.

Urging his friends to withhold judgement on the nature, purposes, and results of the Cultural Revolution, Endicott nevertheless expressed strong doubts about some of its methods: the exaltation of Mao Tse-tung, the rewriting of history for the purposes of dogma, the crude tactics and violence of the revolutionary rebels. The method to be used by the Red Guards, according to the party decision of 8 August 1966 which Mao himself had drafted, was persuasion; yet 'after a brief period, if persuasion fails,' Endicott wrote in 1967, 'one is knocked on the head or dragged before a public denunciation meeting.' According to the same decision the views of the minority as well as the majority were to be respected, but the minority was not being heard. 'Who knows the arguments of the disgraced Mayor of Peking, the Chief of the General Staff, Peng Teh-huai, the old general Chu Teh? Was there an attempt to create an ideological dragon throne in Peking?' Endicott wondered.[7]

Before long he began to moderate his opinion, sensing a grand design below the surface chaos. He accepted the explanation that the struggle was between 'two lines': the one, led by Mao, intended to establish proletarian rule, relying on the masses and organizing them to take an active part in the management of the country; the other, called 'taking the capitalist road,' involved the building of an élite Communist party based on 'self-cultivation' and given to command from the top, bossing the masses rather than inviting them to participate in running the country. Mao, Endicott felt, was dealing with the dark aspect of all the new socialist systems: the growth of a privileged class or group which tended to become self-interested, self-perpetuating, and non-revolutionary. 'It is an effort to organize society on the basis of service above self,' Endicott wrote, 'teaching children to admire and emulate Dr. Norman Bethune in his sacrificial life of service; it is a definite effort to develop revolutionary morality, limit selfishness and make sure bureaucrats and managers are controlled by the people.'[8] He was content to reserve judgement, to wait for history to show what and how much had been achieved. If it succeeded, he grew convinced, the Cultural Revolution would be an extraordinary achievement.

China's foreign policy, under Chou En-lai's guidance throughout most of the Cultural Revolution, remained prudent and restrained. Her rhetorical posture, however, revealed an uncharacteristic fundamentalist zeal and clamour. The 'polemics, philosophical verbosity and claims of infallibility' made no sense to Endicott, and he said so in his *Newsletter*. For a long time also he saw little real evidence for the continuous Chinese refrain that the rulers of the Soviet Union had restored a type of capitalism and were actively colluding with the United States in using nuclear blackmail to divide the world into American and Soviet spheres of influence; nor did he see that they were practising 'social imperialism' and neo-colonialism, as the Chinese claimed.

Then, in August 1968, the Soviet Union marched into Czechoslovakia. The Chinese described Soviet behaviour as socialism in words, imperialism in deeds; by making themselves the judge of right or wrong in other socialist countries, the Soviet leaders redefined the principles of internationalism. Committed peace workers and Communist party members in many countries resigned in distress; they saw the Soviet doctrine of 'limited sovereignty' as blatant imperialism, no different in principle from the arguments used by the American imperialists when they intervened, in the name of freedom, in the affairs of many countries.

How would Endicott react? He, too, was deeply disturbed by the events in Czechoslovakia. 'Another big "credibility gap" has appeared to trouble the minds and consciences of all men of goodwill,' he wrote to peace workers.[9] His first action was to sign a telegram to the Soviet Embassy in Ottawa, which had been drafted by Chandler Davis, Anton Kuerti, and several other members of a new generation of peace activists at the University of Toronto, outspoken critics of American involvement in Vietnam. 'We are shocked by news reports suggesting Soviet forceable interference in Czechoslovakia,' the telegram read. 'As friends of socialism we appeal for immediate withdrawal. Each country must be free to find its own course.' Endicott's signature gave the newspapers headline material for they regarded him as a Soviet camp follower.[10]

In the Canadian Peace Congress executive, where the influence of the old left was strong and pro-Soviet as a matter of principle, he was unable to secure such a forthright stand and had to be content with a general restatement of the peace movement's principles on the right of every country to political, social, and economic independence.

A degree of ambivalence to the crisis was evident in Endicott's response to an appeal for solidarity from the beleaguered Czechoslovak peace committee. 'We have received a great deal of one-sided Soviet propaganda,' he told them, 'which tries to prove the existence of dangerous and imminent counter-revolution in Czechoslovakia. We have heard that the Czechoslovak Academy of Science answered that document but we have not received, nor does the left-wing press publish, such answers.' In his own mind, he explained to them, he had tried to divide the question into two parts. First, there was the question of recent Western activities in West Germany: the NATO manœuvres called 'Black Lion,' he felt, might have been planned for a time when some internal upheaval was expected in the East; if there was danger of this sort, then some joint strengthening of the border defences by the Warsaw Pact allies seemed to be legitimate and reasonable, if it was by mutual agreement. Secondly, there was the question of internal reform and change. Here the principle to be followed was clear: it was absolutely impermissible for one state to undertake forcible intervention in the internal affairs of another state.[11] If the Warsaw Pact allies were concerned about West German intentions, why, he wondered, could their legitimate interests not be satisfied by stationing their forces on the Czech-West German frontier without occupying the whole country? 'We are aware,' he wrote the Czechoslovak peace committee, 'that the peace movement must at this time re-affirm its fundamental principles.'[12]

Although still a member of the presidential committee of the World Council of Peace, Endicott played no part in the deliberations of that body in the months following the Czechoslovak crisis: a painful arthritic condition kept him close to home. His colleague, Isabelle Blume, however, tried unsuccessfully to convene an emergency session of the council in Europe. She argued, correctly, that the peace movement would lose both prestige and influence if it ignored the situation. Her efforts as co-ordinating chairman of that hydra-headed organization were blocked by the Soviet members. When the council finally met in Lahti, Finland, in November 1968, the new general secretary, Romesh Chandra from India, clever and ambitious and known to fellow secretariat members as a 'yes-man' for the Soviets, persuaded the group not to adopt any official resolution on Czechoslovakia.[13] As a result, the World Council of Peace lost its credibility in Europe, East and West. In the future, for those who followed events closely, its only relevance would be as an auxiliary of Soviet diplomacy.

Sometimes the obvious is the most difficult to accept or understand. A deep fund of goodwill for the Soviet people, faith in their honest concern about the welfare of mankind at home and abroad, as well as his own natural optimism, made Endicott reluctant to draw general conclusions about the deteriorating standards of Soviet political leadership. Constantly before him, too, was the official Soviet interpretation of events: visits to Toronto over several years by Vladimir Kulushney, first secretary of the Ottawa embassy, provided a steady stream of opinions, disarming information, and, occasionally, financial aid in the form of bulk purchases of Canadian peace literature. There was, as well, solicitude for his personal health; the Soviet ambassador to Canada kept in touch and invited him to Moscow for treatment of his arthritis.

The culmination of this relationship was a message of appreciation from the Soviet Union on the occasion of the twentieth anniversary of the Canadian Peace Congress and the celebrations to mark Endicott's seventieth birthday in 1969, praising him for 'selfless activity for peace and promoting mutual understanding and friendship between peoples.' In this environment, Endicott was unable or unwilling to penetrate the mysteries of the world that surrounded him, and there followed one of those intervals that occur in every lifetime, when one waits upon the course of events. 'It's easy enough to lecture about the peace movement of yesterday; it is not too difficult to lecture about it today, but I am stuck on tomorrow,' he told his friends at the celebration, smiling somewhat wryly as he prepared to set out in the late spring of 1969 on yet another six-week tour across Canada.[14]

It took evidence of a Russian design to isolate China by trying to have her expelled from the world Communist movement, and of a readiness to overthrow China militarily under cover of a barrage of propaganda, to make up his mind.

Certain facts, like pieces of a jigsaw puzzle, began to make a pattern.

First, there was the shooting between Soviet and Chinese border guards along the Ussuri River in 1969. Harrison Salisbury of the *New York Times*, who was touring the border areas upon the invitation of the Soviet Union at the time, reported on the huge concentrations of well-equipped Soviet divisions he saw in the Far East and predicted a full-scale war.[15] There were also rumours (later confirmed by Major-General George Keegan, US air force chief of intelligence) that the Soviet Union had made discreet suggestions to the United States for a joint surgical strike to destroy China's nuclear establishment.[16]

Endicott entered into correspondence with Salisbury and protested that it was 'monstrous ... breath-taking in its irrationality' to suggest that the Soviet Union and the United States as 'superpowers' would collaborate to intervene in China. Salisbury, who had talked with people he described as 'very distinguished Soviet representatives,' thought otherwise. 'Believe me,' he replied, 'they see the world, rightly or wrongly, in terms of the two super-powers and I am afraid that they somewhat justify the Chinese suspicion that they are interested in a common front with the United States vis-a-vis China.'[17]

Another journalist, the Soviet newsman Victor Louis, who in Endicott's opinion was close to the Soviet foreign office, chose this time to hint in the London *Evening News* that a Czechoslovak-type Soviet intervention to give 'fraternal help' might be in store for China.[18]

Endicott also became aware that the Soviets had begun to assemble a new 'revolutionary central committee ' for China. One of their prime candidates for this committee was the former general secretary of the Chinese Communist party, Wang Ming, who had been living quietly in Moscow under the pseudonym of 'Mamavich' for over a decade and who was suddenly brought into the limelight by a vituperative article he wrote against Mao Tse-tung. Another candidate for the new Soviet-sponsored central committee was Chang Kuo-tao, the only other founding member of the Chinese Communist party besides Mao still alive, and who, by coincidence, was now residing in Toronto. During the course of an excited conversation, when Kulushney asked Endicott to help him meet Chang, the Soviet Embassy official blurted out: 'We are going to discredit and destroy Mao Tse-tung and his regime!'[19] Endicott refused to co-operate.

In retrospect, it was never clear to Endicott why a Soviet attack upon China did not materialize in 1969. Possibly the whole exercise was an act of brinkmanship, a gigantic bluff calculated to bring the downfall of Mao Tse-tung by spreading fear and panic among his subordinates. Perhaps the Soviets drew back, realizing, as the British imperialists had learned long ago, that any puppet government in China, made capable of crushing its opponents through foreign support, would be despised as the servant of that foreign power and before long would fall, leaving the country in chaos, united only in its hatred of the power that had intruded into China's internal affairs. Possibly it was because three-quarters of the Asian Communist parties refused even to attend the Moscow Conference of Communist Parties in June 1969 where Leonid Brezhnev, general secretary of the Soviet party, had hoped to isolate and expel China.[20] Perhaps, as American authorities claimed, it was because President Richard Nixon had signalled the Soviets that the United States was determined to be a friend of China. Whatever the case or combination of reasons, Endicott was thoroughly alarmed by what he considered to be a major and continuing threat to world peace.

Because he was convinced that, for world peace and in the interests of the ultimate co-operation of the two socialist countries, it was necessary for both sides of the debate to be openly stated, he printed the official statements of both parties in the *Canadian Far Eastern Newsletter*. In addition, since he was generally impressed by the manner in which the Chinese were putting their case about the boundary questions, and because he believed that the Russian use of the Wang Ming material revealed a bankruptcy of ideas, he asked for a meeting in Moscow with responsible people: he hoped they could be persuaded to modify their views. His request was granted in April 1970 when he went to Moscow for the Lenin centennial celebrations organized by the Soviet peace committee. During his stay, the Supreme Soviet awarded him a Lenin Centennial Medal in recognition of his leadership in the peace movement. The results of his discussions about China, however, were disappointing. Following a strenuous session with nine Far Eastern experts of the Soviet Academy of Sciences, in which they sheepishly admitted that the Wang Ming article was a mistake, he came away feeling that one would look in vain for any serious scholarship on contemporary China from that prestigious organization.[21] Quite unexpectedly, however, the inner tensions of the peace movement subsided shortly after this, a reflection of temporary improvements in formal state relations between China and the Soviet Union.

On the domestic side, it was a time of happiness. A great source of joy to Endicott was his marriage to Ella Phyllis Hansen in September 1970. Ella, who had grown up on a prairie farm in Manitoba, had moved to Ontario following the breakdown of her first marriage. Jim and Mary had known her for years through the peace movement, where from 1966 she acted as secretary of the Canadian Peace Congress. A lively person with a jolly sense of humour, and some years younger than Endicott, she enjoyed entertaining friends and supporting his numerous hobbies. One of their chief pleasures was feeding a dozen tropical finches which flitted about their living room. As in the Chungchow hills years ago, when he caught dragonflies and moths, 'nature spoke to him remembered things' and brought renewal to his spirit; on sunny afternoons along the country roads north of Toronto, passing motorists gaped in surprise to see a seventy-year-old man and his companion, nets in hand, chasing after grasshoppers as delicacies for the inhabitants of their aviary.

Another source of Endicott's renewed vitality was a successful operation by Toronto's internationally famous orthopaedic surgeon, Dr J.E. Bateman; where traction, exercises, and mineral baths had failed to bring relief to a worn-out left hip, Dr Bateman's scalpel, and his steel and plastic hip-joint, restored mobility and vigour.

The political highlight of 1970 was the long-awaited recognition in October of the People's Republic of China by the government of Canada. Because of his long association with China, and his long fight for recognition, Endicott's comments received wide coverage in the media. In celebration of the event he sent a telegram to Chou En-lai that for two years he had been carrying around in his wallet in anticipation: 'Please accept my expression of pleasure that the Canadian government has at long last established normal relations with your government. We welcome this opportunity to establish friendship between our two peoples.'[22]

When tensions resumed within the peace movement, the issue, as usual, was China. Following recognition by Canada and several other countries, the People's Republic was admitted into the United Nations Organization, and in 1971 President Nixon accepted the invitation for his historic visit to Peking. This turn of events displeased the Soviet Union, and Wang Ming's line began to emanate once more: 'the Mao group' was an illegal leadership; China had become a 'military and bureaucratic dictatorship' with expansionist aims. Even though Vladimir Kulushney urged him to pay no attention to polemics conducted through the Soviet Novesti Press Agency, saying that 'they aren't taken too seriously,' Endicott feared that this was not just another round in the ideological battle; the Soviet Union might still plan to use military force to try to oust the Peking regime. At an Ottawa reception in the Soviet Embassy for Premier Alexei Kosygin, who was touring Canada, he raised his concerns: the Soviet leader brushed them aside, choosing instead to thank Endicott for his past efforts and urging him to continue to help educate and inspire the younger generation in the struggle for peace. Kosygin was not amused when Endicott suggested to Prime Minister Pierre Elliott Trudeau that it would be a fine thing if the next foreign prime minister to be invited to visit Canada was Chou En-lai.

Shortly after this, in December 1971, the Communist Party of Canada sent a deputation, headed by its general secretary William Kashtan, to press Endicott to resign. They reported that their central committee was unanimous in believing that his *Newsletter* was anti-Soviet and harmful to the cause of peace; they felt that he was waging the struggle about China from a privileged sanctuary, sheltered by the prestige of being chairman of the Canadian Peace Congress where they did not feel free to attack him as they otherwise would.

In view of the long years they had worked together harmoniously, they hoped that he would withdraw from the chairmanship with a statement that health and age were the main reasons. Kashtan said he would consider helping to make arrangements for a pension of forty dollars a week.

'Has due consideration been given to trying to strike a balance between the harm that will be done to the peace movement by my withdrawing and the "harm" that will happen by my remaining and continuing to express my opinions freely in the *Newsletter*?' Endicott asked.

'Yes, that has all been carefully considered,' replied Kashtan, a greying, humourless man who did not inspire much confidence. (Later, Kashtan's office would issue a statement to the press claiming it was 'simply not true' that the Communist party or any member of it had put pressure on Endicott to quit.[23])

That evening Endicott called together members of his family. He had made up his mind to resign. Looking remarkably relaxed and fit, he passed around a brief statement that started off by talking about old age and ill health, a description that was greeted first with amazement and then by laughter. He was soon persuaded to keep to the real issue, his opinions on China and the Sino-Soviet differences, for everyone knew his health had considerably improved lately.

To the executives of the World Council of Peace and the Canadian Peace Congress he bade farewell with letters of resignation. After reviewing the disagreements over Sino-Soviet relations and informing them of the position of the Communist party, he said it would be pointless to call a national council to debate his role all over again; the council should plan for the future. Although his resignation, to take effect on 31 December 1971, was rejected by the Canadian Peace Congress executive by a majority of two, with two abstentions, he carried through his intention and resigned.

He also wrote, expressing gratitude and affection, to peace workers with whom he had had the privilege of fellowship, work, and struggle. 'Regardless of differences of opinion and belief,' he told them, 'you all have a permanent dwelling in my heart.' The twenty-three years of interpreting the Chinese revolution to Canadians and of working in the Canadian and world-wide peace movement, he declared, had been the most meaningful and satisfying period of his life. To have worked on the World Council of Peace with such people as Frédéric Joliot-Curie and Professor J.D. Bernal was a rare and precious experience. He was optimistic that a general war could be prevented, and re-emphasized that he did not think anything useful for peace and progress would be accomplished by campaigns suggesting the total infallibility of *Pravda* or the total depravity of the thought of Mao Tse-tung.[24]

After years of minimal attention in spite of his international prominence, Endicott was suddenly newsworthy again in Canada. Local hot-line radio shows and the daily newspapers gave prominent coverage to his resignation; invitations multiplied to speak at high schools, universities, churches, and service clubs.

While the opportunities thus provided to state his case were welcome, there was one troublesome thrust in all the publicity: the gleeful suggestions that the circumstances of his resignation gave final, irrefutable, proof that the peace movement was not independent and had been all along a front controlled by the Communist party. Endicott's critics had always maintained that he was either knowingly an apologist or unwittingly a dupe of Moscow; had he not now delivered himself into their hands?

Endicott had worked on quite a different hypothesis. He saw the world peace movement as an opportunity to advance the causes he believed in. By his record and by the force of his personality he could make a credible case that it was possible for a person of goodwill to work within a coalition and not be controlled by anyone. It was also possible to lose.

'The Peace Movement,' he contended, 'has been controlled by its own program. The communists, being politically intelligent, have worked hard in the peace movement and have usually abided faithfully by the limitations of its program and have respected and fully cooperated with my leadership.'[25] He did not really resent the manner of the demand for his resignation, just the fact of it. For years the Communist party leaders had come and talked to him frankly, giving their views and advice, but always willing to leave the final decisions to himself and his executive. On several occasions he had decided on a different approach or emphasis. If the present group of party leaders wanted him to resign, it showed, in his opinion, that they were politically and perhaps otherwise bankrupt. However, as in the case of his resignation from the West China Mission twenty-five years earlier, he had no appetite for internal wranglings, nor did he wish to contribute to an atmosphere of mindless 'red-baiting' since, he felt, the future of fundamental social progress would still likely require new and better inspired generations of Canadian Marxists. Therefore he resigned without acrimony.

Queried about his attitude to the Soviets, he said he had been willing to give them the benefit of any doubts because for the first fifteen years of his relationship with them in the peace movement he had felt from experience that they were sincere, dedicated, and helpful. Since all modern states had their own interests to protect, it was perhaps inevitable that attempts would be made to intrude national objectives into the struggle for peace. But the lesson in this respect was that in so far as a powerful state succeeded in imposing its narrow necessities, the effectiveness of the international movement was dissipated. When the Soviet Union followed policies that were detrimental to peace, to national independence, and to social justice, he and others like him resisted, criticized, and finally broke with the Soviet Union, opposing behaviour that had become unacceptable.

As for the worth of the Canadian Peace Congress and the World Council of Peace, he believed that in the 1950s and 1960s they had led a genuine and necessary people's movement against the atomic bomb and for disarmament. Popular movements, whether to 'Ban the Bomb' or to establish a Charter of Rights as in nineteenth-century England, or to win the vote as in the suffragette phase of the women's movement, represented a tide in the affairs of humankind. The tide flowed for a time and then ebbed, either because it achieved or partially achieved its goal and thus became irrelevant or because it was overwhelmed by the contending odds. The peace movement after the Second World War had partially achieved its objectives; statesmen everywhere had begun to affirm its slogans. And yet its incompleteness meant that the end of popular international action was not yet in sight. After a time of confusion, in which existing institutional loyalties would dissolve, Endicott felt sure that regrouping would occur, and new initiatives, keeping in mind some of the lessons of the past, would begin to appear. He would take part as circumstances and his energy permitted.

EPILOGUE

UNDERSTANDINGS

'Cast away illusions; prepare for struggle!'

Mao Tse-tung

'A good way to get into trouble today is to try to persuade the Christians of the world to come to terms with the teachings and work of Karl Marx, Lenin, and Mao Tse-tung.'

Dr James G. Endicott
Trinity United Church
Toronto 1977

'We have no reason to suppose that our present condition of civilization is the last masterpiece of universal organization, the highest form of order of which Nature is capable. I believe there are many grounds for seeing in collectivism, of the kind of which we could approve, a form of organization as much above the outlook of middle class nations as their form of order is superior to that of primitive tribes. I think it would hardly be going too far to say that, so clear is the continuity between inorganic, biological and social order, the transition from economic individualism to the common ownership by humanity of the world's productive resources will be a step similar in nature to the transition from lifeless proteins to the living cell, or from primitive savagery to the first community. From this point of view, the future state of social justice is seen not as a fantastic Utopia, not a desperate hope, but as a form of organization with the full force and authority of evolution behind it.'

Dr Joseph Needham, FRS
Cambridge University, 1972

The happy warrior continues

The news of Endicott's resignation from the World Council of Peace was released in China three months later. In Peking on 2 April 1972 the *People's Daily* reproduced parts of his letter of resignation and a summary was broadcast on national radio. Letters of support and welcome from old friends arrived in Toronto and by the end of the year Jim and Ella were on their way for an extended visit to China. Chou En-lai's greeting was as warm as ever, and the two old friends were able to talk over the great changes that had taken place in the thirteen years since they had last met in 1959.

This was to be the first of three trips Endicott made to China in the 1970s, and heralded the fact that his active public life would end as it had begun, as a student and interpreter of the changes in that vast civilization and as a continuing participant in the effort to foster international co-operation, peace, and justice. His travels continued to fire his imagination about how successful the struggle for socialism in China would be by the end of the century. He was not deterred by China's further troubles, as the first generation of outstanding revolutionary figures lost vigour and passed from the scene. Chou En-lai, Chu Teh, and Mao Tse-tung, all died in 1976.

From the evidence he collected about the ensuing struggle for succession, he could not agree with arguments that Mao's widow, Chiang Ching, and the other three leaders who were dubbed 'the gang of four' were honest and intelligent promoters of the revolutionary line of Chairman Mao; they were rather, he decided, 'a gang of unprincipled, arrogant and corrupt conspirators ... fake super-leftists ... extravagant in their personal lives, isolated from the masses and hated by them';[1] the outbursts of rejoicing in China when they were arrested were spontaneous and deeply felt. Endicott expected that the revolutionary process, the dialectic of conflict and change, would continue in China. Over the years since 1949, in hard battles against the rightists and the ultra-leftists, there had been failures, uneven growth, some heart-breaking personal tragedies, but also extraordinary gains.

His main interest was in the moral and spiritual basis of Chinese development. How would the tendency of all people and all revolutions to backslide be counteracted? How would the revolutionary spirit be kept alive?

With his Christian background it was particularly fascinating to discover that during the course of strenuous struggles with old revolutionary comrades who had sacrificed for, won, and administered a successful revolution, Mao Tse-tung had found it necessary to say: 'if you are not completely reborn you cannot enter the door of communism.'[2] With a similar concern for personal transformation, Jesus had said: 'unless a man has been born over again he cannot see the kingdom of God' (John 3:3, New English Bible).

At the time Mao issued his challenge, in 1959, many Chinese believed that social ownership of the means of production had laid a sure foundation for the changing of society and human nature and that what was further required was more technology, a plentiful supply of material goods, and education; then all would be well. Mao felt that the emphasis on material incentives was creating a new class of privileged managers and an élitist party. When he challenged this trend with the slogan, 'put politics in command,' Endicott understood him to mean, 'put human values in command, not economic laws, technology, and profits.'[3]

Endicott singled out several of the moral principles on which Chinese socialism had been built as being of prime significance: of all things people are most precious; self-reliance and hard struggle; promote production and grasp revolution; serve the people. These – not personal fame and possessive individualism – were taught as the main ambitions of a good citizen.

Mao had also warned his people to 'never forget the class struggle,' an unsettling injunction he saw as the key to eliminating the corrupting influence of power and for promoting greater equality. Chou had echoed this when he said: 'recognizing the existence of classes and class struggle is a question of political principle ... if we didn't admit class struggle, how could we direct our work? What would be our guiding principles?'[4]

On this basis, Endicott came to hope China might escape the common rule, that power tends to corrupt those who wield it; the legacy of involving the people in the process of their own emancipation, the revolutionary mass line, was by now too deeply rooted in the consciousness of China to be reversed by any inner-party struggle that might occur. There would be confusions and setbacks, attempts to put China back on the capitalist road, but the theme of fifty *Canadian Far Eastern Newsletters* in the late 1970s was the prophecy that the new moral basis for socialism as taught by Mao would succeed. Combined

with the programme for socialist modernization, it offered hope of an egalitarian, non-bureaucratic society that might well be unique in human history.

But China's rebirth did not represent for Endicott an Eastern utopia that
could be used as a model to compensate for the spiritual impoverishment of
the West. On the contrary, he was openly scornful of the young, rather
arrogant, middle class intellectuals, the so-called Maoists of the North Atlantic countries, who rushed hither and yon proclaiming a new panacea and
demanding blind obedience. He believed it unwise to try to follow the
example or to apply the lessons of China without careful consideration lest, as
Mao had once warned, it became a case of 'cutting the feet to fit the shoes.'
Revolution could succeed only if inspired and fuelled by indigenous sources;
that was surely one of the chief lessons of China's experience of Marxism-
Leninism under Mao's leadership. Apart from that, the Chinese example was
important because it provided refutation of philosophies that taught resignation to fate, retreat into private worlds; it was a powerful affirmation of the
essential creativity of human beings, their rationality and social concern, their
ability to be masters of their own destiny, and their capacity, given appropriate leadership, to serve and enrich their heritage.

Endicott's espousal of social change through class struggle, and his explanation of how the Chinese revolution had become intelligible and acceptable to
him as a Christian, undoubtedly antagonized more people in the West than it
persuaded. Although praised and admired by some, he baffled most of his
generation. Blair Fraser expressed his puzzlement in *Maclean's* in 1952,
declaring that everything in Endicott's environment befitted him to spend
twenty-odd years in the service of Christ, while none of it explained why this
same man 'should now be lending his talents and his influence to the Anti-
christ.' Some of the more thoughtful journalists could not decide whether he
was a congenital liar in the interests of communism or an absolutely sincere
man who was bringing to his followers news of great significance that did not
come through the regular channels of information. Scott Young, writing in
the Toronto *Globe and Mail* in 1975, confessed that he had started many times
to write a column about a sermon of Endicott's entitled 'Revolution and
Christian Response,' but he never finished it. Why? 'I can't be his cutting
adversary with conviction,' he explained, 'but feel I am not wise enough to be
certain that I should become his advocate.'[5]

Much of the controversy that surrounded Endicott's public witness,
throughout his life, arose from his conception of freedom and human rights.
His view of these values was never passive or abstract; it was always dynamic
and vital, related to the contemporary scene. A strong advocate of civil
liberties, he was nevertheless wary of being entangled in 'human rights' as a

catch-phrase regardless of time and circumstances. The advancement of liberty, in his view, was based upon a unity of opposites: individual human rights are very important when the struggle for them is associated with social justice.

Many of his liberal friends parted company over this attitude. When an oppressive party had wielded power over the peasantry and disaffected intellectuals of China before 1949, Endicott had fought hard for freedom to think 'unpopular thoughts,' to promote them by press, public meetings, and organization without fear of arrest by the secret police; during this struggle the predominantly middle class missionary group attacked him as extremist, irresponsible, and lacking in constructive attitudes; they called for understanding. After the liberation, when the peasant-based Communist party was coming into power, the same missionaries became extremely vocal about freedoms of speech and assembly, about human rights, about freedom from the tyranny of arrest by 'people's courts'; Endicott called for understanding.

In spite of the fact that his attitude laid him open to charges of hypocrisy and of being 'soft on communism,' he held to his belief that human rights, seen as an end in themselves, were often sterile, even dangerous. Could any supporter of human rights conscientiously promote the liberties of the racist Ku Klux Klan? A strong believer in certain minority rights, he was also aware that crusaders for social justice could forget to 'love mercy and walk humbly.' He preferred not to be dogmatic about the contours of human rights; each generation would have to redefine for itself the meaning of freedom.[6]

When his views were distorted or newspapers denied him space to reply to attacks and state his case, he fumed for a time and then relaxed with the recollection of Lincoln's advice: 'If I were to try to read, much less to answer all the attacks made on me, this shop might as well be closed for business. I do the very best I know how, the very best I can and I mean to keep doing so until the end. If the end brings me out all right, what is said against me won't amount to anything. If the end brings me out wrong, ten angels swearing I was right would make no difference.'[7]

Or if assailed occasionally by self-doubt about his own stand, he reflected upon the American president's polemical writing on the subject of liberty, made in the midst of the civil war that brought about the end of slavery in America barely a hundred years earlier: 'The shepherd drives the wolf from the sheep's throat, for which the sheep thanks the shepherd as his liberator, while the wolf denounces him for the same act, as the destroyer of liberty, especially as the sheep was a black one. Plainly, the sheep and the wolf are not agreed upon a definition of the word liberty; and precisely the same difference prevails today among us human creatures ... all professing to love liberty ... Recently, it seems the people ... have been doing something to define liberty, and thanks to them ... the wolf's dictionary has been repudiated.'[8]

More than once Endicott had to adjust his frames of reference when the causes he espoused turned into blind alleys. This was the case in his lifelong attempt to find real foundations for international friendship and co-operation as an alternative to war. First came the failure of his hopes for the international missionary movement and the League of Nations as successful instruments for peace in the 1920s and 1930s. Thereafter, he was guided by the belief that capitalism's control of markets and plunder of resources abroad were at the root of the war system and could be checked only by the advent of socialism. Following the defeat of European and Japanese fascism in 1945 and the survival of socialist Russia, he believed that there was only one remaining major source of war, United States imperialism; once this pillar was toppled or else collapsed under its own weight, the other obstacles to human emancipation posed by the exigencies of corporate capitalism would rapidly disintegrate. He never abandoned this reasoning, even though his general analysis was overtaken by events and rendered obsolete by the manner in which numerous post-capitalist societies conducted their external relations. All too often countries that had been established by Marxist revolutionaries, that declared themselves to be socialist, interpreted the lofty ideal of proletarian internationalism to mean support for their own national interests and policies at the expense of other people's revolutions. Some went to war not only in self-defence but also to impose their will upon others. Endicott often repeated in this context Shakespeare's lines from the end of the 94th Sonnet: 'For sweetest things turn sourest by their deeds; / Lilies that fester smell far worse than weeds.'

A most glaring example of the fallibility of socialist states, in Endicott's view, was the invasion and occupation of Kampuchea (Cambodia) by the Socialist Republic of Vietnam, which began at the time of his eightieth birthday in December 1978. Hanoi's outrage in Kampuchea appeared to him to be a straight case of one country marching into another with manifest imperial intent.[9] Vietnam was backed fully by the Soviet Union and opposed by the Chinese, who later sent a limited, punitive expedition across the border, lasting three weeks. When Kampuchea's Prince Norodom Sihanouk went before the United Nations Security Council to state his charge of military aggression against Vietnam, a resolution sponsored by seven non-aligned countries calling for a ceasefire and withdrawal of all foreign troops passed by a vote of thirteen to two; but it was vetoed by the Soviet Union. Endicott thought he was seeing ghosts of the 1930s: there came to mind the lonely figure of the emperor of Ethiopia asking for justice from the old League of Nations when Mussolini invaded his country in a similar fashion.

Endicott viewed with sorrow his former colleagues in the peace movement, who justified Vietnam's aggression while shouting loudly about peace and socialism. He, meanwhile, defended China's intervention in Vietnam as a response to border provocations in a manner reminiscent of his earlier justification of China's interventions in the Korean War and in India in 1962. In the absence of any satisfactory theoretical explanation for the failure of socialist nations to live in peace, he turned, as he often did, to the poetry of Wordsworth:[10]

> Earth is sick,
> And Heaven is weary of the hollow words
> Which States and Kingdoms utter when they talk
> Of truth and justice.

As a result of his understanding of the facts, Endicott joined with his old friend Chester Ronning and others, including a new generation of young Canadian militants and anti-imperialists, to form a Kampuchea Support Committee.[11] With his hopes for peace amongst socialist nations shattered, the search for real foundations for international fraternity would have to begin again; to many of his friends, a far-away and confused corner of South-East Asia seemed a most unlikely, ill-advised, and perhaps insignificant place to begin a new crusade.

As Endicott began his ninth decade, however, his rare gifts of optimism and good humour remained intact, as did his fighting spirit. His 'faculty for storm and turbulence,'[12] like Wordsworth's happy warrior, continued to attract many people as an example to follow, as a ray of hope – a Christian person who dared to take another road to the Kingdom.

The source of his resilience was, in one part, the compelling influence of his Christian beliefs, the moral imperatives of the prophets of Israel and the meaning of the life and spirit of Jesus as he understood them. The other part, always more difficult, was an openness to new truths and a willingness to test them out in practice. If Christians are 'to meet the challenge of modern Marxism,' he told the congregation of his church in 1977,[13] 'we will have to change the method of putting almost total emphasis on faith and dogmatic belief, and much more on social justice and human brotherhood. We need to re-emphasize in social life the warning of the writer of the Epistle of John to the select group of believers: "We know that we have passed out of death into life, because we love the brethren ... No man hath beheld God at any time: if we love one another, God abideth in us, and his love is perfected in us ... If a man say, I love God, and hateth his brother, he is a liar: for he that loveth not his brother whom he hath seen, cannot love God whom he hath not seen"' (1 John 3:14, 4:12,20).

Within his church there began to grow a feeling, here and there, that Endicott's chief mistake through the years had been to be ahead of his time. To some, 'his witness, his resolve, and his vision of a better future' bore the hallmarks of a prophet. 'It's time this prophet was recognized,' declared an editorial in the *United Church Observer* of May 1979, suggesting that if the General Council of the United Church rescinded its 1952 repudiation of Endicott's stand it would be an appropriate way to recognize 'a man of vision and courage' who had often been without honour in his own country.[14]

Some prominent church leaders wished to go further. In spite of the intense struggle that had swirled around him, they argued, he had never become bitter; he had remained a lay member of the church and had continued to struggle for his beliefs and his point of view. Thus, impressed by his strength, they tried to persuade him to withdraw his resignation from the Toronto Conference and to 'rejoin the fellowship.' Endicott declined to do this, fearing that it would raise a bitter quarrel and objections from many of the ministers who remained unfriendly. He felt also that the suggestion was based upon sentimental grounds, without any rethinking by the church of the issues involved.

How did his case relate to the scores of other United Church ministers, in Saskatchewan and elsewhere, who were not celebrities but had been pushed out of their pulpits for their advanced social and political views without adequate protest by the church headquarters? Would such an action help them or recognize their struggle in any way? Would it help such people in the future? Would it mean that the church was now a more open place both theologically and politically? And why had the late editor of the *Observer*, A.C. Forrest, one of his strongest supporters, periodically raised the anxious question: 'You are not a Communist, are you?' If the proposed withdrawal of a thirty-year-old resignation did not first provoke answers to some of these questions, he thought, it would not say anything that needed to be said.

Although Jim Endicott campaigned on political issues and valued the opportunities for democratic expression in the parliamentary system, he never sought national political office; he chose to work out his mission in the international arena. From his experiences there he presented a view of the world that sometimes seemed to be irrelevant to comfortable Canadians, who, if they were reform-minded, preferred the more familiar approaches established earlier by men such as J.S. Woodsworth.

A comparison of the two men adds perspective to Endicott's contribution to Canadian politics. Both were the sons of clergymen; both began their life's work as ordained ministers; later, as a result of strong criticism from within the church, both resigned from the active ministry to work as laymen in the broader social and political environment. Each was a man of principle, compassion, and integrity, genuinely concerned about his country but internationalist in outlook as well. Woodsworth, who died in 1942, was a convinced pacifist and had become a doctrinaire anti-communist; his place in Canadian history rests securely on his leadership for some twenty years, both in and out of Parliament, of the social democratic movement in Canada and the Co-operative Commonwealth Federation.

Endicott was a bearer of harsher news and more difficult remedies. He had come to an acceptance of class struggles, social violence, and just wars against imperialism as inevitable elements in the liberation of exploited and oppressed peoples. Living a full generation after Woodsworth, he saw dogmatic anti-communism as a negative religion in Canada and elsewhere, used as a smokescreen to blind people to the increasing necessity for fundamental social change. 'The struggle in the world today,' he contended, 'is not between Marxists, Communists and atheists on one side, and Christians as saviours of the world on the other. The struggle is between exploitation, poverty, ignorance and disease on one side and imperialism, capitalism and entrenched privilege ... on the other.'[15]   He shared with Woodsworth the idea that the competitive, acquisitive society of capitalism should be replaced by a co-operative one; he differed on who could and should be allies in such a campaign and on the range of tactics that might be involved. He was more certain than Woodsworth that men of privilege, power, and profits would always try to squash the opposition, and that it was therefore necessary to build a broader base in the struggle for social justice.

As a champion of world peace and social change in the Canadian context, Endicott has a reputation, compared to Woodsworth's, that is far from secure; his achievements fall short of his high purposes. Yet history demonstrates that many must fail before someone wins. Through their struggles those that appear to lose may demonstrate the moral value and truthfulness of their ideas, thereby helping to create a new and higher consciousness. The distinguished Quebec historian, Michel Brunet, once told Endicott that the vindication of his position about China's revolution was a vivid illustration of the way our interpretation of history changes: the ideas presented yesterday as certainties turn out to be but the prejudices of preceding generations.[16]

Notes

J.G.E.   James Gareth Endicott
M.A.E.   Mary Austin Endicott
CBC   Interview with J.G. Endicott by Marjorie McEnancy, 1966, Canadian
         Broadcasting Corporation Archives, Toronto
CFEN   *Canadian Far Eastern Newsletter*, Toronto, edited by J.G. Endicott
DEA   Department of External Affairs (Historical Division), Ottawa
EP   J.G. Endicott Papers, Public Archives of Canada, Ottawa
WCM   West China Mission Papers, United Church of Canada Archives, Victoria
         University, Toronto

PART ONE: BEGINNINGS, 1898–1925

1 IN THE SHADOW OF THE WHITE PAGODA

1 EP, James Endicott, Sr, to Rev. W.A. Cooke, 14 July 1892
2 For background, see Jean Chesneaux, Marianne Bastid, and Marie-Claire Bergère,
  China: From the Opium Wars to the 1911 Revolution (New York 1976); Victor
  Nee and James Peck, eds., *China's Uninterrupted Revolution: From 1840 to the
  Present* (New York 1975).
3 Kang Yu-wei, speaking in 1895, quoted in S.Y. Teng and J.K. Fairbank, *China's
  Response to the West* (New York 1967), 152
4 Chinese merchants were being ruined by road-toll taxes (likin), collected twenty
  times over a distance of seventy miles in one case, to raise money to pay the war
  indemnities; meanwhile, privileged foreign companies travelled the same route on
  a transit pass, exempt from the likin. Foreign competitors, paying only 5 to $7\frac{1}{2}$ per

cent duty, were able to ship out timber, oil, silk, opium, and tobacco at one-fifth of the cost to a Chinese company. The missionaries apparently had no awareness of the real background to the riots. See Han Suyin, *The Crippled Tree* (London 1965), 86–7.

5 For details of the Canadian West China Mission, see E.W. Wallace, *The Heart of Szechuan* (Toronto 1905), and Missionary Society of the Methodist Church, *Our West China Mission* (Toronto 1920).

6 CBC, McEnaney

7 Interview by author with J.G.E.

8 CBC, McEnaney

9 EP, letters of 1907; interview by author with J.G.E. and with his sister, Mary Endicott Manning

10 Interview by author with Norman J. Endicott

11 CBC, McEnaney

12 Interview by author with Mary Endicott Manning; EP, interview by M.A.E. with James Endicott, Sr, 1949

13 For an extended contemporary discussion of this question by an American missionary, see F.L.H. Pott, *The Outbreak in China* (New York 1900), 95 ff.; see also Victor Purcell, *The Boxer Uprising* (Cambridge 1963); Hu Sheng, *Imperialism and Chinese Politics* (Peking 1955), 131–54.

14 EP, letter book of 1902–8

15 CBC, McEnaney

16 Interview by author with J.G.E.

17 EP, J.G.E. to his daughter, Shirley Endicott, 9 Feb. 1945

18 Interview by author with J.G.E.; also EP, war diary, 5 Aug. 1917

19 EP, J.G.E. to Shirley Endicott, 24 Dec. 1946

20 CBC, McEnaney

2 THE METHODIST SOLDIER

The quotations in this chapter, unless otherwise noted, are extracts from Endicott's letters home and from a war diary he kept during 1917–18, to be found in the J.G. Endicott Papers in the Public Archives.

1 6 June 1917, quoted in Richard Allen, *The Social Passion: Religion and Social Reform in Canada, 1914–28* (Toronto 1971), 35

2 EP, James Endicott, Sr, 'Report to the Bishops and Delegates of the General Conference of the Methodist Episcopal Church, Saratoga Springs, New York, 1916' (typescript)

3 See Gerald A. Hallowell, *Prohibition in Ontario, 1919–1923* (Ottawa 1972).

4 See Chow Tse-tsung, *The May Fourth Movement: Intellectual Revolution in*

Modern China (1960; Stanford 1967), 35–46. Among the activists in France with whom Endicott later became acquainted in China were Chou En-lai, Chen Yi, Li Fu-chun, Ms Tsai Chang, and Teng Hsiao-ping.

5 Capt. J.D. Craig, comp., *The 1st Canadian Division in the Battles of 1918* (London 1919), 7–12

6 George F.G. Stanley, *Canada's Soldiers: The Military History of an Unmilitary People*, rev. ed. (Toronto 1960), 330

3 AT UNIVERSITY

1 See, for example, D.G. Creighton, *Canada's First Century* (Toronto 1970), 149 ff.; Kenneth McNaught, *The Pelican History of Canada* (London 1969), 215 ff.; and Norman Penner, ed., *Winnipeg 1919: The Strikers' Own History of the Winnipeg General Strike* (Toronto 1973).

2 William Beeching and Phyllis Clarke, eds., *Yours in the Struggle: Reminiscences of Tim Buck* (Toronto 1977), 95 ff.

3 Kenneth McNaught, *A Prophet in Politics: A Biography of J.S. Woodsworth* (Toronto 1959), 132–53

4 *Methodist Journal of Proceedings*, 1918, pp. 341–2, as cited in Richard Allen, *The Social Passion* (Toronto 1971), 74, and McNaught, *Pelican History of Canada*, 224

5 See Charles B. Sissons, *A History of Victoria University* (Toronto 1952).

6 *Torontonensis* (Toronto), 1923

7 Interview by author with J.G.E.

8 *Toronto Star*, 11 June 1926

9 Sharman's important books include *Records of the Life of Jesus* (1917), *Studies in Jesus as Teacher* (n.d.), *Jesus in the Records* (1919), *Jesus as Teacher* (1935), *Son of Man, Kingdom of God* (1943), all published in New York.

10 Student Christian Movement of Canada, *This One Thing* (Toronto 1959), 43–4

11 Interview by author with J.G.E.

12 Hooke wrote many books, including *Christ and the Kingdom of God* (New York 1917), *Christianity in the Making* (1926), *The Kingdom of God in the Experience of Jesus* (1949), *Myth, Ritual and Kingship* (1958), *Babylonian and Assyrian Religion* (1962), published mainly in London.

13 Tawney, *Religion and the Rise of Capitalism*, Pelican ed. (New York 1947), 233–4

14 CBC, McEnaney

15 From *Prometheus Unbound*, in *The Complete Poetical Works of Percy Bysshe Shelley* (London 1960), 268

16 From 'To Toussaint L'Ouverture,' in *The Shorter Poems of William Wordsworth* (London 1927), 129

17 Interview by author with J.G.E.; EP, file on S.H. Hooke; 'What Does the United

Church Believe?' *United Church Observer*, 1 Jan. 1957, especially articles v, xiii, and xiv

18 As quoted by Endicott in his *Canadian Far Eastern Newsletter* (Toronto), no 183 (Sept. 1965); see also Albert Schweitzer, *My Life and Thought: An Autobiography* (London 1933), 72 ff.

19 EP, sermon, 'Building on a Rock,' 14 Aug. 1977; interview by author with J.G.E.

4 CIRCUIT-RIDING IN SASKATCHEWAN

Quotations in this chapter are from several letters Endicott wrote home in the summers of 1921 and 1922, now in the Endicott Papers in the Public Archives, and interviews with him by the author in the course of seeking explanations of photographs in a family album.

1 For a general account of the organization of the wheat pool, see Vernon C. Fowke, *The National Policy and the Wheat Economy* (Toronto 1957), 196 ff.

5 IDEOLOGY AND ORDINATION

1 For background on the svm, see *The Student Volunteer Movement after Twenty-five Years, 1886–1911* (New York 1911); John R. Mott, *Five Decades and a Forward View* (New York 1939); and Valentin H. Rabe, *The Home Base of American China Missions, 1880–1920* (Cambridge, Mass. 1978), 90 ff.

2 *A Brief History of the Student Christian Movement in Canada, 1921–1974* (Toronto 1975), 7–9

3 Student Christian Movement of Canada, *Some Canadian Questions* (Toronto 1922), 34. See also the *Varsity* (Toronto), 2 Nov. 1921; *Canadian Student*, Dec. 1922, p. 8; SCM, *Foundations* (Toronto 1927), 56.

4 SCM Archives, Victoria University, Toronto: Minutes of the svm Convention held in Toronto, 27–8 Dec. 1922; see also Helen R. Nichol to Hugh MacMillan, 17 April 1923, and 'Reply of John R. Mott,' 21 Jan. 1927, in same location.

5 Interview by author with J.G.E.

6 SCM Archives, Minutes of SCM General Committee, 2–3 Jan. 1924; Nichol to MacMillan, 17 April 1923; Canadian Committee of the svm, Minutes, 2 and 23 Jan. 1923. Also interview by author with J.G.E.

7 *Varsity*, 11 Jan. 1924, special SCM supplement

8 3 Oct. 1924

9 EP, J.G.E. to M.A.E., 5, 6 Aug. 1928

10 Rauschenbusch, *Christianity and the Social Crisis* (London 1912), and *A Theology for the Social Gospel* (New York 1917)

11 José Bonino, *Doing Theology in a Revolutionary Situation* (Philadelphia 1975),

151–2. Bonino asks, p. 101, if it is 'altogether absured to reread the Resurrection today as the death of the monopolies, the liberation from hunger or the solidary form of socialism?' See also Antonio Perez-Esclarin, *Atheism and Liberation* (New York 1978), 96 ff., and José Miranda, *Marx and the Bible: A Critique of the Philosophy of Oppression* (New York 1974).

12 Tennyson, 'In Memoriam,' XCVI, stanza 3

13 Interview by author with J.G.E.

14 Tennyson, 'Morte d'Arthur,' line 242, in *Representative Poetry* (Toronto 1946), II, 385

15 EP, 'Address' by Rev. James Endicott, DD, secretary of the Methodist Foreign Missions, speaking as the representative of the Methodist Church entering Union, June 1925. For a general account of church union, see C.E. Silcox, *Church Union in Canada* (New York 1933).

6 THE GATES OF EDEN

The material in this chapter is taken from letters exchanged between Mary Austin and Jim Endicott between 6 February and 14 June 1925 (now in the author's possession), as well as interviews with them.

1 EP, M.A.E., notes for 'Life with Jim,' 1963

PART TWO: THE MISSIONARY YEARS, 1925–1944

7 APPRENTICESHIP IN CHUNGCHOW

1 This account of the Endicotts' first year in China is based upon their letters to Canada (all quotations, unless otherwise noted, are from letters written between 9 December 1925 and 26 November 1926, and are to be found in the Endicott Papers, 1925, 1926, correspondence files), a chapter of Mary Endicott's unfinished manuscript 'Life with Jim,' and interviews by the author with Alex and Ida Pincock and J.G. Endicott.

2 Endicott met Kuo Mo-jo in Peking in January 1952. Kuo repeated this opinion to the American writer, Ross Terrill; see his *800,000,000: The Real China* (New York 1972), 72.

3 For fuller explanation of the unequal treaty system, see Stephen L. Endicott, *Diplomacy and Enterprise: British Policy in China, 1933–1937* (Vancouver 1975), 2–10.

4 WCM, W.J. Mortimer to James Endicott, Sr, Board of Foreign Missions, 1, 12 June 1926, box 1, file 3. For the attitude of the executive officers of the mission in

Canada and the missionaries on furlough, more sympathetic to the abolition of the unequal treaties, see in *ibid.* the resolution adopted at a conference held in Toronto on 18–19 February 1926.
5 Interview by author with J.G.E.
6 *Ibid.*
7 The classic description of river travel between Chungking and Ichang on the upper Yangtze is Cornell Plant's *Glimpses of the Yangtze Gorges* (Shanghai 1926).

8 CHINA IN FERMENT

1 Li Chien-nung, *The Political History of China, 1840–1928* (Stanford 1967), 277
2 James E. Sheridan, *Chinese Warlord: The Career of Feng Yuxiang* (Stanford 1966), 1. See also Robert Kapp, *Szechuan and the Chinese Republic* (New Haven 1973), and Jerome Ch'en, *Military-Gentry Coalition* (Toronto 1979), for background to the warlord period.
3 C. Brandt *et al.*, *A Documentary History of Chinese Communism* (New York 1967), 66; on Dr Sun, see Lyon Sharman, *Sun Yat-sen: His Life and Its Meaning* (Stanford 1934).
4 Ho Kan-chih, *A History of the Modern Chinese Revolution* (Peking 1959), 93
5 Harold Isaacs, *The Tragedy of the Chinese Revolution*, 2nd rev. ed. (New York 1966), 70–1
6 WCM, George E. Hartwell to James Endicott, Sr, 16 July 1925, box 5, file 61
7 *Ibid.*, 28 April 1925, file 60, 15 Aug. 1924, file 58
8 WCM, Endicott, Sr, to Hartwell, 29 June 1925, box 5, file 61
9 WCM, Kilborn to Dr E. Shore, superintendent of missions, 14 May 1913, box 3, file 42a
10 See Chow Tse-tsung, *The May Fourth Movement: Intellectual Revolution in Modern China* (1960; Stanford 1967)
11 WCM, Kern to Endicott, Sr, 12 Jan. 1922, box 5, file 51
12 See John W. Foster, 'The Imperialism of Righteousness: Canadian Protestant Missions and the Chinese Revolution, 1925–1928,' unpublished PHD thesis, University of Toronto, 1977, pp. 140 ff., and Paul Varg, *Missionaries, Chinese and Diplomats* (Princeton 1958), 180–93, 208–11
13 Foster, *ibid.*, 24, 331–3

9 THE WANHSIEN INCIDENT

1 For details, see Arnold J. Toynbee, *Survey of International Affairs, 1926* (London 1928), 301 ff., and Peter G. Clark, 'Britain and the Chinese Revolution, 1925–1927,' unpublished PHD thesis, University of California at Los Angeles, Berkeley, 1973, pp. 234–76.

2 EP, J.G.E. to Minnie Austin, 13 Aug., to James Endicott, Sr, 26 Aug. 1926
3 See Clark, 'Britain and the Chinese Revolution,' 238, 264–9, for evidence of the British navy's desire to take forceful action in China. Also WCM, box 1, file 7, for the circular letter by S.H. Frier, secretary of the Chungking local committee of the mission, 19 September 1926, explaining that a number of missionary families had already been evacuated because of advice from the Chengtu British consul 'as to the attitude of the Foreign Office. It was realized that the presence of so many women and children in the country made it difficult for the British authorities to deal with the situation in China, as they might otherwise desire to do.'
4 This reconstruction of the Wanhsien affair is from EP, ciruclar letter by J.G.E., 1 Nov. 1926, and Joseph Beech, president of West China Union University, to Sir Joseph Flavelle, 4 Oct. 1926, as cited by John Foster, 'The Imperialism of Righteousness,' unpublished PHD thesis, University of Toronto, 1977, pp. 360–2
5 EP, J.G.E. to James Endicott, Sr, 9 Sept. 1926
6 EP, J.G.E. to University of Toronto Historical Club, 24 Oct. 1926
7 WCM, Ashley W. Lindsay, ed., *The Daily Lyre*, a journal of extracts translated from local Chinese newspapers, Chengtu, 8 Oct. 1926, box 1, file 13. Lindsay was dean of dentistry at West China Union University.
8 WCM, Beech to Flavelle, 23 Nov. 1926, box 2, file 10
9 *Ibid.*; also WCM, S.H. Frier to Dr J.H. Arnup, 21 Sept. 1926, box 1, file 7; EP, Harold Swann to J.G.E., 17 Sept. 1926
10 EP, Swann to J.G.E., 26 Sept. 1926
11 EP, J.G.E. to Endicott, Sr, 10 Oct. 1926
12 EP, J.G.E to Charles Austin, 10 Oct. 1926. The British intention to use force again is corroborated in Clark, 'Britain and the Chinese Revolution,' 238.
13 EP, circular letter by J.G.E., 14 Jan. 1927
14 CBC, McEnaney
15 Foster, 'The Imperialism of Righteousness,' 370
16 See also WCM, Beech to Flavelle, 23 Nov. 1926, box 2, file 10
17 EP, J.G.E to Endicott, Sr, 10 Oct. 1926

10 EXODUS TO SHANGHAI

1 EP, circular letter by J.G.E., 14 Jan. 1927
2 *Ibid.*; also CBC, McEnaney
3 Carl Crow, *Handbook for China* (Shanghai 1925), 137, and F.C. Jones, *Shanghai and Tientsin* (London 1940), 1–7
4 WCM, Kenneth Beaton, acting secretary of the mission, to Dr J.H. Arnup, 11 March 1927, box 2, file 2; George E. Sokolosky, editor of an American business journal, in the *China Yearbook, 1928* (Shanghai 1929), 988, 931, 934

5 Ho Kan-chih, *A History of the Modern Chinese Revolution* (Peking 1959), 143 ff., and Harold Isaacs, *The Tragedy of the Chinese Revolution* (New York 1966), 130–45

6 Interview by author with J.G.E.

7 John Swire & Sons Archives, London, England, T.H.R. Shaw (Butterfield and Swire), Shanghai, to J. Swire & Sons, 31 Dec. 1926, correspondence, vol. 1079, Political China, 1926–27; Shaw to Swire, 29 March 1927, *ibid.*, China and Japan, vol. 42; Public Record Office, London, Foreign Office, memorandum, 5 Nov. 1934, *FO 18122/*F6568, pp. 19–20.

8 For discussion of the 'December Memorandum of 1926,' see Sir Frederick Whyte, *China and the Foreign Powers* (London 1928), 51–6.

9 According to H.B. Morse and H.F. MacNair, *Far Eastern International Relations* (Shanghai 1928), 1050–1, the number of foreign troops in Shanghai rose from 16,000 on 21 March 1927 to 40,000 a month later. A British fleet sailed from Portsmouth for Shanghai in January 1927, accompanying a full division of 12,000 men consisting of brigade each from India, the Mediterranean, and Great Britain. Winston Churchill, a member of the British cabinet, strongly supported the dispatch of the armada, urging systematic bombing of the Chinese army as well as the use of poison gas. Churchill to Prime Minister Stanley Baldwin, 22 Jan. 1927, Baldwin Papers, Cambridge University, vol. 115, pp. 205–8, as cited by Peter G. Clark, 'Britain and the Chinese Revolution, 1925–1927,' PHD thesis, Berkeley, 1973, p. 492

10 EP, M.A.E to Minnie Austin, 22 March 1927

11 EP, J.G.E. to Minnie Austin, 2 April 1927

12 Du Yu-sheng, who acquired the reputation of being a philanthropist, was the guest at a New Life Movement dinner in Chungking in 1940, at which time he told Endicott about his role in the Shanghai events of 1927. Interview by author with J.G.E.

13 WCM, 'The Present Situation in China,' sent by F.C. Stephenson, secretary of missionary education, to ministers in Canada, 26 Sept. 1927, box 2, file 14; Gordon R. Jones to J.H. Arnup, 23 Dec. 1927, box 3, file 3; Jones to Harold Swann, 23 Dec. 1927, box 2, file 8; M.P. Smith to Stephenson, 'Our Last Days in Chungking,' n.d., box 14, file 210. At this time Colonel C. Starnes, commissioner of the Royal Canadian Mounted Police, Ottawa, proposed to recruit a paid informer in Toronto to detect any Bolshevist tendencies among the Chinese community in Canada. Public Archives of Canada, RG 25, O.D. Skelton to Starnes, 8 April 1927, vol. 1470, file 529, part 2

14 EP, minutes, Thirty-first Annual Council of the West China Mission, 19 March–7 April 1927

15 EP, address of the moderator, Dr J. Endicott, to West China Mission Council in Shanghai, 21 March 1927

16 WCM, speech at dinner meeting of committee of West China Union University, Shanghai, March 1927, box 2, file 11
17 EP, 'Addresses and synopsis of discussion, West China Mission Council, Shanghai, March 19–31, 1927,' address of Dr Cheng Ching-yi; Dr Willard Lyon, in *ibid.*, and 'Should the Missionary be Discouraged?' *China Weekly Review*, 30 April 1927, pp. 221–3; Shen Ti-lan, 'The Christian Movement in a Revolutionary China,' *Chinese Recorder*, Aug. 1928.
18 EP, J.G.E to Arnup, 22 Nov. 1927
19 WCM, Beaton to Arnup, 10 June 1927, box 2, file 2
20 EP, minutes, Thirty-first Annual Council of the mission, 1927, 'Resolutions regarding devolution,' 7–8
21 See WCM, 'Statement to the Board of Foreign Missions,' 1939, box 8, file 167

11 PREACHING AND TEACHING IN CHUNGKING

1 EP, J.G.E. to Katherine Willmott, 11 April, to M.A.E., 30 March, to R.O. Jolliffe, 10 April, to James Endicott, Sr, 1 June 1928, to Charles Austin, 14 March, to T.G. Rogers, superintendent of Timothy Eaton Memorial Sunday School, 22 March 1929, to Endicott, Sr, March 1930, to Austin, 17 Feb. 1931
2 Information based on Richard Gunde, 'Land Tax and Social Change in Sichuan, 1925–1935,' *Modern China* (Beverley Hills), II, 1 (Jan. 1976), 23–48
3 WCM, Endicott, Sr, to G.E. Rackham, 25 March 1930, box 5, file 6, Endicott, Sr, to Bell, 1932, box 7, file 1
4 WCM, Bell to Dr J.H. Arnup, 6 Sept. 1932, box 7, file 2; Veals, 'Report of Work for 1930,' box 5, file 10
5 WCM, J.G.E., 'Report of Work for 1931,' box 6, file 7; 'Report of Work for 1932,' box 7, file 11; interview by author with J.G.E.
6 WCM, J.G.E., 'Report of Work for 1929,' box 4, file 9; EP, J.G.E. to Jolliffe, 12 Feb. 1932
7 EP, J.G.E. to Rogers, 3 Feb. 1931
8 Interview by author with J.G.E.
9 WCM, Bell to Endicott, Sr, 1 March 1933, box 8, file 1; EP, J.G.E. to Li Ni-ming, pastor of Little Cross Roads Church, Chungking, 10 Oct. 1932, to Bell, 22 Aug. 1934
10 WCM, appendix to J.G.E., 'Report of Work for 1931,' box 6, file 7; EP, 'Basic Ballyhoo Needs De-bunking,' n.d.
11 J.E. Moncreiff, head of the Department of Foreign Languages, West China Union University, in *Educational Review, 1936* (Shanghai), 229–31
12 EP, M.A.E. to her family, 3 Oct. 1932, 24 Feb. 1933; WCM, J.G.E., 'Report of Work for 1932,' box 7, file 11 – see also Frank Dickinson to Endicott, Sr, 18 Sept. 1933, box 8, file 5

13 EP, M.A.E. to her family, 29 Sept., 7 and 29 Dec. 1932; interview by author with J.G.E.
14 EP, J.G.E. to Freda Waldon, Hamilton, 17 Sept. 1928, to Charles Austin, 10 March 1926
15 EP, J.G.E. to M.A.E., 5 Aug. 1928; M.A.E. to J.G.E., 13 July 1928, to Minnie Austin, 11 Dec. 1928, 24 March 1931, to S.H. Hooke, 23 Sept. 1931

12 FURLOUGH IN CANADA

1 See Kenneth McNaught, *The Pelican History of Canada* (London 1969), 246
2 CBC, McEnaney
3 *Co-operative Commonwealth Federation Programme*, pamphlet (Ottawa 1933), 1, 8. On CCF development, see Norman Penner, *The Canadian Left: A Critical Analysis* (Toronto 1977), 171–217, and Walter D. Young, *The Anatomy of a Party: The National CCF, 1932–61* (Toronto 1971).
4 Scott and Vlastos, eds., *Towards the Christian Revolution* (Chicago 1936), preface, 255 ff.
5 Interview by the author with J.G.E.
6 *Ibid.*
7 WCM, Jan. 1932, box 6, file 123
8 Stanley High, *A Digest of Re-Thinking Missions: A Layman's Inquiry after One Hundred Years* (Chicago, n.d.), 21–2
9 International Missionary Council, *The World Mission of Christianity* (New York 1928), 11; also United Church of Canada, Board of Foreign Missions, *My Church and Its World Mission*, pamphlet (Toronto 1929), 3
10 EP, M.A.E. to her family, 22 Jan. 1934; interview by the author with J.G.E.
11 EP, C.A. Williams, Hamilton, to J.G.E., n.d.; see also resolution of Saskatoon presbytery in Rev. J.L. Nicol to J.G.E., 23 Oct. 1933
12 *Rotary Voice* (Toronto), 31 Jan. 1934; *Chatham Daily News*, clippings, in EP, correspondence file, 1933
13 *Chatham Daily News*, 16 Aug. 1934
14 Interview by author with J.G.E.
15 EP, Bell to Endicott, Sr, 12 July 1934
16 EP, J.G.E. to Bell, 22 Aug. 1934
17 EP, Endicott, Sr, to J.G.E., 25 Aug., 5 Sept. 1934, to Bell, 2 Oct. 1934

13 EXPERIMENTS IN MISSIONARY WORK

1 EP, M.A.E. to Effie Lafferty, Chatham, 31 Aug. 1937
2 EP, Endicott, Sr, to J.G.E., 18 March 1936

3 CBC, McEnaney; EP, M.A.E. to Endicott, Sr, 19 Feb. 1937, and file on 'The Three Chinese Boys.' Other Chinese young people whose education was supported by the Endicotts were Marjorie Lee, Wang Dzai-min, and Chou Ya-lun.

4 EP, N.A. Endicott to Austin grandparents, 23 April 1936

5 EP, J.G.E. to Hughes, 12 Nov. 1936

6 EP, J.G.E. to Jane Wright, Chatham, 15 March 1936

7 EP, Mills, Chungking, to J.G.E., 31 Dec., Roy Spooner, Chengtu, to J.G.E., 29 Nov., J.G.E. to Chungking Municipal Government, 24 Dec., M.A.E. to Charles Austin, 21 Nov. 1936; interview by author with J.G.E.

8 CBC, McEnaney. A similar opinion was expressed in WCM, G.S. Bell, Chengtu, to Endicott, Sr, 26 Dec. 1936, box 11, file 1. For information on the Sian incident, see Jerome Ch'en, *Mao and the Chinese Revolution* (London 1965), 229 ff.

9 EP, J.G.E. to Endicott, Sr, 19 Dec. 1937

10 See Barbara W. Tuchman, *Stilwell and the American Experience in China, 1911–1945* (New York 1971), 206–7; Munroe Scott, *McClure: The China Years* (Toronto 1977), 284–5

14 MADAME CHIANG'S NEW LIFE MOVEMENT

1 Interview by the author with J.G.E. Confidential reports of British consuls reported earlier anti-opium drives along the Yangtze River to be a farce, with proceeds of the 'banned' traffic being remitted directly to Chiang Kai-shek's field headquarters. Public Records Office, FO 371, 18083/F7057, 29 Nov. 1934, and 19393/F3591, J.W. Davidson, Chungking, to Sir Alexander Cadogan, London, 3 June 1935

2 The 'Gung Ho' or Industrial Co-operative Movement was initated by Rewi Alley, Edgar Snow, Sir Archibald Kerr Clark-Kerr, who was British ambassador in China, and a few other people in 1938. Soon there were 30,000 co-ops engaged in such production as making shoes, weaving cloth, surface coal-mining, etc. Endicott considered the New Zealander, Rewi Alley, to be the most remarkable and best-informed foreigner in China: 'He has travelled the length and breadth of the country preaching the gospel of mobile co-operative units as the answer to Japan's attempted destruction of China's industrial life. He has a genius for organization and for making the best use of make-shift and inadequate materials.' Broadcast, 23 Nov. 1941, Canadian Broadcasting Corporation, *We Have Been There* (Toronto 1942), 66–7

3 EP, M.A.E. to Freda Waldon, 25 Nov., J.G.E. to Endicott, Sr, 24 Dec. 1939; CBC, McEnaney

4 J.G.E., 'With the New Life Movement,' in *West China Missionary News* (Chengtu), May 1939, pp. 255–8; EP, J.G.E. to Endicott, Sr, 4 Feb. 1939; CBC, McEnaney

5 Details of Endicott's relief work following Japanese bombing raids are found in EP, J.G.E. to Jane Wright, 1 June, to Dr J.H. Arnup, 20 Sept. 1939, and in file of speeches, 1942, CBC broadcast 'In the News'; see also WCM, box 15, file 5
6 EP, file on Madame Chiang Kai-shek; M.A.E. to her family, 14 Jan., J.G.E. to Endicott, Sr, 1 March 1940
7 J.G.E., 'A Comment on the County Governments of the Kuomintang,' in DEA, enclosure in C.A. Ronning to Secretary of State, Ottawa, 17 Dec. 1946, file 11578-B-40, vol. 7
8 EP, file on General Chang Chun. Details of the Endicotts' personal friendship with the Chang Chuns are in WCM, J.G.E. to Arnup, 1 Dec., M.A.E. to Arnup, 2 Dec. 1940, box 15, file 4. The 'CC Clique,' named after Ch'en Li-fu and his brother Ch'en Kuo-fu, controlled the KMT central secretariat.
9 WCM, copy of Willmott letter received by Dr Arnup, box 15, file 4
10 EP, J.G.E. to Endicott, Sr, 1 March 1940
11 Hahn, China to Me (New York 1944), 127
12 EP, J.G.E. to Endicott, Sr, 1 March 1940, to Vincent Sheean, New York, 12 Nov. 1943, file on Madame Chiang Kai-shek, file of Endicott's reports to the US Office of Strategic Services, p. 20; CBC, McEnaney; interview by author with J.G.E.

15 FURLOUGH AGAIN

1 EP, file of speeches, 1941, 'The Missionary Contribution to China's Struggle for Self-Preservation'; 'Speech at the Empire Club' (Toronto); Canadian Broascasting Corporation, We Have Been There (Toronto 1942), 63–9. The Chinese guerilla song was composed by Lu Ho-ting.
2 EP, M.A.E. to Gordon Jones, Chengtu, 29 June 1942; WCM, Arnup to J.G.E., 29 Sept. 1941, Arnup to M.A.E., 8 May 1942, box 17, file 10
3 EP, Arnup to G.S. Bell, Chengtu, 30 Nov. 1942, J.G.E. to Roy and Kathleen Spooner, Chengtu, 30 Jan. 1944
4 EP, file of speeches, 1942, 'Address' at Timothy Eaton Memorial Church, 30 Nov. 1942
5 Kenneth McNaught, A Prophet in Politics (Toronto 1959), 288–300
6 CCF Policy Statement, For Victory and Reconstruction, pamphlet (Toronto 1942); EP, letters about pacifism, J.G.E. to Endicott, Sr, 19 Dec. 1937, to Charles Austin, 24 June 1940
7 Saturday Night (Toronto), 14 Aug. 1943, from 'The New Commonwealth' (Regina); also in F.R. Scott and A.J.M. Smith, eds., The Blasted Pine (Toronto 1957), 39
8 EP, file on CCF; M.A.E. to Gordon Jones, 29 June 1942; J.G.E. to the Spooners, 30 Jan. 1944; J.G.E. to M.A.E. enclosing 'Speech to Nanking University,' 23 Oct. 1944, dealing with Canadian politics

9 Vincent Sheean, *Between the Thunder and the Sun* (New York 1943), 368. Sheean was an American war correspondent in Chungking.

10 EP, files of speeches, 1943, 1944, 'What 7,000 Japanese Bombers Taught Me'

11 EP, Lady Eaton to J.G.E., 16 Sept., J.G.E. to Lady Eaton, 18 Oct. 1943. Dr Arnup wrote Gerald Bell, 10 Sept. 1943, to say: 'we have had a series of protests about [Endicott's] political activities, most from leading members of Timothy Eaton Memorial Church.' The proper text from Genesis 5:24 is 'And Enoch walked with God: and he *was* not; for God took him.'

12 EP, J.G.E. to M.A.E., 24 Sept., 2, 7 Oct. 1943. These letters reveal his strong temptation to become a CCF organizer.

13 DEA, Odlum, Chungking, to King, Ottawa, 31 May 1943, Odlum to Hugh Keenleyside, Ottawa, 3 June 1943, file 4558-P-40C; WCM, Arnup to Bell, 6 Nov. 1942 and 10 Sept. 1943, boxes 17 and 18, file 1

14 EP, J.G.E. to Minister for Air, Ottawa, 10 June 1943; Frank W. Price, Washington, to J.G.E., 13 March 1944

15 WCM, H.D. Robertson to Arnup, 12 Sept., Arnup to Robertson, 19 Nov. 1943, box 18, file 11, Arnup to Bell, 29 March 1944, box 19, file 1

16 DEA, Lester Pearson, Washington, to Norman Robertson, 9 June 1943, file 25-B(s); memorandum by E.H. Norman, 'Conversations with Mr. J.K. Fairbank,' 15 Jan. 1944, file 11578-B-40

17 EP, J.G.E. to L.S. Albright, New York, 17 Aug. 1944

18 EP, file of speeches, 1944

PART THREE: CHINA IN REVOLUTION, 1944–1947

Ronning letter: DEA, file 102-AZW-40C

16 ABOARD THE S.S. PRIAM

1 Barbara Tuchman, *Stilwell and the American Experience in China, 1911–1945* (New York 1971), 455 ff.; John Gittings, *The World and China, 1922–1972* (London 1974), 104 ff.; US Department of State, *United States Relations with China: White Paper* (Washington 1949), 65–70

2 EP, J.G.E. to M.A.E., n.d., written while en route to Capetown, July 1944

3 EP, file on *Gin I English Weekly*, no 3 (19 Sept. 1938), 'Mr. Mellon and Mr. Mao Tse-tung.' Mellon was an American millionaire.

4 EP, Norman Endicott to M.A.E., 16 Aug. 1944

5 *Ibid.*, 21 Aug. 1944

6 *Ibid.*, 16 Jan. 1945

7 EP, J.G.E. to Stephen Endicott, 12 Nov. 1944

8 Professor Fei wrote *Earthbound China* (Chicago 1945) and *China's Gentry* (Chicago 1953)
9 EP, J.G.E. to M.A.E., n.d., en route to Bombay, July 1944
10 EP, M.A.E. to J.G.E., 6 Nov. 1943
11 WCM, J.H. Arnup, 'Address to the London Ministerial Association,' Dec. 1948, box 22, file 507

17 SAVE CHINA BY DEMOCRACY

1 See Lawrence K. Rosinger, *China's Wartime Politics, 1937–1944* (Princeton 1945), 100–3
2 Some of the prominent Democratic League members with whom Endicott became well acquainted were Chang Lan (chairman), Lo Lung-chi (vice-chairman), Ms Shih Liang (National Salvation Association), Chang Po-chun (Third party), Carson Chang (State Socialist party), and Li Huang (Youth party).
3 DEA, enclosure in G.S. Patterson to Secretary of State for External Affairs, 20 Oct. 1944, file 11578-B-40, vol. 2; also in EP, J.G.E. to M.A.E., 10 Oct. 1944
4 EP, J.G.E. to M.A.E., 30 Oct. 1944
5 EP, 'Notes on a speech to the Sun Yat-sen Memorial Meeting of Nanking University, Monday, 23 Oct. 1944,' enclosed in J.G.E. to M.A.E., 1 Nov. 1944. Nanking University was located in Chengtu during the war.
6 *Hsin Hua Ji Bao* (Chungking), 18 Dec. 1944, translation by the Canadian Embassy, headed 'Save China by Democracy, Canadian Advises,' enclosed in DEA, Patterson to Secretary of State for External Affairs, 22 Dec. 1944, file 11578-B-40, vol. 3
7 EP, file of speeches, 1944
8 Interview by author with pastors Wang Chun-hsieh and Shu Yao-guang, and Ms Peng Shu-hsien, in Chengtu, May 1975
9 CBC, McEnaney

18 SECRET AGENT 'HIALEAH'

1 EP, J.G.E. to M.A.E., July 1945 and 9 Aug. 1945; *Toronto Star Weekly*, J.G.E., 'Why There Is Civil War in China,' 13 Dec. 1947; interview by author with J.G.E.
2 WCM, G.S. Bell, Chengtu, to J.H. Arnup, 11 Oct., ? Dec. 1944, box 19, files 1 and 11; DEA, F. Olin Stockwell, Chengtu, to Esther B. Stockwell, Oberlin, 19 Dec. 1944, file 25-B(s)
3 DEA, G.S. Patterson, Chungking, to H. Keenleyside, assistant under-secretary of state for external affairs, 'Re: Dr. Jas. G. Endicott,' 23 Dec. 1944, file 6466-40C
4 EP, J.G.E. to M.A.E., 10, 22 Oct. 1944
5 EP, telegram, John Coughlin, New Delhi, to J.G.E., Chengtu, 5 Oct. 1944

6 Barbara Tuchman, *Stilwell and the American Experience in China, 1911–1945* (New York 1971), 483 ff.

7 EP, J.G.E. to M.A.E., 15 Dec. 1944, 25 Feb. 1945; file of reports, J.G.E. to OSS, 1944–45; interview by author with J.G.E.

8 Tai Li's secret police were described by A.R. Menzies, head of the China desk at the Department of External Affairs in Ottawa, as follows: 'Tai-li is an ex-gangster ... started his present activities in Shanghai ... much along Gestapo lines with quantities of information about personalities. By instinct a sort of super cop and strong man, he is by election a distinct bumper-offer and blower-upper. He is uncultured, unscrupulous, cunning and capable ... He is loyal to Chiang Kai-shek and has direct access to him ... apart from Tai-li's ability to be actively nasty [he] is basically anti-foreign and probably more anti-British than anti-American.' DEA, 'Memorandum: Chinese Secret Intelligence Organization,' 8 May 1944, file 50055-40, vol. 1

9 DEA, G.S. Patterson, 'Interview with Dr. Endicott,' 13 Dec., Patterson to Keenleyside, 'Re: Dr. Jas. G. Endicott,' 23 Dec. 1944; interview by author with J.G.E.

10 EP, file of reports, J.G.E. to OSS, 1944–45, and J.G.E. to Philip M. Endicott, 6 June 1946; *Toronto Star Weekly*, 13 Dec. 1947; DEA, Patterson, 'Interview with Dr. Endicott,' 13 Dec. 1944, and J.G.E. to Under-Secretary of State for External Affairs, 22 Jan. 1945, file 11578-B-40, vol. 3

11 EP, file of reports, J.G.E. to OSS, 1944–45; interview by author with J.G.E.

12 Sevareid, *Not So Wild a Dream* (New York 1947), 327 ff.

13 EP, file of reports, J.G.E. to OSS, 1944–45; DEA, 'Conversations with Mr. J.K. Fairbank,' by E.H. Norman, 15 Jan. 1944, file 11578-B-40

14 EP, J.G.E. to M.A.E., 30 Oct. 1945

15 US Department of State, *United States Relations with China: White Paper* (Washington 1949), 71, 92, 99–100, 132–3, 1042 ff.

16 *CFEN*, 1, 14 and 15 (21 Oct. 1948), 'Appeal by Nine Democratic Parties of China to Mr. Trygve Li, General Secretary of the United Nations'

19 THE MICE OF NO 11

1 EP, J.G.E. to M.A.E., 9 Jan., 2 Feb., 24 March 1946, 10 Oct. 1944; interviews by author with Hsieh Tao in Chengtu, April 1975, with Wang Yu-guang and Chia Wei-yin in Chungking, May 1975

2 DEA, J.G.E., 'Student Demonstrations in Chengtu,' 10 Dec. 1944; dispatches or commentaries on the demonstrations by G.S. Patterson, Chungking, 12 Dec. 1944, R.M. Macdonnell, Ottawa, 9 Feb. 1945, Lester B. Pearson, Washington, 27 Feb. 1945, file 11578-B-40, vol. 3; EP, J.G.E. to M.A.E., 8 Nov. 1944, and Pearson to M.A.E., 18 April 1945

3 EP, J.G.E. to M.A.E., 22 Aug., 28 and 30 Oct., 2 Nov. 1945
4 For background, see Jerome Ch'en, *Mao and the Chinese Revolution* (London 1965), 260–73. John P. Davis, *Dragon by the Tail* (New York 1972), 410 ff., gives an account of American policy in China.
5 EP, J.G.E. to his family, 14 Oct., 2 Nov. 1945
6 For an analysis of the anti-war movements of students between December 1945 and May 1948, see Suzanne Pepper, 'The Student Movement and the Chinese Civil War, 1945–1949,' *China Quarterly*, no 48 (1971), 698–735.
7 EP, J.G.E., sermon, 'Strength for Action,' at Trinity United Church, Toronto, 11 March 1979
8 EP, J.G.E. to M.A.E., 8 Dec. 1945
9 *Yenching News* (Chengtu edition), 13 Dec. 1945; see also DEA, Victor Odlum to Mackenzie King, 'Kunming Student "Incident,"' 18 Dec. 1945, file 11578-B-40
10 EP, J.G.E. to James Endicott, Sr, 14 Feb. 1946, J.G.E. to M.A.E., 11 Dec. 1945
11 EP, J.G.E. to M.A.E., 13 April 1945; also J.G.E., 'A Sermonette for the Times,' n.d. [1945]

20 THE BATTLE OF THE EMBASSY

1 DEA, Victor Odlum, Chungking, to Mackenzie King, prime minister and secretary of state for external affairs, 26 Nov. 1943, file 11578-B-40
2 EP, Odlum to J.G.E., 18 May 1946
3 DEA, A.R. Menzies, Ottawa, to Ralph Collins, Chungking, 1 Dec. 1944, file 4558-V-40. See also Public Archives of Canada, W.L. Mackenzie King Papers, MG 26 J1, files 3291 and 2490 on Odlum; DEA, Norman A. Robertson to King, 18 Jan. 1943, file 4-F(s)
4 DEA, Commercial relations between China and Canada, 1940–52, file 9030-40C, especially documents of 3 March 1945, 26 Feb., 23 July, 12 Oct. 1945, Jan. 1946; Export credit arrangements for purchases from Canada by China, file 6993-C-40, letter, 'Guarantee of Credits to China,' 15 Oct. 1946; Odlum to King, 11 Dec. 1945, file 11578-B-40
5 DEA, Odlum to J.G.E., 8 June 1945, file 50055-40, vol. 2. Other references, in the order they apply following the previous note, are DEA, J.G.E. to Odlum, 18 May 1946, file 11578-B-40, Odlum to King, 10 April 1945, file 50055-40, vol. 1, minute by E.H. Norman, 19 May 1945, and Odlum to King, 30 July 1945, file 11578-B-40, Odlum to J.G.E., 19 Dec. 1945, file 6466-40C, Odlum to King, 28 Aug. 1943, file 50056-40, Odlum to King, 10 April 1945, and minute by G.S. Patterson; EP, Odlum to J.G.E., 3 May 1945, 16 April 1946
6 EP, Odlum file, Odlum to J.G.E., 2 May 1946, 3 May 1945, 18 May 1946; DEA, Odlum to King, 10 April 1945, file 50055-40, vol. 1, Odlum to J.G.E., 18 May 1946, file 11578-B-40

7 EP, J.G.E. to Odlum, 27 May 1945, 24 April, 11 May 1946; DEA, minute by G.S. Patterson, 'Dr. Endicott's Case against the National Government,' 14 June 1946, file 11578-B-40, vol. 6

8 DEA, Odlum to King, 'Dr. James G. Endicott and the Communists,' 8 June 1945, file 5005 5-40; EP, Odlum to J.G.E., 18 May 1946; DEA, Odlum to King, 27 Aug., 30 July 1945, telegram of 6 July 1945, 25 June 1946, file 11578-B-40, 8 Sept. 1945, file 6466-40C, 12 June 1946, file 11578-B-40; King Papers, 'Interview of General Odlum with Mao Tse-tung,' 28 Sept. 1945, C163972; EP, J.G.E. to Lester B. Pearson, 4 Oct. 1946; DEA, Odlum to King, 25 July 1945, file 11578-B-40; EP, Odlum to J.G.E., 18 May 1946; DEA, R.E. Collins, 'The Communist Areas,' 7 Nov. 1944, file 6466-40C; King Papers, Odlum to King, enclosing report by the military attaché, 'The Chinese "Communists," ' 16 Jan. 1945, file 2490

9 DEA, marginal notes on Odlum to King, 30 May 1944, file 11578-B-40, minute on Odlum to King, 16 Oct. 1945, file 5005-40, Odlum to Hugh Keenleyside, 17 Dec. 1943, file 4558-P-40, Odlum to King, 4 Sept. 1946, file 5005 6-40

10 DEA, Odlum to King, 18 May 1946, file 11578-B-40; King Papers, Hume Wrong, 'Memorandum for the Prime Minister,' 5 Feb. 1945, C163945

11 DEA, J.G.E. to King, quoting D. Copland, 12 Oct. 1946

12 DEA, minute by Patterson on Odlum to King, 31 Dec. 1945, file 11578-B-40, King to Odlum, 17 Sept. 1945, Menzies, 'Memorandum,' 16 July 1946, file 5005 5-40

13 EP, J.G.E. to Odlum, 7 March 1946

14 DEA, Odlum to King, 'Dr. Endicott's Case against the National Government,' with comments by Wang Bin-nan, a Chinese Communist representative, 18 May 1946, file 11578 B 40

15 EP, J.G.E. to Shirley Endicott, 30 April 1946

16 DEA, J.G.E. to King, 12 Oct. 1946, file 11578-B-40; EP, Pearson to J.G.E., 21 Nov. 1946. See DEA, Patterson to King, 12 Dec. 1944, file 11578-B-40, and E.H. Norman, 24 July 1945, file 5005 5-40, for the department's assessment of the quality of Endicott's reports from China.

17 DEA, Menzies, 'Memorandum,' 16 July 1946, file 5005-40; King Papers, Hume Wrong to King, 5 Feb. 1945, C163945

18 *Toronto Daily Star*, '150 Mosquitos Going to China as "Mutual Aid," ' 16 Sept. 1947; reference to Bethune in DEA, Odlum to King, 26 Oct. 1945, file 6466-40C; EP, J.G.E. to Chester Ronning, Nanking, 25 Oct. 1946, for Chou En-lai's comment

21 RESIGNATION

1 WCM, H.D. Robertson, Chengtu, to J.H. Arnup, 21 Sept. 1944, box 19, file 9; EP, J.G.E. to M.A.E., 25, 28 Feb. 1945; interview by author with J.G.E.; EP, J.G.E. to M.A.E., 2 Feb. 1945, 8 May 1946, to A.W. Lindsay, 2 Aug. 1946; WCM, Lindsay

to Arnup, 18 Nov. 1947, with enclosures, Arnup to G. Stanley Russell, Toronto, 13 Nov. 1947, box 21, file 29

2 EP, J.G.E. to Roy and Kathleen Spooner, 30 Jan., to Cecil Hoffman, 25 Oct. 1944, to M.A.E., 28 Feb. 1946, to G.S. Bell, 20 Jan. 1948, to Shirley Endicott, 9 Feb. 1945, to M.A.E., 20 Dec. 1945

3 EP, J.G.E. to MacLennan, 16 Aug. 1946, to Stephen Endicott, 10 Nov. 1945; CBC, McEnaney

4 EP, J.G.E. to M.A.E., 19 Feb. 1945; James Endicott, Sr, to J.G.E., 18 March 1936; J.G.E. to M.A.E., 26 Nov., 15 Dec. 1944, 8 May 1946, 12 Feb. 1945

5 Interview by author with J.G.E.; EP, J.G.E. to M.A.E., 10 Oct., 24 Dec. 1944

6 EP, J.G.E. to M.A.E., 9 Feb., 5 April 1945; file on Y.T. Wu; Donald Evans, *Communist Faith and Christian Faith* (Toronto 1964)

7 EP, Arnup to J.G.E., 27 March 1945

8 EP, M.A.E. to J.G.E., 25 Feb., 21, 23 March 1945

9 EP, J.G.E. to M.A.E., 5 April, 1 May, 14 Oct. 1945

10 WCM, Leslie Kilborn, Chengtu, to Bell and Arnup, 3 Feb. 1946, Bell to Kilborn, 27 Feb. 1946, box 21, file 12; EP, file on Chang Chun, J.G.E. to M.A.E., 25 Feb., 24 March 1946; *West China Evening News* (*Hua Hsi Wan Bao*, Chengtu), ' "Soviet Spy" James Endicott Laughs,' 24 April 1946

11 Public Archives of Canada, RG 25, G2, vol. 2412, Bell, Toronto, to J.G.E., 23 Jan. 1946, from Department of External Affairs, file 102 AZW 40, 'Activities of Dr. James Endicott and reports re: and *Shanghai Newsletter*, 1945–1963,' 2 vols. Endicott had sent Bell's letter to Ambassador Odlum as a matter of information, and this is the only surviving copy.

12 EP, J.G.E. to Endicott, Sr, 14 Feb., to M.A.E., 20 Feb., to the executive of the West China Mission of the United Church of Canada, 28 Feb., to M.A.E., 3 March 1946

13 EP, file on resignation, 1945–48; WCM, H.J. Veals, Chengtu, to Bell, 4 March 1946, box 21, file 1

14 Interview by author with J.G.E.; EP, J.G.E. to Veals, 2 March, to M.A.E., 3 March, George C. Li, Chia Wei-ying *et al.* to J.G.E., 23 March, J.G.E. to M.A.E., 8 April, to MacLennan, 4 May, to Mary's sister Jane Wright, Chatham, 4 May, to Arnup, secretary of the Board of Foreign Missions, 5 May, to the secretary of the Toronto Conference of the United Church of Canada, 5 May, to Endicott, Sr, 8 May, to M.A.E., 3 June 1946; WCM, M.A.E. to Arnup, 1 March 1948, box 21, file 478

22 THE SHANGHAI NEWSLETTER

1 Interview by author with J.G.E.; EP, J.G.E. to M.A.E., 3 June 1946. See also DEA, Victor Odlum to W.L. Mackenzie King, Ottawa, 'top secret' telegram, 31 May, file 5005 5-40, Odlum to King, 29 May 1946, file 6466-40C

2 CBC, McEnaney

3 EP, J.G.E. to M.A.E., 3 June 1946

4 EP, J.G.E. to Philip M. Endicott, 6 June, to M.A.E., 4 July 1946

5 Interview by author with J.G.E.; EP, J.G.E. to M.A.E., 12 June, to Shirley Endicott, 27 Sept. 1946

6 DEA, Odlum to King, 'Dr. Endicott and Communist Propaganda,' 10 July 1946, file 6466-40C

7 EP, J.G.E. to M.A.E., 1 Aug. 1946

8 EP, file on Chinese personalities, Li Chao-chi to J.G.E., ? 1946; interview by author with J.G.E.

9 DEA, Davis, Nanking, to Louis St Laurent, Ottawa, 'General Situation in China,' 16 June 1947

10 DEA, 'top secret' telegram, 7 June 1947

11 DEA, 'General Conditions in China,' 1 Nov. 1947

12 See WCM, M.A.E. to J.R. Mutchmor, on draft letter for 'Principles for Canadian Aid to China,' 13 Aug. 1946, box 19, file 411; also DEA, Dr Robert B. McClure, secretary of sponsoring group for 'Principles ...' to King, 21 Sept. 1946, file 11578-B-40

13 Interview by author with Chiao Kuan-hua in Peking, April 1975

14 DEA, Norman A. Robertson to Lester Pearson, Washington, telegram, 19 Sept. 1946, file 102-AZW-40C; EP, M.A.E. to Dr Ed Cunningham, 22 Sept. 1946

15 EP, J.G.E. to Stephen Endicott, 7, 29 Jan., 8 April, M.A.E. to Charles Austin, 30 Jan., to Earl and Katherine Willmott, 17 March, to Stephen Endicott, 28 Feb., 8 April 1947

16 EP, J.G.E. to Charles Austin, 3 March 1947

17 Interview by author with J.G.E.

18 Ibid. See also DEA, P.G.R. Campbell, Shanghai, 'Dr. Jim Endicott on Present Affairs in China,' 3 March 1947, in G.S. Patterson to St Laurent, 10 March 1947, file 5005-40

19 CBC, McEnaney

20 EP, file of speeches, 1947, 'Open letter to my Chinese friends on the occasion of my leaving China,' 16 June 1947

23 THE 'ENDICOTT CONTROVERSY'

1 For evidence of the Canadian ambassador's private view that Chiang's regime could not last long, see DEA, T.C. Davis to Louis St Laurent, 7 June 1947, 'top secret' telegram, file 5005-40.

2 Toronto Star, 16 Sept. 1947

3 University of Toronto Archives, minutes of the Students' Administrative Council, 19 March 1947, 14, 28 Jan., 18 Feb., 3 March 1948; DEA, E.A. Macdonald, secretary of the SAC, to W.L. Mackenzie King, 25 Feb. 1946, file 11578-B-40

4 EP, Coldwell, Ottawa, to A.O. Smith, Regina, 18 Feb. 1948

5 EP, Victor Butts to M.A.E., 10 Feb. 1948

6 EP, M.A.E. to A.J. Wilson, editor of the *United Church Observer*, 18 Feb., J.G.E. to M.A.E., 4, 24 Feb., Bruce Collier, Saskatoon, to M.A.E., 28 Feb. 1948

7 World Council of Churches, *Findings and Decisions, Amsterdam, August 22– September 4, 1948* (Geneva 1948), 43–5; *CFEN*, nos 13, 14 (Oct. and Nov. 1948)

8 EP, file of articles and speeches, 1948

9 See DEA, Davis to St Laurent, 16 June 1947, file 5005 5-40; and EP, file on arms to China, 1947–48, letters of the Secretary of State of Canada to Irene Howard, Vancouver, with enclosure, 'Persecutions of Christians by Reds Reaches Horrifying Levels in China,' 28 Jan. 1948, and C.C.I. Merritt, MP, to John Howard, 7 Feb. 1948

10 EP, J.G.E., 'A Memorandum on the Present Crisis in China,' in file of speeches and articles, 1947

11 EP, J.G.E. to James Endicott, Sr, 8 May 1946; *CFEN*, 15 Jan., 15 Feb. 1948

12 WCM, G. Stanley Russell to J.H. Arnup, 14 Nov. 1947; see also Andrew Roddan to Arnup, 11 March, Norman Rawson to Arnup, 15 March, and E.E. Long to Arnup, 27 Feb. 1948, box 21, file 479

13 WCM, Arnup, 'Notes for Address at London,' Dec., box 22, file 507, Hoffman to Arnup, 1 March, Long to Arnup, 27 Feb., Homer R. Lane to Arnup, 20 Jan. 1948, box 21, file 479; EP, file on libel suit, Endicott *v.* Toronto *Telegram*, 1948, I.G. Perkins to J.G.E., 1 April 1948; interview by author with Rev. Perkins, Feb. 1976

14 EP, J.G.E., 'Reply to the Board of Overseas Mission,' 23 March 1948, in file on resignation; see also the *United Church Observer*, 15 April 1948 and Jan. 1975

15 WCM, Melville Buttars to Arnup, 21 April 1948, box 21, file 479

16 EP, Bland to J.G.E., May, Bowles to Endicott, Sr, 5 Nov. 1948; interview by author with J.G.E.

17 EP, M.A.E. to Mary and Bruce Collier, 16 Dec. 1947

18 *Ibid.*

19 EP, 'Mission Policies in Present Day China,' 5 Jan. 1948, file on James Endicott, Sr

20 EP, file on Christianity and communism, 1941–49, 'Mission and Politics in the Far East'; *United Church Observer*, 15 Jan. 1950, 'Missions under Communist Domination in China'; *CFEN*, no 28 (Feb. 1950)

PART FOUR: THE PEACE MOVEMENT, 1948–1971

24 FOUNDING THE PEACE MOVEMENT

1 *Toronto Daily Star*, 14 Oct. 1948, report of Dr Ward's speech in Toronto

2 Writing in 1956, George F. Kennan, former US State Department expert on the

Soviet Union, said: 'The image of a Stalinist Russia poised and yearning to attack the West, and deterred only by our possession of atomic weapons was largely a creation of the Western imagination.' Quoted in David Horowitz, *From Yalta to Vietnam* (London 1967), 21. Likewise, the British historian, A.J.P. Taylor, concluded that 'the detailed records ... destroy the accepted legend completely. They show perhaps too emphatically that the Cold War was deliberately started by Truman and his advisers.' 'The Cold War,' *New Statesman*, 71 (24 June 1966), 930–1. See also DEA, Escott Reid, 'The United States and the Soviet Union,' 30 Aug. 1947, file 52 F(s), p. 3

3 This view was supported in later years by Arnold J. Toynbee who stated, in 1962, that 'America is today the leader of a world-wide anti-revolutionary movement in defence of vested interests. She now stands for what Rome stood for. Rome consistently supported the rich against the poor in all foreign communities that fell under her sway; and, since the poor, so far, have always and everywhere been far more numerous than the rich, Rome's policy made for inequality, for injustice, and for the least happiness of the greatest number. America's decision to adopt Rome's role has been deliberate, if I have gauged it right.' *America and the World Revolution* (London 1962), 92

4 CBC, McEnaney; interview by the author with I.G. Perkins who recalled Dr Ward's participation, in Toronto, Feb. 1976

5 EP, files of speeches and articles, 1948–50

6 Among the recommendations adopted by the Toronto peace movement in December 1948 were a policy of adherence to the principles of the UN Charter, opposition to reliance on regional pacts outside the United Nations, prohibition of the atomic bomb and support for the principle of reduced armaments as adopted by the UN General Assembly in December 1946, condemnation of war propaganda, support of the struggle for self-determination in the colonial countries, support for the UN decision on the establishment of Jewish and Arab states in Palestine and recognition of the state of Israel at once, opposition to the inclusion of the Franco dictatorship of Spain in the United Nations because of its record in the war and its alliance with fascism. See *A Call to Peace*, pamphlet (Toronto 1948), keynote address by J.G.E., 3 Dec. 1948.

7 'Snaring Us in the Face,' *Gazette*, editorial, 29 March 1951; see also Gerald Waring, 'The Canadian Peace Congress,' syndicated series in the *Vancouver Sun*, *Montreal Star*, and many other papers, 16–18 Aug. 1950. Waring, who was unsympathetic to the peace movement, set out to answer the question, 'Who, then runs the Canadian Peace Congress? The Canadian people? Or the Communists?' He discovered that of one hundred members of the National Council, '19 of them are either self-admitted Communists or so blatantly Communistic that their roseate political hue is obvious to everyone.'

8 *Prince Albert News Herald,* 2 March 1949

9 EP, 'Keynote Address to the Canadian Peace Congress, Toronto, 6 May 1949,' file of speeches, 1949

10 *Ibid.*

11 DEA, 'The Communist Peace Movement,' n.d., file 10833-A-40 on the Canadian Peace Congress, vol. 2; National Archives, Washington, Records of the US Department of State, Eugene M. Hinkle, Montreal, to Dean Acheson, Dispatch no 81, 9 May 1949, 842.00B/5-249

12 EP, 'The Canadian Struggle for Peace,' address in Paris, April 1949; see also J.G.E. to M.A.E., 24 April 1949

13 *Ottawa Journal,* 25 April 1949. For an account of the way American requests to carry out various military operations on Canadian territory began 'arriving thick and fast' by the summer of 1946, and of Mackenzie King's reluctance to accept too many projects for fear of undermining Canadian sovereignty and seeming provocative to the Soviet Union, see James Eayrs, *In Defence of Canada: Peacemaking and Deterrence* (Toronto 1972), 351–6. Endicott based his charges about the US presence in Canada's north on various press items such as: Associated Press (Washington), 9 March 1949, 'Two defense moves, in cooperation with Canada, were passed by the House ... a radar fence and a 3000-mile range for testing guided missiles'; a polar map in the *Globe and Mail,* 21 March 1949, marking fourteen installations used by US forces; a reference in the *Toronto Star,* 22 July 1949, to a 'hitherto secret plan' for US heavy bombers to refuel in northern Canada and Greenland on their way to potential targets in the heartland of the Eurasian continent.

14 Interview by the author with J.G.E.

15 Henry Kissinger, *Nuclear Weapons and Foreign Policy* (New York 1957), 375

16 Canadian government officials reported claims of 400 million signatures to the Stockholm Appeal, of which 300,000 for Canada were considered 'approximately valid.' See DEA, 'The Communist Peace Movement.'

17 J.G.E., foreword to *The Dean Speaks,* pamphlet (Toronto 1948), 6. For other details, see the *Toronto Star,* '10,000 Cheer Red Dean,' 8 May 1950; EP, M.A.E. to Charles Austin, 1 June 1950; Hewlett Johnson, *Searching for Light: An Autobiography* (London 1968), 280, 267

18 Canadian Chamber of Commerce, *The Communist Threat to Canada,* pamphlet (Montreal 1947), 25

19 *Watchman What of the Night?* sermon by Very Reverend James Endicott, DD, LLD, 4 June 1950, pamphlet (Toronto 1950), 7. Rev. Willard Brewing, moderator of the United Church of Canada, found it 'a rather startling situation' that some preachers had been pilloried for signing the Stockholm peace appeal because it was 'sponsored by the wrong people.' See EP, mimeo., file on ban the bomb campaign,

1949–50, opening address, 14th General Council of the United Church of Canada, 12 Sept. 1950

20 EP, M.A.E. to Dr Winnifred Thomas, 16 May 1950

21 *Ottawa Evening Journal,* 4 May 1950; see also EP, Coldwell to J.G.E., 4 May, J.G.E. to Coldwell, 5 May 1950

22 *Across Canada* (Ottawa), III, 3 (March 1949), 4

23 EP, file on CCF, J.G.E., 'An explanation offered to the Editor of "Across Canada,"' mimeo., n.d.

24 Douglas to the author at Atkinson College, Toronto, June 1974

25 EP, M.A.E. to Bruce Collier, 15 Dec. 1947 and 5 June 1950

26 Interview by the author with J.G.E.

27 *Ibid.*

28 *National Affairs Monthly* (Toronto), IX, 1 (Jan. 1952), 24; also see Joseph Stalin, *Economic Problems of Socialism in the U.S.S.R.* (Moscow 1952), 37–41, and Clemens Dutt, ed., *Fundamentals of Marxism-Leninism,* 2nd ed. (Moscow 1963), 464–5.

29 See, for example, *Calgary Albertan,* 13 June 1950, *Maclean's* (Toronto), 15 July 1952.

30 EP, notes of speech at World Council of Peace, Stockholm, March 1950, and J.G.E to Claude Morgan, editor of *In Defence of Peace* (Paris)

31 EP, letter from the Prime Minister's Office to the Canadian Peace Congress, 4 Feb. 1950

32 Interview by the author with J.G.E.

33 EP, J.G.E. to M.A.E., 9 March 1950

34 *Ottawa Citizen,* 30 March 1950; Lester B. Pearson, *The Four Faces of Peace* (Toronto 1964), 181; statement on 'The Colombo Conference' in the House of Commons, 22 Feb. 1950; speech in 1958, quoted in R.D. Cuff and J.L. Granatstein, *Canadian-American Relations in Wartime* (Toronto 1975), 118

35 Public Archives of Canada, L.B. Pearson Papers, MG 26 N1, vol. 53, Pearson speeches, vol. 2, draft by R.G. Riddell, 27 April 1950; EP, file on founding of Canadian Peace Congress, 'Canadian Peace Congress Answer to Government Charges,' mimeo., May 1950; file of correspondence, 1950, St Laurent to Canadian Peace Congress, 26 April 1950

36 EP, file of speeches, 1950, J.G.E., 'Statement on Mr Pearson's Reception of the Peace Congress Delegates,' keynote speech to the Canadian Peace Congress, Massey Hall, Toronto, 6 May 1950; see also Blair Fraser, 'How Dr. Endicott Fronts for the Reds,' *Maclean's,* 15 July 1952, p. 51, and *CFEN,* no 56 (Sept. 1952).

37 See John Swettenham, *McNaughton* (Toronto 1967), III, 124

38 EP, file on L.B. Pearson, 'Memorandum of conference with Mr. Pearson,' 4 May
   1950
39 EP, file of speeches, 1950, 'Keynote Speech,' 6 May 1950

25 WAR IN KOREA

1 Endicott's information was based mainly on Mark Gayn, *Japan Diary* (New York
   1948), and George McCune, *Korea Today* (London 1950); see *CFEN*, no 32 (June
   1950), no 33 (July 1950). For more background, see Bruce Cumings, 'American
   Policy and Korean Liberation,' in Frank Baldwin, ed., *Without Parallel: The
   American-Korean Relationship since 1945* (New York 1974), 39–108, and Gavan
   McCormack and Mark Selden, eds., *Korea North and South: The Deepening Crisis*
   (New York 1978).
2 *Winnipeg Free Press*, 27 June 1950; EP, file of speeches, 1950, 'Notes on the Truth
   about Korea'
3 *Winnipeg Free Press*, 26 June 1950; see also *New York Times*, same date.
4 *CFEN*, no 39 (Feb. 1951). See Karunakar Gupta, 'How Did the Korean War
   Begin?' in *China Quarterly*, no 52 (1972), for a reconstruction of South Korean
   provocation in attacking Haeju.
5 See Gabriel and Joyce Kolko, *The Limits of Power* (New York 1972), 576, 581,
   592, 605, for an explanation of the South Korean retreat in the summer of 1950,
   which suggests that MacArthur and Rhee conspired to provoke the North Korean
   attack and then retreated needlessly in July and August to ensure a massive US
   commitment to a larger war in Asia. Jon Halliday, 'The Korean War,' *Bulletin of
   Concerned Asian Scholars*, XI, 3 (July 1979), concludes that although the United
   States was not well prepared for the Korean War in 1950 the possibilities remain '(1)
   that elements in the U.S. state and military apparatuses were in favor of eliminating
   the DPRK [Democratic People's Republic of Korea] and encouraged Rhee to that
   end; (2) that Rhee provoked war in order to force the U.S. in to prop up his regime,
   and, if possible, to overthrow the DPRK.'
6 SEE *CFEN*, no 35 (Oct. 1950), *National Guardian* (New York), 11 Oct. 1950, and
   Far East Spotlight (New York 1951): 'Documents and Materials Exposing the
   Instigators of the Civil War in Korea,' Ministry of Foreign Affairs of the Democratic People's Republic of Korea, 1950
7 EP, file on Sir John Pratt. For illustration of Pratt's contention about the suppression or distortion of UN Document s/1496, see Denis Stairs' treatment in *The
   Diplomacy of Constraint* (Toronto 1974), 36, and Glenn D. Paige, *The Korean
   Decision* (New York 1968), 107. The complete text of the UN document is in DEA,
   file 8254-D-40, and in *CFEN*, no 49 (Jan. 1952).

8 *Mike: The Memoirs of the Right Honourable Lester B. Pearson* (Toronto 1975), II, 137, 140, 149, 150
9 Canadian forces were first placed under General MacArthur's command on 15 July 1950. See Thor Thorgrimsson and E.C. Russell, *Canadian Naval Operations in Korean Waters, 1950–1955* (Ottawa 1965), 4–5
10 *Ottawa Evening Journal* and *Ottawa Citizen*, 7 Sept. 1950
11 *Mike*, II, 166
12 EP, file of speeches, 1951, 'Make Peace Triumph over War'
13 National Archives, Washington, Records of the US Department of State, G.J. Haering, consul-general, Toronto, to John Foster Dulles, 15 May 1952, encl. 'Memorandum' by J.F. Burt, 12 May 1952, Serial no 1164; Office of Naval Intelligence, Washington, 'Canada: Report on current political, labour and subversive developments,' from J.T. Holmes, Vancouver, 19 Feb., 13 March 1953
14 Interview in *Life* magazine, 25 Sept. 1950
15 EP, M.A.E. to Stephen Endicott, 14 Oct. 1950; also *CFEN*, no 33 (July 1950), no 36 (Nov. 1950), no 42 (July 1951)
16 DEA, 'Communism and the Peace Campaign,' an address by L.B. Pearson to the Sudbury Chamber of Commerce and Kiwanis Club, 20 April 1951, file 10833-A-40
17 World Peace Movement, *Resolutions and Documents* (Vienna), 47, 61, 137
18 Interview by the author with J.G.E.; also EP, file on RCMP, 'A statement on searchings of my baggage and person by RCMP officers,' n.d.; and CBC, McEnaney
19 DEA, Pearson speeches, in Toronto, 10 April 1951, file 50208-40; in Sudbury, 20 April 1951, file 10833-A-40
20 Interview by the author with J.G.E.
21 EP, M.A.E. to Mr Nieme, Fort William, 24 April 1951, describing a gang of hoodlums blockading the doors of Massey Hall, Toronto, during a peace meeting, and singing 'the Nazi song "Horst Wessel"'; *Toronto Telegram*, 9 April 1951
22 *Canada, House of Commons Debates*, 25 June 1951, pp. 4632–3
23 *Gazette*, 26, 27 May 1950. A similar example of the RCMP's disruptive tactics was revealed at the Quebec Keable Judicial Inquiry of 1977–78, when it was proved that the security service had issued a fake terrorist communiqué in December 1971, calling for 'violence to liberate us from the capitalist tyrants.' *Globe and Mail*, 10 Jan. 1978
24 EP, J.G.E. to the editor, *South End News* (Ottawa), 5 Jan. 1962. See also *South End News*, 30 Nov., 14 Dec. 1961, for articles by Pat Walsh, former RCMP agent; EP, file on RCMP, M.A.E. to J.G.E., 8 June 1950.
25 EP, file on CCF-NDP, T.C. Douglas speech in Saskatchewan legislature, 'Bread or Bombs,' 1951; file on Christians and peace, 1950, for Hunter letter

26 CHARGES OF GERM WARFARE

1 From Mao Tse-tung's poem, 'Snow,' quoted in Mary A. Endicott, *Five Stars over China: The Story of Our Return to New China* (Toronto 1953), 35–6
2 Interview by the author with J.G.E.
3 See 'Peking Protestants and Catholics Join in Protest,' 7 March 1952, *Stop U.S. Germ Warfare!* pamphlet (Peking 1952), 45
4 EP, J.G.E. to Victor Odlum, Canadian ambassador to Turkey, 21 May 1952
5 EP, file on germ warfare charges, J.G.E., 'My Investigation of American Germ War in China,' statement to Canadian Press in London, 26 April 1952
6 Western leaders were puzzled by the absence of Russian equipment among the Chinese forces in Korea. They speculated the reason was that the Russians were only providing equipment on a barter or payment basis which the Chinese were unable to meet. From captured documents they found that there had been no free delivery of Russian equipment to North Korea. See L.B. Pearson, *Mike* (Toronto 1973), II, 179.
7 As cited in Jack Scott, 'Jelly, Not Germs,' *Vancouver Sun*, 1 May 1952
8 Cutforth, *Korean Reporter* (London 1952), 174
9 For text of Geneva Protocol, see J.G.E., *I Accuse!* pamphlet (Toronto 1952), 6. E.L.M. Burns, president of the United Nations Association of Canada, wrote to Pearson, 22 August 1952, urging that it would be 'morally advantageous' if the United States could be persuaded to sign the 1925 protocol. DEA, file 50208–40
10 Hsin Hua News Agency, *Daily News Release* (Peking), 14, 16 April 1952, copies in DEA, files 50208–40 and 102–AZW–40
11 *Ibid.*; see also J.G.E., 'Repeating All the Myths,' *The Last Post* (Toronto), Jan. 1975, pp. 47–50. Later, O.M. Solandt denied making the statement attributed to him in the *Standard* of 15 October, and Gerald Waring denied writing it, 'making it,' Endicott commented, 'the first known case to date of spontaneous composition by the linotype machine.'
12 Canada, House of Commons, Standing Committee on External Affairs, minutes of 24 April 1952
13 *Ibid.*; see also report in the *Vancouver Province*, 25 April 1952
14 DEA, 'Memorandum for the Minister: Dr. Endicott,' 25 April 1952, files 50208–40 and 102–AZW–40
15 *CFEN*, M.A.E., 'Life with Jim,' supplement to no 198 (Aug. 1967)
16 Standing Committee on External Affairs, 2,5,7,8 May 1952
17 *Telegram*, 12 May 1952
18 EP, Vlastos to J.G.E., after reading *My Son*, pamphlet (Toronto 1952), 26 July 1952
19 *Toronto Daily Star*, 14 April 1949

20 EP, file of speeches, 1952
21 Marjorie Lamb, 'The Canadian Peace Congress and the World Peace Movement,' *The Alert Service* (Toronto, n.d.)
22 *Telegram,* 12 May 1952
23 *Canada, House of Commons Debates,* 12 May 1952
24 *Ibid.*; see also *Toronto Star,* 14 May 1952: 'Death, or Life Term Seen for Aiding China, Revise Treason Law'
25 *Canada, House of Commons Debates,* 25 June 1952
26 DEA, 'Dr. James Gareth Endicott,' 17 July 1952, file 50208–40
27 Public Archives of Canada, Pearson Papers, Pearson to Wrong, 16 April 1951, MG 26 N1, vol. 35; also see Pearson, *Mike,* II, 176, 181–3
28 PAC, Escot Reid, 'Memorandum on the Korean War and the Situation in the Far East,' 19 Feb. 1952, MG 26 N1, vol. 42; Wrong to Pearson, 16 Feb. 1951, MG 26 N1, vol. 35
29 In the spring of 1952, when Endicott was making his germ warfare charges, Pearson learned from Canadian intelligence sources that US fighter aircraft were secretly making 'deliberate and repeated' flights over northeastern China as far as Mukden, in defiance of the standing orders of the UN Command. Pearson raised questions through diplomatic channels but refrained from pressing Washington as to the purposes of such flights. See PAC, Pearson to Wrong, 29 May, Wrong to Pearson, 5 June 1952, MG 26 N1, vol. 35. Documents of the US joint chiefs of staff, partially declassified in the 1970s, reveal that 'toxic chemical-agents ... specifically requested by Commander-in-Chief Far East,' were shipped overseas from the United States sometime after 21 December 1951. In the light of hindsight, the germ warfare charges do not seem so fantastic, flimsy, or ridiculous as they were alleged to be in 1952. For further evidence of a prima facie case that the United States used germ warfare, see Stephen Endicott, 'Germ Warfare and Plausible Denial in the Korean War, 1952–53,' *Modern China* (Beverly Hills), V, 1 (Jan. 1979)
30 Pearson, speech at Iroquois United Church, 25 May 1952, in EP, file on L.B. Pearson; see also *Canada, House of Commons Debates,* Stuart Garson on 27 June 1952
31 DEA, G.P. de T. Glazebrook, defence liaison, 'Memorandum for the Under-Secretary,' 21 June; 'Memorandum for the Minister,' 20 June; and 'Canadian Scientists Refute Germ Warfare Charges,' Circular Document no B71/52, 11 July 1952; all in file 50208–40
32 *Report of the International Scientific Commission for the Investigation of the Facts Concerning Bacterial Warfare in Korea and China, with Appendices* (Peking 1952)
33 For the report of the three scientists, see *External Affairs* (Ottawa), IV, 7 (July 1952), 249 ff. Among the scholars using this report as conclusive refutation of the germ warfare charges were H.F. Angus, *Canada and the Far East, 1940–1953*

(Toronto 1953), 39; Denis Stairs, *The Diplomacy of Constraint* (Toronto 1974), 262; H.F. Wood, *Strange Battleground* (Ottawa 1966), 200

34 The student newspaper, the *Gateway* (Edmonton), gives the details on 16 Feb. 1952, and in a retrospective feature 4 April 1978. See also A.R.M. Lower, *My First Seventy-five Years* (Toronto 1967), 317, and the *Edmonton Journal*, 7 July 1952.

35 *Winnipeg Tribune*, 2 July 1952, and letter to the author from Eric Wells, 24 June 1976

36 Interview by the author with J.G.E.; *Globe and Mail*, 'Endicott Not Unfrocked, Still Minister,' 11 Sept. 1952; EP, Gordon A. Sisco to J.G.E., 29 Sept., J.G.E. to E. Crossley Hunter, 16 Sept., M.A.E. to Stephen and Lena Endicott, 2 Oct. 1952

37 EP, file on Vienna Congress, 1952, Jean-Paul Sartre, 'What We Saw in Vienna Was Peace,' mimeographed pamphlet (Toronto 1952)

38 For Endicott's account of the Vienna meeting, see *CFEN*, no 59 (Jan. 1953)

27 THE STALIN PEACE PRIZE

1 *Globe and Mail* (Toronto), 6 Jan. 1953

2 EP, file on the Stalin Peace Prize

3 *Pravda* (Moscow), editorial, 21 Dec., and articles, 22, 24 Dec. 1952

4 Quoted in Anna Louise Strong, *The Stalin Era* (Altadena, Calif. 1956), 117

5 EP, file of speeches, 1953

6 See Seymour M. Hersh, 'The Angleton Story,' in the *New York Times Magazine*, 25 June 1978, for the way Khrushchev's secret speech was obtained by Western news sources, and the claim that the CIA's James Angleton planted 'disinformation' in the text. Khrushchev's speech has never been officially released by the Soviet Union.

7 EP, J.G.E. to Hunter, written from Moscow on Easter Sunday, 1953

8 Interview by the author with J.G.E.

28 RETURN TO CHINA

1 Sources and all quotations in this chapter, unless otherwise noted, are from interviews by the author with J.G.E. or from letters written by the Endicotts from China in 1952, 1956, or 1959.

2 EP, file of speeches, 1956, broadcast on Radio Peking, Nov. 1956

3 EP, file of reviews of *Five Stars over China* (Toronto 1953)

4 As quoted in *CFEN*, no 58 (Dec. 1952)

5 *Vancouver Daily Province*, 8 March 1954. For Endicott's comments on Kilborn and Allen, see *CFEN*, no 98 (Nov. 1956).

6 *Shanghai News*, 'Dr. Endicott Welcomed at Local Meeting,' 20 March 1952

395 Notes to pages 313–26

7 For background on the Great Leap Forward and the People's Communes, see Bill
Brugger, *Contemporary China* (London 1977), 149 ff.; Mark Selden, ed., *The
People's Republic of China: A Documentary History of Revolutionary Change*
(New York 1979), 381–464; and Nicholas Lardy, *Economic Growth and Distribu-
tion in China* (Cambridge 1978).

8 Joseph Alsop, 'Matter of Fact: The Commune Comes,' *Calgary Albertan*, 25 Nov.
1959

9 See M.A.E., *Five Stars over China*, 227–68. For additional background, see John
Gardner, 'The Wu-fan Campaign in Shanghai,' in A. Doak Barnett, *Chinese
Communist Politics in Action* (Seattle 1969), 477–539; and Kuan Ta-tung, *The
Socialist Transformation of Capitalist Industry and Commerce in China* (Peking
1960).

10 For further insight into the Chinese prisons of the 1950s, see Allyn and Adelle
Rickett, *Prisoners of Liberation* (New York 1957).

11 EP, Chen Wei-hsi to J.G.E., 25 June 1978

12 EP, J.G.E. to M.A.E., 27 May 1957

13 A letter from Chengtu from Rev. Clarence G. Vichert of the American Baptist
Board of Missions, reporting the results of a conference between Chou En-lai and a
group of Chinese Christian leaders in June 1950, is quoted in *CFEN*, no 34 (Sept.
1950).

14 EP, file of speeches and articles, 1952, J.G.E., 'Report on the State of Religion and
the Christian Church in China'

15 *CFEN*, no 122 (May 1959)

16 Wu Yao-tsung, *The Chinese Christian Church Rids Itself of Imperialist Influence*,
pamphlet (Peking 1951), 17

17 EP, file on Y.T. Wu, 'Some thoughts about a new orientation in Christian Theology,' and M.A.E. to her family, 29 March 1952

18 EP, J.G.E. to Y.T. Wu, 8 April 1952

19 J.G.E., 'My Impressions of Sun Yat-sen,' *Peking Daily*, 11 Nov. 1956

20 Mao Tse-tung, 'A Single Spark Can Start a Prairie Fire,' *Selected Works* (Peking
1967), I, 127

21 EP, file of articles and speeches, 1972, J.G.E., notes of unpublished 'Epilogue to
Five Stars over China,' quoting Dr Charles Hendry, director of the School of
Social Work of the University of Toronto, who visited China in 1959.

29 ONE DIVIDES INTO TWO

1 EP, J.G.E. to Bruce Mickleburgh, 10 May 1956

2 EP, J.G.E. to Dr Marion Hilliard, 19 Dec. 1957

3 World Council of Peace, *Resolutions and Documents* (Vienna, n.d.), 47, 'Resolution Defining Aggression'
4 EP, J.G.E. to Rev. Ernest Hunter, Dec. 1956
5 EP, file on Helsinki meeting of the World Council of Peace, 18 Nov. 1956
6 *Ibid.*, 'Declaration of conference of members of the Executive of the World Council of Peace and leaders of National Peace Movements, Helsinki, November 18, 1956'; see also EP, Canadian Peace Congress, 'Information Service' (mimeo.), 26 Nov. 1956
7 Interview by author with J.G.E.
8 *Ibid.*
9 EP, J.G.E. to Katherine and Earl Willmott, 11 Feb. 1957
10 Gary Moffat, *History of the Canadian Peace Movement* (Toronto, n.d.), 80
11 Interview by author with Yoshitaro Hirano in Tokyo, May 1975
12 Interviews by author with Goro Hani in Tokyo, May 1975, with Mrs Sandra Ranghet in Bucharest, September 1976, and with Roy Gore in London, September 1976
13 Interviews by author with Vladimir Brusskov, Ivy Zaslawski, Mary Prager, and Heinz Badner in Vienna, September 1976
14 *Bulletin of the World Council of Peace* (Vienna), 15 July 1957, p. 9
15 EP, J.G.E., 'Memorandum on some internal problems of the World Peace Movement' (mimeo., not for publication), 23 March 1959
16 *CFEN*, no 166 (Sept. 1963); see also EP, Scott Nearing to J.G.E., 19 Sept. 1963, protesting Endicott's line 'In a word: while war goes on, the thing to do is wage war,' saying that if the World Council of Peace had nothing better to offer the human race 'it should shut up shop.'
17 *Bulletin of the World Council of Peace*, 15 July 1957, p. 6
18 *Ibid.*, 22
19 EP, J.G.E., 'Memorandum on some internal problems,' 23 March 1959
20 Interview by author with J.G.E.; see also *CFEN*, no 199 (Sept. 1967)
21 *CFEN*, no 166 (Sept. 1963); interview by author with Ivor Montagu in London, September 1976
22 Mao Tse-tung, 'On Contradiction,' *Selected Works* (Peking 1967), 1, 332
23 For a detailed discussion of Chinese and Soviet disagreements in the peace movement, see John Gittings, *Survey of the Sino-Soviet Dispute* (London 1968), 193 ff.
24 EP, J.G.E. to M.A.E., 6 Oct. 1963
25 V. Marchetti and J.D. Marks, *The CIA and the Cult of Intelligence* (New York 1974), 52, 395. See also EP, file on British Guiana, 'Note on the trade union movement in British Guiana showing how it is under the domination of the United States' trade union movement, whose aim is the overthrow of the government of British Guiana' (mimeo.), 12 June 1963. For background on Great Britain's

relations with the Jagan government, see Audrey Jupp, *Facing Facts in British Guiana*, pamphlet (London, n.d.)

26 *Thunder* (Georgetown), 24 Feb. 1962, p. 4; see also *CFEN*, no 151 (March 1962), supplement, for Endicott's experience in Georgetown.
27 Interview by author with J.G.E.
28 *CFEN*, no 140 (Jan. 1961); EP, *Peace Letter* (Toronto), 11 Jan. 1961
29 EP, J.G.E. to M.A.E., 1 Oct. 1964
30 See Marchetti and Marks, *The CIA and the Cult of Intelligence*, 30–1, 310, for evidence of continuing CIA-sponsored raids against Cuba until the mid-1960s. See also *Globe and Mail* (Toronto), 10 Jan. 1977, 'Fever Virus Sent to Cuba.'
31 EP, J.G.E. to M.A.E., 1 Oct., and to J.D. Bernal, 7 Oct. 1964
32 'Speech by President Ho Chi Minh,' in *Bulletin of the World Council of Peace*, Dec. 1964, p. 11
33 EP, file on Hanoi Conference, Nov. 1964, 'Report by Mme Isabelle Blume on Vietnam' (mimeo.), n.d.
34 The Geneva Agreements of 1954 provided for a temporary dividing line between North and South Vietnam at the 17th parallel pending elections to be held within one year to determine a government for the entire country. These agreements were signed by Great Britain, France, the Soviet Union, and the People's Republic of China; US Secretary of State John Foster Dulles refused to sign the agreements but stated that the United States would not oppose their implementation. Later, fearing that the Vietnamese Communists would win in a free election, the United States 'recognized' South Vietnam as a separate country and set up a puppet government under Ngo Dinh Diem. See Committee of Concerned Asian Scholars, *The Indochina Story* (New York 1970), and Marvin E. Gettleman, ed., *Vietnam: History, Documents and Opinions* (New York 1970).
35 Interview by author with J.G.E.
36 EP, file on Berlin meeting of the presidential committee of the World Council of Peace, 6–9 Dec. 1964, minutes, declarations, etc.

30 A TIME OF DECISION

1 Ivor Montagu, 'The Story of the World Peace Movement,' in *New Perspectives* (Helsinki), 1, 2 (Aug. 1971), 92–5
2 EP, *Peace Letter*, 30 Nov. 1962; see also *CFEN*, no 129 (Dec. 1959), nos 157 and 158 (Oct., Nov. 1962), no 226 (April 1971), on the border war, and EP, Neville Maxwell to J.G.E., 19 April 1971. Maxwell, who was *The Times* correspondent in New Delhi until 1967, and author of *India's China War* (London 1970), said he had read earlier issues of the *Canadian Far Eastern Newsletter* with some bitterness. 'What a long, long time it took me to see clearly the realities of the Sino-

Indian dispute,' he wrote Endicott. 'I thought my reporting of it to *The Times*, while it was at its height was objective, but I had been gulled.'

3 Interview by author with J.G.E.; also EP, letters from Ivor Montagu, 28 Aug., from F. Scholl, 28 Aug., from A.L. Walker, 9 Sept. 1963; and World Council of Peace, *Information Letter*, no 32 (14 Aug. 1963)

4 EP, M.A.E. to China Publications Centre, 12 Feb. 1965

5 See *CFEN*, no 198 (Aug. 1967)

6 EP, J.G.E. to Stephen Endicott, 5 Nov. 1967

7 *CFEN*, no 191 (July-Aug. 1966), no 195 (Feb. 1967)

8 *CFEN*, no 212 (June-July 1969); see also J.G.E., 'On the Passing of Mao Tse-tung,' *This Magazine* (Toronto), XIX, 5 and 6 (Nov.-Dec. 1976).

9 EP, *Peace Letter*, 22 Aug. 1968

10 *Toronto Daily Star*, 21 Aug. 1968, '"Withdraw" Endicott Urges Soviets'

11 EP, J.G.E. to Jiri Stepanowsky, Prague, n.d.

12 EP, letter of J.G.E., 17 Sept. 1968

13 Interviews by author with Dr H. Badner, Mary Prager, and Ms C. Grundorfer in Vienna, 1976; with Sandra Ranghet in Bucharest, 1976. See also EP, Isabelle Blume to J.G.E., 24 Aug. 1968, and file on the Lahti meeting of the World Council of Peace, Nov. 1968

14 EP, *Peace Letter*, April 1969

15 Salisbury, *The Coming War between Russia and China* (London 1969)

16 *Globe and Mail* (Toronto), UPI interview with Keegan, 18 Feb. 1978

17 EP, Harrison Salisbury to J.G.E., 26 Feb. 1969

18 *CFEN*, no 213 (Sept. 1969)

19 Interview by the author with J.G.E.

20 'The Moscow Conference of Communist Parties,' *Keesing's Contemporary Archives* (London), 23437–41, 5–12 July 1969

21 EP, J.G.E. to Stephen Endicott, 16 April 1970, and J.G.E., 'Report on Soviet Far East experts meeting,' n.d.

22 *CFEN*, no 223 (Nov. 1970)

23 *Globe and Mail*, 20 Jan. 1972, 'Endicott Not Pressed to Resign, Party Says'

24 EP, J.G.E. to fellow workers for peace, 12 Jan. 1972

25 EP, J.G.E. to Janet Wringer (CBC Toronto), 15 Jan. 1972

EPILOGUE

31 THE HAPPY WARRIOR CONTINUES

1 *CFEN*, no 290 (April 1978), in reply to Jock Brown, 'China Reconstructs?'

2 As reported on 11 Sept. 1959 in Stuart Schram, ed., *Mao Tse-tung Unrehearsed* (London 1974), 149

3 For an extended discussion of Mao's moral and spiritual ideas, see Raymond L. Whitehead, *Love and Struggle in Mao's Thought* (Maryknoll, NY 1977).

4 William Hinton, 'Interview with Chou En-lai in 1971,' *China Now* (London) no 53 (July-Aug. 1975), 8

5 Blair Fraser, 'How Dr. Endicott Fronts for the Reds,' *Maclean's*, 15 July 1952; Jack Scott, 'Strange Music,' *Vancouver Sun*, April 1952; Scott Young, 'Unwritten Columns,' *Globe and Mail* (Toronto), 1 Jan. 1975

6 See EP, files of speeches, 1948 and 1962, and *CFEN*, no 293 (Sept. 1978), for Endicott's views on human rights.

7 EP, quoted by J.G.E. in letter to Marion Hilliard, 19 Dec. 1957

8 Roy P. Basler, ed., *The Collected Works of Abraham Lincoln* (New Brunswick, NJ 1953), VIII, 301, 302

9 For background on the conflict between Vietnam and Kampuchea, see Noam Chomsky and Edward S. Herman, *After the Cataclysm: Postwar Indochina and the Reconstruction of Imperial Ideology* (Montreal 1979).

10 *The Longer Poems of William Wordsworth* (London 1927), 522

11 See *CFEN*, nos 299 and 300 (March and April 1979).

12 From Wordsworth, 'Character of the Happy Warrior,' in *Representative Poetry* (Toronto 1946), II, 62

13 EP, file of speeches, 1977, sermon at Trinity United Church, Toronto, 'Building on a Rock,' 14 Aug. 1977

14 'It's Time This Prophet Was Recognized,' *Observer* (Toronto), May 1979; see also Barrie Zwicker, 'The Right to Say What No One Wants to Hear,' *ibid.*, Sept. 1972.

15 Quoted in *Observer* article, Sept. 1972

16 EP, Michel Brunet to J.G.E., 21 Feb. 1968

Index

Acheson, Dean 263, 282, 284
Ackerman, Bill 247
Adamic, Louis 130
Alberta 247, 261, 293, 300–1
Alexei, Patriarch 267
Allen, Stewart 311
Allende, Salvador 288
Alley, Rewi 144, 377 n2
Arnup, Dr Jesse 61, 63, 91, 108, 229, 230, 379 n11; seeks J.G.E. as chairman of Student Volunteers 51; on J.G.E.'s fund-raising 156; on KMT Youth Corps on West China Union University campus 220; on J.G.E.'s resignation from mission 223, 226–7, 233; controversy about Chinese revolution 252–3, 256
Atwood, C.E. 300
Austin, Allan 60
Austin, Charles 59, 75, 109, 234
Austin, Minnie (née Chapman) 59, 109, 131, 373 n2
Austin, Warren 320
Austria, International Institute for Peace in 330–1

Baker, A.W. 300
Baldwin, Stanley 130, 374 n9

Barth, Karl 156
Bateman, Dr J.F. 351
Batista, Fulgencio 338
Beaver Lake, Endicott cottage 261, 344
Beech, Joseph 97
Beethoven, Ludwig 110, 171
Beijing see Peking
Bell, Rev. Gerald 113, 132, 178, 219, 229–30, 231, 253
Bennett, R.B. 126
Bernal, J.D. 333, 336, 353
Best, Dr and Mrs Edward 190
Bethune, Dr Norman 217, 297, 346
Bevin, Ernest 263, 273
Bible: Adam 40; Amos 4, 204, 223; Belshazar 4; Daniel 4, 15, 18, 44; Darius 4; Dives 160; Elijah 4, 246; Enoch 161; Isaiah 204; Jesus: teachings about a life of service 37, 364, on sin and the nature of salvation 40–1, 360, on social justice 114, 182, 230–1, Schweitzer on 41, J.G.E.'s views on church doctrine about 54 ff., 223, J.G.E. teaches Chinese about life of 112, 115–16, 119, Y.T. Wu on possibility of salvation through unexpected channels 321–2; Job 94; King Uzziah 17; Lazarus 160; Moses 4, 5,

15, 44, 46, 223, story of, and socialism 181–2; Nebuchadnezzar 4, 15, 44; Paul 15, 57, 79; Peter 57; Pharaoh 4, 15, 44, 46; Pharisees 115–16; Pilate 227; Sampson 22; Solomon 266

   Texts cited: Acts 4:29 23; Genesis 5:24 379; Hebrews 11:8–10 261; Isaiah 6:1 17; Joel 3:9–10 259; John 3:8 112, 3:13 360; 1 John 3:14, 4:12, 20 364; Luke 17:33 37, 15:11–32 40, 4:15–20 114, 1:52 206, 18:19 224; Matthew 7:20–1 46, 5:48 224, 23:24 xi; Micah 4:3 259; Revelations 21:2, 4 39; Timothy 1:7 93

Biological warfare *see* Germ warfare
Bland, Rev. Salem 19, 35, 56, 254
Blume, Isabelle 340–1, 347
Bonino, José 370 n11
Borodin, Michael 87, 105
Bowles, Isaac 56, 57, 58
Bowles, R.P. 37, 254
Boxer Uprising 15, 89
Brace, Capt. Bert 27
Brecht, Bertolt 288
Brezhnev, Leonid 349
British Columbia 328
British Guiana *see* Guyana
Brittain, W.H. 300
Brotchie, Capt. Donald 121–2
Brown, Harold 238
Brunet, Michel 366
Buck, Tim 271, 272
Burton, C.L. 159

Cambodia *see* Kampuchea
Campaign for Nuclear Disarmament 329
Canada, politics, J.G.E. perceptions of: at the time of the Great War 19–20, 22; post-war situation 33–5; results of the Great Depression 124–6; chang-ing views of empire 129–31; World War II and its aims 157; the CCF in Ontario and support for 157–62; on relations between social democratic and communist parties 172–3, 269–72; religion and politics 38–42, 46–7, 50 ff., 125–6, 132, 160, 224 ff., 305–6, 364–6; need for peace movement to oppose the Cold War and the direction of Canadian foreign policy 263–4, 388 n13; the Korean War and opposition to participation in 282 ff.; use of the RCMP for political purposes 285–8
Canada, relations with China 209, 215, 217, 245; public support for Chinese resistance to Japan 155; embassy in Chungking 185, 208–17; J.G.E.'s advice on policy towards China 209, 216–17, 297; 'hands off China' campaign in late 1940s 245–56; Department of External Affairs opinions on J.G.E.'s reporting 167, 208, 214, 216–17; departmental advice on China rejected by cabinet 217; arms sales to Kuomintang 217, 245; Sino-Canadian Development Corporation inactive 209; recognition of People's Republic in 1970 351
Canadian Chamber of Commerce 269
Canadian Communist party: formed 34; supported by radical Christians 126; and Liberal-Labour coalition 172; J.G.E. questions split with CCF 173; and Canadian Peace Congress 264, 270, 272; J.G.E. decides not to join 270–1; J.G.E. relationship with 271–2, 343, 351–2
Canadian Council of Churches 292
Canadian Far Eastern Newsletter 270, 280, 331, 350, 360; begun in 1948 247;

pressure to cease publication of 343–4, 346, 351–2
Canadian Institute of International Affairs 246
Canadian Peace Congress: founded 1949 264; programme of 387 n6; organization and history of 328–9; media attack on 264; and Christians 269; circulates 'ban the bomb' petition 264, 270, 273, 275; second national conference of 275–6; public support for 277; opposes Korean War 283; attempts to discredit, as subversive 286–8, 387 n7; amendments to criminal code extending definition of treason 287; rally to oppose germ warfare and debate on in Parliament 294–8; United Church disassociates itself from 300; and use of Stalin Peace Prize award 304, 306; and revelations about Stalin 326; and Suez Canal crisis 1956 326–7; and Soviet intervention in Hungary 1956 326–8; and Soviet intervention in Czechoslovakia 1968 347; J.G.E. resignation from 343, 352–3; worth of 354
Cantlie, Dr James, son of 323
Canton 86, 87, 89, 140, 310; and May 30th Movement 88
Capetown, South Africa 173
Carnegie, Dale 199
Castro, Fidel 338, 339
Caughey, Col. J. Hart 236
Chamberlain, Neville 201
Chandra, Romesh 348
Chang, C.C. 209
Chang Chu 243
Chang Chun and Madame Chang 209; friendship with Endicotts 146, 181, 183, 200–1, 202, 206–7, 229; denies

KMT acting against Communists 147; tutored in English by J.G.E. 146, 180, 198; position with KMT 187, 229; and student unrest 199, 203–4; on impossibility of coalition government with Communists 201
Chang Han-fu 323
Chang Kuo-tao 349
Chang Lan 178–9, 180, 188
Chang Yu-yu 193–4
Chatham 59, 62; Park Street United Church in 60, 128; J.G.E. speech to Rotary Club 1934 129–31
Cheer, Miss 17
Chen Chia-kang 323
Chen Li-fu 144, 147, 197, 201, 206
Chen Wei-hsi (Gerald) 136, 316–18
Chen Yi 243
Cheng Chen-min (Richard) 136
Cheng Ching-yi 107
Chengdu see Chengtu
Chengtu 10, 16, 75, 90, 92, 93, 100, 169, 175, 187, 193; J.G.E. grows up in 11–12; mission press in 11, 12, 14; Canadian School in 14, 136, 151; J.G.E. gives sermon at Sze Shen Szi Church in 181–3; military draft pool in 191; J.G.E. leaves 1946 234; Endicotts return to visit 1956 311–12
Christian universities in 174, 197; J.G.E. at 175, 196–207; Youth Corps on campus 174, 175, 199, 202; J.G.E. protests latter 219–20; student unrest at 177–9, 196–207, and Chengtu Students' Self-Government Associations 202, and Union of Sympathizers and Supporters of the Kunming Students 202, J.G.E. speaks at Sao Chen Park rally 203–6, 228, 231; see also West China Union University

Chia Wei-yin 196, 381 n1, 384 n14
Chiang Ching 359
Chiang Ching-kuo 186
Chiang Kai-shek 5, 135, 192, 193, 198, 213, 243, 253, 288, 319, 381 n8; heads Whampao Academy 87; suppresses Shanghai uprising of 1927 103–5; relations with Chinese Communists 104–5, 139–40, 150–1, 175, 185, 186; kidnapped at Sian 1936 139–40; J.G.E. opinions on 140, 151, 153–4, 164, 175, 194, 209, 211–12, 245, 265; forms New Life Movement 141–2, 146, 147; interviews J.G.E. on NLM 141–2, 150–1; and *China's Destiny* 163–4; on democracy 177, 179; negotiates with Mao Tse-tung 200; Odlum on 210; Arnup on 252; James Endicott, Sr, on 255; on alliance with US against Japan 170, 185, 188; and involvement of US in China's civil war 194–5, 250, 251; possible role for in Korean War 284
Chiang Kai-shek, Madame 245, 317; leads New Life Movement 140 ff.; interviews J.G.E. for NLM 142–3; J.G.E. on 143, 144–5, 164; speaks to US Congress for aid 163
Chiao Kuan-hua 192, 238, 239, 385 n13
China Democratic National Construction Association 316
China, Republic of (1912–49): and World War I 27; unequal treaties 78, 104, 367 n4, 371 n4; extraterritorial rights in 78, 95, 96, 103; toleration clauses 78, 79; May 4th Movement 90; anti-foreign sentiment in 9–10, 73, 78, 79, 80, 88 ff., 92, 97; poverty in 82–3, 113, 114, 134; James Endicott, Sr, on landlords in 255–6; warlords in 77, 86, 94, 97, 100, 103, 112–13,

187–9; democracy in 143, 177–83, 235, 237; J.G.E. on democracy in 154, 159, 180–1, 204, 237–8; and war of resistance against Japan 154, 162–3, 170–1, 185, Canadian public support for 155, 162, Western democracies stance on 159, J.G.E. and 184–95; growth of fascism in 163; ideology of universities in 174, 197, 221–2; and opium trade 188, 377 n1; Odlum on growing corruption in 210; Endicotts leave 1947 245–6; *see also* entries below under Chinese, Missionaries, New Life Movement
China, People's Republic of: Endicotts visit in 1950s 289–94, 309–24, and report on status of peasants 312, 313–15, heavy labour of cargo carriers 312, aims and results of the Great Leap Forward 313–15, role of former capitalists 315–17, the legal system 317–18, the Christian community 318–22; position of the peace movement of 267, 333–4, 343 ff.; border war with India 343–4; the Great Proletarian Cultural Revolution 345–6; split with the Soviet Union 343 ff.; foreign policy during Cultural Revolution 346; diplomatic recognition of 285, 351; the 'gang of four' in 359; policy towards Vietnam 339–41, 363–4
Chinese Christians 79, 84–5, 91, 94, 98, 154, 183, 265, 318–22; National Christian Council of 107–8; discouraged and isolated 112; invitation to J.G.E. as pastor of Little Cross Roads Church 115; role in New Life Movement 142, 145–6; Student Christian Movement of 147; in anti-

civil war movement 203; and participation in social change 221, 320; and US germ warfare 290; and church in 1950s 318–19; and Western Christians 319–20; *see also* Y.T. Wu, K.H. Ting

Chinese civil war 200; grows from breakdown of KMT-Communist united front against Japan 162–3, 175, 178–9, 186, 188, 192; US involvement in 194–5, 200, 206, 216, 235, 251, 263; Canadian involvement in 217, 245, 263; and anti-civil war movement: J.G.E. joins 175, 202, 203–7, and *Shanghai Newsletter* 235–44, and Szechuanese landlords 188, committee established in Chungking 1945 202; analysis of by Communist party 235, 242–3; J.G.E. on 201, 237, 244, 245–7; and United Church of Canada 247–56

Chinese Committee for World Peace 289, 309, 333–4

Chinese Communist party: founded in 1921 87; alliances with KMT 87, 91, 92, 139–40, 148, 154, 162, 178–9, 200–2; and Shanghai uprising 1927 103–5; missionary attitude to 105–6; members taught English by J.G.E. 119–20; J.G.E. becomes acquainted with 191–4; J.G.E. views on 140, 171, 194, 209, 212–13, 248–52, 360–1; Odlum on 214, 215; and Eighth Route Army 140, 171, 192, 193; *Guerilla Song* 154; J.G.E. on Eighth Route Army 147–8, 154, 163; appeal to peasantry 167, 184–5; and underground movement 189; and New Democratic Youth League 196, 234; requests J.G.E.'s aid 235–6, 242; provides information

for *Shanghai Newsletter* 238, 242–3; theories and policies of: two-stage revolution 193, mass line 314, policies provide informal legal framework 318, on Christians and religion 252, 319, 322, 360

Chinese Democratic League: organized in 1941 178; opposition to KMT 178, 188, 189, 236; members assassinated 238; J.G.E. on 209, 213; and J.G.E. 242, 380 n2

Chinese Industrial Co-operative Movement 377 n2

Chinese language: J.G.E. learns 76–7, 102, and fluent in 111, 119, 152

Chinese Nationalist army: Whampoa military academy formed 87; northern expedition of 103; J.G.E. appointed officer instructor in 142; failure of resistance against Japan 170, 188; corruption in 179, 243; and fascism 188; relations with Szechuanese generals 187–9; conscription scandals of 190–1; Tung Bi-wu predicts defeat of in 1947 242–3; McArthur proposes to use in Korean War 284

Chinese Nationalist party (Kuomintang): founded 86–7; alliances with the Communist party 87, 139–40, 154, 162, 178–9, 186, 200–2; proclaims national government at Canton 89; takes Hankow 99; division into right and left wings 104; betrays Shanghai labour 104–5; and democracy 144–5, 146, 147, 148, 177–9, 194; plans to exterminate Communists in 1940 146–7; and fascism in 140, 146–7, 149, 163, 195, 244; threatens to deport J.G.E. 228–9; and San Min Chu I Youth Corps 149, 174, 175, 199, 202,

219, 242; corruption in 162–3, 167, 170, 184, 189, 194, 197; secret service of 169, 179, 191, 199, 203, 222; student opposition to 175, 189, 196–207; gains US support 194–5, 200, 235; J.G.E. harassed by 229, 242; J.G.E. on 151, 163, 175, 209, 212, 238, 245
Chinese peasantry 188; and taxation by landlords 112–13; need for social change 114; J.G.E. prediction on agrarian revolution in 1947 167; appeal of communism 184–5, 312; fear of conscription 190, 221–2; introduction of people's communes in 1958 313–15
Chinese revolution: Sun Yat-sen promotes 86–7; May 30th 1925, movement of 88–9; Wanhsien incident in 92–101; the Shanghai coup in 1927 103–5; Communist party on theory of 193; imperialism as cause of 250–1; J.G.E. explains nature of to Canadian audiences 245–7, 265, urges churches to reconsider attitude towards 247–56; James Endicott, Sr, on 255–6; J.G.E. on results of Great Proletarian Cultural Revolution 360–1
Chinese student movement: student unrest 77–8, 97, 175, 177–9, 196–207; Double Eleventh movement 199; December First movement 202; Chengtu Students' Self-Government Associations 202; Union of Sympathizers and Supporters of the Kunming Students 202; and 'the Sparks' 196–207; J.G.E. gives cover to 'the Sparks' 196, 198; 'the Sparks' bid farewell to J.G.E. 234
Chkhikvadse, Victor 334–5

Chongqin see Chungking
Chou En-lai 9, 105, 193, 214, 217, 238, 368 n4, 261, 271, 290, 346, 351; at Communist headquarters in Chungking 191, 192; J.G.E. meets 192, 322–3, 359; criticizes J.G.E. for resignation from mission 232; requests assistance of J.G.E. in publicity work 235–6; on situation in China 1946 235; J.G.E. on 251; supports freedom of religion 319, 395 n13; gives views on the class struggle 360
Chou Ya-lun 377 n3
Chown, S.D. 56
Christianity: influences on theology of J.G.E. 13, 15, 17, 24–5, 26–7, 36–42, from Y.T. Wu 224–6, 320, 321–2; ideas of J.G.E. about 53–6, 111–12, 115–16, 204, 364; May 4th Movement on 90; view of Chinese converts 107–8, 224 ff., 320 ff.; and Marxism 225–6, 271, 366; class origins of Christians 207, 321; and 'above politics' mentality 225; need for social justice as shown in story of Moses 181–2; and the Chinese revolution 17, 250, 252, 360; at universities 221–2; radical Christianity 125–6; in China after the revolution 318–22; and the peace movement 269, 305–6; theology of liberation 55, 370 n11; see also Missionaries
Chu Teh 9, 140, 185, 345, 359
Chuhaldin, Alexander 127
Chung Hwa Book Company, Shanghai 243; publishes J.G.E.'s English texts 118, 196, 237
Chungchow 80–2, 93, 95, 97
Chungking 12, 72, 79, 81, 95, 128, 139, 140, 174, 188, 193; description of 73–

4, 141; anti-foreign sentiment in 89; response to Wanhsien incident 97; protest at the Da Chang Ba 105; J.G.E. in 1927 110–23; bombing of 143, 159, 204; Communist headquarters in 191–2; Endicotts return to 1956 312–13

Churchill, Winston 157, 170, 201, 205, 262, 374 n9

Ci see Tzu

Clarke, Ernest 5

Cockchafer, H.M.S. 94

Cohen, Morris 'Two-Gun' 323

Cold War 275, 325; J.G.E. on 248–50; Dr Harry Ward on 261–2; and theory of 'Red imperialism' 262; origins of 262, 386 n2; and American policy 263, 327; and 'spirit of Geneva' 325

Coldwell, M.J. 160, 246, 270, 283

Collier, Bruce 247

Collins, Ralph 214

Committee for a Democratic Far Eastern Policy, New York 239

Committee on Principles for Canadian Aid to China, Toronto 239, 385 n12

Communism: development of J.G.E.'s thinking on 131, 175, 193–4, 360; World Council of Churches on 247; J.G.E. on alliance of non-communists with 248–52, 270–1; Arnup on 252–3; see also Canadian Communist party, Chinese Communist party, Marxism

Confucianism 90, 116, 144, 197; and New Life Movement 142; concept of crime and punishment 317

Co-operative Commonwealth Federation (CCF) 132; and the 'Regina Manifesto' 125; J.G.E. joins 157; and pacifism 157; on conscription 158;

strength in Ontario 157–8; and 'Hymn to the Glory of Free Enterprise' 158; campaign against 158–9; Lady Eaton on 160; J.G.E. defends against comparison to fascism 161; J.G.E. decides between, and church 161; M.A.E. wins Board of Education seat for in 1944 161; Communist view of 172; J.G.E. questions communist (LPP) split with 173; in Saskatchewan 173, 247; and Make This YOUR Canada 180; rejects J.G.E. membership 1948 269; and peace movement 269–70; denounces J.G.E. in Across Canada 270; on communism 270; and Woodsworth 366

Copland, Douglas 215, 216

Coughlin, Col. John 186

Creighton, W.B. 19, 63

Cromwell, Oliver 57, 248; revolution of, compared to Chinese 250

Cuba 338, 339

Curzon, Lord 262

Cutforth, René 292

Czechoslovakia 130, 144, 346–8

Dai see Tai

Darwin, Charles 39, 54

D'Astier de la Vigerie, Emmanuel 332

Davis, Prof. Chandler 346

Davis, T.C. 239

Democracy: J.G.E. speaks on 159, 180–1, 274–5, and reflects on nature of while detained by RCMP 285; concepts of liberty: advanced by the Dean of Canterbury 268, by J.G.E. 361–2, by Lincoln 362

Deng see Teng

Dickinson, Frank 100

Diefenbaker, John 287, 294, 297
Diggers club 38
Dineen, Jacqueline 328, 331
Ding *see* Ting
Domm, Rev. Gordon 246
Dong *see* Tung
Douglas, T.C. 173; invites J.G.E. to speak to Saskatchewan legislature 247, 328; and peace movement 270, 288; on J.G.E. 270
Drew, George 283, 287, 298
Du Yu-sheng 105, 374 n12
Dubois, W.E.B. 288, 296
Ducharme, Yvan 302
Duckling Pond (Chungking): Endicotts live at 76, 171; old ways at 120; J.G.E. teaches at Gin I Middle School 134, 137; Endicotts revisit in 1956 313
Dulles, John Foster 250, 279, 281

Eaton, Lady Flora McCrea 160–1, 379 n11; *see also* Timothy Eaton Memorial Church, Timothy Eaton Company
Eddy, Sherwood 51
Edwards, Rev. Simon 301
Egypt, Suez Canal crisis 326
Ehrenburg, Ilya 266, 288, 304, 327
Empress of Australia 67, 71; *of Asia* 123; *of Russia* 133
Endicott, Dr Charles 46
Endicott, Ella 350, 359
Endicott, Enid 11
Endicott, Very Rev. James 16, 23, 371 n15; speech 1952 3–5, 296; arrives in Kiating 7, 9–10; background on 8; as parent of J.G.E. 13–18, 19, 62, 108, 133, 135, 222, 254–6; defends J.G.E.'s position on China and calls for change in church policy 1948 255–6; theology

of 15, 17, 55; and British empire 15–16, 254; on World War I 20; and church unity 53; at founding conference of the United Church of Canada 56–8; and Mary Austin 60; on missionaries in China 89, 91, 106
Endicott, James Gareth: birth and childhood in China 11 ff.; relationship to Chinese people 12, 79–80, 111–12, 136, 167, 185, 190, 209, 311; life in Canadian army 19 ff.; enters university, wins Moss scholarship 35; influences and attitude to theology 13, 15, 17, 24, 25, 26–7, 36–42, 53–6, 115–16, 156, 204, 219–34, 364; first censured by church authorities 46–7; appointment as missionary to West China 52; ordination 52 ff.; marriage 1925 66; arrives in China 1925 71–3, 75–6; response to nature 93, 136, 261, 350, dedication v; attitude to danger 93–4; gets typhus fever 110; learns to play violin 121–2, 127; raises children 122, 136–7, 170–2; prophetic sense of 131, 163, 167, 212, 232, 243, 365; predicts outcome of Chinese civil war 245; furlough in Canada 124 ff., 153 ff.; receives honorary doctor of divinity 156; joins CCF 157; returns to China 1944 164; transformed to committed revolutionary 206–7; self-criticism 222–3, 224; resigns from mission 223, 228, 232 ff.; reunion with M.A.E. in Shanghai 239–42; leaves China 1947 243–4; decides to enter peace movement 263; wins Stalin Peace Prize 303 ff.; attitude to human rights 361–2; awarded Lenin Centennial Medal 350; marriage to Ella

Hansen 350; resignation from peace movement 252 ff.; on learning from China 361

Speeches of cited: in Chungking, list of 119; across Canada to raise mission funds 1933 128–31, 1941–44 153–60; to Empire Club in Toronto 1941, on Chiang Kai-shek and democracy in China 153–4; to Toronto Board of Trade 1944, on social change 158–60; on CBC 'Danger Signals in the Far East' 163; on democracy 180–1; sermon on 'Moses and the Principle of Livelihood' 181–2; at Szechuan University under KMT 199; at Sao Chen Park 204–6; to Shanghai friends on departing from China 244; across Canada to publicize nature and purposes of the Chinese civil war/revolution 245–7; to Paris Congress of the Partisans of Peace 1949 266–7; to Manitoba Peace Council on Korean War 278–80; in Toronto on General MacArthur 284; at Maple Leaf Gardens, Toronto, on germ warfare 295–8; in Moscow on receipt of Stalin Peace Prize 305–6; at 90th birth anniversary of Sun Yat-sen, Peking, 1956 323; sermons at Trinity United Church, Toronto, 'Building on a Rock' 1977 364; 'Strength for Action' 1979 203

Endicott, Mary Elsie (née Austin): family background 59 ff.; marriage to J.G.E. 66; letter on arrival in China 1925 71 ff.; on being a missionary's wife 83–4, 121, 128, 134, 135, 155, 241, 242; raises children 122, 131, 135; teaches English 136; wins York Township Board of Education seat

161–2, 240; reacts to J.G.E.'s letter of resignation from mission 226–8; joins J.G.E in Shanghai 1946 236, 239–42; and Communist party 271; writes *Five Stars over China* 310; works with J.G.E. in peace movement 331; death of 345

Endicott, Norman Austin 76, 136, 164, 204; questions about Communist prisoners 120; letter of 137; influences father on Marxism 170–1, 379 n4

Endicott, Norman J. 11, 14, 35

Endicott, Philip Michael 122

Endicott, Sarah (née Diamond) 7 16 *passim*

Endicott, Shirley Jane 122

Endicott, Stephen 109, 128, 241; on germ warfare 393 n29

Engels, Friedrich 173

English teaching: methods used in China 117–18; and *Gin I English Weekly* 137–9; Chinese boys live with Endicotts 136; and J.G.E.: teaches at West China Union University 151, 152, trains interpreters for US army in China 186, meets members of business and official community through 209

Ethiopia, compared to Kampuchea 363

Fairley, Margaret 38

Fascism: just war against 157, 363; J.G.E. on 161; *see also* Chinese Nationalist party

Fei Hsiao-tung 173–4

Fellowship for a Christian Social Order 126

Fellowship of Reconciliation 329

Feng Yu-hsiang 142, 289

Fenn, William P. 228–9
Fong, S.H. 220
Forrest, Rev. A.C. 365
France 96, 130, 263, 266, 326; J.G.E. in army in 24–9; Chinese revolution compared to French 250; in Algeria 326; and World Council of Peace 330
Franco, Gen. Francisco 161
Fraser, Blair 361
Frazer, James 111
Fulton, Davie 286

Galileo, Galilei 54
Gandhi, Mahatma 159
Gardner, Ray 328
Garibaldi, Giuseppe 15
Garson, Stuart 286, 287, 293, 294, 300
George, Lloyd 20
Gerlach, Telitha 238
Germ warfare: US failure to sign Geneva Protocol 292, 392 n9; J.G.E. investigates reports of in Northeast China 290–1; J.G.E. reports on findings 291–8; background to American use of 292; Canadian government responds to charges of 294, 295, 298–300; American citizens are tried for sedition based on germ warfare charges 323; US military shipment of toxic agents to Far East 393 n29
Germany 90, 157, 172, 265; imperialism of 19; consul in China complains about J.G.E. 139; provides advisers to Chiang Kai-shek 140
Gong see Kung
Gordon, Huntley 38
Gore, Roy 330
Gould, Randall 239
Graydon, Gordon 294, 297
Great Britain 9, 16, 263, 326; J.G.E.

with Canadian army in 22–3; press criticizes missionaries 71–2; protects missionaries in China 97–101; in World War II 163; see also Imperialism
Gundy, Dorothy (née Endicott) 11, 16
Gundy, Joyce and Carolyn 345
Guo see Kuo
Guomintang (KMT) see Chinese Nationalist party
Guyana 337, 338, 396 n25

Haeju (Korea) 280, 281
Hahn, Emily 149
Haig, Field Marshal Douglas 25
Halliday, Clarence 35
Hani, Goro 329–30
Harlan, Bryan and Elizabeth 198
Harris, Walter E. 286
Hartwell, George E. 89, 91
Heakes, Air Commodore Vernon 162
Hikmet, Nazim 288
Hilliard, Dr Marion 63, 395 n2
Hirano, Yoshitaro 329
Hitler, Adolf 144, 158, 160, 254, 330; and empire 129, 130; attacked in the English Weekly 139; and fascism 161
Ho Beh-hen 119, 189, 209
Ho Chi Minh 340
Ho Ying-chin, Gen. 144, 148, 213
Hoffman, Rev. A.C. 253
Hooke, Samuel H. 41, 46, 48, 55, 60, 61, 369 n12 and 17, 376 n15; and Bible study 37–8
Howey, Rev. Bill 23
Hromadka, Rev. Josef L. 270, 288
Hsieh Tao 196, 381 n1
Hsu, Milton 237
Huang see also Hwang
Huang, Col. J.L. 151

Hughes, Leslie 138
Hungary 284, 303, 326–8
Hunt, Miss 13
Hunter, Rev. Ernest Crossley 288, 307
Hurley, Patrick 194–5, 200, 215
Hwang Gang-wei (George) 136
Hwang Min-an 135–6, 316

Ilsley, J.L. 217
Imperialism: empire defined by J.G.E. 129–30; in Suez Canal crisis 326; *American* 251, 280, 282, Arnold Toynbee on 387 n3, and Truman Doctrine 262, J.G.E. analysis of 263, 279, 296, 343, 363, Chinese analysis of 333–4 (*see also* United States); *British* 154, Canadian missionary respect for 15–16, J.G.E.'s attitude towards 16, 31, 86, 95–6, 129, 138–9, uses gunboat diplomacy in China 15, 92, 94–5, 99–101, and May 30th incident 88–9, and Wanhsien incident 94–5, 97, 373 n4, military forces in China increased 374 n9, business community of in China supports Chiang Kai-shek 104, aids Japan against China 143–4, and Europe 130; *Chinese* 164; *Japanese* in China 128, 129, 130, 139, 140, 170–1, 205, 250, bombs Szechuan 143, aided by US and Britain 143, attacks Pearl Harbor 156, and Ichigo offensive 170, Chiang Kai-shek negotiates with 188; *Soviet* 'Red imperialism' 262, 279, social imperialism 363; *see also* China, Missionaries
India 155, 185, 364; Bombay 169; Calcutta 169; India-China war 343–4
International Institute for Peace 330–1, 344

Irvine, William 19, 34, 270
Italy 96, 130, 139, 157
Ivens, William 19

Jackson, Prof. Gilbert 38
Jacoby, Annabel 178
Jagan, Cheddi and Janet 337–8
Japan 9, 90, 155, 157, 279, 329, 363
Jennison, Mary 264, 328
Jia *see* Chia
Jiang *see* Chiang
Jiang, Hilde 233–4, 241
Johnson, Hewlett, Dean of Canterbury 171, 267–9, 274
Johnson, Lyndon 340
Joliot-Curie, Frédéric 266, 305, 332, 333, 336, 353
Jolliffe, E.B. 158, 160
Jolliffe, R.O. 77, 125
Jones, Miss 13
Jones, Gordon R. 374 n13, 378 n2
Judd, Walter H. 51, 214, 311

Kampuchea 363, 364
Kang Tseh, Gen. 150
Kang Yu-wei 9
Kashtan, William 271, 351–2
Kay, Brig. Orville 210, 301
Keegan, George 348
Kell, Rev. Jack 55
Kellerman, Jack 247
Kelly, Dr C.B. 79–80
Kennan, George F. 386 n2
Kennedy, John F. 340
Ker, Leah 14, 16
Kern, D.S. 90, 91
Kerr, John 43
Ketchum, Davidson 49–50, 158
Khrushchev, Nikita 306–7, 326, 394 n6
Kiating 7–11, 89, 99, 143, 185; Mount

Omei 7, 191; Bei Ta Gai (White Pago-da Street) 11

Kilborn, Dr Leslie 12, 229, 230, 311, 384 n10

Kilborn, Dr O.L. 9, 89

Kim Yen-song 302

King, W.L. Mackenzie 34, 162, 210, 213, 239; and World War II politics 158, 172, 173; and Odlum 208; 215; and Canadian policy on Korea 282

Kipling, Rudyard 129, 138

Kitchlew, Saifuddin 302

Kobler, Dr Fritz 241

Kong see Kung

Korean War: origins of 280, 281, 390 n4–7; Sir John Pratt on origins of 282; J.G.E. on origins of 278–9; missionaries in China support American role in Korea 320; UN on 278; Yvan Ducharme on 302; Americans tried for sedition over charges of germ warfare 323; forces in: Canadian 283, 391 n9, American 280; and J.G.E. on US involvement 279–80; absence of Soviet arms 392 n6; and J.G.E. on Soviet involvement 279; J.G.E. on UN stance 282–3; Chinese People's Volunteers 283–4, 287

Kosygin, Alexei 351

Kuerti, Prof. Anton 346

Kulushney, Vladimir 348–9, 351

Kung, H.H. 201

Kung, Madame H.H. 145, 189

Kung Peng 192–3, 290, 322

Kunming 174; December 1st Movement in 202; Alumni Association of Lienta University of 205

Kuo Mo-jo 77, 289, 302, 331, 371 n2

Kuomintang (KMT) see Chinese Nationalist party

Labour Progressive party 172; see Canadian Communist party

Laymen's Foreign Missions Inquiry, report on role of missionaries 127–8

League of Nations: and imperialism 128, 129, 130; and Lytton Commission 159; failure of 363

Lee Yeh-yeh 84

Lenin, Vladimir 159, 171, 172, 192, 357; on war 272; centennial medal 350; and 'key link' 335

Leshan see Kiating

Lewis, David 161, 270

Li see also Lee

Li Chao-chi 196, 236–7, 384 n14, 385 n8

Li Hsien-nien 235, 238

Li Huang 178

Li Kung-po 238

Li Pei-lin 291

Li Teh-chuan 142, 289

Liao Cheng-chih 333–4

Liberalism: in China 90; of the middle class 362

Lincoln, Abraham 15, 20, 130, 150, 153; on liberty 362

Lindsay, Dr Ashley 219–20, 229, 230–2, 373 n7, 383 n1

Lindsey, Benjamin B. 122

Lippmann, Walter 276

Liu Hsiang, Gen. 117

Liu Po-cheng 243

Liu Wen-hui, Gen. 100, 188

Lo Lung-chi 242

Loshan see Kiating

Louis, Victor 349

Lu Tso-fu 209, 229

Luce, Henry 215

Luckock, Mrs Rae 270, 286

Lukács, Georg 288

Ludendorff, Gen. Erich von 29

Ma Yin-chu 238

McAree, J.V. 304

MacArthur, Gen. Douglas 280, 281, 283, 284, 390 n5

Macaulay, Thomas B. 248, 311

McCarthy, Joseph 272, 274

McClung, Nellie 19

McClure, Dr Robert 156, 385 n12

MacDonald, Donald 270

MacDonald, Evelyn 17

MacDonald, Ramsay 173

McGee, Harry 44

MacInnis, Angus 270

MacKenzie, Norman A. 51

MacKillop, Rev. Charles 8

MacLennan, Rev. David 221

MacMillan, Hugh 51

McNaughton, Gen. A.G.L. 276

Mair, Austin 45–6

Malraux, André 105

Manchuria: Japanese occupation of 139, 159; KMT army in 243; effects of germ warfare 291

Manitoba: Brandon 156; Winnipeg 34, 267, 278; J.G.E. speaks at Manitoba Peace Council 278

Manning, Harold 38

Manning, Mary (née Endicott) 9, 11, 13, 368 n9 and 12

Mao Tse-tung 5, 9, 140, 171, 175, 193, 214, 226, 238, 279, 357; Endicotts meet 309; and 1945 negotiations with KMT 200; on law of contradiction 259, 335; on need for personal transforma-tion 318, 360; and peasants 184, 312; on how to learn from others 361; on the 'mass line' and class struggle 314, 360; on the inevitability of revolution 323; Soviet hostility to 349; J.G.E. critical about personal exaltation of 345; death of 359

Marshall, Gen. George 216, 235, 236

Marx, Karl 173, 199, 357

Marxism: enters China 90, 199, 361; J.G.E. and son argue about 171–2; J.G.E. wishes to know more about 171–3; studied by Chinese university students 198; and Christianity 225–6, 271, 364, 366; and USSR foreign policy 262, 363; Communist Manifesto 172, 250, J.G.E. on 173

Maxwell, Neville 397 n2

Meighen, Arthur 34, 157–8

Menzies, Arthur 217, 381 n8

Methodist Church of Canada 8, 10, 40; supports World War I 19; challenged by social gospel 34; appoints J.G.E. as missionary 52; and church unity 53; finances China missions 91; Chinese Communist legal system similar to old-fashioned Methodist class meeting 317

Mickleburgh, Bruce 294, 326, 328

Mikoyan, Anastas 338

Mills, E.W.P. 139

Milton, John 57, 311

Missionaries, in China 15, 50, 71, 92, 94; obstacles to work in China 77–9; re-sponse to Chinese nationalism 79–80, 89, 90–1, 106–8; and Wanhsien incident 97–100; protected by warlords 100; heyday in China ends 100, 102–8; and education 174, 197, 312; as defenders of the status quo 220–2; as agents of imperialism 100–1, 107, 138, 207, 220, 320; and anti-communism 105–6; and 'accepted framework of the church' 230–2; Arnup on role of 252; Chinese com-munists on 171; criticized by Cana-dian newspapers 127, by Laymen's Foreign Missions Inquiry 127–30; North American Foreign Missionary

Conference 60; International Missionary Council 1928 128; and J.G.E.: views on 52, 95, 100–1, 131, 134–5, 153, sees work as foundation of international co-operation 154–5, experiments with types of mission work 135, work and theology criticized by 116, 132, 206, 219, 229–30, relations with 1944 219, 230–2, views as narrow and overly cautious 219, writes 'The Christian Good Samaritan Passes By on the Other Side' to expose missionary attitude towards oppressed Chinese 221–2, on proper role of 230–1; see also West China Mission, West China Union University

Molotov, V.M. 273
Montreal 217, 246, 285, 295
Moore, Rev. T. Albert 45
Morgan, Rev. John 345
Morgan, J.P. 284
Morgan, Wesley and Hattie 80, 84
Morris, Leslie 271–2
Moscow 87, 273, 276–7, 305
Mott, John R. 8, 48, 50, 51, 370 n1 and 4
Movement for peaceful coexistence: J.G.E. views missionaries as agents of international co-operation 154–5; communists in 272, 387 n7; Paris Congress of the Partisans of Peace 266; J.G.E. helps draft Stockholm Appeal 267; sends delegation to USSR 273, 276–7; J.G.E. on significance of 296; J.G.E. wins Stalin Peace Prize for role in 303–8; China's position on 333–4; in Canada: J.G.E. helps to organize 263, grows 264–77, government responds to 265, Dean of Canterbury speaks to 268–9, opposition to 268, 269, and Christians 269, and

CCF 269–70, and business 269, and government 275, 276; see also Nuclear disarmament, Canadian Peace Congress, World Council of Peace
Mussolini, Benito 129, 130, 139, 161, 363

Nanking 89, 99, 104, 105, 139, 140, 188, 228, 234
National liberation: American attitude towards 263; in British Guiana 336–8; in Cuba 338–9; in Vietnam 339–41; China on 333–4; see also Chinese revolution
Nearing, Scott 396 n16
Needham, Joseph 300, 357
Nehru, Jawaharlal 159, 302, 344
Neruda, Pablo 288
New Life Movement 154, 317; begun by Madame Chiang 140; J.G.E.'s assistance requested 140, 151; J.G.E. works for 140–51, 175; Madame Chiang defines 142; and People's Anti-Opium Movement 142; and war of resistance against Japan 142; composition of 142, 150; and Women's War Service Clubs 144; and War Service Clubs 145; and anti-communism 145; and anti-democratic KMT link 149–51; J.G.E. criticizes move to the right 149–51
New Testament 15, 53, 223
New York 124, 169, 266, 268
Niagara Falls 269, 323
Nichol, Helen R. 51
Niebuhr, Reinhold 125–6, 226, 322
Nikolai, Metropolitan 305
Nixon, Richard 350, 351
North Atlantic Treaty Organization (NATO) 263–4, 275, 347

Noseworthy, Joseph 157, 160
Nuclear disarmament: Baruch Plan for 276; China on 334; Stockholm Appeal 1950 285, 388 n16, J.G.E. helps to draft 267, international response to 267, church response to 269, presented to Soviet government 273–4, presented to Canadian government 275–6, press attempts to remove signatures from 288; see also Canadian Peace Congress, Movement for peaceful coexistence, World Council of Peace

Odlum, Gen. Victor 208–17, 238, 239; requests J.G.E.'s services 162; description of 208; on Chiang Kai-shek 209–10, 212; and J.G.E. 211, 214; on J.G.E. 208, 209, 211, 216; and attempt to deport J.G.E. 229; on China situation 194, 210, 214, 215; world view of 214–15; on China-Canada relations 209; on Chinese Communists 214
Old Testament 15
Ontario 157–8, 283
Opium Wars 9

Pacifism 157, 265, 331–2, 378 n6
Palmer, Harold E. 117
Pan Wen-hua 187
Peaceful coexistence see Movement for peaceful coexistence
Pearson, Lester 274, 276, 297, 326; friend of Mary Austin 60; helps arrange her passage to China 239–40; thanks J.G.E. for reports on development of Chinese revolution 167, 217; supports us leadership in world affairs 263, 275; rebukes J.G.E. as having

'sold his soul to Moscow' 275; on Canadian policy about Korea 282, 284, 299, 393 n29; on atomic war 285; condemns Canadian Peace Congress 286; and germ warfare issue 291, 294, 295, 298, 393 n29; critical of American foreign policy 299; advises against prosecuting J.G.E. for sedition 298
Peking 88, 89, 174, 289, 359
Pen Chi-ling 11
Peng Teh-huai 345
Perkins, Rev. I.G. 55, 252, 262, 386 n13
Pham Van Dong 341
Picasso, Pablo 288
Pincock, Dr Alex and Ida 80, 82–3, 84, 95, 99, 100, 371 n1
Platts-Mills, John 273
Plisetskaya, Maya 273
Poland 266, 284, 285
Powell, J.B. 104
Powell, J.W. (Bill) and Sylvia 238, 290, 323
Pratt, Sir John 282, 390 n7
Purcell, Henry 122

Qiao see Chiao
Quebec 159, 274, 275, 283

Ranghet, Sandra 330
Rauschenbusch, Walter 55, 370 n10
Red Lantern Society 92
Reliable Exterminators Inc. 162
Renison, Rev. R.J. 247–8
Rhee, Syngman 279, 281, 288, 319, 390 n5
Rhodes, H.G. 280–1
Robertson, Gen. Walter 215
Robeson, Paul 288, 304
Robinson, Lukin 345
Rodd, Nora 298

Rogge, John 274–5
Ronning, Chester 167, 240, 364
Roosevelt, Franklin D. 194, 274; Four
 Freedoms 157, 204, 207; and Amer-
 ican army in China 185, 206
Rowell, Hon. Newton 129
Royal Canadian Mounted Police 374
 n13; detains J.G.E. on return from in-
 ternational travel 285–6, 295;
 attempts to disrupt the peace
 movement 287, 391 n18, 23, and 24;
 on J.G.E. 299
Russell, Bertrand 122
Russia see Union of Soviet Socialist Re-
 publics
Rutherford, Gertrude 51
Ryerson, Stanley 271

St John's University, Shanghai 237, 242
St Laurent, Louis: and Canadian involvement in a third world war 266; refuses
 to meet Canadian Peace Congress 273,
 274; arranges for Congress meeting
 with Pearson 275; and Korean War
 282; on People's Republic of China
 311
Salisbury, Harrison 348–9
Sanderson, Eva 264, 270
Sapiro, Aaron 46
Sargeant, Clyde 186
Sartre, Jean-Paul 288, 302
Saskatchewan 247, 281; J.G.E. circuit-
 riding in 43–7; J.G.E. helps wheat
 pool organization 45–6; CCF in 125,
 173; and role of religion to preserve
 status quo in 220; peace council brief
 to legislature on Hungary 1956 327–8
Schnierson, Vic 238
Scholl, Dr Friedrich 330, 344

Schuman, Julian 323
Schweitzer, Albert 41, 223, 370 n18
Scott, Prof. R.B.Y. 126
Seeger, Alan 31
Sevareid, Eric 193
Shakespeare, William 35, 363
Shanghai 67, 71, 78, 87, 95, 185, 200; and
 May 30th Movement 88; French con-
 cession in 102, 237; discontent in
 1927 103, 104–5; International
 Settlement 103; universities domin-
 ated by Kuomintang 174; J.G.E. lives
 in to write Shanghai Newsletter 235–
 44; J.G.E. on 236; J.G.E. gets job at
 Medhurst College 237; and Shanghai
 Club 238; and Endicotts re-united in
 1946 239–42
Shanghai Newsletter: J.G.E. publishes
 235–6; content of first edition 19 June
 1946 237–8; readers of 238–9; tenor
 of 238; role of, to counter American
 official version of events in China 239;
 M.A.E. assists with 241; continuation
 of as Canadian Far Eastern
 Newsletter 247
Sharman, H.B. 36, 40, 41, 60, 369 n9
Sheean, Vincent 163, 378 n12, 379 n9
Shelley, Percy B. 39
Shen Ti-lan 107, 203, 230–2, 234, 375
 n17
Shenyang (Mukden) 290–1, 293
Sheridan, Dr W.J. 116
Shih Liang 317
Shortliffe, Glen 274
Shostakovich, Dmitri 273
Sian incident 1936 139–40
Sibley, Mrs W.E. 92, 99
Sichuan see Szechuan
Sihanouk, Prince Norodom 363

Sims, Charles 280–1
Sino-Japanese War, 1894–95 9
Sisco, Rev. Gordon 301
Sissons, C.B. 254
Skelton, O.D. 35
Skobeltsyn, Dimitri 303
Small, Walter 100
Smedley, Agnes 171
Smith, Howard K. 304
Smith, Rev. Laval 246
Smith, Lloyd 46
Social change: and missionaries xi–xii;
  movement for in Canada 124–6; the
  development of J.G.E.'s understand-
  ing of 124–32, 160, 181–3, 191, 206–
  7, 361; J.G.E. speaks to Toronto
  Board of Trade on need for 159;
  J.G.E. on 'hero' theory of history
  211; J.G.E. questions the ability of the
  church in China to be part of the strug-
  gle for 220–2; and Christian belief in
  226; J.G.E. on need for missionaries to
  participate in 230–1; Joseph
  Needham on 357; see also Commun
  ism
Socialism see Social change, Marxism,
  Christianity
Society of Friends 329
Solandt, O.M. 293, 295, 297, 392 n11
Soong Ching-ling 145, 163, 288, 305
Soong, T.V. 201, 209, 213
Sorokin, Valentine 334
Sparling, George 230–2
Sri Lanka, World Council of Peace meet-
  ing at Colombo 1957 331–5
Stalin, Joseph 192, 264, 273, 318, 326;
  and China 195; and peace 268, 272;
  Stalin Peace Prize 303; dies 304;
  J.G.E. on repudiation of 306–7

Stevens, Col. Harley 186
Stevenson, R.L. 24, 27
Stewart, Jean 328
Stilwell, Gen. Joseph 175; in China 169;
  and KMT corruption 170; and alliance
  with Communist forces 170–1, 185;
  and J.G.E. as liaison officer with forces
  of 185–95
Stockholm Appeal see Nuclear dis-
  armament
Strachan, Bishop John, on Egerton
  Ryerson 254
Strong, Anna Louise 238, 254
Strong, Dr Margaret 65
Student Christian Movement of Canada
  35; J.G.E. in 48–50; 'Poisoning the
  Student Mind' 49; and SVM 50–2; and
  radical Christianity 126
Student Union for Peace Action 329
Student Volunteer Movement for
  Foreign Missions (SVM): J.G.E. volun-
  teers with 48; Indianapolis
  convention 51–2
Sun Yat-sen 9, 86–7, 148, 159, 175, 192,
  253; and Three Principles of the
  People 87, 91, 141, 199, 204; and Prin-
  ciple of Livelihood 137; J.G.E. on
  181–2; J.G.E. speaks at weekly
  memorial meetings held for 180;
  J.G.E. speaks at Peking rally on 90th
  birth anniversary of 323
Sung see Soong
Swann, Rev. Harold and Donalda 76,
  80, 98–9, 100
Szechuan 7, 8, 75, 89, 94, 97, 99, 105,
  109, 185; landlords in 112–13, 188–9;
  Mount Omei 136–7; lags in war
  effort 140; bombed 143; discontent
  with KMT in 177, 187–9; J.G.E.

assigned secret service work in 187;
Old Brotherhood Society in (Ge Lao
Hui) 188, 189; University of 205;
capitalists invite J.G.E. into part-
nerships with 234

Tai Li, Gen. 146, 186, 188, 192, 381 n8
Taiping Rebellion 9, 250
Tao Hung-chi 238
Tawney, R.H. 38
Taylor, A.J.P. 387 n2
Taylor, E.P. 209
Temple, William 161
Teng Hsi-hou, Gen. 97, 187
Teng Ying-chao 142, 242, 322
Tennyson, Alfred Lord 55, 57
Thexton, Annie 230
Thomas, Rev. Ernest 44
Thompson, Dr J.E. 76
Timothy Eaton Company, Toronto 18,
44
Timothy Eaton Memorial Church 44,
116, 156, 172
Ting, K.H.: and Sui Mei 290; on mis-
sionaries and social change ix; on
J.G.E. ix–x; on labour by religious
workers 320
Tito, Marshal Josip 273
Toronto 58, 62, 89, 234, 236, 262, 359;
Oakwood Collegiate 17; founding
conference of United Church of Cana-
da at Mutual Street sports arena 56;
Endicotts on furlough in 124, 126;
South York election 1942 157, 158;
J.G.E. gives speech at King Edward
Hotel 159; Endicotts return to 1946
245; Canadian Peace Congress founded at Bathurst Street United Church
1949 264; peace movement in 268,
269, 275–6; South York CCF refuse

J.G.E. membership 269; Peace Con-
gress headquarters in 328; peace rally
at Maple Leaf Gardens 3–5, 264, 269,
277, 295–8; peace rallies at Massey
Hall 264, 268, 284, 338
Toynbee, Arnold J. 372 n1, 387 n3
Treaty of Shimonoseki 9
Trudeau, Pierre Elliott 351
Truman, Harry 279, 284; and China
195; and Cold War 262, 280, 284, 386
n2; and Korean War 280; and atomic
bomb 284
Tung Bi-wu 191, 235, 242–3
Tung Sao-sen 209
Twain, Mark 12, 335
Tzu Hsi 9

Ulanova, Galina 273
Union of Soviet Socialist Republics
(USSR) 186, 215, 265; aids Chinese
nationalist movement 87, 92; in World
War II 163; J.G.E. gains respect for
130–1, 171; J.G.E. on democracy in
254; J.G.E. on distortion of news
regarding 249; and Ukraine 222; and
Western view of war with 216, 239;
and nuclear war 267, 277; church in
305; Dean of Canterbury on 268;
J.G.E. opinions on 272, 307, 363;
J.G.E. visits 273–5; and death of
Stalin 306–7; Committee for International Stalin Prizes awards J.G.E. 303,
305–6; requests return of Stalin prizes
308; foreign policy of: and China 195,
343 ff., and Marxism 262, 363, in Eastern Europe 262, in Hungary 326–7,
and Vietnam 340–1, doctrine of
'limited sovereignty' as a new
imperialism 343, 346, and

Czechoslovakia 347–6, Ehrenburg on 327

Union Theological Seminary, New York 62, 261

United Church of Canada 40; founding conference 56–8; sends delegation to West China Mission council meeting 1927 106; faces difficulty in raising mission funds 127–8; J.G.E. tours Canada to raise mission funds 128–31, 153–60; criticizes *English Weekly* 139; notified of threat to deport J.G.E. from China 228–9; and Marxism 226; J.G.E. resigns from ministry of 221, 233–4, 254; controversy with J.G.E. over response to Chinese revolution 247–56; and Stockholm Appeal 388 n19; disassociates itself from J.G.E. and Canadian Peace Congress 300; passes resolution to recognize the People's Republic of China 301; suggestion that J.G.E. withdraw resignation from 1979 365; Board of Overseas Missions 16, 60, 61, 89, 253, J.G.E. takes music lessons through 127, criticizes J.G.E.'s work in China 229–30, J.G.E. defends his work 230–2

United Nations: Atlantic charter 157; and world peace 276; J.G.E. on 264–5; and recognition of China 276, 297; and Kampuchea 363; and Korean War 281, 282, 305, security council declares North Korea aggressor 278, commission in 282, forces in 283, declares China aggressor 284, J.G.E. on 282–3

United States 19, 96, 100, 101; and war against Japan 170–1, 184; Stilwell's plans to work with Chinese Communists 170–1, 185, 189, 192; J.G.E. asked by us Army to do liaison work 163, 171, 186, and becomes part-time intelligence officer in the oss 184–95; decides to support kmt in civil war against Communists 194–5, 215, 216, 236, and later to undermine Peking government 299; prevents Peking government from taking seat at un 279; 'Truman Doctrine' and Cold War with ussr 216, 262; J.G.E. criticizes China policy of 216, 311; version of Korean War origins termed 'a deliberate lie' 282; charged with using germ weapons in Korea and China 290 ff.; described by Toynbee as world-wide anti-revolutionary leader 387 n3; uses cia to disrupt Third World countries 337, 338 ff., 344, 396 n25, 397 n30; war in Vietnam 340–1, 397 n34; J.G.E. banned from entry into 329

University of Toronto 33; J.G.E. at 35–42, 48, 61, 102; J.G.E. letter to Historical Club 96; M.A.E. at 59, 60, 126; Victoria University confers honorary doctorate on J.G.E. 156; and 'hands off China' policy 246; engineers raid peace council 286

Veals, Howard J. 113, 230–2

Veloff, Olga 328

Vienna 241, 284; Congress of the Peoples for Peace in 301–2; and World Council of Peace 330–1

Vietnam 263; Geneva conference to end war in 325, 341; American attacks on 339; J.G.E. at Hanoi conference 1964 339–40; occupies Kampuchea 363–4

Vlastos, Prof. Gregory 126, 296

Walmsley, Lewis 196
Walmsley, Rev. Omar 345
Wang Bin-nan 322, 383 n14
Wang Chun-hsieh, Pastor 183
Wang Dzai-min 377 n3
Wang Lieh-guang, Pastor 114
Wang Ming 349, 350, 351
Wang Shu-hua 105
Wang Yu-guang 196, 381 n1
Wanhsien incident 92–102 passim, 373 n4
Wanxian see Wanhsien
War: Woodsworth on 157; J.G.E. on 157; Nearing on 396 n16; J.G.E. on main danger areas for 1948 263; see also specific wars: World War I, World War II, Korean War, Chinese civil war
Ward, Dr Harry 261–2
Waring, Gerald 293
Warsaw Pact 347
Washington Conference, 1922 95
Washington, George 250
Wedemeyer, Gen. Albert C. 186, 215
Weiss, Ruth 191
Wells, Eric 301
Wen I-do 238
Wen Yueh-hua see Endicott, Mary Austin
Wen Yiu-chang see Endicott, James Gareth
Wesley, John 35, 57
West, Michael 118, 127, 132
West China Mission 105, 185, 312; response to Chinese nationalism 90–1; Exodus Council of 102; on devolution 106–8, 319; on rural poverty 113–14; critical of J.G.E.'s work 132; loans J.G.E. to New Life Movement 140; values J.G.E. for China work 162, 219; J.G.E resigns

from 175, 221; notified of threat to deport J.G.E. 228–9
West China Union University 75, 218; J.G.E. offered position in English department 151, 197; requests J.G.E. return to China 162; and Youth Corps building 174, 219–20; meeting on democracy in China at 177–9; J.G.E. at 1944 180, 196–207, 219; and No 11 Hua Hsi Ba 196; student unrest at 196–207; becomes Szechuan Medical School 312
White, Theodore H. 163, 178
Willmott, Earl and Katherine 147, 313, 385 n15, 396 n9
Wilson, A.J. 301
Women's International League 329
Wong Wen-hao 210
Woodsworth, J.S. 19, 34, 130, 131; leader of CCF 125; encourages J.G.E. to take part in CCF 132; takes pacifist position in World War II 157; Arnup on 227; compared with J.G.E. 365–6
Wordsworth, William 35, 39, 42, 93, 95, 364, 369 n16, 399 n12
World Council of Churches 247, 267, 320
World Council of Peace: purposes of 342; definition of aggression 285, 326; conducts petition campaign for a 'pact of peace among the five great powers' 285; and 'Congress of the Peoples for Peace' 301–2; views on internal politics of nations 307; delegation invited to China 1959 309; on Hungary 1956 327; Soviet view on role of 327; Chinese view on role of 333–4; establishes International Institute for Peace 330–1; debate on national liberation vs

peaceful coexistence 331 ff.; Sino-
Soviet schism in 343 ff.; and J.G.E.:
delegation to USSR 273, role in 284,
329–41, at Congress of the Peoples for
Peace 302, position in debate on
policy 331 ff., resigns from 343, 352,
359
World Partisans of Peace see World
Council of Peace
World War I 19–31, 32, 90, 266
World War II 157, 163, 169, 170, 217,
238
Wrong, Prof. George 33
Wrong, Hume 299
Wu I-fang 178
Wu, Y.T. 203, 228, 290; influence on
J.G.E. 224–6, 232, 322; ideas about
Christianity 224–6, 271, 320, 321–2;
target of KMT attack 229; refutes mis-
sion criticism of J.G.E. 230–2; bids
farewell to J.G.E. 234; on religion in
China 318, 319; and Christian reform
movement of the Protestant church
318, 319

Xian see Sian
Xie see Hsieh
Xu see Hsu

Yang, Lao 10, 12
Yang Sen 94, 97, 99
Yang Tin-yin 196
Yang Tsao-ran, Pastor 114
Yang Wu-hsin 145–6
Yangtze River: trips on 16, 72, 81, 102,
123, 234, 310; description of gorges
72; boatmen talk religion to J.G.E.
111–12
Yeomans, Nina 61–3
Yin Wei-tai 315
Young, Scott 361
Yugoslavia 130, 282

Zhang see Chang
Zheng see Cheng
Zhong see Chung
Zhongzhou see Chungchow
Zhou see Chou
Zu see Chu

This book
was designed by
WILLIAM RUETER
and was printed by
University of
Toronto
Press